An Egg at Easter

Accipe ovum & igneo percute gladio.

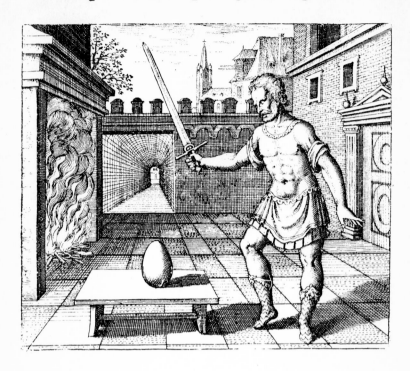

EPIGRAMMA VIII.

Est avis in mundo sublimior omnibus, Ovum
  Cujus ut inquiras, cura sit una tibi.
Albumen luteum circumdat molle vitellum,
  Ignito (ceu mos) cautus id ense petas:
Vulcano Mars addat opem : pullaster & inde
  Exortus, ferri victor & ignis erit.

Michaël Maier, *Scrutinium chymicum* (Frankfurt 1867)

The Philosopher's Egg

An Egg at Easter
A Folklore Study

Venetia Newall
M.A., F.R.G.S., F.R.S.A.

Foreword by
Robert Wildhaber

Je vous donne des œufs. L'œuf en sa forme ronde
Semble au Ciel, qui peut tout en ses bras enfermer,
Le feu, l'air et la terre, et l'humeur de la mer
Et sans estre comprins comprend tout en ce monde.
Ronsard: La Pléiade

INDIANA UNIVERSITY PRESS
BLOOMINGTON

Library of Congress catalog card number: 72–146724

ISBN 253–31942–0

Printed *in* Great Britain

To Richard Dorson and Katharine Briggs, who enabled
the first Anglo-American Folklore Conference to take
place at Ditchley Park, Oxfordshire, in September
1969

Contents

Contents

List of Plates

BLACK AND WHITE PLATES

Foreword

Not only is it an honour for me to be asked to write a few words of introduction to this exciting and learned book but, at the same time, it is also a great pleasure. Never before – at least to my knowledge – has the egg been treated in such a comprehensive monograph, in all its aspects, usages, beliefs and implications. A book, indeed, which has been made possible only because of its author's wide range of knowledge drawn from personal experience, travel and a superior mastery of literature.

The subject in itself is delightful, and one wonders why nobody, up to now, has taken it up. One of the reasons may be that it can be treated in a satisfying way only by doing comparative work, and this is just what Venetia Newall has done, and for which she deserves our admiring praise.

Again and again man has been attracted by the perfect beauty of the form of an egg, by the loveliness of its shades, and by the mysterious symbolism of a seemingly dead object bursting through the containing shell and coming to life. Peasants and herdsmen tried to understand it, putting into it their beliefs and ideas of the world; philosophers and theologians marvelled at it, building up their systems of a cosmos eternally dying and eternally living. In his fine collection of *The Exempla of the Rabbis* Moses Gaster mentioned the following exemplum[1] (in the form of an abstract): 'Wicked man, very ill, asked for an egg. A poor man at the door asked for some food. The man who had never given any alms told them to give the egg to the poor man. After death he appeared to his son whom he exhorted to give charity, for the single egg had sufficed to weigh down the scale in his favour and to grant him place in Paradise.' Whereas in this story the emphasis may be more on the good deed than on the egg as such, in another exemplum it is clearly the egg which is the subject of an ambiguous and enigmatic philosophy as Jewish authorities on the Scriptures would especially enjoy. It is the old story of the three questions which cannot be answered by the man to whom they are put, and which are solved by the 'fool' who acts as his remplaçant. 'An emperor once called the Jews together and ordered them to tell

[1] Reprint, New York, 1968, 153, no. 397.

him his thoughts in three days on pain of death. The people decreed a fast. On the third day a deaf man was seen walking in the
street eating cheese. Rebuked by the people, he asked the cause of
the fast and when told, asked them to allow him to answer for
them.' For us the second question only belongs to our problem;
it was not put into words (as the man was deaf), instead 'the
emperor showed an egg whereupon the deaf one pulled out a
cheese from his bosom'. After the emperor had declared himself
satisfied with the solutions, the Jews asked the deaf one what it
had all meant and he answered: 'The emperor showed me that he
had food (the egg), whereupon I replied by showing that I had
what I wanted (cheese).' But when the courtiers asked the emperor the meaning of his signs, he answered: 'I showed him an
egg to signify that Jesus was born not from a man; he replied by
showing the cheese, which could not curdle without the sperm,
and so Jesus could not be born otherwise than other human
beings.'[1]

In this exemplum one is fully aware of the abysses and even the
traps of theological philosophy; in a way the same symbolic
references are made use of – only in a much more playful manner
– in the manifold riddles.[2] In most of them the egg is described
either according to form, or as house and stronghold, or in terms
of colours, or, finally, in terms of function. It may be 'a stone wall
with a golden lady'. The full beauty of the symbol as employed in
a poetic riddle shines forth in the following example: 'In marble
walls as white as milk, Lined with a skin as soft as silk, Within a
fountain crystal clear, A golden apple doth appear, No doors
there are to this stronghold, Yet thieves break in and steal the
gold.' The Arabs in Palestine describe the egg thus: 'It has
neither foot nor head, nor tail, is neither living nor dead.'

The symbolism is more pronounced, covering every aspect and
every corner of the world, in alchemistic belief. According to this
the egg is the symbol of the four elements: the shell is the earth,
and the membrane is air; the white of the egg is water, and the yolk
fire. A picture from the beginning of the eighteenth century shows
an alchemist endeavouring to get the philosopher's stone out of an

---

[1] *Ibid.*, 177, no. 443.

[2] Taylor, Archer, *English Riddles from Oral Tradition*, Berkeley & Los
Angeles, 1951, 919 f.

egg; he destroys the egg with fire and sword, not to annihilate it completely, but to make it grow and receive new life. So, somehow, life and death are bound together; the egg is connected with both of them. In his recollections of High Albania,[1] the French consul A. Degrand tells of a usage when visiting a woman in childbed. Before leaving, each visitor is shown the baby bound down in his cradle, and offered an egg, with which he touches the baby's body, wishing that it will always remain white, that is, that he will never do anything dishonest which might cause him to blush.

In the Swiss Museum of Folklife in Basle we have the costume of Death hung all over with wreaths of eggshells: the egg in connection with death, the egg as the symbol of resurrection, of hope in future life, in life to come, in Eternity. That is why in religious ceremonies of medieval times it was the custom to put an egg into Christ's tomb. Piero della Francesca painted a wonderful picture (circa 1472), in which the Virgin Mary sits with the Infant Christ in the centre; above her head hangs an egg which is fastened to the ceiling of a small cupola (the picture is now in the Brera, Milan). This egg may be a symbol of Christ's Incarnation, of Eternal Life, of all the strength and vitality embedded in the small shell: who knows! But one thing is certain: there is so much solemnity, so much of the arcanum in it that you will be deeply touched. Also in the Basle Museum is a small glass box, made by a nun, who felt such motherliness for the Infant Christ, that she clothed a wooden doll and decorated the cradle with artificial flowers and shiny metalwork; but over the Baby she hung an egg, maybe without clearly realizing the mystic relationship that she had created.

There are so very many strange conceptions about the egg: on the one hand it is pure and sacred and the bearer of radiant new life; on the other hand there is the secret inside, out of which anything may come to life: good and joyful, or bad and filled with hatred. In 'white magic' you may give an egg to the incubus, whereupon its power is broken, and you will not be troubled by it any more.[2] At the turn of the century nobody in High Albania dared to set an egg for hatching without first drawing the sign of the cross on it; otherwise some monstrous creature might creep

---

[1] Degrand, A., *Souvenirs de la Haute-Albanie*, Paris, 1901, 43.
[2] Henssen, Gottfried, *Volk erzählt*, Munster, 1954, 44.

out of it.[1] In a way this idea is already to be found in the Old Testament. Isaiah (Chapter 59, verses 4, 5) has a vision of the Jews' enormous sins; so, he admonishes them: 'None calleth for justice, nor any pleadeth for truth; they trust in vanity, and speak lies; they conceive mischief, and bring forth iniquity. They hatch cockatrice' eggs, and weave the spider's web: he that eateth of their eggs dieth, and that which is crushed breaketh out into a viper.'

We find cosmogonic conceptions in which the world has arisen out of an egg; we know of ancient deities who have sprung from an egg. That Goddesses of this type are goddesses of fertility is understandable: Aphrodite/Venus. A poetic vision in Syria speaks of a big egg found by fish in the Euphrates; they pushed it to the shore; there it was hatched by a dove, and a Venus was born from it.[2] But strangely enough, the egg has not become the attribute of a Christian saint. In the Christian world it is the Easter egg that has lived on into our times, the red egg of the Orthodox Church. More and more in our tradition it is the hare that brings and lays these eggs.

These are a few ideas which came into my mind; the full range of the whole topic will be spread out in the following chapters. They have been thought over with so much authority by Venetia Newall that it will be a rare pleasure to be guided by her, all the more so as in many previous articles she has already proved her superiority and mastery of the field.

Basle   Robert Wildhaber

[1] Degrand, 289.
[2] Siecke, Ernst, *Götterattribute und sogenannte Symbole*, Jena, 1909, 198.

Author's Preface

It is often difficult to trace one's interest in a particular subject to a definite source. But in my case the study of eggs arose from a visit to central Europe eleven years ago, when I first saw the elaborately coloured specimens sold by market-women at Easter. Later, while living in the Far East, I noticed how often eggs are used as temple offerings, especially among the Chinese.

Subsequently the magnitude of the study, and its pitfalls, dawned upon me. For example, do the temple gift eggs possess any intrinsic ritual or symbolic significance or are they just a convenient offering? Often it is difficult to judge, but in pruning my material I have tried to exclude references where this might have been the case – for instance, in the post-bereavement traditions of the Chinese. The standard pattern which these follow is widely documented. But I discovered one account where the road to the other world – represented by a long, white cloth – was provided with eggs as well as with the usual paper-money. They were picturesquely laid around a sand castle, together with candles and incense, and it is tempting to see in this a special significance. But, since this description is unique, I concluded that here the eggs were just a random choice of foodstuff.

For my errors of interpretation, omissions and mistakes, I naturally accept full responsibility. But in the field of information provided, of practical help and advice given, and of encouragement in this lengthy task, I owe a great debt to friends and acquaintances. Apart from the acknowledgments, which appear elsewhere, of permission to quote copyright passages, I must thank the following who assisted me by providing information: Archbishop Alexis van der Mensbrugghe, Miss Violet Alford, Vytautas Beliajus, Sol Cohen (Curator of the Jewish Museum), F. J. Collins (Historic Buildings Dept., Greater London Council), Dr H. R. Ellis Davidson, Sister Gabriella of the Convent of the Annunciation, Alex Helm, Mrs Herdman, Mrs Mary Hudleston, Arthur Hulme, the Rev. Vassily James, Dr Ildikó Kriza, Dr Siegfried Kube (Institut für Deutsche Volkskunde, Dresden),

F. A. Litvin, Eric Maple, Mrs Kathleen Mitchell, Mrs Ruth Noyes, Mrs Peter Opie, Silvio Van Rooy, D. P. Snoep (Rijksuniversiteit, Utrecht), Karl-Heinz Vick.

For both information and invaluable gifts of eggs, I must thank Miss Cornelia Belcin, Mrs Terěza Budiṇa-Lazdiṇa, Miss Gemma Donati, Willy Hess, Mrs Laura Huyett, Miss Marta Jenkala, Mrs Olena Jenkala, the Rev. Willfred Jennings, Captain Miodrag Jovanovič, Miss Ida-Marie Kaplan, Miss Salme Pruuden, Mr David Streeter, Mrs Cyril Thompson, Mrs Jiři Tondlová, Edmund de Unger, Miss Mary Warren, Frau Gertrud Weinhold and Hans Zühlke.

In building up my collection, and greatly enhancing my possibilities for studying decorated eggs, I must specially thank Dr Wolfhilde von König, who so very kindly provided me with an extensive collection of Easter eggs from all parts of Germany. With her wide knowledge of the subject, she also allowed me to benefit from her personal commentary on the eggs in her own large collection, and on those which she gave to me. My mother-in-law, Mrs Norman Newall, was also exceptionally generous in augmenting my collection, and went to endless personal trouble.

The Dove Cottage Trust, through the good offices of Mr L. V. Rickman, the Hon. Secretary, kindly provided facilities for study and photography of the Wordsworth family pace eggs. The London Museum made arrangements for me to visit their storage vaults in Lancaster House, and the Society of Antiquaries gave me assistance in obtaining one of the illustrations. I must also thank the Editor and Librarian of the *Jewish Chronicle* for their helpfulness and cooperation, and Miss E. M. Loughran, former Assistant Secretary of the Folklore Society.

For help with translations, and for much additional useful material, I am grateful to Henk Arends, Miss Marina Gorodeckis, Georg Jenkala, Miss Jacqueline Simpson, Dr Ihsan Toptani and Alec Wilkinson. Miss Gorodeckis and Miss Simpson also kindly made me gifts of eggs, and Miss Simpson was among those members of the Folklore Society's Committee for whose encouragement I was particularly grateful. I must also specially mention, in this connection, Dr H. R. Ellis Davidson and the Rev. Professor E. O. James.

Finally, there are four further people whom I would like particularly to mention. Firstly—because she was the first person to give an opinion on my work – Miss Christina Hole, Editor of *Folklore*, who read my original essay on the subject, and gave me the encouragement to start out on something more ambitious. Secondly, Dr Robert Wildhaber, until his recent retirement Director of the *Schweizerisches Museum für Volkskunde* in Basle, who edited the many papers on eggs which appeared on his initiative in the *Schweizerisches Archiv für Volkskunde*. Not only have I drawn on this material, but I have benefited from Dr Wildhaber's generous help and wide experience, based on the immense collection of eggs which he has assembled at Basle, and from the study of his most interesting exhibits. Thirdly, I would like to mention Dr Katharine Briggs, former President of the Folklore Society, who was kind enough to give me encouragement after reading an earlier draft. Lastly, I must mention my husband, who has at all times been a source of help and inspiration, not only providing me with many of my eggs, but assisting with translations and many other tasks connected with the preparation of a manuscript. Without his aid it would never have been completed.

Acknowledgments

The author is grateful to the following for permission to quote copyright passages from the books named:

Abelard-Schuman, Ltd, for *Easter*, by Alan W. Watts; All Rights Reserved; Copyright year 1950.

Artia and Vladimir Sís for *Chinese Food and Fables*, by Vladimir Sís.

Cambridge University Press for *The Folklore of Chios*, by Philip Argenti and H. J. Rose.

The Clarendon Press for *Gulliver's Travels*, by Jonathan Swift, edited by A. B. Gough.

Council of the Early English Text Society for *Mandeville's Travels*, edited by P. Hamelius.

Faber and Faber Ltd for 'The Dry Salvages', from *Four Quartets* by T. S. Eliot.

Government of India, North East Frontier Agency for *Myths of the North-East Frontier of India*, by Verrier Elwin.

George G. Harrap & Co. Ltd for *The Fellahin of Upper India*, by Winifred Blackman.

Harvard University Press for *The Kalevala*, compiled by Elias Lönnrot and translated by Francis P. Magoun, Jr; Copyright, 1963, by the President and Fellows of Harvard College.

The Harvill Press Ltd for *Images and Symbols*, by Mircea Eliade.

Jewish Observer and Middle East Review and Reuben Ainsztein for 'The Jewish Background of Carl Marx', by Reuben Ainsztein.

P. J. Kenedy and Sons for *A Dictionary of Mary*, by Donald Attwater; Copyright © 1956 by P. J. Kenedy and Sons, New York.

Oxford University Press for *The Thirteen Principal Upanishads*, edited by R. E. Hume.

Penguin Books Ltd for *Faust* (Part I), by Wolfgang von Goethe, translated by Philip Wayne.

Laurence Pollinger Ltd and The Estate of the Late Mrs Frieda Lawrence and The Viking Press for 'Fish', from *The Complete Poems of D. H. Lawrence*.

Routledge & Kegan Paul Ltd for *Folksongs and Folklore of South Uist*, by M. F. Shaw.

Winant, Towers Ltd for *A Mirror of Witchcraft*, by Christina Hole.

Portions of this manuscript have already appeared in *Folklore, The Journal of American Folklore, Lore and Language* and *Viltis*, and the author wishes to thank the editors of these publications for permission to incorporate the material.

An Egg at Easter

PHOTOGRAPHIC ACKNOWLEDGMENTS

The colour photographs are by Derrick E. Witty. Warm acknow-ledgment must be made to Dr Wolfhilde von König of Munich, without whose generous help many of these colour photographs would not have been possible.

Acknowledgment for other photographs is made to the indi-viduals, institutions and other organizations listed below, and the author is indebted for permission kindly given to reproduce illustrations. Numbers following the names provide reference to the relevant illustrations.

Associated Press Ltd, London (18)
Gemeentemuseum (Musikbibliotheek), The Hague (7, 8, 9)
Institut Royale du Patrimoine Artistique, Brussels (4)
Marta Jenkala, London (19)
Keystone Press Agency Ltd, London (17)
Musée de l'Homme, Paris (12)
Museo del Prado, Madrid (5a)
Museu Nacional de Arte Antiga, Lisbon (5b)
Pennsylvania Folklife Society, Kutztown (13a, 16)
Pinacoteca di Brera, Milan (3)
Portuguese Ministry of Education, Lisbon (5b)
Revue Archeologique (Third Series, No. 40; 1902) (2)
Rijksmuseum, Amsterdam (6)
Emil Schlagintweit (*Indien in Wort und Bild*, Vol. I; Leipzig, 1880) (11)
Schweizerisches Landesbibliothek, Bern (10)
Schwenkfelder Library, Pennsburg (14)
Trustees of the British Museum, London (1)
Dr Don Yoder, University of Pennsylvania, Philadelphia (13a, 16)
The Yorkshire Post, Leeds (20a, 20b)
(Illustrations 13b and 15 are the author's own)

Chapter 1

Creation Myths

We must make use of myths, not entirely as histories, but by taking out of them that which is to the purpose, as in the form of a similitude.

Plutarch

Hail, thou city Akesi, which art hidden from the gods, the Khus knows the name of which the gods are afraid. None can enter therein and none can come forth therefrom except that holy god who dwelleth in his egg. . . . He hath made the city so that he may dwell therein at will, and none can enter therein except on the day of great Transformations.

The Book of the Dead

THE PRIMEVAL WATERS

'Bless, O Lord, we beseech Thee, this Thy creature of eggs, that it may become a wholesome sustenance to Thy faithful servants, eating in thankfulness to Thee, on account of the Resurrection of Our Lord.'[1]

So runs a prayer appointed by Pope Paul V for use during Mass at Eastertide. Already in the fourth century[2] eggs were presented in church, to be sprinkled with holy water and blessed. And by the twelfth century the *Benedictio Ovorum* had been introduced, authorizing the special use of eggs on the holy days of Easter.

Today our traditional feast would be dull indeed without a supply of gaily coloured eggs. But why, after all, use eggs? They have no obvious Christian significance, like the pelican, the lamb or the fish, and yet we still exchange eggs at Easter, as our ancestors did before us. In 'Praying Child', a painting by Hieronymus Bosch, the artist shows us a Christmas scene: two shepherds sit by the fire, warming themselves and holding an egg in their hands. Bosch loved obscure symbols and the meaning here is not obvious. We need a commentary to explain that for him the

---

[1] *The English Missal*, London, 1933, supplementary p. 156.
[2] Becker, Albert, *Brauchtum der deutschen Osterzeit*, Jena, 1937, 43.

egg represented the world and the origins of life – a fitting emblem for the Christ Child.[1]

To discover more we must look back into the remote past, when primitive man lived in a world over which he had no control and where nature was unpredictable, often hostile and destructive. Inevitably the elements, and even familiar useful objects, were regarded with a mixture of fear and awe. Invested by the simple mind with magical powers, the trees and stones, water, sun, moon and fire were worshipped and deified. Even our household egg was an object for wonder and amazement, its smooth, symmetrical shell enclosing the mystery of newly formed life. The young creature, suddenly breaking out from what seemed a lifeless object, evidently stimulated early speculation about the creation of man and the universe around us. The words *atyi akan*, meaning 'the hip egg', still used by the Bulu people of the Cameroons to describe the bone in the hip, express the same idea and recall God creating Eve with a bone from Adam's rib.[2]

Abstractions are difficult for the primitive mind to grasp, especially something as complex as the creation. But all around him in nature early man could watch a parallel process – the hatching of an egg. The idea of a world egg as the origin of the universe, and of the creator and all life itself, developed naturally from this.

And so we find that the egg figures prominently in creation myths all over the world. For it embodied the idea of a silent universe, all at once bursting into activity and chaos, which occurs in the Old Testament and in many other stories of creation.

These accounts often start by depicting a primeval ocean, limitless and immortal, which existed before the world began; in the stirring lines which open the Book of Genesis, the Spirit of God broods over the silent waters of creation, like a great bird tending its nest.[3] Water is a popular female symbol; the Vedic writings of India refer to it as *mâtritamâh*, the most maternal one, a pattern of the womb, containing within its depths the source of life.[4] The expression 'living water' is common in Judaeo-Christian thought.

---

[1] Wildhaber, Robert, 'Zum Symbolgehalt und zur Ikonographie des Eies', *Deutsches Jahrbuch für Volkskunde*, vi (Berlin, 1960), 77.

[2] Weinhold, Gertrud, *Das schöne Osterei in Europa*, Kassel, 1965, 8.

[3] Gen. i.2.

[4] Cirlot, J. E., *A Dictionary of Symbols*, London, 1962, 345.

Living waters were those inhabited by fish, a striking symbol for a people within reach of the Dead Sea, and moreover they flowed from the side of the Temple in Ezekiel's Vision.[1]

The word 'fish' came to be used as an acrostic for Jesus Christ, God's Son Saviour, a sign of recognition among the early Christians. But it also denoted a creature associated with baptism and with water. Tertullian said, 'We, little fish, are born in water', and paintings in the Catacombs, connecting them with baptismal water, are traceable back to Jewish art, where water filled with fish signified the idea of resurrection.[2] D. H. Lawrence suggests something of the mystery of this symbol in one of his poems:

> *They are beyond me, are fishes.*
> *I stand at the pale of my being*
> *And look beyond, and see*
> *Fish, in the outerwards,*
> *As one stands on a bank and looks in . . .*
> *In the beginning*
> *Jesus was called The Fish . . .*
> *And in the end.*[3]

In baptism man is spiritually born through the agency of life-giving waters. For the modern Church of England this only means a token gesture. But in the early church, as in paintings of Our Lord's baptism in the waters of the Jordan, it probably involved total immersion, a practice still common among certain Non-conformist sects. Immersion implied not only a return to the primeval state, but also birth, since water contained the mystic life force.

It is easy to see how a fish came to represent the Christian soul, emerged from the waters of baptism. The ancient Assyrians eschewed its flesh because of divine associations; for it was fish which pushed ashore from the River Euphrates an egg containing their goddess Atargatis and from which, in due course, she hatched.[4] A Chinese myth, dating from the sixth century B.C.,

[1] Ezek. xlvii.1–12.

[2] Daniélou, Jean, *Primitive Christian Symbols*, London, 1964, 50.

[3] Lawrence, D. H., *Selected Poems*, London, 1950, 89–90.

[4] Frazer, Sir James G., *Pausanias's Description of Greece*, London, 1913, iii.339. Mackenzie, Donald A., *Myths of Babylonia and Assyria*, London, 1915, 28.

describes how an egg swam out from the creative waters, much like a fish, and spread itself to form dry land.[1]

Indeed, these legendary accounts often tell of an egg, which floats in water and is the source of all things: the gods, the dry land, mankind, and food. Bread, the staple diet of many races, is often held in a certain awe on account of its life-giving properties, and the Populuca people of Mexico tell the following myth of the origin of maize: A childless woman, who went to fetch water, saw the reflection of an egg on the cliff above. Her husband fetched it, and in seven days it hatched a small child with golden hair, which was soft and silky like maize. The child grew quickly and was well developed after seven days. But people teased him because he was 'only a little egg taken out of the water'.[2]

This tale is perhaps an inversion of the idea that the life-giving water causes the grain to grow, so that there must be its origin. As a rule these stories are linked closely to local conditions. In Minahassa, northern Celebes, the objects which produce mankind are of egg-shaped foam, which appeared on the waves of the sea when it beat upon a rock[3] – a gift from the water, which brings both life and death to a seafaring people. The Bād tribe of north-west Australia also have a sea story, of fishermen working in Disaster Bay. There they found a rainbow egg which had fallen from the sky. They brought it home, lit a fire, and roasted it. But this caused a mighty storm to break, and suddenly the egg cracked. Water and a rainbow came out of it, but the sky rained still harder and a sorcerer changed them all into ducks to save them from drowning.[4]

The primeval waters often reappear in these flood stories. A Peruvian account, with echoes of Noah and his Ark, describes five eggs, which remained on a mountain-top after the waters receded; the Inca hero, Paricaca, was born from one of them.[5] Another important mythical figure, the Great-Coyote-Who-was-Formed-in-the-Water of the North American Navaho, also

[1] Burdick, L. D., *Foundation Rites*, London, 1901, 65.

[2] Hellbom, Anna-Britta, 'The Creation Egg', *Ethnos*, i (Stockholm, 1963), 89.

[3] *Larousse Encyclopaedia of Mythology*, London, 1959, 457.

[4] Hellbom, 84.

[5] Bellamy, H. S., *Moons, Myth and Man*, London, 1936, 128.

hatched from an egg.[1] Other more esoteric creatures inhabited the early water. To the Chinese it was the dwelling-place of the dragon, in their system of thought a highly important symbol of rhythmic life, representing lightning, rain and fecundity.[2] Here we have an idea rather than a natural feature, as in the cosmogony of the Mesopotamians, where the mysterious depths of the sea symbolized unfathomable wisdom.[3]

This must be the idea behind the *Kathâsaritsagara*, an eleventh-century Indian collection of tales by the poet Somadeva. He tells us that Shiva created the world from a drop of blood which fell into the primeval water. An egg formed from this and out of it came Purusha, the Supreme Soul. Heaven and earth emerged from the two halves of this egg. In the words of Shiva: 'Moreover, this world, resembling a skull, rests in my hand; for the two skull-shaped halves of the egg are called heaven and earth'.[4]

Generally the skull represents death and the transitory nature of earthly things, especially in Christian art and literature. But because it remains behind after the disintegration of the flesh, it is also regarded as the repository of life, the dwelling place of the soul after death, and the seat of thought and power.[5]

THE EGG OF THE SUN

The waters of wisdom and the seat of wisdom – both these ideas are implied in the world skull-egg of Shiva. But the conception is not common. The first recorded reference to a world egg as such appears to be in an Egyptian papyrus of the New Kingdom period:[6] 'O Egg of the water, source of the earth, product of the Eight, great in heaven and great in the underworld, dweller in the thicket, chief of the Isle of the Lake of the Two Knives, I came forth with thee from the water; I came forth with thee from thy rest.'[7]

Egyptologists have not decided who it is that this text refers to. Probably it is Thoth, god of the moon, who appeared in the form

---

[1] O'Bryan, Aileen, 'The Dîné, Origin Myths of the Navaho Indians', *Bureau of American Ethnology* (Washington, 1956), clxiii, 3.

[2] Cirlot, 83, 345.　　　[3] *Ibid.*, 345.　　　[4] Hellbom, 68.

[5] Ferguson, George, *Signs and Symbols in Christian Art*, New York, 1961, 50.

[6] 1580–1085 B.C.

[7] Brandon, S. G. F., *Creation Legends of the Ancient Near East*, London, 1963, 44.

of an ibis, and who is described variously in different legends, both as having hatched the world egg at Hermopolis and as having emerged from it himself.[1] Petosiris, the priest of Hermopolis, tells us 'Part of the Egg was buried in this place, and here were found all beings who came forth from the Egg.'[2]

Another cycle of myth describes the god Amun forming his own egg and creating himself in the waters at Hermopolis.[3] In yet another we are told that the ark carried in procession to honour Osiris on his festival days always contained an egg, as well as a phallus and a serpent.[4] A New Kingdom greeting to the sun god Re reads: 'Thou art ascended on high, coming forth from the secret egg as the child of the Eight.'[5] A similar inscription from the sixth century B.C. runs: 'Thou didst raise thyself from the waters out of the secret egg.'[6] The criminals in Re's great hall, which symbolizes the world, are those who insulted him on earth: 'Those who have cursed that which is in the egg.'[7] This ancient idea of a primeval egg which hatched the sun god occurs in other mythologies, and at a much later date. It is very striking how often there is an explicit or implied connection between the world egg and the egg of the sun. Perhaps it was because the world egg floated in the waters of creation, and in the same way it was often thought that the sun, when it sank below the horizon each evening, was floating in the depths of the sea:

> *So, when the sun in bed,*
> *Curtained with cloudy red,*
> *Pillows his chin upon an orient wave*[8]

writes Milton.

The round, yellow yolk of the egg was an obvious emblem for the sun. But, more important, the egg, like the sun, was seen as the source of all life. For the ancient Lithuanians the world egg did not resemble the sun, the warming rays of which brought the earth into being. The sun, moving for centuries around the great egg-shaped mass of primeval chaos, gradually caused it to form the

[1] *Larousse*, 26.   [2] Brandon, 49.   [3] *Ibid.*, 53.
[4] Waterman, Philip, *The Story of Superstition*, New York, 1929, 91, 130.
[5] Brandon, 45.   [6] *Ibid.*, 45.
[7] Wallis Budge, E. A., *The Gods of the Egyptians*, London, 1904, i.180.
[8] Milton, John, 'On the Morning of Christ's Nativity', *English Religious Verse*, ed. G. Lacey May, London, 1937, 89, verse xxvi.

6

earth.[1] Human beings, it was sometimes thought, and animals too, were born from the heat of the sun, just as it was once supposed that living creatures were hatched from the life-giving mud of the Nile when it overflowed its banks. A hymn composed by the outstanding Eighteenth Dynasty Pharaoh, Amen-hotep IV or Akhnaton – the first individual who worshipped one god in Egypt – in honour of the sun god Aton, describes how the sun creates the chick within the egg, and brings it forth:

> *When the chicken cries in the egg shell*
> *Thou givest him breath therein, to preserve him above.*
> *When Thou hast perfected him*
> *That he may pierce the egg,*
> *He comes forth from the egg*
> *To chirp with all his might.*
> *He runneth about upon his two feet*
> *When he hath come forth therefrom.*[2]

Khnum, a god of creation whose name signifies 'The Moulder', formed the world egg from a lump of Nile mud on his potter's wheel.[3] To these early peoples the waters of the Nile were life itself and provided the means for growing the crops. When the river flooded its banks, it left a deposit of fertile mud behind. What more fitting symbol could there be for the creation of the world egg? In ancient drawings one also finds Ptah of Memphis seated on his throne, moulding an egg on a potter's wheel. In this case the egg is golden, the colour of the sun.[4] Other sources describe him emerging from the egg laid by the celestial Chaos Goose, the father of beginnings, creator of sun and moon.[5]

The goose in its role as mate of Seb the gander, god of the earth, lays the sun egg.[6] From this the phoenix, symbol of the sun, arose. Seb is also the Egyptian name for a type of goose, and god and bird were often confused. Sometimes he is called the Great

---

[1] Beckers, Hartmut, *The Myth of the Origin of the World according to the Mashafi Räsh*, unpublished MS, 5.

[2] Information kindly supplied by Edmund de Unger. See also Brandon, 59.

[3] Spence, Lewis, *An Introduction to Mythology*, London, 1921, 165. *Larousse*, 37.

[4] James, E. O., *The Ancient Gods*, London, 1960, 71.

[5] Mackenzie, Donald A., *Myths and Traditions of the South Sea Islands*, London, 1930, 180. Meyerowitz, Eva L. R., *The Divine Kingship in Ghana and Ancient Egypt*, London, 1960, 65–8.

[6] O'Neill, John, *The Night of the Gods*, London, 1897, ii.767.

Cackler,[1] and in the *Book of the Dead*: 'I protect the egg of the great divine Cackler. If I thrive, it thrives, if I live, it lives, if I breathe the breath of air, it breathes.'[2] Egg and creation are frequently linked by the Egyptians; again from the *Book of the Dead*: 'I shine in the egg in the unseen world. . . . He is in the Solar Eye, an egg to which life is given among you.'[3]

The *Harris Magical Papyrus* records a ritual intended to protect a man on board ship from hostile animals and monsters. He must hold an egg in his hand and repeat the following:

> O Egg of the Water, which has been spread over the earth, essence of the divine apes, the great one in the heavens above and in the earth beneath; who doth dwell in the nests which are in the waters. I have come forth from thee from the water, I have been with thee in thy nest. I am Amsu of Coptos, I am Amsu, Lord of Kebu.[4]

Egyptian myth of this kind is varied, sometimes no doubt because of the many races which succeeded each other as immigrants or conquerors. But the sun egg of the water is a fairly constant idea and we find it in many other cosmogonies. It appears, through the agency of a bird, in the Finnish *Kalevala* epic. Lunnotar, Daughter of Nature, floats upon the waters of the sea. A duck arrives, builds its nest on her knee and lays in it a number of golden eggs. After it has sat on them for three full days, she feels her knee is burning – and the heat of the egg suggests that it is really the sun. She jerks her leg and the eggs roll down in the abyss:

So then the mother of the water, mother of the water, virgin of the air,
Raised her knee from the sea, her shoulder blade from a billow,
For the goldeneye as a place for a nest, as an agreeable dwelling place;
That goldeneye, graceful bird, flits about, soars about.
She discovered the knee of the mother of the water on the bluish open sea;
She thought it a grass grown tussock, fresh turf.
She soars about, flits about, settles down on the knee.
On it she builds her nest, laid her golden eggs,

---

[1] Wallis Budge, ii.96.

[2] Davis, C., ed., *The Egyptian Book of the Dead*, New York, 1894, 24 (Intro.).

[3] *Ibid.*, xlii.95.

[4] Pap. Mag. Harris, Recto Col. VI, 10–12, in Kees, H., *Religionsgeschichtliches Lesebuch* (*Aegypten*), Tübingen, 1928, 10. See also Chabas, F. J., *La Papyrus Magique Harris*, Paris, 1860, and compare text in Brandon: see above, page 5, footnote 7.

Six golden eggs, the seventh an iron egg.
She began to brood the eggs, to warm the top of the knee.
She brooded one day, brooded a second, then brooded a third too.
Now because of that the mother of the water, mother of the water, virgin of the
*   air,*

Feels burning hot, her skin scorched;
She thought her knee was burning, all her sinews melting.
Suddenly she twitched her knee, made her limbs tremble.
The eggs tumbled into the water, are sent into the waves of the sea;
The eggs cracked to pieces, broke to bits.
The eggs do not get into the ooze, the bits not get mixed up with the water.

The bits were turned into fine things, the pieces into beautiful things:
The lower half of one egg into the earth beneath,
The top half of another egg into the heavens above.
The top half of one yolk gets to glow like the sun,
The top half of one white gets to gleam palely as the moon;
Any mottled things on an egg, those become stars in heaven,
Anything black on an egg, those indeed become clouds in the sky.[1]

Here the agent is a bird, the catalyst which galvanizes the stillness
and the spirit into activity. Again we are reminded of Genesis,
where the Spirit of God appears like a mighty bird. Describing
the creation in *Paradise Lost*, Milton writes:

> *Thou from the first*
> *Wast present, and with mighty wings outspread*
> *Dove-like, satst brooding on the vast Abyss*
> *And madst it pregnant.*[2]

But here the bird plays a lesser role. In the *Rig Veda* of India it is
the mighty spirit Prajapati who fertilizes the waters of creation,
transforming them into the Golden Egg. Inside sits Brahma, the
Golden Person, where he remains for a thousand years, floating
in the waters of creation, his miraculous power shining through
the seven shells of the egg, infusing it with a golden radiance.
Within the egg with Brahma are the continents, oceans, mountains, planets, divisions of the universe, gods, demons and
humanity.[3] The *Chandogya Upanishad* says:

[1] Magoun, Francis, tr., *Kalevala*, Cambridge, Mass., 1963, i.202–26.
[2] Milton, John, 'Paradise Lost', *Poetical Works*, Oxford, 1922, 182, Book
I, 19–22.
[3] Agrawala, Vasudeva S., *Sparks from the Vedic Fire*, Varanasi, 1962, 26–7.

9

Colour Plate I Eggs from the *Berliner-Porzellan-Manufaktur* (c. 1820–1880). They show, respectively, two soldiers in eighteenth-century uniform, a bunch of daisies (dated *Ostern 1879* on the reverse), Strasbourg Cathedral (probably commemorating the German acquisition of Alsace in 1871), the Berlin *Schloss,* and Frederick the Great.

Colour Plate II (a) Russian nineteenth-century porcelain eggs, three of them depicting the Resurrection. The fourth shows St Evgenia.

(b) Eggs of the type made at the Russian Imperial porcelain factory as Easter gifts from members of the Royal family to friends and dependants. Those at the top right and left show, respectively, the monogram of the last Tsarevich and the Grand Duchess Olga. The other two monogram eggs show the monogram of the last Tsarina, and the same appears on the reverse of the red cross egg. This last was of a type specially made in World War I, the black ribbon also being a wartime gesture. During peace a yellow ribbon was normal, and the other eggs would have been threaded in this way. The eggs, as is usual with Russian eggs, are hollow and have a hole at each end. That at the bottom left is inscribed *Christos Voskresi* (Christ is Risen) and the remaining egg (centre right) shows Our Lord praying in the garden of Gethsemane.

An Egg at Easter

The Sun is Brahma – this is the teaching. A further explanation thereof [is as follows]. In the beginning this world was merely non-being. It was existent. It developed. It turned into an egg. It lay for the period of a year. It was split asunder. One of the two egg shell parts became silver, one gold. That which was of silver is this earth. That which was of gold is the sky. . . . Now what was born therefrom is yonder sun. When it was born shouts and hurrahs; all beings and all desires rose up toward it. . . . He who, knowing it thus, reverences the Sun as Brahma.[1]

Again, in *The Laws of Manu*:

He, having willed to produce various beings from his own divine substance, first with a thought created the waters, and placed in them a productive seed. The seed became an egg bright as gold, blazing like the luminary with a thousand beams; and in that egg he was born himself in the form of Brahma, the great forefather of all spirits. . . . In that egg the great power sat inactive a whole year of the Creator at the close of which, by his thought alone, he caused the egg to divide itself. And from its two divisions he framed the heaven above and the earth beneath. In the midst he placed the subtil ether, the eight regions, and the permanent receptacle of waters.[2]

In the *Bhagvata-Purana* the separate elements at the beginning of time came together through the influence of fate and formed an egg in the waters of creation. For a thousand years the first deity sat inside it. Then a lotus, shining like 1,000 suns, sprang from his navel, and from this Brahma was born.[3] *Hiranyagarbha*, the golden world egg, appears in a variety of forms in different traditions. In *Brihadaranyaka Upanishad* Brahma becomes Viraj, the first of all living creatures, who appears from the golden egg.[4] A bird symbol is often used for *hiranyagarbha*, and Prajapati sometimes appears as the cosmic cow who produces a golden egg, representing the essence of life. It floats in the Cosmic Moisture, and contains within itself all existence.[5] In *Aitareya Upanishad* Prajapati creates the Cosmic Person actually in the shape of an egg.[6]

[1] Hume, R. E., ed., *The Thirteen Principal Upanishads*, London, 1931, 214–15.
[2] Haughton, G. C., ed., *Mánava-Dherma-Sástra*, London, 1825, ii.2–3.
[3] Haavio, Martti, 'Väinämöinen, Creator of the World', *F. F. Communications*, lxi–lxii (Helsinki, 1952–3), 56.
[4] Radhakrishnan, S., ed., *The Principal Upanishads*, London, 1953, 164.
[5] Agrawala, 28.
[6] Radhakrishnan, 516.

Sometimes the egg-born sun gallops across the sky each day, like Apollo in the Greek pantheon.[1] The *Vedic Hymns* describe eight sky divinities. One of these, the Aditya Surya, was 'born from the dead egg':

> *Eight sons there are of Aditi,*
> *Who from her body were produced.*
> *With seven she approached the gods*
> *But the egg-born she cast away.*[2]

He drives a chariot, drawn by red horses; a myth in the *Rig Veda* describes how he dropped an egg which rolls through space.[3] Here we have the sun in its diurnal course. A Hindu symbol reproduced in *Les Religions de L'Antiquité* shows the Cosmic Tree growing up from the primeval egg which lies deep in the waters of creation. It spreads out into three branches and each of these carries a sun at its extremity. A fourth and larger sun is located against the trunk at the point where the branches are joined to it. The whole represents the sun at the three stages of its course: rising, zenith and setting.[4] Vedic myth personified it as the three steps of Vishnu, and we may compare the old Anglo-Saxon tradition of the sun which leapt three times on Easter Day:

> *But oh! She dances such a way,*
> *No sun upon an Easter Day*
> *Is half so fine a sight.*[5]

– a tradition which persisted in spite of the prosaic observation by Sir Thomas Browne that 'we shall not, I hope, disparage the Resurrection of Our Redeemer, if we say the sun doth not dance on Easter day.'[6] Even now, in northern Friesland, they say that if an Easter egg peels easily the owner will see the sun dance on Easter morning.[7] So closely is the egg associated with the sun in Indian myth that

[1] Wilson, H. H., ed., *Rig Veda Sanhita*, London, 1857, 314.

[2] *Ibid.*, 150.

[3] Hackin, J., *Asiatic Mythology*, London, 1963, 103.

[4] D'Alviella, Goblet, *The Migration of Symbols*, London, 1894, 60–1. Whittick, Arnold, *Symbols, Signs and Their Meaning*, London, 1960, 271.

[5] Suckling, Sir John, 'A Ballad upon a Wedding', *The Works of Sir John Suckling in Prose and Verse*, ed. A. Hamilton Thompson, London, 1910, 30.

[6] Browne, Sir Thomas, *Pseudodoxia Epidemica*, London, 1686, V. xxii, para. 16.

[7] Bächtold-Stäubli, Hanns, ed., *Handwörterbuch des deutschen Aberglaubens*, Berlin, 1934–5, vi, 1,328.

it is even used in magical rites to strengthen the power of its rays, as in the folk-tale of 'Numit Kappa', which comes from Manipur, on the borders of India and Burma. Five times the sun lifted his foot from the earth before he climbed to the peak of a neighbouring mountain. The ten gods looked, and were dismayed to see that his face was pale. 'This must be remedied,' they said. So the priests took water from the River Moirang, and with an egg and some yellow grass they made the sun pure, so that his eyes and face were bright and beautiful again.[1]

Indeed, the egg is so important in Indian myth that we find it set out in a familiar piece of architecture. In Nepal, where beliefs of Buddhist and Hindu are inextricably confused, the cupola of a Buddhist *stupa* is intended to represent the cosmic egg.[2] Not only is the dome a protective covering for the sacred relics which are inside. It is intended to show the structure of the universe, just as the frescoes in an Orthodox church of Slav Macedonia show by their arrangement the construction of the kingdom of heaven.

THE COSMIC MOUNTAIN

A *stupa* may also suggest the stylized representation of a mountain. These temple mountains were not uncommon in various parts of the world – for instance, the *ziggurat* at Ur of the Chaldees, and Borobudur in Indonesia.[3] For the cosmic mountain, at the figurative centre of the world, was a popular conception in cosmology. Its peak represented the point of contact between the heavens and the earth and the axis of the world passed through it.[4] The holy mountain formed the link between different worlds and levels of consciousness, like the world tree of Scandinavian myth.[5] Heroes, like Tannhäuser, came in and out of mountains, which suggested not only ideas of spiritual elevation, as in the case of the Grail Mountain, but also an abode of the living and of the dead.[6] Mountains were anciently worshipped in China and

---

[1] Hodson, T. C., *The Meitheis*, London, 1908, 125–30.

[2] Rowland, Benjamin, *The World's Image in Indian Architecture*, a lecture delivered at the Royal Society of Arts, London, on Thursday, 11 June 1964.

[3] Quaritch Wales, H. G., *The Mountain of God*, London, 1953, 47.

[4] *Ibid.*, 40–1. Cirlot, 209.

[5] Turville-Petre, E. O. G., *Myth and Religion of the North*, London, 1964, 279.

[6] Brewer, E. Cobham, *Dictionary of Phrase and Fable*, London, 1896, 1,271.

the Immortals went to live on K'un Lun, located in the centre of the world.[1]

In Mexico, in pre-Columban times, the sun egg hatched from a mountain which split open.[2] Just as the hero or deity was imagined arising from a magic egg, so among mountains, which were impressive geographical features and hence places of awe and veneration, the sun egg was supposed to arise from their caverns. Artificial mountains like the Pyramids were originally burial-vaults, and in the mythologies of many lands chthonic deities are linked with mountains. Hence we have here the subterranean aspect of the sun. When it descends into the mountain again at dusk we are reminded of the Graeco-Roman myth explaining the seasons: Proserpina, gathering flowers, is snatched into the underworld by 'gloomy Dis' and winter falls on the land for a six months' cycle. The sun descends into its mountain and night falls for a period of twelve hours.

Sometimes the converse process is imagined and an egg appears as an offering from the mountain. A legend from the Hill Miri of the North-East Frontier of India describes Chabobi, a great snow-capped mountain, the older brother of Sichi, the earth. It was inhabited by Hak-Tajum and his wife, Sip-Gilli. They cohabited and soon she laid an egg. But, being round, it rolled down the slope of the mountain to the valley below. There it broke and a river gushed out. This happened many times, until the land was filled with rivers.[3]

This legend seeks to explain a natural phenomenon: the way rivers take their origin from high mountains. It is normal for mountains to figure in the cosmology of peoples from mountainous regions; the taller and more spectacular the mountains, the greater the impact that they make on popular imagination. Thus an Angakkok, a *shaman* of the Greenland Eskimos, described the world as being like an egg; the blue sky stretched above the earth, like an egg-shell revolving around a high mountain far up in the north.[4]

Heroes were born from mountains. We have already seen how

[1] Hackin, 278–82, 381–3.
[2] Mackenzie, Donald A., *Myths of Pre-Columban America*, London, 1924, 56.
[3] Elwin, Verrier, *Myths of the North-East Frontier of India*, Shillong, 1958, 73.
[4] Hellbom, 73.

the Peruvian culture hero Paricaca was hatched from an egg found lying on a mountain after a mighty deluge. The Chinese Imperial White Ape, Sun Hou Tzŭ, a popular figure in both Buddhist and Taoist pantheons, is also said to have appeared from an egg which formed on the summit of a mountain.[1]

Such eggs were sometimes evolved in the bowels of the earth. In Europe as late as the Middle Ages an idea persisted that the earth was an egg itself, and metals grew like an embryo within its yolk. Man, wishing to imitate nature and prepare his own precious metal – the philosopher's stone, which would possess unbelievable magic powers – tried to reproduce what he took to be natural conditions. Hence the vessel used, the *aludel* or retort, was egg-shaped.[2] This was also in imitation of the universe, so that the stars would be sure to influence the operation. The miraculous substance that was supposed to emerge was often called the 'philosopher's egg', and is depicted as such in early woodcuts. Occasionally, with richer invention, it was shown as an infant.[3] This creative aspect is emphasized by the word *Mutterschoss*, mother's womb, a common metallurgical term for a smelting kiln. Alchemists worked on two levels. Some only wanted to manufacture gold. Others, more mystically inclined, saw gold as representing spiritual rebirth. From the heat of the symbolic egg-shaped vessel, the phoenix or new soul would finally arise. An old woodcut shows the traditional alchemist cleaving an egg with a fiery sword, not to destroy it, but to release the new life within.[4]

A portrait of Samuel Hafenreffer of Tübingen, the teacher of medicine, painted by an unknown artist in 1660, represents him holding a text-book in one hand and an egg in the other. The egg is obviously a symbol, but of what? Hafenreffer could well have been a member of the Rosicrucians, or one of the current secret societies which maintained relics of earlier alchemistic belief. Hence the egg would here represent creation, life and the world.[5]

[1] Werner, E. T. C., *A Dictionary of Chinese Mythology*, Shanghai, 1932, 102.

[2] Eliade, Mircea, *The Forge and the Crucible*, London, 1962, 51.

[3] Read, John, 'Alchemy and Alchemists', *The Advancement of Science*, ix (London, June 1952), No. 33, 27.

[4] Majeri, Michaelis, *Chymisches Cabinet*, Frankfurt, 1708, 22. See Frontispiece.

[5] Wildhaber, 'Zum Symbolgehalt', 83.

CHTHONIC SYMBOLS

If metals grew within the yolk of the earth, no great stretch of the imagination was needed to envisage the subterranean facet of the sun, and this dual aspect – the sun in the heavens and the sun in the bowels of the earth – appears in various systems of thought.

The idea of the cosmic egg was used by the Mithraists, an early cult of sun-worshippers. A relief at Borcovicum – Housesteads, in Northumberland – shows their god Mithra appearing from an egg, and one authority, Staudacher, believes that the Orphic egg derived from this.[1] The second of these cults, more interesting in the present context, spread in the sixth century B.C. from Thrace into Greece proper, and was based on the concept of redemption.[2] It taught that the egg was the source of life and hence was forbidden food. Orphic literature is complex and there are many versions of this myth: from Chaos and Ether, surrounded by night, the universe was shaped in the form of an egg, night serving as the shell. The upper part made the vault of the sky, the lower part the earth. In the centre Protogones was formed, a being symbolizing Light, and hence, presumably, the sun:

> O *mighty first-begotten, hear my prayer,*
> *Two-fold, egg-born, and wandering through the air;*
> *Bull-roarer, glorying in thy golden wings,*
> *From whom the race of gods and mortals springs.*[3]

Near Lemisso, in Cyprus, a huge stone vase, thirty feet around, supposedly represents this Orphic egg.

A variant of the myth describes how there was nothing but water at the beginning of creation. This changed into mud, and finally to dry land. From these the dragon Chronos was formed, who created Ether, Chaos and Hell. He also made the egg which hatched the dragon-being Protogones. This personage, who was known by many names, including Phanes, created Heaven and Earth from the shell of his egg.[4] A carving, known as the Modena relief, illustrates the legend. Around its edge is an oval frame containing the signs of the zodiac. In the centre stands Phanes, his

---

[1] Guthrie, W. K. C., *Orpheus and Greek Religion*, London, 1935, 254–5, and pl. 13.
[2] Haavio, 54.
[3] Taylor, Thomas, tr., *The Mystical Hymns of Orpheus*, London, 1824, 18.
[4] Haavio, 54.

feet placed on one half of the egg-shell, his head adorned with the other, and with the disk of the sun. The four winds are shown in the corners since, in Orphic tradition, it was the winds which first stirred the world egg in the waters of creation.[1]

Phanes, in his aspect of a dragon, suggests a chthonic deity. To simple people, as we have seen, the egg of the sun appears to bury itself in the ground each evening, and we find these two thoughts linked in a traditional tale from Korea. A huge golden egg, which was found on a mountain-top, contained a lovely rosy boy. The child grew up and, when he became a man, married the daughter of a well dragon.[2]

In British myth the lady of the underworld, Kreirwy, was called 'the token of the egg'.[3] This was the serpent's egg, revered by the sun-worshipping Druids, to which Pliny attributed the power of swimming against the stream. The *glain*, or red egg of the sea-serpent, figured prominently in the Druids' mysteries.[4] As a badge of office, every Druid wore one around his neck, heavily inlaid with gold. Each was, according to Pliny, 'About the bigness of a moderate apple; its shell a cartilaginous incrustation full of little cavities, such as are on the legs of the polypus'[5] – which has suggested a fossil to certain commentators. An authentic serpent egg, thrown into the river, they claimed, would swim against the current.

The Druids, like the Orphics, would not eat eggs, since this destroyed their vital principle.[6] The *glain* was hatched by several serpents, who bore it in the air by means of their hissing. To obtain one, you caught it in your cloak before it fell and hurried to a flowing stream which the serpents could not cross. The owner was then credited with wonderful powers. He could win lawsuits and obtain access to royalty.[7] In the reign of Claudius a Roman citizen was actually put to death for bringing one of these eggs into court.[8] Pliny's own account is most detailed and colourful:

---

[1] *Ibid.*, 54–5. See plate 2.
[2] O'Neill, ii.767.
[3] *Notes and Queries*, 15 May 1915, XI Series, ii.382.
[4] Graves, Robert, *The White Goddess*, London, 1938, 39, 247, 386.
[5] Jones, William, *Credulities Past and Present*, London, 1880, 468.
[6] *Ibid.*, 450–1.   [7] Brewer, 407.
[8] Bostock, John, ed., *Pliny's 'Natural History'*, London, 1856, v.390.

There is another kind of egg, held in high renown by the people of the Gallic provinces, but totally omitted by the Greek writers. In summer time numberless snakes become artificially entwined together and form rings around their bodies with the viscous slime which exudes from their mouths, and with the foam secreted by them. ... But as it is the way with magicians to be dextrous and cunning in casting a veil about their frauds, they [the Druids] pretend that these eggs can only be taken on a certain day of the moon: as though forsooth it depended entirely upon the human will to make the moon and the serpents accord as to the moment of this operation.[1]

The Phanes of Orphic myth was created by the dragon Chronos and is himself a dragon-being. Serpents, and the dragons to which they are related, are traditional guardians of treasure. Gold and silver eggs, concealed in the ground and protected by a winged dragon, are related to a recurring motif in folklore. Perhaps by some association of ideas, a legend from Schwarzenburg in the Upper Palatinate of Germany relates how the shells and fragments of Easter eggs, scattered around rocks and streams, draw out the hidden treasures of the earth.[2] In other tales, concealment of the riches is merely implied. A Thuringian story about the city of Tost in Silesia describes a golden goose brooding on a nest of golden eggs. The bird sits in the ruins of a castle outside the city, and anyone wishing to find him must first have Mass said in the local church.[3] Here an element of the spiritual is introduced. In another Silesian legend the same theme is stressed even further: only the sinless one can discover the hidden riches. Thus a Jesuit, without stain, came upon a golden goose sitting with its eggs in the ruins of a convent.[4] Here the meaning is surely intended to be symbolic: the hidden treasures represent the superior riches of the spirit, only obtainable after a conscious effort.

Sometimes the attainment of hidden treasure brings death. A village wife in a Pomeranian tale threw away two eggs which had gone bad. As soon as they touched the ground golden coins rolled out of them. These were written on, and the inscription said that they were made by a man who was now in her kitchen. However, as soon as she went in to find him the man died.[5] The other

---

[1] *Ibid.*, v.388–9.   [2] Bächtold-Stäubli, ii. 599.
[3] *Ibid.*   [4] *Ibid.*, 598.   [5] *Ibid.*, 628.

complex ideas in this story will be discussed later on. For the moment it is worth stressing the chthonic significance of the eggs which yield up their hidden gold as soon as they touch the ground.

Just as, often, a treasure egg is concealed inside the earth, the egg itself may contain hidden riches. This mystical idea appears in certain riddles: 'Within marble walls there is a fountain and a golden apple.'[1] Other examples collected by Archer Taylor represent it as a lady in a yellow skirt,[2] a white flower with a yellow heart,[3] and a cup full of honey under ice.[4] Some are charming conceits:

> *My mother made me singing*
> *All dressed in white.*[5]

Many express a sense of mystery and wonder at 'a man without head or limbs'[6] and 'the dead giving life to life':[7]

'Tell me something that you have seen coming from a bird, in either foreign lands or the Arabian lands; it is eaten boiled, fried, roasted; you put it into the fire; it has neither foot nor hand, neither head nor tail; it is neither living nor dead; tell me what this marvellous thing is.'[8]

Something of importance is concealed inside the 'house which has no doors'.[9] A French rhyme comments:

> *A little white cottage*
> *With neither door nor window;*
> *If the king comes*
> *Where will he go in?*[10]

In the Netherlands, *'Iemand het ei uit 't gat vragen'* – to ask for the egg out of someone's bottom – is to request the very utmost of a person.[11] Other traditional conundrums, 'a box which once

---

[1] Taylor, Archer, 'Das Ei im europäischen Volksrätsel', *Schweizerisches Archiv für Volkskunde*, LIII (Basle, 1957), ii–iii.197.

[2] *Ibid.*, 195.   [3] *Ibid.*, 196.   [4] *Ibid.*

[5] Joisten, Charles, 'Le Folklore de L'Œuf en Dauphiné', *Arts et Traditions Populaires* (Paris, January–March 1961), 57.

[6] Taylor, 195.   [7] *Ibid.*

[8] *Ibid.*, 'Ainu Riddles', *Western Folklore* (Berkeley, 1947), vi, No. 2, 167, note 1.

[9] *Ibid.*,'Das Ei', 197.   [10] Joisten, 57.

[11] Information kindly supplied by Henk Arends, of Amsterdam.

opened cannot be closed again',[1] and 'a shirt without a seam',[2] suggest the unity of perfection: one thinks of Our Lord's seamless robe and the flawless whole which, once shattered, cannot be restored again.

The contents of an egg are hidden and mysterious. In mythology, when earth replaces water as the all-embracing element, the egg treasure itself is hidden in the bowels of the earth and the dragon or the serpent, traditional guardians, are often miraculously born from one. A legend of the Mixe in Mexico tells how a woman and her husband find two eggs in a well. They hatch in three days; one brings forth a snake, the other a human called Kondoy, who performs great deeds.[3]

Here we see the birth of a hero. A similar process in a Chinese folk-tale describes the birth of a goddess. A young girl, seeing a beautiful egg floating along a stream, swallows it and becomes pregnant. Her child, which is born in considerable pain, is invisible. But at night something comes and suckles it. Eventually this mysterious being takes the mother along to Hsia-Tung-T'ien, where she becomes a goddess, the holy Dragon Mother.[4]

On Rossel Island, off the New Guinea coast, the snake is ancestor of the human race, like the biblical Adam. The first two people were hatched from an egg laid by Konjini, a young girl, and fertilized by Mbasi, the local snake god.[5] Many countries possess a mighty serpent deity in their pantheons – a figure who may appear in association with the world egg. In southern Borneo, above the Makassar Strait, it is thought that Hatala, ruler of the gods, laid earth upon the Naga's head, and this became an island. Ranying Atala, another god, came down from the skies and found seven earthen eggs upon the ground. One contained a man, another a woman, and the others the beginnings of all the world's plants and animals.[6]

Damballah-Wédo, the great snake spirit of Haiti, pours water over himself, simulating the Flood, and treasures the egg from which all things hatch.[7] This belief, common in Eastern thought,

[1] Taylor, 'Das Ei', 196.   [2] *Ibid.*
[3] Hellbom, 88–9.   [4] *Ibid.*, 81–2.
[5] Mackenzie, Donald A., *Myths from Melanesia and Indonesia*, London, 1931, 148.
[6] *Ibid.*, 308–9, 338.
[7] Huxley, Francis, *The Invisibles*, London, 1966, 123–4.

of a benign snake seems a contradiction. But often unpleasant creatures appear in two contrasting aspects: menacing and protective. Probably the one derives from the other. Creatures of terror are suitable guardians, frightening away evil things, and a guardian is a helpful and therefore benign deity. Evil beings, controlled and utilized, tend to assume a beneficent form. Hence, while the Bād of north Australia have a belief that contact with eggs from the mysterious 'one-eyed snake' brings death,[1] Chinese legends about dragon eggs provide a complete contrast. Somebody finds one and it has the magic property of rendering everything that it touches inexhaustible. Everyone longs to possess the egg, so that the owner swallows it and becomes a dragon himself.[2]

Western legend has a perfect counterpart here in the treasure of the Nibelung and the giant Fafnir, who changes into a dragon in order to guard it. The gold, which is buried in the ground, is forged by dwarfs. And since these creatures, said to be more knowledgeable than men, only frequent the places where precious metals occur, to find them is generally an omen of wealth to come. The dwarf, symbol of subterranean life, is a lesser chthonic deity and the ancient Teutons felt a certain fear of them. Possessed of supernatural powers, they lived in secret places and were often hunchbacked or deformed in some other respect. A tale from Uruguay of a heroic dwarf is interesting in that his miraculous birth takes place from an egg. His mother, a witch, who longed for a child, placed an egg given to her by hunchbacks under her house, and from this the dwarf came forth. One day, while his mother was out, he found and struck a golden cymbal. It had already been foretold that the person doing this would dethrone the king, and so he was commanded to perform a series of impossible tasks. However, he was successful and, having killed the king, reigned for a period equivalent to the lives of seventy mortal men.[3]

THE GOOSE THAT LAYS GOLDEN EGGS

A legend in the Talmud describes God taking up the two halves of an egg. They fertilize each other, and this results in the creation

---

[1] Hellbom, 94.　　　[2] *Ibid.*, 93.

[3] Hansen, T. L., *The Types of the Folk Tale in Cuba, Puerto Rico, the Dominican Republic, and Spanish South America*, Berkeley, 1957, 60–1.

of the world.[1] The idea is not unlike one expressed in an obscure Indian document, *The Playful Treatise on Elephants*, describing the origin of the divine elephant, Airavata. At the beginning of time the sun-bird, Garuda, appeared from its shell. Brahma, the supreme creator, held the two broken halves and sang seven holy songs over them until Airavata was born.[2]

The story of the sun-bird, usually disguised as the fowl which lays golden eggs, appears not only in Europe, but in Africa, where the Hausas tell of the fabulous Fufunda. A king, so the story goes, wanted somebody who would travel to the place where the sun rises in the morning. A poor man named Ataru agreed to go, and he was given a horse to ride on his journey. After a month of travelling he arrived in the land of the storks, and they directed him on his way. He journeyed through a place of darkness, a place of whiteness, and a river of silver. At last he arrived in a place that was completely red, and crossed a golden river. There, before he rested for the night, he saw the Fufunda bird under a tamarind tree. The next day, when the sun began to rise, he galloped away on his horse. But, hurry as he might, the sun scorched him and he could scarcely continue. The Fufunda, which figures in this adventure, is King of the Birds. Its only egg, laid after the creation of the world, has not hatched, and will not do so until the end of time. Good men will be allowed to shelter in the shadow of the bird. But wicked men, although they will see the shadow, will not be allowed to use it. They will stay in the sun until their brains boil.[3]

Another Hausa tale refers to a hen that lays golden eggs with silver whites. The greedy owner kills it to get the eggs which are still inside.[4] This resembles the Aesop fable of the goose that laid golden eggs, probably an Indian story, since a version occurs in the *Jātakas*: a flamingo moults its golden feathers and is plucked bare by the avaricious owner.[5]

Gold and silver represent the mystical aspects of sun and moon.

---

[1] Haavio, 56.

[2] Zimmer, Heinrich, *Myths and Symbols in Indian Art and Civilization*, Washington, 1946, 103–4.

[3] Tremearne, A. J. N., *Hausa Superstitions and Customs*, London, 1913, 128–9.

[4] *Ibid.*, 15.

[5] Jacobs, J., ed., *The Fables of Aesop*, London, 1889, i. 66–7.

A duck which lays a golden egg in the morning and a silver one in the evening is mentioned in the Russian Märchen, collected by Afanasief,[1] and Aldrovandus refers to an egg-laying Moon Woman: she broods a clutch and they hatch into giants.[2]

An unusual version of the moon egg, called Nkosuano, is known to the Akan people of Ghana. Shown with a smaller egg, the two symbolize Nyame, a lunar goddess who gave birth to the sun. Here the relative importance of the two bodies is reversed: the smaller egg stands for the sun. This emblem is a royal tribal symbol. In Bono-Takyiaian State the herald's staff is surmounted by two eggs, and on these two falcons perch, the female actually seated on the eggs. This ensemble, too, represents the moon goddess, special deity of the tribe.[3]

In 'The Lady and the Lion', a fairy tale collected by the Brothers Grimm, the moon again plays a leading role. The lady, searching for her husband, who has been changed into a dove, is given an egg by the moon and told to break it in her hour of need. In due course she does this, and out run a hen and twelve chickens, all made of gold. The enchanting sight so distracts his captor that the lady is enabled to fulfil her plans.[4] Here the moon egg is just a trifle, but the origins of the story may well link up with early creation myth. It may be that a popular belief, recorded in Germany, that anyone eating eggs will commit seven foolish acts,[5] implies some original connection with the moon and lunacy. Perhaps the seven foolish acts are relics of the belief in moon-based madness, the egg resembling the full moon.

Folk-tales often express in poetic form eternal truths and mystic concepts, unformulated because intuitively held in the thoughts of those who pass them on. A story from old Russia of 'Dawn, Twilight and Midnight' suggests a primitive attempt to portray three stages of the moon's light. Three youths, Dawn, Twilight and Midnight, pay a visit to the underworld, where they rescue three princesses enchanted by a wicked serpent. The three princesses, and here the guardian-of-the-treasure motif occurs again, are

---

[1] Müller, F. Max, *Contributions to the Science of Mythology*, London, 1897, ii.635.

[2] Ashton, John, *Curious Creatures in Zoology*, London, 1890, 180.

[3] Meyerowitz, 35.

[4] The Brothers Grimm, *Fairy Tales*, London, 1909, 235.

[5] Bächtold-Stäubli, ii.643.

living in three palaces: one made of gold, one silver, and one copper. When the heroes arrive, each princess folds her palace up into an egg. They at last return to the world again, after a journey through the underworld, and the palaces unroll, each preserved in its magic container.[1]

Sometimes the treasure egg contains a god. The Molionids, sons of Poseidon, Lord of the Sea, were hatched from a silver egg,[2] and Helen of Troy was said to derive from an egg which fell down from the moon,[3] a celestial body often associated with great beauty.

Often in Greek myth and elsewhere rival principals come from an egg. Zeus in the form of a swan mated with Leda, causing her to lay two eggs; one, according to other versions, hatched the two women Helen and Clytemnestra; the other, the Dioscuri, Castor and Pollux, the embodiment of light and shade.[4] The tale is almost paralleled in Peru, but here the contrast is metaphysical. A virgin, seduced by a god, laid two eggs, one containing the Prince of Evil, Apo-Catequil, the other Piguerao-Catequil, a life-bestowing deity who raised his mother back from death.[5]

In the Roman Circus wooden eggs were used to score the progress of different races. A certain number, seven at the most, were laid on a special structure supported by columns. This was set up on the Spina, a lengthwise barrier erected in the Circus. One egg was removed after every contest. Livy, referring to '*Ova ad notas curriculis numerandus*', tells us that these *ovaria* had been constructed since 174 B.C.[6] Agrippa introduced them, according to another source, in 37 B.C. They were thought to afford to the competitors the special protection of the Dioscuri, their patrons, in whose temple at Laconia a large egg marked with hieroglyphs was suspended.[7]

The Dioscuri symbolize the two main aspects of the sun: its appearance and disappearance, day and night. In many folk-tales

---

[1] Curtin, Jeremiah, *Fairy Tales of Eastern Europe*, London, 1906, 15ff.

[2] *Larousse*, 155.

[3] Briffault, Robert, *The Mothers*, London, 1927, iii.140.

[4] *Larousse*, 204. Viski, Károly, *Volksbrauch der Ungarn*, Budapest, 1932, 51.

[5] Gardner, James, *The Faiths of the World*, Edinburgh, 1858, i.797.

[6] Wissowa, Georg, *Paulys Real Encyclopädie der classischen Altertumswissenschaft*, Stuttgart, 1942, xviiia, 1889–90.

[7] Jones, 447.

this darker side is described, and sometimes success can only be achieved by invoking the powers of darkness. In Normandy and other parts of France there is a tradition of a bird that lays golden eggs. To benefit from it, the Devil is summoned by taking a black hen to a cross-roads and calling out loudly: 'Money from my black fowl.' The Devil will appear, bringing a golden egg, but the soul must be pledged in exchange.[1] The Satanic figure appears as a dishonest innkeeper in the German version collected by Wolff. He steals the golden-egg-laying bird from a boy who had obtained it, but is eventually foiled with the aid of a magic walking stick.[2] The tale of 'Jack and the Beanstalk' – one of the hero's achievements is to steal the hen that lays the golden eggs from the giant's castle in cloudland – is perhaps of similar origin.[3]

Here the miraculous fowl lives up in the sky. But in Estonian tradition *Paäsukene Päeva Lindu* – the swallow bird of the sun – flies across the earth and 'over the world's church', looking for a suitable place to lay her eggs. She avoids both a blue bush and a red, finally choosing one that is yellow, the colour of the sun, to build her nest. After three months the eggs hatch a fruit, a stone, the sun and the moon. The feathers of this miraculous bird are also blue, yellow and red, the same colours as the bushes, and sometimes the eggs themselves are described in these colours.[4]

Whereas the Estonian eggs furnish the world, but omit mankind, in Ecuador there is a story of an egg which, with the aid of the sun, produces the human race. The tale, peculiar to the Jivaro, tells how the creator and his wife, Kumpara and Chingaso, give birth to the sun and moon, Esta and Nantu. These two marry and beget children. One day Chingaso gives the children two eggs, with instructions to bury them in the sand beside the river. But next day the heron steals them. The sun goes in pursuit, and in the excitement one of the eggs is dropped. The other is saved and brought home again. It is the very same colour as the sun and, after a time, it hatches the ancestor of the Jivaro tribe; other eggs brought by Chingaso produce birds, animals and food.[5]

[1] *Ibid.*, 468.

[2] Kelly, Walter, *Curiosities of Indo-European Tradition and Folklore*, London, 1863, 210.

[3] Hardwick, Charles, *Traditions, Superstitions and Folklore*, London, 1872, 71–2.

[4] Haavio, 50.   [5] Hellbom, 78.

That a tribe should derive from an egg is a quite common idea. The southern Chin, beyond the Assamese border, will never kill a crow, for it embodies their source of life: it laid the original Chin egg from which they are all descended.[1]

THE CREATION STRUGGLE

Often the idea of procreation involves a struggle – conflict or an act of violence of some kind – and, as with all basic human instincts and behaviour, we find this reflected in myth. On the lowest level, the physical, this is a fact of life in the behaviour of the sexes. The act of procreation often only takes place after a struggle, the ravishing by force of the pure virgin. Such a tale is used to describe the founding of the Korean kingdom, Koguryo. Yuhwa, the daughter of Haback, was abducted and rescued by King Golden Frog. To ensure her safety, she was locked in a room and told to avoid the sunshine. Unfortunately, one ray touched her and she became pregnant, giving birth in due course to a very large egg. This was thought to be a bad omen. The king gave the egg to a pig, but the pig refused it. So did a dog. It was thrown by the wayside, but horses and cows would not step on it. When it was left among the mountains and the fields, birds and animals refused to harm it and protected it instead. Finally, when the king had tried to break it and failed, he returned the egg to its mother. At once it hatched, and out came a male child, Chumong, a descendant of the god Paekha, who performed miraculous deeds and founded Koguryo.[2]

In this tale of rape, the sun is again the operative factor. The same idea, more mystically expressed, is central to the cosmology of Japan. Hirata says the egg of creation was called *ichi motsu*. In the beginning it was chaos, and contained the breath of life and beginnings of creation.[3] *Nihongi*, the Chronicle of Japan, a Shinto work dating from the eighth century B.C., puts it quite clearly: 'Of old, Heaven and Earth were not yet separated . . . they formed a chaotic mass like an egg, which was of obscurely defined

---

[1] Frazer, Sir James G., *Totemism and Exogamy*, London, 1910, ii.337.
[2] *Korea, Its Land, People and Culture of All Ages*, Seoul, 1963, 650. No author.
[3] O'Neill, ii.765.

limits and contained germs. The purer and clearer part was thinly diffused and formed Heaven, while the heavier and grosser element settled down and became Earth.'[1]

A few temples (Daibod, Miyako) contain representations of the world egg floating in water. A bull clutches it between his forefeet and strikes at it with his horns. When he broke it open, the human race emerged.[2] He may here be a symbol of the sun, or perhaps the wind. A Jesuit priest named Vilela, who visited Japan in 1563, heard a tale in which not only mankind, but the heavens, the seas and the earth appeared from an egg broken open by the wind.[3]

The wind also plays a role in the myth of North American Indians. The Chinooks, contending with difficult natural conditions, saw their origin in a conflict between the sun and the elements, and imagined their birth from a thunder egg, with the South Wind as a midwife. Old Man South Wind was travelling north when he met a giantess and, since he was feeling hungry, she gave him a net to catch some fish. He caught a whale, but, instead of splitting it open as she had told him, he cut it across and began to remove some pieces of blubber. At once the whale changed into the Thunderbird, so large that it hid the sun, the noise of its wings causing the earth to shake. The Thunderbird flew to Saddleback Mountain, near the mouth of the Columbia River, where it laid a nest of eggs upon the summit. The old giantess followed and threw all the eggs down into the valley where they broke and were changed into Indians. The Thunderbird and South Wind both looked for the giantess in order to punish her, but could not find her, although they travelled northwards every year.[4] Here the conflict assumes epic proportions as the elements rage.

In Australia, where an emu egg is a popular symbol for the sun, the aborigines say that man quarrelled with his friend the emu and stole one of its eggs. According to the Euahlayi, he threw it into

[1] Aston, W. G., ed., *Nihongi*, London, 1896, 1–2.

[2] Gardner, i.798. Bayley, Harold, *The Lost Language of Symbolism*, London, 1912, i.324.

[3] Haavio, 58.

[4] Chung-I-Wen, 'Bird Ancestor Legends of N.E. Asia, N.W. America and the Pacific', *Bulletin of the Institute of Ethnology*, xii (Taipei, Autumn 1961) 104.

the sky, where it struck a great pile of firewood and burst into flames – the sun.[1]

This strife which brings the world and the elements into being exists, not only on a physical level, but in a metaphysical sphere as well. Creation myths among the sun-worshipping Zoroastrians describe a perpetual struggle between the principle of good, Ahura-Mazda, and the principle of evil, Angra-Mainyu. There is a lengthy truce of several thousand years, and during this time the evil spirit despairs, hurling himself into the abyss, while the spirit of good lays an egg.[2] The *Ninokhired Manuscript* describes how 'Heaven, the earth, water and everything else under the heavens, have been formed the same as a bird's egg. The heaven above the earth and below the earth is like an egg, made by the hands of Ahura the Creator. The earth within the heavens is like the yolk of an egg.'[3]

The *Bundahisn* tells us that Ahura-Mazda created the sky 'Bright and manifest, its ends exceeding far apart, in the form of an egg, of shining metal . . . the top of it reached to the Endless Light.'[4]

The egg represents the universe, the earth hanging suspended from the vault of the sky, midway between the regions of good and evil. This rouses the spirit of darkness. Bent on mischief, he pierces the egg and arrives on earth. The two spirits then contend for its possession till the end of time.[5] Other versions say that each spirit created an egg, and enclosed in it twenty-four genii of his own persuasion. When the two eggs broke, good and evil were brought together into the world. Plutarch says only one egg was made, by Ahura-Mazda. When the twenty-four demons of the evil spirit broke into it, among the twenty-four genii of the blessed spirit, evil and good became mingled in the world.[6]

Manichaeism brought features of a similar dualism both eastwards into China, and to Europe. Something of this seems to be reflected in a legend of the Letts. God, the creator, sent forth His word as a gust of wind, which bore an eagle. He made darkness

---

[1] *Larousse*, 469–70.
[2] Kellett, E. E., *A Short History of Religions*, London, 1962, 385.
[3] Haavio, 56.
[4] Kramer, S. N., *Mythologies of the Ancient World*, New York, 1961, 338–9.
[5] Kellett, 385.
[6] Dragomanov, M. P., *Notes on the Slavic Religio-Ethical Legends*, Bloomington, 1961, 152.

and light, and banished the eagle – evidently the spirit of evil – to the former. The bird rebelled, and was dismembered by God. His blood became the sea, his body mud, and from the two halves of an egg within him came heaven and hell. Inside these were a white, sticky mass and a black, sticky mass, which became angels and devils, and within the lower shell the mud collected, forming the earth. Much of this story closely resembles the medieval dualist heresies, where all matter, living or dead, is seen as stemming from the evil principle.[1]

These tales express the warring of the elements, and the conflict of darkness and light, in terms of the eternal struggle between the forces of good and evil. A story from Bengal sets out the two aspects of the sun, in the day and in the night, united through an act of unnatural violence. 'Blue Lotus and Red Lotus' tells of a king who has two wives, each with a son. One woman is a demon in disguise who eats, first her rival's child, and then her own, when he tries to save his half-brother. As she devours the first boy, a golden ball drops from her mouth; an iron ball appears when she has eaten her own son. Alarmed at this, she buries the two balls in a bamboo grove. Later, in the identical spot, a workman finds a blue egg from which the human child is reborn, and a red egg, out of which the demon child reappears. They are named Blue Lotus and Red Lotus, and have many heroic adventures when they grow up.[2]

This elaborate tale undoubtedly has affinities with the legends of the creator sun god in the *Bhagvata-Purana*. Readers might recall how Brahma sat for 1,000 years inside his egg, until a shining lotus sprang up from his navel and he was born. The golden ball of this tale suggests Brahma's 'golden egg as brilliant as the sun'; the iron ball is its reflection.

The reverse side of the coin is expressed very forcefully in a north Asian tale from a tribe on the River Yenisey, where the egg, symbol of life and creation, brings death and destruction. A man and a woman, so it is said, fell down to earth from heaven. They stayed for the period of a year and produced a child, which was then buried. Then they returned to heaven.

---

[1] Lukas, Franz, 'Das Ei als kosmogonische Vorstellung', *Zeitschrift des Vereins für Volkskunde*, iv (Berlin, 1894), 238–9.

[2] Bradley-Birt, F. B., *Bengal Fairy Tales*, London, 1920, 168–73.

Two years passed by, when the grave broke open and an egg came out. It started rolling and, wherever it went, a bad smell exuded, killing everything that came in its way. At last a human being, who was Lord of the Upper Yenisey, threw a stone at the egg and shattered it into pieces.[1] In a Hrusso legend, from the North-East Frontier Area, rolling eggs also appear, but in creative capacity. In the beginning, they say, no earth or sky existed. There were only two eggs, and these were soft and shone like gold. Instead of remaining quiescent, they rolled until they bumped together. When this happened, both eggs broke open: the earth appeared from one, her husband, the sky, from the other.[2]

Here legend seems to coincide with astronomical fact. Sometimes, however, not even the apparent collision of two heavenly bodies is mirrored, nor is there an external agent. The egg fractures of its own accord, just as the simplest organic growth, the amoeba, divides its own substance involuntarily, for the purpose of procreation. In modern terms, the self-induced fracture of the egg resembles the cataclysmic splitting of the atom. Tangaroa, primeval god of the South Seas, sits brooding in his egg, high in the sky, enveloped in eternal night. Then, so the Society Islanders imagine, this ancestor of the gods, who existed from the beginning of time, became tired of the buffeting wind, and burst out from his shell. He stood up, and this signified the creation of light. His shell became the sky and the god entered yet another one, which provided the foundation of the world. The first shell, which was called Rumia, became his house – the vault of the sky, which enclosed the newly created world.[3] A slightly different story from Ra'iatea describes how the shell was always replaced with one a little larger than the last. The world grew bigger and bigger, until it reached its present size.[4] Hawaians call Tangaroa the bird which laid the creation egg. When this broke, the sky and earth were formed.[5] In Samoa and the Sandwich Islands they say that their archipelagos formed from the fragments of shell. The

[1] Hellbom, 97.

[2] Elwin, 15–16.

[3] Williamson, Robert W., *Religious and Cosmic Beliefs of Central Polynesia*, Cambridge, 1933, 226. Mackenzie, *South Sea Islands*, 179, 307.

[4] Hastings, James, ed., *Encyclopaedia of Religion and Ethics*, Edinburgh, 1911, iv.174b.

[5] *Ibid.*

creator god of Tahiti, Ta'aroa, was an orphan, and quite alone. He flung away his egg, revealed his face, and said:

> *O landless void, O skyless void,*
> *O nebulous, purposeless space,*
> *Eternal and timeless,*
> *Become the world, extend!*[1]

Tales of the original Chinese being, P'an Ku, also describe how, after the dark and the silence, a world egg formed itself, from which this personage appeared. The heavens and lower regions of the earth shaped themselves from the shell, but P'an Ku himself made the sun, the moon, and the stars.[2]

In Eudemus' account, Phoenician mythology describes the cosmic egg splitting itself in half and forming heaven and earth. The egg was produced by the original elements of air and breath, which in turn had been transformed from darkness and desire. The theory of the world egg in this case was borrowed from Egypt, though the Phoenicians, who were famous sailors, must have helped to spread the idea far and wide. However, it seems fanciful to imagine that they gave it to China.[3]

TIMELESSNESS

The concept of timelessness, like other esoteric ideals, exists on different levels. In Buddhist thought man, striving to transcend time, and passing in turn through seven spiritual stages of development, sees the breaking of an egg-shell as equivalent to breaking out of Samsāra, the wheel of existence. A well-known parable illustrates this point:

'When a hen has laid eggs,' says the Buddha, 'eight, ten, or a dozen; when the hen has sat upon them and kept them warm long enough – then, when one of those chicks, the first one to break the shell with the point of its claw or its beak, comes safely out of the egg, what will they call that chick, the eldest or the youngest?'

The answer comes: 'They will call him the eldest, venerable Gautama, for he is the first born among them.' And the Buddha continues: 'So likewise, O Brahman, I alone, among all those who live

---

[1] *Larousse*, 457. Freund, Philip, *Myths of Creation*, London, 1964, 45.
[2] Haavio, 58. Freund, 46. Gardner, i.797.
[3] *Larousse*, 82. Sykes, Egerton, *Dictionary of Non-Classical Mythology*, London, 1961, 66.

in ignorance, and are as though enclosed and imprisoned in an egg, have burst through this shell of ignorance; I alone in this world have attained to the blessed, the universal dignity of Buddha.'[1]

In Western civilization Christian thinking does not constrain man to abandon the usual concepts of time entirely. But above and beyond the reckoning of our normal daily lives is the Christian calendar year, which fulfils its mystical annual round, without regard to the ordinary world of man. A legend from Iceland about the three Magi tells how on Melchior's farmyard there was an ostrich which laid two eggs. On Christmas night both were hatched and from one a lamb came forth; from the other, a lion – the traditional Christian image of peace, drawn from irreconcilable opposites, in the Book of Isaiah.[2]

The night when the lion lay down with the lamb is endless. But in the world of myth all ordinary time is falsified and normal processes are quickened, as in the Russian folk-tale of 'Bábá Yagá'. Zamorýshek, the weakling, and his forty brothers, have a strange life-cycle. As children, they grow up not by days, but by hours. Each is born from an egg collected by an old and childless Russian couple from every house in their village. Eventually Zamorýshek, with his magic horse, outwits the evil Bábá Yagá.[3]

Just as in the timeless world of magic, so in everyday life factors may exist which give the semblance of leading to a celestial, or semicelestial, sphere, where ordinary time is of no importance. To the South Sea Islanders, for whom the ocean was an ever-present frontier, birds must have seemed especially miraculous beings; not only as messengers of Heaven, but also as creatures who soared freely beyond the bounds of land and sea. The origin of man from a bird's egg is a common idea throughout the area. An Easter Island stone-carving in the British Museum shows a bird-headed man carefully clasping an egg.[4] The Fijians, far to the west, seem to echo this in their two hawk eggs, from which a boy and girl, ancestors of the human race, hatched out. The bird had laid these eggs near the house of the god Ngendei, and this so delighted

[1] Eliade, Mircea, *Images and Symbols*, London, 1961, 76–7.
[2] Hellbom, 98. Isai. xi.6–7.
[3] Magnus, Leonard A., *Russian Folk Tales*, London, 1916, 48.
[4] Mackenzie, *Melanesia and Indonesia*, 49. *Larousse*, 457. See plate i.

him that he brooded them himself.[1] For the Mandaya of the Mindanao Uplands around Davao the hawk eggs have become those of the dove. And, while the god no longer plays a part, the two original ancestors, brought forth from the eggs, have now become important spirits, influencing the destiny of the world.[2] In the Admiralty Islands to the south, the doves' eggs again produce the founders of mankind. But in this case they are a man and a bird.[3] The legends are numerous, and one cannot list them all. The Les of Hainan in the South China Sea[4] and the natives of the Torres Strait have similar stories;[5] in a Maori version we originate from an egg, laid on the primeval waters by a giant bird.[6]

In the tales discussed above, the egg is a link between timelessness and real existence as we know it. It can also be used to symbolize a concurrent survival of that other world. The story of Seetetelane from Basutoland tells how a poor man, who had no wife, found an egg in a nearby field. He took it home and saved it for a few days. To his surprise, each evening on returning home, beer and bread were ready prepared for him. One day a girl appeared out of the egg, and told him never to speak of this, not even to himself. She made him into a great chief, who owned many possessions, and he was very happy. But one day, being drunk, he called her 'the daughter of an ostrich egg'. That night he went to sleep as usual, and in the morning woke to find that everything had gone and he was a poor man again.[7] Here the two planes of existence and time are seen as irreconcilable. But, in a similar tale from the Santal Parganas of North Bengal, this dichotomy is eliminated. A herd-boy, finding a flycatcher's egg, asks his mother to cook it, but she forgets. Each day a beautiful magic maiden, the Bonga, comes out from the egg, prepares his food and goes back into the shell again. One day the herd-boy discovers her; they marry, and live happily ever after.[8]

Today we are greatly preoccupied both with time and space, following recent scientific discoveries. This has given rise to a most bizarre interpretation of the egg creation myth which tries

[1] Mackenzie, *Melanesia and Indonesia*, 146–7.
[2] *Ibid.*, 312.   [3] *Larousse*, 477.
[4] Frazer, *Pausanias*, iii.339.
[5] *Larousse*, 477.   [6] Hastings, iv.174*b*.
[7] Jacottet, E., *The Treasury of Basuto Lore*, London, 1908, 108–11.
[8] Bompas, C. H., *Folklore of the Santal Parganas*, London, 1909, 111–13.

to fit it into a purely materialist view of man's thought. A modern Soviet writer refers to a Latin American legend in which eggs dropped down from the sky on to dandelions; presumably this refers to the parachute-like dandelion pollen. He goes on to suggest that ancient man may once have seen a container with a human being in it descend from the sky, and so imagined that the visitor was emerging from a celestial egg. This extraordinary comparison of the creation egg to a flying saucer was put forward quite seriously in an article in 1967.[1]

For those who accept the fantasy, the flying saucer comes to the earth from another planet. As such, the idea is ultra-modern. Aristophanes, writing many centuries ago, suggests how the seasons themselves might have evolved from the timeless mass of chaos:

> *There was Chaos at first, and Darkness, and Night,*
> *And Tartarus vasty and dismal;*
> *But the Earth was not there, nor the Sky, nor the Air,*
> *Till at length in the bosom abysmal*
> *Of Darkness an egg, from the whirlwind conceived,*
> *Was laid by the sable plumed Night.*
> *And out of that egg, as the seasons revolved,*
> *Sprang Love, the entrancing, the bright,*
> *Love brilliant and bold, with his pinions of gold,*
> *Like a whirlwind, refulgent and sparkling.*[2]

These lines are supposed to parody some remarks made by Hesiod in his *Theogony*. But the birth of Eros from an egg does not originate from Hesiod, who never specifically mentions it in his accounts of the creation.[3] More likely it arises from the countless legends of the Orphics.

THE UNIVERSE EGG

In the beginning, according to many creation myths, the universe was a formless void, but containing a cosmic mass which resembled an egg. Glele, a famous King of Dahomey, had a son, Behanzin, whose throne-name translates: 'The universe carries

---

[1] Zaitsev, Vyacheslav, 'Visitors from Outer Space', *Sputnik* (Moscow, January 1967), 166–7.

[2] Rogers, Benjamin B., ed., *The Birds*, London, 1906, 93.

[3] Hesiod, *Théogonie*, Paris, 1928, 37.

the egg the world desires.'[1] There seem to be several ideas compounded here. One is that the origins of being gave rise to chaos, from which the world egg, which personifies form, at last derived. The universe itself is represented as a creator, and the act of creation does not produce a passive object: the pre-formative world desires to be given form.

The nature of this form is sometimes rather curious. The *San-Wu-Li-Chi*, an obscure Chinese work of the third century A.D., describes the heaven and earth blended together like the contents of an egg, in a condition called *hun-tun*. This formation broke up after eighteen thousand years, and the bright part formed the heavens, the dark the earth. Astronomical theory in Han times taught that the earth was enclosed by the sphere of the heavens, just as the yolk of an egg is completely enclosed by its shell. In modern Chinese, *hun-tun* is the name of a small sac-like dumpling, popular in soup: a quantity of chopped-up meat is enclosed in a shell of dough – a miniature universe.[2]

The state of flux, represented by the contents of this small dumpling, was taken in medieval Europe to represent the elements. A Paris miniature from the *Codex Ovide Moralise* shows a teacher sitting at a desk, pointing to an egg and explaining that the membrane symbolizes air, white the water, and yolk the earth.[3] Only the element of fire is lacking, and the shell serves instead as an emblem of the sky. This error could have been due to ignorance or, more likely, the impossibility of finding anything in the egg which resembled fire. Old Russian manuscripts use the same image, substituting cloud for air.[4]

Tibetans imagined five elements instead of the customary four, and each of these appears from an egg of different colour and material: wind from dark red sardonyx comes 'like a black year', fire from red copper, water from blue iron, and earth from gold. In the beginning, they say, there was only existence, followed by moisture and fire, which combined to produce these four kinds of egg. Lastly came a white mussel shell, a bright beam of light playing over it, for it contained a rainbow and the brilliance of

---

[1] Scofield, John, 'Freedom Speaks French in Ouagadougou', *National Geographic* (Washington, August 1966), 176–7.

[2] Kramer, 382, 384.

[3] Wildhaber, 'Zum Symbolgehalt', 79–80.

[4] Haavio, 53–4.

the sky.[1] A tribal variant, set down in the Bon texts, describes one gigantic egg, created in eighteen layers, from which the elements and mankind appear.[2]

But it is the weather, rather than the elements, which figures in the minds of another Asiatic people, the Iglulik of northern Canada, struggling to exist in highly adverse conditions. Arctic regions are dangerously deceptive and sudden violent storms of mist and rain are common during periods of apparently cloudless weather. This group of Eskimos believe in giant game animals, similar to the Abominable Snowman, which govern these sudden changes. They are said to hatch out of eggs and to be so enormous that it takes days to cut a single one up. When one appears among the herds of caribou, it is like a great mountain of snow, and when it runs torrential rain and fog sweep over the land.[3]

Arctic storms are heavy and dangerous. But, of course, in the heat of central Asia the rain is a cool, refreshing phenomenon; a legend of the Hill Miri, on the Assamese-Tibetan border, describes it as the very source of life. Chingum-Erum, wife of Wigu Chungum-Irum, was sleeping one day when some rain from the sky fell into her. After a six-month cycle she laid an egg, and from it came Sichi the earth, Togle the mountains, and Togji the little hills.[4]

This myth recalls others from Europe, where fertilization is brought about by the sun. Local conditions clearly govern the choice of the operative element in these stories: they tend to dictate the whole fabric of the tales. Naturally, a mountain tribe would stress the creation of the mighty hills, just as the Estonians describe in some detail the formation of their islands from the creation egg.[5]

LEVELS OF CREATION

In myth, an egg represents something difficult to define: the beginning of time and all things, the source of life itself. From the waters of creation and the primeval flux, the desire for procreation stirs and arises in the form of an egg. Plutarch wrote: 'It is

---

[1] *Ibid.*, 57–8. Talbot Rice, Tamara, *Everyday Life in Byzantium*, London, 1967, 148. In this account, ostrich eggs are used.
[2] Hellbom, 68–9.   [3] *Ibid.*, 97.
[4] Elwin, 15.   [5] Hellbom, 72.

consecrated to the sacred ceremonies of Bacchus, as a representation of the author of nature, who produces and comprehends all things in himself.'[1]

Statues of Dionysus in Boetian tombs are represented clasping an egg, for the emblem was carried in procession at the celebration of the Mysteries, and was later sanctified, signifying the world.[2] As in the Osiris processions of early Egypt, when various items – diamond dust, fig flour, and aromatic spices – were shaped into an egg, the sacred casket which held a real egg also contained a phallus.[3] Caps worn by the statues of certain Roman and Greek gods, Mercury, Vulcan, and the Dioscuri, are egg-shaped, a form of dress which stood for freedom and emancipation among the Greeks and Romans.[4] We probably see the descendant of this cap worn in present-day Albania, where white woollen egg-shaped hats of very ancient design are still common.

Social position is connected with the magic egg in other countries too. It is surprising to find the escutcheon of an English family figuring three eggs.[5] But in the East it is quite common for certain races and classes to visualize their origin in birth from an egg. According to the Khampti, a Thai tribe on the Indo-Burmese border, the Rajahs appeared from one. In the beginning, so they say, there was water all over the earth. Then the god Phra ordered a female to lay an egg, which he cut in two halves. One of these he placed on the ground, the other was fixed to the summit of a hill which he had built, forming the sky. It was from this elevated half that the Rajahs derived.[6]

The Palangs, living rather further east, trace their ancestry to the Naga princess who laid three eggs,[7] and the Tonkinese tell of Princess Au-Leo, who laid a hundred, all of which hatched out male babies.[8] These mystical evolutions often have a pronounced element of class distinction. The mythical progenitor is a royal or

---

[1] Arundell of Wardour, Lord, *Tradition, Principally with Reference to Mythology and the Law of Nations*, London, 1872, 306.

[2] Eliade, Mircea, *Patterns in Comparative Religion*, London, 1958, 415.

[3] *Ibid.* Waterman, 91.

[4] O'Neill, ii.924–5. Payne Knight, Richard, *The Symbolical Language of Ancient Art and Mythology*, New York, 1876, 96.

[5] *Notes and Queries*, 9 January 1932, clxii.27.

[6] Elwin, 17.

[7] Frazer, *Totemism*, ii.337.

[8] Gardner, i.797.

privileged personage. This is also apparent in the spirit worship of Burma. The *nats* or spirits are mostly the ghosts of dead royal heroes and heroines. Taungmagyi and Myauk Minsinbyu, two of the most important shades, were both originally from eggs.[1]

Elaborate legends detailing the evolution of the class system emphasize the point. One such is preserved in Peru, where it was collected by a sixteenth-century Augustine friar. Vichama, the Inca hero, was greatly distressed to find no men in the world, and hence no one to worship the Huacas and the god of the sun. He asked the father of the sun god for help, and three eggs fell from the sky – one of gold, one of silver, and a third of copper. These provided the three social classes: the *curacas* or chiefs from the golden egg, the nobles from the silver, and from the copper the common folk.[2] A primitive myth from the island of Anaa, east of Tahiti in the Tuamotu Archipelago, puts the idea in an even more basic form. Where the Peruvian myth uses three different types of metal to express a social conception, the class levels are here defined spatially. The cosmos was shaped like an egg containing Te Tumu and Te Papa. When it burst there were three levels inside – the two creator gods on the lowest one, together with all the animals and plants of the universe. The process of creation continued, and when the bottom level became too crowded a hole was knocked in the middle of the next. People moved up, bringing plants and animals with them. Finally, some went to the highest layer, so now the human race has three levels on which to live.[3]

The gods are often thought of as literally high above the world of men; Christian children tend to imagine that God is an old man up in the clouds. A myth from Sumatra telling how the world was furnished from eggs and from a magic ring is based on this idea. Sitapi, daughter of the ruling god, Bataru Guru, looked down at the earth from her vantage-point in the sky. She was distressed to see such a bare plain below, and begged her father to send down a swallow to seek information. High winds prevented its return, so Sitapi sent down another bird and again the same thing happened. She then carefully lowered seven eggs and a magic ring. The eggs contained all plants and trees, and the ring provided houses and

[1] Ridgeway, William, *The Dramas and Dramatic Dances of Non-European Races*, Cambridge, 1915, 246.
[2] Haavio, 59.   [3] Freund, 45.

cattle.[1] The skies too were equipped with stars formed from an egg created by a god, though this belief is recorded from Java.[2]

This legend stresses the gap between the gods and the race of man. And often it is the mystic rather than the social differences between the different strata that are emphasized. A thirteenth-century Tibetan manuscript describes six eggs resulting from intercourse of Yi Dam, the monkey king, with a rock demon. Six different types of creature appear: a spirit, a titan, an animal, an infernal being, a hunger demon and a human – whose child, the Ye Smon king, becomes the ancestor of the Tibetan people.[3]

Some Chinese families claimed origin from an ancestor miraculously born, but these tales only appear in south China. The Sea Dyaks of the South China Sea believe mankind as a whole came out of an egg,[4] and a woman in a cave in Huang Shan is said to have found two big eggs. She broke them open and was amazed to find human beings inside.[5]

The Ch'en family of Kwangtung presumed relationship with the god of thunder, because one day during a thunderstorm an egg dropped down into their home. A child came out of this egg, which the thunder suckled. Heads of leading Chinese families often claimed descent from a thunder egg. Another family had a hunting dog which found twelve eggs. When it thundered the eggs burst, but the shells were saved. Seeing this as a divine omen, the clan chiefs from then on asserted their ownership of these shells.[6]

A magic dog with nine ears, in another tale, finds an egg which is brought home. There is thunder and lightning and the egg hatches a child, who becomes Governor of Laichow and is still worshipped as the god of thunder.[7] Newberry describes such a hero, who seems to have acquired his divinity as a reward. Soldiers of Wên Wang found an egg beside an ancient tomb, and it brought forth a young man. He found two magic apricots and, having eaten them, acquired so much strength that he was able to rescue his imprisoned father. Filial piety was a great virtue in China, so perhaps this is why he was made into the god of thunder and lightning.[8]

[1] Mackenzie, *Melanesia and Indonesia*, 310–11.
[2] Haavio, 59.   [3] Hellbom, 73.   [4] Haavio, 59.
[5] Hellbom, 74.   [6] *Ibid.*   [7] *Ibid.*
[8] Newberry, J. S., *The Rainbow Bridge*, London, 1934, 72.

Sometimes gods seem to appear in the guise of animals; a dog figures in several Chinese legends mentioned above, and a princess of Cochin China united with a dog, which was born from an egg. These two are the mythical ancestors of the Les of Hainan.[1] The Jivaro of Ecuador tell of a jaguar, who married a local woman and made her pregnant. They quarrelled and he ripped her belly open. From the dead woman's womb rolled out two little eggs. The jaguar's mother hung them in a kettle on the ceiling and in time two boys appeared from them. It seemed dangerous for them to remain in that house, even though they had been well looked after, so one day the boys shot a number of arrows in the air. These clung together and formed a ladder which they were able to mount up into the sky. For, as the story says, originally the stars were human.[2]

Divinities often hatch from an egg, but it is interesting how in so many different cultures the birth of an outstanding person or heroic figure is imagined in the same way. The famous Miao scribe Mi Wang Sen was born from an egg, laid by a pigeon and hatched by a dove. He was able to write at once, and went to Ntzi, the heavenly land. Here, although the personage is human, his divine associations are referred to. Another Miao figure, the war-leader Mma Ngao Mi, was born from a grasshopper egg. She was an Amazon, who led her people bravely in their fights against the Chinese.[3]

Not all these popular folk-heroes are from the Chinese area. The Finnish legendary figure, Munapoika, was born in a similar way; his name means 'Egg Boy'.[4] The Danes have Holger Danske, the warrior born from an egg, who will ride on an egg-born steed. A magpie will build its nest on a tree in Viborg Lake, and from its egg Holger Danske will come again to fight for Denmark. When he comes riding on his mighty horse, there will be a battle, so fierce and gory that an iron hat could float in the blood that is shed.[5]

Magical beings often have some weak spot. Chinese folklore is fond of the toad, and in one tale it is described how, long ago, there was a childless man and wife. One day an egg appeared out of her knee and hatched a toad. The distressed parents tried to

[1] Hellbom, 75.   [2] *Ibid.*, 87.
[3] *Ibid.*, 81.   [4] *Ibid.*, 93.   [5] *Ibid.*, 93, 98.

Colour Plate III (a) Two Russian porcelain eggs. That on the left is probably a fanciful elaboration of the famous twelfth-century icon known as 'The Goldenheaded Angel' (The Archangel Gabriel); the second egg shows the Virgin of Kazan, and preserves a less Italianate style of painting than is usual in much nineteenth-century Russian work of this type.

(b) Eight Russian porcelain eggs. At the bottom right is the reverse of the similarly placed egg in colour plate II (b), and top right is the reverse of the horizontally adjacent egg in the same plate. The reverse of the eggs decorated with a chalice is also shown: the smaller example in colour plate II (b) (centre right), the larger in colour plate II (a) (on the right).

Colour Plate IV (a) St Anne and a Prophet, probably Elijah, on two Russian porcelain eggs.

(b) St George and two red eggs. In the centre the Saint, probably after the icon in the Cathedral of the Assumption at Moscow. He is flanked on the left by an egg bearing the Russian initial letters for 'Christ is Risen' (*Christos Voskresi*), and on the right by a Russian glass egg which also shows predominantly the common Easter-egg colour, red.

kill it, but the toad escaped and, when he matured, took a wife. She found him one day – a beautiful young man and not a toad any more. In her joy she burnt the toad skin, but the young man died.[1]

A reversal of the tale from Basutoland has a happier ending. The wife of a chief lays an egg. They hide it, and when the egg is of age, obtain a bride. One day she hears a voice laughing: 'Ha! Ha! My father has given me a wife.' The bride and her father discover the egg and transform it into a man, whom she then marries. But the egg-man ungratefully soon takes a second wife. The unhappy girl then fetches the egg-shells and buries them beside her husband's headrest. He changes back into an egg and is obliged to remain in that state until he promisest o discard the second wife.[2]

Here a member of the highest social caste is forcibly returned, though this is only temporary, to his original humble state. The idea, a human truth expressed in simple form, is one which we also find in the complex philosophy of Japan. 'Earth to earth, ashes to ashes, dust to dust', we say in the Christian burial service and *daruma* toys, which are found in every Japanese home, represent this thought. Japanese toys, or *omocha*, of which the *daruma* is one, are in many cases more than simple playthings. Often they are votive figures or charms with an ancient history, and they fufil functions which include bringing good luck, health and happiness to the owner, and protecting him and his household from misfortune and hard times. Such is the *daruma*, a small, round egg-shaped figure with no limbs, the head and body formed all in one. It represents the Indian saint Bodhidharma, who went to China in the sixth century A.D., where he founded the Ch'an Buddhist sect from which Japanese Zen derives. In Kyoto the *darumas* are female – *himedaruma*, they are called, recollecting an event of long ago, when the Empress Jingu Kogo stopped at the Matsuyama hot springs in the course of her journey to Korea. According to popular legend, Bodhidharma meditated upon a mountain peak for nine years, and during this time his legs grew into the ground, his arms fused into his body.[3] This shows how, in old age, we return to the egg whence we came.

[1] *Ibid.*, 82.   [2] *Ibid.*, 91.

[3] Hrdlicka, V. and Z., 'Daruma, A Japanese Folk Toy', *New Orient* (Prague, March 1966), 48.

Chapter 2
Sacrifice

Humpty Dumpty sat on a wall,
Humpty Dumpty had a great fall;
All the king's horses,
And all the king's men
Couldn't put Humpty together again.

FOUNDATION CEREMONIES

The egg was a rich and very ancient symbol of life: first consciousness, the creator gods and the universe itself arose from it. And indeed there are grounds for supposing that in popular belief it is sometimes even used as a substitute for human life.

Primitive peoples shared an idea that foundations of any new building must be laid on a blood sacrifice.[1] Without a basis in something living a new structure would surely collapse, and a variant of the same idea involved enclosing a living person in the walls.

The original point of the ceremony is no longer entirely clear. Was it intended to propitiate the offended local deity, or was it to create from the sacrifice a ghost to be a guardian spirit, who would watch over the new construction? The two ideas are not incompatible; and there is no reason why a sacrifice offered to the indwelling god should not have gradually developed into a new guardian spirit.

These practices were widespread. An early example in Britain was the sacrificial burial of two old women, whose bodies were excavated beneath the wall of a house at Skara Brae – the Stone Age village in Orkney.[2] This is not remarkable at such an early date; more surprising are similar accounts in a Christian setting, and it is especially interesting where the building is not secular, but consecrated to the service of God. Tradition imputes to St Columba the sacrifice of St Oran to prevent the collapse of Iona, and there is a Gaelic proverb based on the legend: 'Earth! Earth!

[1] Burdick, L. D., *Foundation Rites*, London, 1901, 16ff.
[2] Gordon Childe, V., *Skara Brae*, Edinburgh, 1950, 13.

45

– on to the mouth of Oran, that he may blab no more.' Apparently three days after the burial Columba had the foundation reopened for a last look at the corpse of his old friend, wherupon Oran raised swimming eyes and said, 'There is no wonder in death, and hell is not as it is reported.' Columba was so outraged that he ordered the earth to be flung back, uttering the words of the proverb.[1] Another persistent legend asserts that the wall of fifteenth-century Holsworthy Church was built over a living human being.[2] There was a further incident in Algeria in 1569, when a Spaniard called Geronimo was seized by the local people and walled into a fortress.[3] But, of course, in this case, as an enemy infidel, the Christian was a highly suitable victim.

Human sacrifice was usual to protect the walls of a new dwelling in Alaska long ago,[4] and in this case it seems that no special type of person was required. But in general, stories, legends and known fact tend to imply that, if it is to be meaningful, the sacrifice must represent something quite special. God required the ancient Jews to offer their first-fruits, the crops and the animals, to the glory of His Holy Name, and Abraham was prepared to slaughter his only son. Nothing is more precious to a man than his wife and child, and many folk-tales describe the plight of a builder obliged to make just this terrible sacrifice to ensure the stability of what he has made.

In Albania, at the northern town of Shkoder, they still tell visitors about the demon who damaged the fortress of Rosafat. So assiduous were his wrecking tactics that in the end the builder was obliged to sacrifice his wife. Because she was young and nursing a child, they built her into the walls with a small aperture left open, so that the baby could continue to feed. Local people insist that a trickle of cloudy water which runs down off the walls is the milk of the unfortunate mother.[5]

---

[1] Burdick, 34–5. Jamieson, John, *An Historical Account of the Ancient Culdees of Iona*, Edinburgh, 1811, 20–1. Baring-Gould, Sabine, *Strange Survivals*, London, 1892, 10–11. Thomas, Northcote W., ed., *Examples of Printed Folklore Concerning Northumberland*, London, 1904, 147. Scott, Sir Walter, *Minstrelsy of the Scottish Border*, Kelso, 1802–3, ii.334, 371; iii.398.

[2] Burdick, 43–4.

[3] *Ibid.*, 36.

[4] *Ibid.*, 49.

[5] Recounted to the author in Shkoder, July 1958.

It was the first person passing the site of a proposed new city gate who was seized and buried alive in old Thailand.[1] While the element of surprise was clearly important – or the victim would have escaped – the significance of the first arrival, a recurring theme in folk-tales of this kind, echoes the original sacrifice of the first-fruits. In neighbouring Burma the famous palace at Mandalay was built over no less than fifty bodies, specially slaughtered for the occasion.[2] Perhaps one corpse was thought insufficient to protect a remarkable royal dwelling.

Not only in folk-lore, but in mythology too, these ideas appear, and then the ritual death assumes a cosmic significance: the giant Ymir of Norse creation legend was slain so that his body could form the foundations of the universe.[3] Behind this lay the thought, however inarticulate, that without a death, a sacrifice, there can be no creation and nothing new. But as man progressed in development human bloodshed became less acceptable and gradually substitute rituals evolved.

At one time people imagined that a shadow was the outward and visible image of the soul. And so, in lieu of a sacrifice, builders secretly tried to measure the shadow of a passing man and bury it under the stones.[4] Animals were used too, especially in northern Europe.[5] Swedes buried a lamb below the altars of their early churches, curiously blending Christian and pagan belief with a common symbol.[6] Danes did the same, and also put pigs and hens beneath their houses.[7] In Greece the first person to enter a new house would die within the year unless an animal was buried where the first stone had been laid.[8] As recently as 1901 there is a Greek account of foundation ceremonies involving a death, although it was only a lamb. In the presence of a priest, the creature was slaughtered and its blood smeared on the foundations; then it was buried in the same place.[9] Theodore Storm, in his novel *The Rider of the White Horse*, describes how a horrified overseer

---

[1] Burdick, 48.

[2] *Ibid.*, 47.

[3] Ellis Davidson, H. R., *Gods and Myths of Northern Europe*, London, 1964, 27.

[4] Hole, Christina, ed., *Encyclopaedia of Superstitions*, London, 1961, 303.

[5] Baring-Gould, 5–6. Burdick, 5ff.

[6] *Ibid.*, 57.   [7] *Ibid.*, 57–8.

[8] *Ibid.*, 58.   [9] *Ibid.*, 57.

rescued a puppy from his group of Dutch workmen – they had tried to bury it in the ditch which they were digging.[1]

Even today the foundation of a building is still important. The ancient Romans concealed leaden seals, imprinted with the emperor's image, inside the walls of their houses. Christians preferred a portrait of Our Lord.[2] Hence, perhaps, our modern custom of putting a penny into the mortar wall of a new cottage. If the building is important, a member of the royal family may be asked to lay the first stone. Richard Wagner, performing a similar ceremony for the opening of his Bayreuth Opera House, buried a letter from his patron, King Ludwig II, together with the following lines:

> *Hier schliess ich ein Geheimnis ein,*
> *Da run es viele hundert Jahr.*
> *Solange es verwahrt der Stein*
> *Macht es der Welt sich offenbar.*[3]

At some stage in the past blood sacrifice of any kind was dropped, and among the substitutes was an egg – the symbol of life.[4] Natives of Borneo lay some out to propitiate the spirits of a newly cleared village site,[5] and in the last century, or even this, builders in Bombay put an egg and milk into the foundations of new buildings.[6] Professor Westermarck, visiting Morocco, was told in Andjara that an egg, salt and wheat are concealed in the ground where a new house is going to be built and then, when all the work has been completed, a goat is slain on the threshold.[7] Of course there are no rigid dividing lines in the study of local custom, and this particular example shows a transition between the two stages.

Sometimes it is not one building only but a whole city which is involved. A legend from Italy refers to the founding of the city of Naples on a base of eggs,[8] and Thoms, in his *Early Prose*

[1] Reference kindly supplied by Herr Willy Hess of Winterthur.
[2] Burdick, 101.
[3] Information kindly supplied by Herr Willy Hess.
[4] Baring-Gould, 29.
[5] Bächtold-Stäubli, Hanns, ed., *Handwörterbuch des deutschen Aberglaubens*, Berlin, 1929–30, ii.617.
[6] *Ibid.*, 618.
[7] Westermarck, Edward, *Ritual and Belief in Morocco*, London, 1926, i.315.
[8] Burdick, 65.

Romances, alludes to it in the story of the magician Virgilius – who is, of course, Virgil:

> And Virgilius was sore enamoured of that lady. Than he thoughte in his mynde howe he myght mareye hyr, and thoughte in his mynde to found in the myddes of the sea a fayr towne with great landes belongyng to it; and so he did by his cunnynge, and called it Napells, and the foundacyon of it was of egges; and in that towne of Napells he made a tower with iiij corners, and in the toppe he set an apyll upon a yron yarde, and no man coulde pull that apyll without he brake it; and throughe that yron set he a botel, and on that botel set he an egge, and he henge the apyll by the stauke upon the cheyne, and so hangeth it styll. And when the egg styrreth so shulde the towne synke. When he had made an ende, he lette call it Napels.[1]

From early times Italians had thought of Virgil as a demi-god: Martial tells us that the October Ides were sacred to him,[2] and Pliny describes a religious visit to his Naples' monument, as though it were a temple.[3] Soon Christians were to find a prophecy of Christ's coming in the fourth *Ecologue*.[4] By the twelfth century stories of his magic powers were accumulating in Naples, a city which he had loved and where his remains were buried.[5] In time he became the protecting genius of the city. Writing from Italy in 1194, Conrad of Querfurt describes how Virgil provided Naples with a palladium – a model of the city enclosed in a bottle.[6] Later, in the fourteenth century, this was described as an egg, and the old *castello di mare* of 1154 became *castel dell'uovo*.[7] The statutes of a religious house – The Order of St Esprit – refer to it as *castellum ovi incantati*,[8] and the first record of this is dated 1352. Hasluck quotes two lines from that period:

> *Ova mira novo sic ovo non tuber ovo,*
> *Dorica castra cluens tutor temerare timeto.*[9]

Such legends appear to be founded on fact. Apollo, according to Callimachus, was a builder of towns and he himself laid the

---

[1] Morley, Henry, ed., *Thoms' Early Prose Romances*, London, 1889, 207ff.

[2] *Ibid.*, 18–20.   [3] *Ibid.*   [4] *Ibid.*

[5] *Ibid.*   [6] *Ibid.*   [7] *Ibid.*

[8] Jones, William, *Credulities Past and Present*, London, 1880, 473. See also Montfacon, *Monuments de la Monarchie Française*, ii.329.

[9] Hasluck, F. W., *Letters on Religion and Folklore*, London, 1926, 97–8, 127.

foundations.[1] There are statues of this god with a heap of eggs underneath him or at his side,[2] and an egg hung in the Temple dedicated to his daughters, Phoebe and Hilaria.[3] Archaeological finds have been numerous. A striking early discovery was the goose egg found in a cavity between blocks of unbaked brick in Nippur Temple, placed there more than 2,000 years ago.[4] But it is the later survivals which are of such particular interest. Bächtold-Stäubli lists a number from Germany, without unfortunately supplying the dates, though he does mention hens' eggs found at Grossweitzschen in Saxony, which were buried in the foundations of a house dating from the early eighteenth century.[5] Other items on his list and elsewhere include egg-shells in the base of a chimney on a forest hut in Altenhagen,[6] a single egg built into the walls of the Kirchspiels Church at Iserlohn,[7] and seven in the walls of the old Town Hall at Schötmar.[8]

Ralph Merrifield notes that an earthenware tripod-pitcher containing egg-shells was found beneath a fifteenth- or sixteenth-century house at Deventer in Holland,[9] and many discoveries have been made in France. At Bellecombe (Isère) in 1960, a M. Leonce Dumas was having his house rebuilt. Workmen demolishing the old structure, which was probably seventeenth- or even eighteenth-century, found an egg embedded in the mortar about forty centimetres below the entrance door.[10] In 1956 a M. Boisse was excavating the Romanesque chapel of St Peter at Serves-on-Rhone in Dauphiné when he found a crumbling brick coping at a level of thirty metres. In the wall, about forty centimetres beneath the coping, he discovered two hen's eggs. One was close

---

[1] Burdick, 62.

[2] Payne Knight, R., *The Symbolical Language of Ancient Art and Mythology*, New York, 1876, 95.

[3] Frazer, Sir James G., *Pausanias's Description of Greece*, London, 1913, iii.339, note 16.1.

[4] Peters, John P., *Nippur*, New York, 1897, ii.123.

[5] Bächtold-Stäubli, ii.618.

[6] Leland, C. G., *Gypsy Sorcery and Fortune Telling*, London, 1891, 77.

[7] Burdick, 65.

[8] Bächtold-Stäubli, ii.618.

[9] Merrifield, Ralph, 'Witch Bottles and Magic Jugs', *Folk-Lore*, lxvi (London, March 1955), 205.

[10] Joisten, Charles, 'Le Folklore de L'Œuf en Dauphiné', *Arts et Traditions Populaires* (Paris, January–March 1961), 59.

to the door, in a walled niche.[1] An article in the periodical *Arts et Traditions Populaires* describes how M. Charles Joisten came across an egg inscribed with the letter M, and the numerals 1373, during demolition of a house in Moisse in April 1964. It is conceivable, as the author suggests, that this is a date commemorating the original construction.[2]

One last story from a M. Schaudel in the *Revue de Folklore Français* describes in some detail finding a hen's egg during demolition of a house at Badonviller in 1921. Certain buildings in the lowest part of the town partially surrounded a form of large courtyard, built underneath the walls of the ancient fortified enclosure. This area, called Famine Castle, presumably commemorated a siege of the fortress. While demolishing a house on the east of this site, workmen found a small cavity in the exterior wall containing a hen's egg. Nearby, on a slightly lower level, was an elegantly carved oval stone. M. Schaudel continues:

> As a result of my recommendations to the contractors, I was informed of this the same day. But, although I came in great haste, I arrived too late to save the egg which, although discovered intact, was immediately broken, because the workers thought that perhaps they had found something of the chicken which lays the golden eggs. They were disappointed to discover that the shell only contained some dried-out matter.

They were probably no less disappointed than M. Schaudel, who continues:

> The remains were therefore contemptuously thrown into the rubble-heap, where it was impossible for me to retrieve them. The proprietor kindly presented me with the mutilated oval stone, which is only slightly chipped around the base.[3]

This sort of thing is unfortunately not unusual in archaeology. An equally interesting discovery in London recently appeared in a basket, and by the time experts had arrived to examine it, the contents had been dumped out on the floor and the basket thrown away. The find, which came to light five years ago, is particularly

[1] *Ibid.*, 59.

[2] *Ibid.*, 'Folklore de l'Œuf', *Arts et Traditions Populaires*, (Paris, January 1965), 56.

[3] Schaudel, L., 'Œufs Talismans dans les Murs des Maisons', *Revue de Folklore Français et de Folklore Colonial*, iii (Paris, March–April 1932), No. 2, 88–9.

interesting on account of its associations. The building, Lauderdale House, is located in Waterlow Park.[1] Lady Arabella Stuart was a prisoner there on her way to the Tower, Cromwell's son-in-law was the owner when he was Lord Mayor of London, and later the Earl of Lauderdale – the 'L' member of Charles II's 'Cabal' Ministry – occupied it. Samuel Pepys came to visit him there, and heard Scottish music for the first time. Waterlow Park itself inspired Andrew Marvell to write his famous poem, 'Thoughts in a Garden'.

Five years ago workmen doing restoration discovered in a bricked-up recess near a first-floor fireplace: four chickens, a glass goblet, a candlestick, two odd shoes and an egg. The style of the sole of one of the shoes, which is thickened with cork, dates the find at about 1600. Experts who were called in considered that one of the chickens might have laid the egg before it died. But I see no particular reason for not surmising that it was deliberately placed there. Two of the chickens had obviously been strangled; in the case of the other two this was not established for certain. But if all four chickens were not dead by some method or other at the time of their entombment, it seems extraordinary that they did not consume the egg. Chickens are notorious cannibals in this way, and there was in fact nothing else for them to eat inside the recess.

A popular legend of the same period, still current in the Shetlands, refers to Scalloway Castle. It was built by the tyrant Earl Patrick Stuart, a nephew of Mary Queen of Scots, in 1600, and people said that the mortar was blended with a mixture of eggs and blood:[2] the curious account of the ingredients probably reflects some of the fear felt by the local people for their terrifying ruler.

Another dreaded building, the Tower of Death in Bukhara, was also said to have been built with eggs.[3] This minaret, saved from the ravages of Genghis Khan by its outstanding

[1] I am indebted to F. J. Collins, of Historic Buildings, Greater London Council, for this information; also to the London Museum, who kindly allowed me to view the objects in their storage vaults; also to Eric Maple, who first drew my attention to the find. For further details, see the article by John Crossland in the *Sunday Telegraph*, 24 January 1965.

[2] Thomson, W. P. L., *Islands of the North*, Lerwick, n.d., 8.

[3] Information kindly supplied by John Massey-Stewart.

height and beauty, served as a beacon for travellers in the desert, who watched for the fires kept burning at the top in order to find their way into the city. Genghis Khan destroyed everything, with the exception of this one remarkable tower – which was used to fling convicts to their death – and, of course, stories multiplied about it. According to one, the mortar was made of eggs; another said that the actual bricks were a blend of sand from the deserts of Bukhara and Samarkand, the milk of camels and eggs. Late sixteenth-century England, a comparatively civilized environment, provides evidence of similar practices. An account for repairs to the spire of Newark Church reads:

> The whole charges for pointinge the steple to the Battlements, donne and Begonne in Easter weke and ended the weke before Crosse weke in the yere of Our Lord a thousand five hundreth seventye-one, and in the thirteenth yere of the Reign of our Sovereign Ladye Quene Elizabeth, and in the time of Mr John Brignell, their Alderman:
> Item, 7 quarter lyme   4s.
> Item, three hundreth and a halfe eiggs to temper the same lyme with   4s 8d.[1]

On reading this first, it seemed to me that eggs were an improbable material to use for this purpose, and rather expensive; that here was another example of a sacrificial rite, or rather the half-remembered relics of it, in this case to prevent the spire of the church from falling down. I discussed these examples with Mr Collins, the historic buildings restoration expert at County Hall, and, while he does consider that both eggs and Scalloway's blood would in fact have had some merits from a practical point of view, you will see he shares my opinion that there is nothing incompatible between this and their magical use. What he says is this:

> Church spires were built in lime mortar, each stone being held in position by the stone above, but the top section of a spire would need to be 'cemented' with something stronger than lime. Portland cement and/or a long iron rod is the modern solution, but in the Middle Ages an adhesive of lime and egg would seem to me a very reasonable method. White of egg with ground burnt oyster shells as a filler is an old adhesive for pottery, and I feel sure that egg and lime would be ideal for coarser work; in addition it would provide an almost waterproof joint between the stones. To a certain extent

[1] *Notes and Queries*, 11 December 1858, vi, 2nd series, 478.

blood, 7% albumen, as against 12% in white of egg, would have been used for a similar purpose. I wonder where to draw the line between function and magic? If blood or egg is 'sticky', what better material to stick one's castle together with, when it also represents strength.

The idea that buildings must be founded with the sacrifice of a life – that is, with the spilling of blood – is reflected in other human activities. Blood brotherhood, the founding of a friendship in blood, is not only performed by English schoolboys. It is a practice of numerous cultures from the Congo to the Balkans and elsewhere. An interesting version of this ceremony was observed in Albania.[1] Drops of blood from the arm of each man are placed on separate lumps of sugar by Moslems there, and consumed by the other partner. Christians, who were allowed wine, took it in this instead. Perhaps the Moroccan ceremony observed by Westermarck echoes the same principle: the egg talisman used during confinement is given to the baby's brother to eat, so that they will like each other. The egg, as a blood substitute, is interesting here, since it contains not only the seeds of friendship, but also of enmity. If someone else should happen to eat it, the infant would grow up to hate his mother.[2]

In Yugoslav Macedonia, if a person dies leaving a surviving relative born on the same day, or even in the same month, the living man is also doomed. He can only save himself if he is really far-sighted, and shares the yolk of an egg with this relative before he dies, on the opposite sides of a stream.[3] A sick man can save himself from death if he performs a similar ceremony, that of the 'adopted brother', with someone prepared to oblige him. This involved eating a sugared egg together on the threshold of his house.[4]

HOUSEHOLD SPIRITS

Eggs are often used to propitiate local spirits; not only those who might be offended by a new construction, but more specifically the local deities of houses, water, trees and other natural features.

[1] Durham, M. E., *Some Tribal Origins, Laws and Customs of the Balkans*, London, 1928, 153–5.

[2] Westermarck, ii.391.

[3] Kemp, P., *Healing Ritual: Studies in the Technique and Tradition of the Southern Slavs*, London, 1935, 93.

[4] *Ibid.*, 93.

House spirits, the genii of the family, are popular in many countries and enjoy a variety of names. Most people are familiar with the German *Kobold*, an unreliable sprite whose name – which also means a gnome – gives us our modern cobalt. German miners named it after the well-known goblin because they thought the metal, which is slightly magnetic, both useless and troublesome. They attributed these qualities to the sprite who lived in the mine.[1]

Danes have the *nis*, the French their *esprit follet* and every English child knows the *brownie*. In Spain there is the *duende*, in Finland the *para*, and the Faroese have the *niagruisar*. Even the Neapolitans have their own local sprite – the *monaciello*.[2] The *domovoi*, an important creature in Russia, takes his name from *dom*, meaning a house. But the peasants thought it unlucky to call him by his name; instead, they referred to 'the grandfather'.[3]

Sometimes the *domovoi* assumed the form of a snake and conferred all kinds of benefits on the master who treated him well. But it was important to offer him egg pancakes – the Russian *bliny* – and these were laid out on the roof or the threshing floor. If this gift was overlooked, the house was burnt down in reprisal.[4]

The *domovoi* resembled the Czech *hospodaricek*, another serpent, who brought both food and money and also warned the family in times of danger.[5] Both house spirits appear in the guise of a snake, and it is worth noting the frequent connection between serpent and egg, sometimes in the form of a food-offering to tribal deities – the founders of the clan. The Hausa greatly revere Mai-Ja-Chikki, the Drawer along of the Stomach. He is chief of the Black Spirits, and always offered eggs.[6] And a high priestess among the Hausa of southern Libya offers eggs and milk to her snake totem.[7]

A Chinese legend describes how a woman found an egg which hatched a male child, Chüeh. When he was four years old, the Turkish ruler, Lüi Yüan of Ping Yang, tried to build a wall around his capital and failed. The child then transformed himself into a snake and gave instructions as to how the wall should be

[1] Brewer, E. Cobham, *Dictionary of Phrase and Fable*, London, 1896, 267.
[2] *Ibid.*, 631.
[3] Roucek, Joseph L., ed., *Slavonic Encyclopaedia*, New York, 1949, 328.
[4] Jones, 472.   [5] Roucek, 327.
[6] Tremearne, A. J. N., *The Ban of the Bori*, London, 1914, 328.
[7] *Ibid.*

built.[1] This story, with its background of an initially unsuccessful building project, not only suggests a link between snake and foundation deity – and this is quite feasible, since snakes appear to inhabit the ground – it shows how close a connection can exist between the sacrifice which is offered and the new guardian spirit. In fact, the distinction is difficult to make.

The *domovoi's* shape could be vague, sometimes human and sometimes animal. Local lore describes how a band of rebel spirits revolted against God and were hurled down out of the heavens so that they fell on people's roofs, or into their yards. These house spirits were friendly creatures who liked to live close to the stove, where it was warm. If a peasant family moved, the house-wife put a slice of bread beneath the stove to tempt the *domovoi* along into the new house.[2] Maxim Gorky, in the account of his *Childhood*, refers to these beliefs. His grandmother is telling fairy tales: 'And then it was like this – under the stove sat the hearth goblin, a splinter of noodle in his paw. Rocking he sat, and moaning: "Oh, little mice, little mice! Oh, I shall die, little mice."'[3] But later it is clear that this is more than just a fairy tale:

> Grandfather rented two dark rooms in the cellar of an old house in a blind alley. During the moving, grandmother took an old bast shoe with long laces and thrust it under the stove. Squatting down, she began to call the hearth goblin: 'Come, goblin, come goblin, climb inside and take a ride to bring us luck in the other house.' Grandfather, who was out in the yard, glanced through the window. 'Taking it along, are you? I'll show you, you heretic! Disgracing me like this!' 'Oh, watch out, father! It'll mean bad luck for sure!' she warned, but grandfather flew into a rage and forbade her taking the goblin along.[4]

If the *domovoi* was annoyed for any reason, the head of the family was obliged to go out in the courtyard at midnight, turn his face to the moon, and say: 'Master stand before me as the leaf before the grass, neither black nor green but just like me. I have

---

[1] Hellbom, Anna-Britta, 'The Creation Egg', *Ethnos*, i (Stockholm, 1963), 89.

[2] *Larousse Encyclopaedia of Mythology*, London, 1959, 298.

[3] Gorky, Maxim, *Childhood*, tr. Wettlin, Margaret, Moscow, n.d., 24. First Russian edition, 1913–14.

[4] *Ibid.*, 342–3.

brought thee a red egg.'[1] The sprite then assumed its human form and was appeased.

Guardian spirits often lived under the threshold. Since ill-omened strangers might easily come in, bringing bad luck and misfortune, it was a vital part of the house and needed particularly careful protection. The Malers of Chota Nâgpur (Bihar State, India) call their local god Dwara Gusaîn, 'Lord of the house door'. In times of calamity he has to be propitiated. So the head of each household prepares a place in front of the door, and sets up a branch of the sacred *mukmum* tree. Near the branch they place an egg, supposed to contain the god. Meanwhile, a hog is slaughtered, and there is great feasting with friends and neighbours. When this is over, the branch is placed on the roof and the egg broken, so that the god can come out and put the disaster right.[2]

THE BLAJINI

Russian peasants buried a few eggs beneath the threshold during the annual festival of Death Week, which marked the end of winter and beginning of spring.[3] The part which eggs play in feasts of the dead is connected with the notion of rebirth – but more of this later. For now it is enough to note the close link between the cult of the dead and the upsurge of nature. In spring, when vegetation reappears, the dead are thought to draw nearer the living and hope to return to life.

Some such idea must lie behind the widespread and rather pathetic cult of the *Blajini* in the distant parts of eastern Europe. This is their name in Russia, Byelorussia and Rumania, and similarly in the Ukraine they are the *Blazhenni*. Known in Galicia as the *Rakhmane*, and as *Rochmen* in Bukowina, they are the Kindly Ones – worthy beings who live far away to the south, on the banks of a river fed by all the streams of the world. They inhabit a Never-never Land beyond the distant waters – on the edges of the earth – variously known as Saturday River and Sunday Water. A lost race, meek and worthy and beloved by God, they are said by some to be the souls of children who died before their baptism, dwelling where they can never see the sun. They know

---

[1] Jones, 472.

[2] Crooke, William, *Popular Religion and Folklore of Northern India*, London, 1896, i.104–5.

[3] Burdick, 65.

nothing of the world of men, and so at Easter-time the women, who celebrate their festival, throw red eggs into the streams – it is done by children in Byelorussia. The flowing waters carry these tokens away to that distant land, bringing the message that Easter has been celebrated, so that they may observe the festival themselves. They lead a holy life and eat no meat, except on the day when they celebrate Easter, and this is when the red egg-shells have reached them. Their feast day – Rumanians call it *Sărbătoarea Blajinilor* – is on the second Monday after Easter, except in Bukowina, where the *Rochmen* receive their Easter egg-shells after a period of forty days.[1]

Behind this cult, largely one supposes the prerogative of bereaved mothers, lies the belief that the soul of an unbaptized child, shut off from eternal bliss, inhabited for ever a grey and nebulous sphere of existence.[2] In Byelorussia they say that the brightly coloured shells will bring the message of spring to the race which lives in darkness and never sees the sun – a literal form of a metaphysical idea.

In fact, longing for the little dead children has become confused with primitive ideas of sun renewal, for the *Blajini* live in darkness and never see the daylight. After winter, when the sun's rays were weak, rituals were common to invoke it and renew its full strength and power. In Austria peasants in villages bordering the Danube place egg-shells containing oil and lighted wicks upon the waters, which carry them gently away.[3] At Rotterswil (Lucerne), where similar floating lights are called *Lichterschwemma*, they are allowed to drift away as a sign that dark evenings are over, and it is no longer necessary to work with lights.[4] But this is a modern rationalization of the older belief.

WATER SPRITES

A bridge was a very important structure, and the same precautions were taken as with a building to ensure the steadiness of its

[1] Jones, 456. Slătineanu, Barbu, 'Les Œufs de Pâques en Roumanie', *Schweizerisches Archiv für Volkskunde*, LIII (Basle, 1957), ii–iii, 182. Murgoçi, Agnes, 'Rumanian Easter Eggs', *Folk-Lore*, xx (London, September 1909), 297. Dmytrikw, Olga, *Ukrainian Arts*, New York, 1955, 101–2. Stratilesco, T., *From Carpathian to Pindus*, Boston, 1907, 180.

[2] Addis, William, ed., *A Catholic Dictionary*, London, 1959, 63, 512–13.

[3] Cooper, Gordon, *Festivals of Europe*, London, 1961, 12–13.

[4] Bächtold-Stäubli, iii 1,195.

1   Bird-headed man with egg; carved stone from Easter Island

3*

2 The Orphic deity Phanes, between two halves of the cosmic egg;
a bas-relief from Modena (c. 2nd century A.D.)

3 Madonna and Child beneath a suspended egg (1472); Piero della
Francesca (c. 1416–92)

4 *Concert in the Egg*, by Hieronymus Bosch (c. 1462–1516); in the clearly negative context, it is interesting that the egg is specifically associated with the tree, here a blighted symbol of life

foundations. Recently people queued all night to be the first over
the new Tay Bridge, but at one time it was thought most unlucky
to be first over such a structure. A common European tradition
describes a bridge built by the Devil, who claims the first living
thing to cross it as his payment – that is, as a sacrifice.[1] A Czech
legend of the 200 cartloads of eggs – one from every town in
Bohemia – used to secure the mortar of the Charles Bridge in
Prague, is a later version of the same idea.[2]

If this applied to the bridge, it was certainly true of the water
which flowed beneath it. The sprites required a sacrifice, and the
river god would claim a number of lives each year by drowning
individuals or by flooding surrounding areas. This became a
way of explaining the havoc caused by inundations and swift-
flowing rivers. Ideas of sacrifice faded but left their mark. For it
was long thought that daemons of rivers and pools selected their
quota of victims. The spirit of the Tweed claimed a life every year
and fishermen threw a plaid into the water to appease it.

> *Bloodthirsty Dee, each year needs three*
> *But bonny Don, she needs none.*[3]

reflected another Scottish tradition of this kind. Sacrifice was
essential to calm the angry sprite, and again eggs replace the
original human offering – though in Haiti, Simalo, the spirit god
of the waters, eats both eggs and men.[4] Gipsies often buried eggs
on the banks of rising streams,[5] and the French offered eggs,
bread and cheese to wells.[6] In Morocco, if a child stumbled into
water he immediately had to provide a gift for the *djinn*. The
parents gave him an egg, which was thrown in at once.[7] Crying
children, who are troubled by *djinni*, are also given an egg,
which must be dropped into a well.[8] Later we shall see how the
djinn is born from an egg, which is the emblem of his master.

---

[1] Hole, 68.   [2] Information kindly supplied by Eric Maple.
[3] McPherson, J. M., *Primitive Beliefs in the North-East of Scotland*, London,
1929, 64.
[4] Huxley, Francis, *The Invisibles*, London, 1966, 123–4.
[5] Bächtold-Stäubli, ii.617.
[6] Runeberg, Arne, 'Witches, Demons and Fertility Magic', *Commentationes
Humanorum Litterarum*, xiv (Helsinki, 1947), Nos. 1–4, 153.
[7] Legey, F., *Folklore of Morocco*, London, 1935, 71.
[8] *Ibid.*, 162.

In England and France it was popularly supposed that eggs would never hatch if carried over running water,[1] presumably since the water sprites appropriated the contents: in Czissova (Silesia) one was actually seen sitting inside an egg.[2] These creatures were particularly important in Slav areas, where they sometimes became confused with ancestor-worship. The Russian *rusalka* were virgins, drowned by choice or accident; sometimes they were friendly, more often voracious beings.[3] Their counterparts, the *samovily* of Bulgaria – the souls of unbaptized maidens – were also associated with water. Like the *Lorelei*, they sat on the banks of rivers and streams combing their hair; they were also connected with wells.[4] The *rusalka*, who lighted will-o'-the-wisp fires and caused floods by combing their hair – another common feature – often floated in egg-shells.[5] During *rusalka* week relatives of those who had been drowned or shipwrecked poured eggs and spirits over their graves. The idea behind this practice, which will be discussed later on, is more complex, since the *rusalka* had two aspects: spirits who drowned people, but who also originated themselves from the drowned.

TREE SPIRITS

Until the beginning of summer, *rusalkas* lived in the water. But during *rusalka* week, the seventh after Easter, they emerged and went into the trees, particularly weeping willow or birch which overhangs the water. Russian peasants believed that the souls of their ancestors inhabited these birch trees[6] – the famous *berioska*, which play so great a part in Russian folk-tradition. Like the egg trees of Germany, their branches were decorated with ribbons – on the Wednesday before Trinity, which was one of the Ancestor Festivals – and maidens from the village marked out certain trees. The following day, or on the Saturday, they returned with fried eggs and again adorned the trees which had been selected. Each girl carried a dish, which she put beside a particular tree, and then a dance was performed to the accompaniment of their song:

[1] Hole, 149.   [2] Bächtold-Stäubli, ii.616.
[3] *Larousse*, 302.   [4] Roucek, 326.
[5] Bassett, F. S., *Legends and Superstitions of the Sea*, London, 1885, 162.
[6] *Larousse*, 303. Sokolov, Y. M., *Russian Folklore*, New York, 1950, 192.

To you the maidens have come,
Birch tree, birch tree,
Be garlanded, curly one!
To you the fair ones have come,
They have brought you cakes,
With fried eggs.[1]

At the ceremony of the Christening of the Cuckoo, when the first bird returned, two girls walked in different directions around the birch trees, met in a circle made from their branches, kissed through this three times, and gave each other a yellow egg[2] – a prettier custom than spitting on your money and turning it.

Sprites of the water and of the trees are also confused in a superstition from the Oberberg: woodland elves, said to bake themselves delicious egg cakes, were offered eggs at May-time, and these were laid beside the streams.[3] The same applied to *Kobolds* – Bächtold-Stäubli mentions one who was actually banished into an egg. The Swiss, to prevent a house on the edge of a river from slipping in, put a hen's egg in the space between the water and the outer walls.[4] In Jamaica, if someone is ill and orthodox medicine fails, the people gather round a magic tree. They sing and drum and pelt it with eggs, to persuade the spirits of the dead to give up the shadow of the man they have stolen.[5] The eggs – a valuable item of food in such a poor country – are offered to the tree as a sacrifice of propitiation.

On a neighbouring island Haitians smash an egg against a post for *grand bois*, an important spirit who appears in the form of a tree. Probably this too is a kind of sacrifice. But Huxley, who saw it done in 1965, believed that it was to invoke *damballah*, the snake *loa*, in a man standing near the post.[6] This spirit, *damballah wedo*, is said to treasure the egg from which all things hatch;[7] the idea of sacrificing the most precious thing in the world might derive from muddled recollections of the Sacrifice of the Mass. Haitians, though nominally Catholic, have confused many Christian doctrines and concepts with their native voodoo practices.[8]

---

[1] *Ibid.*, 193.   [2] Jones, 470.
[3] Bächtold-Stäubli, ii.616.   [4] *Ibid.*, 618.
[5] Beckwith, Martha, *Black Roadways: a Study of Jamaican Folk Life*, Chapel Hill, 1929, 144.
[6] Huxley, 158, 211.   [7] *Ibid.*, 152, 189.
[8] Métraux, Alfred, *Voodoo in Haiti*, London, 1959, 323ff.

Chapter 3
Witchcraft and Magic

The devil should think of purchasing that egg-shell
To victual out a witch for the Burmoothies.
Beaumont and Fletcher: *Women Pleased*

DIVINATION AND PROPHECIES

In ancient times sacrifice and divination were closely linked: a favourite Roman method was to slaughter an animal and read the future from its writhing entrails. The egg, as a life emblem, had been a substitute for real people in sacrificial offerings, and in the same way it could have come to replace the slaughtered-animal augury. For it contained new life in embryo, the seeds of the future:

> *If you can look into the seeds of time,*
> *And say which grain will grow and which will not,*
> *Speak then to me,*[1]

said Banquo to the witches, who spoke prophecies. Nothing could better represent the nebulous future than an egg, its contents providing the promise of life to come, its shell of spherical boundless shape. The glass ball of the fortune-teller contains the same idea. The Khasis do nothing of any importance without first breaking an egg. They throw it, muttering appropriate words, on to a board made specially for the purpose, and augur from the position of the fragments.[2]

Egg-divining rites were practised in many countries, particularly in Britain, but also in Mexico, Portugal, Spain, Italy, France, Germany, Poland and Russia, to mention only a few. The time of year chosen was generally for obvious reasons. Halloween, when spirits are thought to walk, was popular; so were St Agnes' Eve and New Year – when people wish to know what the future has in store. The procedure was usually much the same. An egg was pierced and drops of the white caught in a glass of water; in

---

[1] *Macbeth*, i.iii.
[2] Quoted by Burne, C. S., in *The Handbook of Folklore*, London, 1914, 132, from *The Khasis*, by Gurdon, P. R. T., London, 1907.

France it was broken on somebody's head. The shapes which formed were carefully studied and interpreted.[1]

Young girls wanting to know the name of their future husband particularly enjoyed doing this. The Scots used an *eirack*'s egg – the first which a hen had ever laid – and saved it specially.[2] In some Adriatic ports they broke an egg into the harbour before bedtime. Next morning, when the fishing boats returned, the shapes were noted.[3] The custom was widespread in Greek Macedonia on the Feast of St John the Baptist – known as St John of the Divination because of the fortune-telling which took place at that time. Young girls drew water from a well and left it out of doors all night in a jug, with the white of an egg.[4]

This was a time for divination in England too: West Country girls put egg-white and water in the sun at noon and left it for five minutes before examining the result.[5] Evening too was a suitable time. Aubrey writes: "Tis Midsommer-night, or Midsommer-eve (St Jo. Baptist) is counted or called the witches night . . . of the breaking of hen-egges this night, in which they may see what their future will be."[6]

In Scotland both egg and water were retained inside the mouth, which was much more difficult to do. The correct way was for a girl to go outside at midnight, and wait until she heard the name of a boy being called. Then she had to swallow her mouthful immediately.[7] Of course, when girls were doing this the boys were not far away, calling out different names when a popular girl appeared.

A dreadful custom, shared with the Irish, involved removing the yolk from a hard-boiled egg and filling the cavity with salt. The whole thing had to be eaten – egg, salt and shell. This must have been difficult enough, but, worse still, the victim was not allowed a drink of water until the morning. And if she dreamed

[1] Bächtold-Stäubli, Hanns, ed., *Handwörterbuch des deutschen Aberglaubens*, Berlin, 1929–30, ii.620.

[2] Jones, William, *Credulities Past and Present*, London, 1880, 457.

[3] Bächtold-Stäubli, ii.618.

[4] Abbott, G. F., *Macedonian Folklore*, Cambridge, 1903, 52.

[5] *Notes and Queries*, 8 July 1905, 10th Series, iv.27.

[6] Aubrey, John, *The Remaines of Gentilisme and Judaisme* (1686–87), London, 1881, 133.

[7] Guthrie, E. J., *Old Scottish Customs*, London, 1885, 74–5.

that her lover was bringing one, it meant she was going to be jilted.[1] Aubrey knew this too, and writes of 'A magiall Receipt to know whom one shall marry. Egges roasted hard and the yelke taken out and salt putt in its sted, sc. filled up: to be eaten fasting without supper when you goe to bed.'[2] He adds rather surprisingly: 'I think only one egge.' Could anyone have possibly eaten two?

With minor variants, the pleasanter egg-and-water method was known in many countries. Thuringians put their eggs in boiling water.[3] Russian girls dropped just the yolk into a glass on the Eve of Epiphany[4] – a very important festival in the Orthodox Church. Faroese left the egg-white mixture overnight on their window-sills on the Eve of Candlemas,[5] and Austrians whisked a whole egg the night before Good Friday, poured water on the top, and waited until morning to have a look. The shape which they found would show how the coming fruit-crop would be.[6]

These blobs of egg were always anxiously studied for anything recognizable. Girls watched hopefully for a ship, or a hoe, or book – something which might give a clue to their intended husband's profession. But a recipe from South Uist may just be a disguised phallic symbol: 'Put a wee bit of the white in a glass of water, and if it comes up in wee trees you may look for your sweetheart, but if it stays at the bottom it is a bad lookout.'[7] An old song from the same island goes:

> *Sad am I*
> *At this time of winter*
> *On Hallowe'en night*
> *And I without eggs.*[8]

For Drap Glasses, as the Scots called it, could be quite a merry occasion. Sometimes a group got together and each person chose an egg, which was then given to the woman in charge. She dropped each white one by one into an ale glass, sealed the brim

[1] Jones, *Credulities*, 458.   [2] Aubrey, 62.

[3] Bächtold-Stäubli, ii.620, note 257.

[4] Spicer, Dorothy, *The Book of Festivals*, New York, 1937, 288.

[5] Williamson, Kenneth, *The Atlantic Islands: a Study of the Faroe Life and Scene*, London, 1948, 236.

[6] Bächtold-Stäubli, ii.619.

[7] Shaw, M. F., *Folksongs and Folklore of South Uist*, London, 1955, 14, 237.

[8] *Ibid.*, 237.

with her hand, and inverted it. When all the fortunes had been told in this way, the eggs were carefully collected and used for baking bannocks – known as 'dumb cakes', for no one was allowed to speak during divination.[1]

This was the most popular method of reading the future, but there were others too. Double yolks were an obvious symbol of marriage in Sweden as well as in England.[2] But if the egg was peeled and fragments were left behind, sticking to the shell, it meant that the bridegroom would be pock-scarred.[3] Austrians peered through two holes pierced in the shell before sunrise on New Year's Day.[4] What they hoped to see is not recorded – perhaps their true love's face. But it was very important to use a fresh egg. To find out if he is thinking of you, put an egg-shell over the fire, and if the inside skin rises it is a good sign – or so they say in Mexico.[5]

Yugoslavs used eggs for divining hidden treasure, but dark spots in the yolk were a warning of evil to come.[6] Black, of course, was a very sinister, ill-omened colour. Indeed, in Morgentheim if anyone was seriously ill and thought to be dying, a white thread was wound round an egg and placed on the fire in his name. The token was anxiously watched, and if the shell turned black in the flames it meant death was not far off.[7]

More innocuously eggs were supposed to inform us about curious freaks of nature. Some had what were thought to be comets or eclipses marked upon them. The comet of 1680 caused a great sensation and the *True Protestant Mercury*, probably rather sarcastically, wrote:

> We have many nights been surprised with the sight of that prodigious blazing phenomenon in the heavens. But that which more amazes us is that since its appearance a hen in the house of Seignior Massimi de

[1] McNeill, F. Marian, *The Silver Bough*, Glasgow, 1961, ii.43. Banks, M. Macleod, *British Calendar Customs: Scotland*, London, 1937, i.7.

[2] Briggs, K. M. and Tongue, R. L., *Somerset Folklore*, London, 1965, 145. Eskeröd, Albert, 'Ostereier in Schweden', *Schweizerisches Archiv für Volkskunde*, LIV (Basle, 1958), 14.

[3] Bächtold-Stäubli, ii.619.   [4] *Ibid.*

[5] Espinosa, Aurelio M., 'New-Mexican Spanish Folk-Lore', *Journal of American Folklore*, xxiii (Boston, October–December 1910), 416.

[6] Kemp, P., *Healing Ritual: Studies in the Technique and Tradition of the Southern Slavs*, London, 1935, 140.

[7] Bächtold-Stäubli, ii.631.

Campidoglio in this city [Rome], laid an egg in which there is very conspicuously seen the perfect figure of this comet, the inward part of the egg being very clear, and the shell transparent. In the greater end is the star, whence a blaze or luminous beam shines very bright to the other end. It was first taken notice of by a servant of the said Massimi who, with wonder showed it to his master, and it hath since been carried to be viewed by the Pope, who as wise and infallible as he is does not know what to make of it. The Queen of Sweden and most of the Grandees of Rome have likewise beheld it with admiration, and have ordered it to be carefully deposited where it administers not a little matter of speculation to our philosophers.[1]

Indeed, as late as 1911 it was thought in Hamburg that there was a connection between a misshapen egg and a comet.[2] It is not surprising that such absurdities led to abuse: in 1819 an egg was exhibited in Boston, U.S.A., supposed to have been found in a farmhouse near Bordeaux, and inscribed: '*Cici avertit, que Napoleon Bonaparte remontera sur la trone de France, le 15me Novembre 1818.*' The egg, discovered by a certain Lieutenant Patterson, was sold in London for 300 guineas – a comparatively even greater sum in those days – but a commentator observed some years later:

We should hardly have supposed that the good folk of Boston could be deceived by such a miserable hoax as this. Nothing is more simple or more easy than the art of making inscriptions upon eggs. Write any word you please upon an egg with grease, and boil the egg in limewater with a little onion juice, or place the egg in strong vinegar for a few hours, and the inscription will appear prominent. We have likewise seen letters raised upon an egg so ingeniously as hardly to be discovered, with no other instrument than a sharp knife. The Yankee who can manufacture WOODEN NUTMEGS can make PROPHETIC eggs with as little trouble or expense.[3]

The man who wrote these lines probably had no idea how genuinely prophetic an egg could seem to many people – especially in dreams, which are a way of linking the everyday with the enormous, unexplored realms of the subconscious. Immense importance was and still is attached to them. An egg could be used to induce a desired dream: an English girl would see her

[1] Jones, *Credulities*, 459.
[2] Bächtold-Stäubli, ii.602.
[3] *Percy Anecdotes, The*, London, 1868, i.865.

husband to be if the first laid by a white pullet was tucked beneath her pillow.[1] But actually to dream about eggs was a very different matter. A seventeenth-century German work, *The Dream Book* of Artemidori, suggests that it could be lucky for certain people.[2] But as a rule, in Germany as at home, it meant death, quarrels and terrible misfortune of some kind. Negroes in the southern part of America take note of the quantity – a lot means riches, a few poverty – and it is also important whether they are whole or broken. As one might expect, a broken egg means tragedy is on the way.[3]

SUPERNATURAL SIGHTS

If superstitions about dreams are sometimes confused, those related to second sight are more straightforward. American Negroes wanting to see a ghost break a rain-crow's egg into some water and wash their faces in it.[4] And in Germany, if you wish evil spirits to appear, go to Christmas Mass carrying an egg in each armpit. Enter the church backwards and look through one of the eggs: the invisible evil spirits will materialize, with haloes like butter-sieves around their heads.[5] It is surprising, that evil spirits should have been present at Christmas Mass. Certainly in English popular lore they would have had no power to do harm:

> *Some say that ever 'gainst that season comes*
> *Wherein our Saviour's birth is celebrated,*
> *The bird of dawning singeth all night long;*
> *And then, they say, no spirit can walk abroad;*
> *The nights are wholesome; then no planets strike,*
> *No fairy takes, nor witch hath power to charm,*
> *So hallow'd and so gracious is the time.*[6]

One could pick out those destined to die during the coming year by taking the first egg from a young hen to church on New Year's Day. The doomed would all be revealed, wearing crowns of thorns.[7]

Both these German customs are examples of Christian influence on occult practice. In the Caribbean area, witchcraft is still widely

[1] Jones, *Credulities*, 469. [2] Bächtold-Stäubli, ii.643–4.
[3] Puckett, N., *Folk Beliefs of the Southern Negro*, Chapel Hill, 1926, 500–1.
[4] *Ibid.*, 139. [5] Bächtold-Stäubli, ii.609, 619.
[6] *Hamlet*, i.i. [7] Bächtold-Stäubli, ii.619.

practised as such. In Haiti, during voodoo ceremonies, *veve* – emblematic magic drawings – are laid out on the floor, compelling the spirits to appear. They are made with flour, but if an egg is added too the magic becomes so powerful that the spirit cannot resist it.[1]

Huxley, writing in 1965, describes how he saw the remains of paraphernalia from a voodoo rite, which included twenty-one gourds filled with eggs.[2] Jamaicans say, if you want a ghost to help you and bring good luck, go to the churchyard at night and visit the grave of a friend or relative – one's mother would be the most suitable. Take an egg, rice and rum, and mash the egg beside the grave. The ghost will come up and eat it, and will then do as you wish.[3]

Ancestors and dead members of the family generally watch over the fortunes of a household if properly treated. Probably this is why the African Bantu offer an egg to the spirit of a child, placing it on a tuft of grass on a clean path near the hut.[4] The Mandari of the Sudan lay it out neatly in the evening on a pile of ash in a pathway, which must be forked. This, however, is for finding witches, and an elder of the village addresses the egg, urging it to do its work: 'You egg! If there is a witch, locate him! Let the egg be eaten if there is a witch: if not, let it remain!'[5] In the morning he returns to see whether the egg has been consumed.

A folk-tale from Germany, collected by the Brothers Grimm, tells of a supernatural change which takes place in the egg itself. Murder has been committed, and the egg mysteriously stains with blood which cannot be removed. The story, 'Fitcher's Vogel', is a variant of the Bluebeard legend. A young girl captured by a wizard has been forced to stay in his house. One day he sets off on a journey, leaving her an egg which she must take great care of, together with a bunch of keys. On no account must she unlock a certain room and look inside. Of course, overcome by curiosity,

[1] Métraux, Alfred, *Voodoo in Haiti*, London, 1959, 164–5.

[2] Huxley, Francis, *The Invisibles*, London, 1966, 105.

[3] Beckwith, Martha, *Black Roadways: a Study of Jamaican Folk Life*, Chapel Hill, 1929, 136.

[4] Wagner, Günter, *The Bantu of North Kavirondo*, Oxford, 1949, i.280.

[5] Middleton, John and Winter, E. H., *Witchcraft and Sorcery in East Africa*, London, 1963, 120.

she disobeys and is horrified to find a bloody basin filled with the limbs of his murdered victims. In her confusion she drops the egg, which stains and she cannot clean it, no matter how hard she tries.[1] This is an echo of the old idea that 'murder will out'. Bloodstains stubbornly remain, bearing witness to a crime, and no amount of water will remove them.[2] Shakespeare refers to this in Macbeth's famous speech:

> *Will all great Neptune's ocean wash this blood*
> *Clean from my hand? No, this my hand will rather*
> *The multitudinous seas incarnadine,*
> *Making the green one red.*[3]

THE DEVIL'S EGG

Eggs often represented a vicarious human sacrifice, so it is perhaps not surprising that they were considered suitable food for evil creatures. Germans offer one to the bad night spirit or to a troublesome witch, to prevent them from coming back,[4] and an account dated 1577 describes how demons sat down to a meal of beer, butter and eggs; they enjoyed egg pancakes too.[5] Proteus mentions a devil in Döttingen who used to rob eggs of their contents, and some sprites had the power to do this quite effortlessly – a Swiss pixie could attract whole eggs to himself, like a magnet.[6]

There were demons who kept flocks of chickens, feeding them magic food to ensure a good supply of eggs. Many comic folktales, quite widespread in Germany from Swabia to Pomerania, describe the discomfort of farmers and monks who accidentally eat this kind of food, and begin to lay eggs themselves. Bächtold-Stäubli says that Swiss witches can do this with the aid of magic grease, selling their produce in the market to unsuspecting purchasers.[7]

---

[1] Grimm, The Brothers, *German Folk Tales*, Carbondale, Ill., 1960, 164–7.
[2] Hole, Christina, ed., *Encyclopaedia of Superstitions*, London, 1961, 149.
[3] *Macbeth*, ii.ii.
[4] Wildhaber, Robert, 'Zum Symbolgehalt und zur Ikonographie des Eies', *Deutsches Jahrbuch für Volkskunde*, vi (Berlin, 1960), 81.
[5] Bächtold-Stäubli, ii.605.
[6] *Ibid.* See also Erasmum Francisci, *Der höllische Proteus*, Nuremberg, 1690.
[7] Bächtold-Stäubli, ii.605.

Even the Devil made eggs. In medieval times, when the fear of witchcraft raged through Europe, it was supposed that he came by night and slept with certain women. Sometimes this happened without their knowledge, and then they were 'possessed' against their will. Others readily consented. In either case an apple with a worm in it, or an egg, appeared beside the bed; with it, the woman could obtain amazing wealth. This corresponds to a Central European notion that fairies were given eggs and apples after intercourse with the Devil; these gifts were often handed on to their especial favourites.[1] Perhaps an old German prohibition against taking apples and eggs on a journey was in some way connected with this.[2] Apples were fairy fruit in the northern countries where they grew, and in Norse myth the apples of Idun symbolize eternal youth, enabling the gods to remain forever young.[3]

The fact that an egg was the accompaniment of this unholy intercourse, may have accentuated the suspicion aroused by any of unusual appearance. There were so many different kinds: small eggs, yolkless eggs, and eggs without a shell were particularly unpopular. In England yolkless eggs were thought unlucky if brought into the house.[4] Shell-less eggs were 'wind eggs', a name which arose from a curious idea that the hen laying them had been impregnated, not by the cock, but by the wind. Dr Johnson, too, pointed out that these eggs would never hatch out into chicks.[5] In Hungary a soft-shelled egg from a black hen was always smashed at once, for it meant *fold meglágyult alatta* – the earth would grow soft beneath one of the family, a euphemism for death.[6]

Ideas of this kind are not exclusively European. Madagascar, in the Indian Ocean, possesses many strange beliefs connected with unusual eggs – a pregnant woman who eats one will lose the foetus and with it her capacity for bearing future children. Any that are infertile bring disaster and damage to property.[7]

---

[1] Wlislocki, Heinrich von, *Volksglaube und religiöser Brauch der Magyaren*, Münster, 1893, 162–3, 165.

[2] Bächtold-Stäubli, ii.643.

[3] Brewer, E. Cobham, *Dictionary of Phrase and Fable*, London, 1896, 57.

[4] Hole, *Encyclopaedia*, 149.   [5] Brewer, 1,304.   [6] Wlislocki, 77.

[7] Ruud, Jørgen, *Taboo: a Study of Malagasy Customs and Beliefs*, Oslo, 1960, 92–4, 241.

In Europe eggs considered as bewitched could be thrown backwards over the house, to avoid bad luck.[1] These could be variously malformed – apart from those which lacked a proper shell, there were empty eggs and ones where yolk and white had merged. They were supposed, besides, to have been laid by the cock. From earliest times this bird was thought to possess oracular powers. Mahommed found one in the first Moslem heaven, so huge that its comb touched the second, and its crowing aroused all creation from their sleep: the day when it ceases to crow will be the Day of Judgment.[2]

Revered by the Teutons, the cock was also an ensign of the Goths, and was often used to decorate their churches. In Greek and Roman times it was a symbol of Minerva, Apollo and Aesculapius. From Minerva, in fact, the Goths may have taken their emblem. She was goddess of war, but her association with the bird is obscure. Perhaps it derives from its famous pugnacity – cock-fighting, after all, was a popular sport in Roman times and earlier.[3] The connection with Aesculapius is purely practical, for he was the god of medicine and a cock is herald of the dawn, when it is healthy to get up. Invalids used to sacrifice one to him. So did Socrates, after drinking the cup of hemlock, to show that he regarded death as a cure and not with fear.

Dawn, of course, is also the sunrise – hence the association with Apollo. A Peruvian tale relates how a peasant was stranded in the mountains one night with nothing to eat except an egg. The Devil and his legions came and tormented him, but at midnight the egg broke open and out came a cock crowing, 'Now it is beginning to get light,' and the evil spirits fled.[4]

Because of the cock's magic powers, misshapen eggs were attributed to it and greatly feared. In fact, the bodies of aged roosters sometimes contain a small, white, egg-shaped globule, which may help to account for the superstition, particularly as it was only an aged rooster that was supposed to lay a 'cock's egg'.[5] This was generally imagined to be when the bird was seven years

---

[1] *Notes and Queries*, 9 December 1882, 6th Series, vi, 477.

[2] Brewer, 267.

[3] *Ibid.*, 268.

[4] Hansen, T. L., *The Types of the Folk Tale in Cuba, Puerto Rico, the Dominican Republic and Spanish South America*, Berkeley, 1957, 98.

[5] Lum, Peter, *Fabulous Beasts*, London, 1952, 38.

old,[1] and our modern word cockney underlines the popularity of the belief. Literally it meant 'cock's egg', from the Middle English *coken* and *ay* (egg). Hence it came to mean an undernourished town-dweller – a typical attitude among country folk.[2] In Devonshire in 1882 a small 'cock's egg' was known as a *cockernony*,[3] and the term was current in Shakespeare's day: 'Cry to it, nuncle, as the cockney did to the eels when she put 'em i' the paste alive; she knapped 'em o' the coxcombs with a stick, and cried, "Down, wantons, down!"'[4]

In 1474 legal proceedings were actually instituted at Basle against a cock, which was accused of laying an egg for purposes of witchcraft. The prosecutor pointed out that cocks' eggs were very valuable for mixing magic potions: all sorcerers longed to possess one. Satan was known to employ witches for brooding these eggs, and dreadful creatures hatched out of them. Not surprisingly, the cock was convicted as a sorcerer in the form of a bird, and was burnt at the stake together with its egg.[5]

Lapeyronie, writing in the *Mémoires de l'Academie des Sciences* for 1710, notes that even well-educated people believed in cocks' eggs.[6] The bird was supposed to use snakes or toads to hatch them out, and monsters appeared such as the basilisk or cockatrice, whose blazing eyes killed all who looked at it: 'This will so fright them both that they will kill one another by the look, like cockatrices',[7] writes Shakespeare in *Twelfth Night*; again in Isaiah: 'The weaned child shall put his hand on the cockatrice' den.'[8]

Belief in this monster was common throughout Europe, even as far north as Iceland. In England it hatched from a little, yolkless egg, the *cent*, so called because it was the hundredth to arrive. The other ninety-nine were all quite normal.[9] Fifty years ago French children of the Hautes Alpes were told that this little egg was laid each Easter and hatched a flying serpent, which brought bad luck

---

[1] Gregor, W., *Notes on the Folklore of North-East Scotland*, London, 1881, 140.

[2] Brewer, 270–1. Skeat, Walter W., *A Concise Etymological Dictionary of the English Language*, Oxford, 1882, 97.

[3] *Notes and Queries*, 9 December 1882, 6th Series, vi.477.

[4] *King Lear*, II.iv.   [5] Lum, 37. Bächtold-Stäubli, ii.601.

[6] Jones, *Credulities*, 301.   [7] *Twelfth Night*, III.iv.

[8] Isai. xi.8.   [9] Jones, *Credulities*, 462.

to all who saw it.[1] Pliny and other ancient writers described the basilisk in considerable detail,[2] but they do not refer to its fabled birth from an egg. This idea was especially popular in the Middle Ages. Bächtold-Stäubli found the first reference in Cassian's *Contra Nestorium*: '*Ex ovis volucrum, quas in Aegypto hibes vocant, basilisios serpentes gigni indubitabile est.*'[3]

In modern times people in Brittany have said that shell-less eggs, laid by the cock, are actually gifts from the Devil, and the early Church Fathers saw the basilisk as the Fiend in one of his manifestations – an idea which first appears in a German work, *Physica*, by the nun Hildegard von Bingen: '*Basilisius de quibusdam vermibus nascitur, qui aliquid de diabolicis artibus in se habent, scilicet quod rubeta.*'[4]

When the egg hatches, sulphurous fumes burst out and the basilisk splits the earth around with its fiery tongue, growing till it fits the chasm, which is five ells deep. Its burning breath and dreadful gaze wither everything in sight. Only the cock, who gives it life and whose crowing kills it, can withstand its power. Konrad von Megenberg mentions the legend in his *Book of Nature* (1340): 'It is also known everywhere that from the egg laid by a cockerel when it is nine years old a basilisk is born.'[5]

The Bolognese Aldrovandi says in his *Ornithologia* of 1610 that he saw many of these eggs.[6] One unfortunate Italian cock, which had even brooded and hatched an egg, at once had its neck wrung and the chicken was crushed by the local people, who feared a basilisk.[7] Probably the whole thing was a case of mistaken sex.

The account given in the *Journal of Pforzheim* (1787) suggests a connection with the weather. The small egg laid by a seven-year-old cock, if put in a moist place, will produce a dragon capable of living for hundreds of years. Before it has time to hatch, the egg must be hurled over the roof, or leaks will develop during the winter storms.[8]

In France a freak egg placed in warm horse-dung hatched the *farfollet*, or house spirit, which tormented children in the guise of

[1] Joisten, Charles, 'Le Folklore de L'Œuf en Dauphiné', *Arts et Traditions Populaires* (Paris, January–March 1961), 60–1.

[2] Bächtold-Stäubli, ii.600.

[3] Petschenig, M., ed., *Corpus Scriptorum Ecclesiasticorum* (Vienna, 1888), v.xvii.360.

[4] Bächtold-Stäubli, ii.600.   [5] *Ibid.*

[6] *Ibid.*, 600–1.   [7] *Ibid.*, 601.   [8] *Ibid.*

Colour Plate V (a) Wax eggs made by Arab Sisters of the Convent of the Annunciation. The letters on the central egg, XB, are the initials of the Russian words *Christos Voskresi* (Christ is Risen), and the technique of decoration with beads was taken to the Holy Land from Russia. A sister house of the original Palestinian Convent now exists in London, and this traditional art has therefore been carried to England; but the precise method remains a secret of the Arab Sisters.

(b) Glass and Battersea eggs, scent bottles, a vinaigrette. The three glass eggs on the left are, from top to bottom, Bohemian, Russian (see caption above for meaning of XB), and Austrian. The last is an egg-shaped scent bottle in which the egg is topped by a silver bird-head stopper. Two further egg-shaped scent bottles, at the bottom, are probably Continental (nineteenth century), and that patterned after a peewit's egg is English. The silver egg (c. 1800) is a vinaigrette, and the two remaining eggs (yellow speckled at top right, and small floral in the centre) are early nineteenth-century Battersea enamel.

Colour Plate VI (a) Russian necklace eggs. Among the collection of nine eggs are niello work, silver inlaid with enamel, silver, and semi-precious stone examples. The large central egg is dated 1901 on the reverse, and two eggs are inscribed XB (see caption to colour plate V (a) for meaning).

(b) Eggs for special uses and as hobbies. On the left three eggs carved in boxwood or similar material, a not unusual hobby in the latter nineteenth century. The bone egg below them is probably of similar origin. Top centre is a sugar egg, hollow and open at one end, with a rural scene inside (recent, Czech). Next to it (striped) is a Mexican *cascarone*, or confetti-filled egg. In the centre is an English chocolate-egg mould, and below it plaster casts made with a German marzipan-egg mould. Centre right is a wooden egg, open and containing a nutmeg-grater (English, nineteenth century). Below it, a similar egg as container for a sewing cotton spindle. The picture partly visible on the bottom half is of Osborne House.

a cock.[1] Since an egg would probably hatch under these conditions, and might well produce a cock, this superstition is not difficult to understand. The grandfather of a peasant interviewed by the French folklorist Joisten had seen 'a large egg unlike the others' laid out on the straw in the barn where he worked as a farmhand. He did not touch it, knowing that it contained the *farfollet*.[2]

A host of European sprites and elves – brownies, *Kobolds*, *Spanzifankerl* and Golden Dove, *Lauterfresser* and Chick of the Devil – appear from a cockerel's egg which has been brooded in the armpit.[3] Be sure not to talk or laugh until it is ready, warn the Pomeranians, or the *Kobold* will not survive. Some take on semi-human form. *Coqwergi* is a Swiss dwarf known in the Valais Alps,[4] and the Czech *sotek* appears as a little boy with claws on hands and feet.[5] Hungarians feared *lidércz*, their will-o'-the-wisp, and smashed any small eggs as a precaution.[6] But for the most part these are amiable, helpful sprites, whose names reflect their nature. The Tyrolese were especially fond of *Lauterfresser*, who lived on a diet of raw eggs, because he helped to build up one's strength.[7]

A Magyar tale, 'The Three Princes, Three Dragons, and the Old Woman with the Iron Nose', describes how Ambrose is given by his fairy godmother a black, five-cornered egg. She places it in his armpit and he carries it for seven years, the usual period for incubating a basilisk. On Ash Wednesday of the eighth year out jumps a horse with five legs and three heads. It is a *tátos*, a friendly, supernatural animal which can speak in human language.[8]

Outside Europe these egg-born creatures sometimes retain alarming characteristics. The Vugusu of Kenya place an egg outside their neighbour's door, in the hopes that an *omulosi* will haunt him. For if he leaves and goes elsewhere, they can seize his land.[9] In Arabia the *ghaddar* and other types of *djinn* – demons which entice men, terrify and torture them – are also born from

---

[1] Joisten, 61.

[2] *Ibid.*

[3] Roucek, Joseph L., ed., *Slavonic Encyclopaedia*, New York, 1949, 327. Bächtold-Stäubli, ii.604.

[4] Joisten, 61.   [5] Roucek, 327.

[6] Wlislocki, 122.   [7] Bächtold-Stäubli, ii.604.

[8] Jones, W. H., ed., *The Folk Tales of the Magyars*, London, 1889, 197.

[9] Wagner, i.280.

eggs.[1] They occur, in pre-Islamic myth, in the Yemen and Upper Egypt, and their egg could conceivably have been the world egg of creation:[2]

'*Djinni*,' said to him Aladdin, 'there is wanting to this dome a roc's egg hung from the centre of the vault; I demand of thee in the name of the Lamp I hold, that thou doest in such sort that this defect be made good.' (Now Aladdin had been counselled hereto for his destruction by the false Fatima, who was the evil brother of the dead magician.) Aladdin had not finished speaking these words before the *djinni* raised a cry so loud and so appalling that the hall was shaken with it, and Aladdin staggered ready to fall. 'What wretch!' said the *djinni* to him, in a voice fit to make the boldest man tremble, 'doth it not suffice thee that I and my companions have done all things in consideration of thee, but thou must ask of me, with an ingratitude without its like, that I should bring thee MY MASTER, and hang him in the midst of the arch of this dome! This insult deserves that thou shouldst be reduced to ashes on the spot; thou, thy wife, and thy palace!'[3]

In Morocco a woman troubled by a *djinn* is carried to the room where she became afflicted. An egg is laid in each corner as an offering, and this is the cure.[4] Certain cave *djinni* will also heal sickness. The sufferer must go to a holy cave, bringing presents for the *mqaddem*, its guardian; these include eggs. When sleeping in the cave the sick man must place one egg beneath his head, another under his feet. Each Wednesday the *mqaddem* fills an eggshell with oil and sprinkles it over the passages leading into the mountain cave. Then the *djinni* will appear and cure the sick man.[5]

CHANGELINGS

Recurring folklore themes tend to be rooted in human psychology. Few more so than the tale of the changeling child where, as in the cult of the *Blajini*[6] and similar traditions built around children, the superficial quaintness of the observance conceals a genuine human grief. For an old idea, which still persists today, is

[1] Lane, E. W., *Arabian Society in the Middle Ages*, London, 1883, 43.
[2] Sykes, Egerton, *Dictionary of Non-Classical Mythology*, London, 1961, 66.
[3] O'Neill, John, *The Night of the Gods*, London, 1897, ii.767–8.
[4] Westermarck, Edward, *Ritual and Belief in Morocco*, London, 1926, i.338.
[5] *Ibid.*, 287.   [6] See ch. 2.

that a defect in a child reflects a defect in the parent. This is one of a number of cruel oversimplifications which still clutter the human mind, causing untold distress – in this case to the parents of backward children.

Defence mechanisms vary. Anyone who has ever lived in the country knows that parents of a mongol will always say that 'he was dropped on his head when he was little', or something of the kind. In earlier times the catastrophe would have been blamed on an unpropitious grouping of the stars. The child of a doctor friend is very backward, and his father always blames this on the war, which, he claims, made his wife so nervous that it affected her milk when the baby was nursing. If a London doctor, admittedly personally involved, can suggest such a curious theory, it is not surprising that less-educated people entertain similar ideas.

In Britain, Germany and France, and possibly elsewhere too, there are many folk-tales referring to the changeling, the name for a sickly and unprepossessing child. Simple folk, ashamed of such an offspring, excused it to themselves by saying it was not really their own – the fairies had taken the real baby away and left this wretched substitute in its place. Such extravagant wishful thinking was clearly at one time a seriously held belief and, as so often, one catches an echo of this in Shakespeare:

> *O! that it could be prov'd*
> *That some night-tripping fairy had exchang'd*
> *In cradle-clothes our children where they lay,*
> *And call'd mine Percy, his Plantagenet.*
> *Then would I have his Harry, and he mine.*[1]

The group of folk-tales dealing with this theme tends to follow a certain pattern. In each case the sprite must be so startled and shocked that he speaks, revealing his true identity. Then the housewife can drive him away. As a rule he inadvertently tells his age: 'I was seven before I came to my nurse. I have lived for years since, and never did I see so many milk-pans',[2] says a Scottish changeling. In another Gaelic story the creature is 'more than three hundred years old',[3] and in an Irish variant he has 'been in the world 1,500 years'.[4] A Breton song and a German tale, make the

[1] *I Henry IV*, i.i.
[2] Grimm, Jacob, *Teutonic Mythology*, London, 1883, ii.469.
[3] Bett, Henry, *English Myths and Traditions*, London, 1952, 31.
[4] Grimm, ii.469.

sprite older than historical event: 'I have seen the egg before the white hen, and the acorn before the oak, but never aught like this'[1] runs the song. The German version is a dialect rhyme:

> *Ik bün so old*
> *As Böhmen gold*
> *Äwerst dat heff ik minleder nicht truht*
> *Wenn man't bier dörch'n eierdopp bruht.*

> *I am as old*
> *As Bohemian gold,*
> *Yet for the first time now I see*
> *Beer in an egg-shell brewed to be!*[2]

The technique used to trick the changeling is generally much the same, and in this eggs play a prominent part. In the Gaelic story the afflicted mother makes a circle with the shells and tells the changeling it is a brewing cauldron for beer; the other version describes how she puts twenty-four shells on the fire for boiling milk. In the Breton song she cooks for ten servants in one shell and, according to a tale from Wales, she halves an egg at noon, throws one piece away and mixes the other 'backwards and forwards': she tells the sprite that this is a pasty for the reapers.[3]

Other stories suggest a link with the changeling motif. Bächtold-Stäubli refers to a tale from Buchholz about a dog which drove a whole family away when they cooked a meal in an egg, and the *Norggelle*, a Tyrolese woodland elf, is expelled by standing a row of eggs around the grate.[4] In Germany the black-dog apparition – a shaggy creature which strikes dead those who touch or speak to it – is exorcized from cottages by filling 100 eggs with water and dropping them on the fire.[5] The same technique succeeded with the wild woman or mountain goat, and with a French fairy – *le sauvageon*.[6]

In all these tales the egg is used for some cooking process –

---

[1] *Ibid.*

[2] *Ibid.*, iii.927. According to Hartland, this is a Mecklenburg corruption of the correct version, which appears in a tale from Schleswig-Holstein as *Behmere Wœlt*, or Bohemian Forest (Hartland, E. S., *The Science of Fairy Tales*, London, 1891, 114–15).

[3] Rhys, John, *Celtic Folklore*, Oxford, 1901, 62–3, i.220.

[4] Bächtold-Stäubli, ii.690. See also Zingerle, Ignaz, *Sagen aus Tirol*, Innsbruck, 1891, 82–6.

[5] Bächtold-Stäubli, ii.690–1.   [6] *Ibid.*, 691.

often the brewing of beer, a theme preserved in the *Hervarer Saga* and in certain riddles where an egg is described as a barrel containing two kinds of liquid and a cask without rims or plug.[1] Odin in *Gestumblindi's Vision* refers to an egg as a beer barrel.[2]

The meaning in these stories, as they are left to us, is puzzling. But possibly there was a common basis. Perhaps in an earlier version the householder performed some intelligible counter-magic against the sprite: the circle on the floor and the ritual stirring at noon all point to this. But why is cooking such an important theme? Maybe because it implies the use of heat. In certain of the tales the shells are actually put on the fire. We know that sprites and elves often derived from eggs, and it may be that there is some suggestion here of an attempt to hurt the creature. The cry of surprise in the later versions may have originally been a cry of pain. Many supernatural beings, as we will see later on, housed their soul in an external object, such as an egg, which was susceptible to pain. Conceivably here is the relic of an attempt to injure the creature's soul and so force it to leave. Unless an earlier version comes to light, this must, of course, be pure supposition. But clearly the egg is an object with which the sprite is very familiar, though not in the context of the actions described. Taken at their face value, moreover, the tricks to which he reacts so strongly do not seem sufficiently startling.

WITCHES' BOATS

An account of witchcraft dated 5 February 1673 tells how:

> Anne Armstrong of Birks-wook, saith that being servant to one Mabel Fouler, of Burtree House, in August last her dame sent her to seek eggs of one Anne Forster, of Stocksfield, but as they could not agree for the price, the said Anne desired her to sit down, and look her head . . . and about three days after, seeking the cows in the pasture, a little after daybreak, she met, as she thought, an old man with ragged clothes, who asked this informant where she was on Friday last. She told him she was seeking eggs at Stocksfield so he told her that the same woman who looked her head should be first that made a horse of her spirit, and who should be the next that should ride her, and into what shape and likeness she should be changed if she would turn to their god. And withall told this in-

[1] Taylor, Archer, 'Das Ei im europäischen Volksrätsel', *Schweizerisches Archiv für Volkskunde*, LIII (Basle, 1957), ii–iii.196.

[2] Bächtold-Stäubli, ii.690.

former how they would use all means to allure her; first by their tricks, by riding in the house in empty wood dishes that had never been wet, and also in egg-shells.[1]

In April of the same year a certain Anne Baites of Morpeth was also accused of riding on wooden dishes and in egg-shells.[2] The objects used in witchcraft often seem odd and unrelated. But among the Chrovotes there is a belief that witches use egg-shells as cups and dishes for their meals,[3] and the South Slavonian gipsies in eastern Croatia smash them to prevent the witches doing this.[4] Once, they say, a witch saddled her sleeping husband and rode him to the Sabbath without his knowledge. The others there had egg-shell pots and jars, which they set down and danced around. In time, the man found out what was happening and his wife was burned to death as a witch.[5]

The Swedes say that trolls cause damage with egg-shells, and in many countries people smashed the shell after they had eaten an egg, to avoid it being used by the witches. A collector of folk-customs saw the Scots Highlanders doing this in the mid-1920s.[6] But Catholic children on the island of Barra saved their Easter morning's egg-shells very carefully and sailed them on the burn or in a tub. It was safe to do this, so they believed, because the shells had been consecrated and no witch would want to use them for, as they express it, her aircraft.[7]

Witches needed a vehicle for travelling to their Sabbaths, and children's story-books of an earlier generation have pictures of them whirling through the sky, not in aircraft admittedly, but on broomsticks. Legends, stories and superstitions collected from all over Europe – Sweden, Holland, France, Portugal, Russia and Yugoslavia – also suggest that an egg-shell was a usual means of transport. Tales of a witch travelling in this way even come from Puerto Rico,[8] and Mexico where a half-breed woman named Juana was accused of it in 1631.[9]

---

[1] Hole, Christina, *A Mirror of Witchcraft*, London, 1957, 43–4.
[2] Hardy, James, ed., *The Denham Tracts*, London, 1895, ii.299.
[3] Bächtold-Stäubli, ii.688.
[4] Leland, C. G., *Gypsy Sorcery and Fortune Telling*, London, 1891, 73–4.
[5] *Ibid.*
[6] Polson, Alexander, *Our Highland Folklore Heritage*, Inverness, 1926, 69.
[7] McNeill, ii.49.   [8] Hansen, 85.
[9] Parsons, E. C., *Pueblo Indian Religion*, Chicago, 1939, ii.1,068, note 1.

Sometimes witches flew through the air and sometimes they sailed across the sea. The stories that we have from Holland, Mexico and Puerto Rico possibly derive from Spain. All were at one time Spanish, and Portugal shares the same Iberian traditions. There the witches voyage to the Indies and suck the blood from children's veins.[1]

Certainly the influence of the Renaissance played a part, with its wonderful accounts of voyages of discovery, and distant unknown lands. A Slavonian gipsy story, steeped in this atmosphere, describes how a clever girl remembered all she had heard about the witches, made a hole in an egg, removed the contents, put the shell on some white sand near a stream, hid, and waited. At night a witch came, spoke a word over it and changed it into a boat, which carried her away across the sea. The girl carefully noted all this, ate another egg and then transformed that shell into a boat. It took her all over the world and, by trading knives and scissors for gold, she acquired many possessions and grew rich. One day an envious woman spied on her, to discover where the wealth all came from, and heard her say, 'To Africa!' before the egg-shell boat set sail. After the girl had returned, laden with goods, the woman stole her vessel and put it in water. 'To Africa!' she said, getting in. But she did not know the spell for magic speed, and so it moved very slowly. She urged it on, but nothing made any difference. At last she lost her temper. 'In God's name get on with you,' she cried, but the boat at once changed to an egg-shell and the woman drowned.[2]

Witches could be kind. Another Slavonian gipsy tale tells how a girl noticed everyone smash the shell when they had eaten an egg. She asked why, and was told:

> *You must break the shell to bits for fear*
> *Lest the witches should make it a boat, my dear.*
> *For over the sea, away from home,*
> *Far by night the witches roam.*

'I don't see why the poor witches should not have boats as well as other people,' said the girl, and she threw an egg-shell as far as she could, crying: 'Witch – there is your boat!' To her amazement, it was caught up by the wind and whirled away until it was invisible. A voice cried out: 'I thank you.' Some time later the girl

---

[1] Bächtold-Stäubli, ii.688.   [2] Leland, 74–5.

was on an island, when a great flood rose and washed her boat away. The island was almost swamped when a white vessel came in sight. It contained a 'woman with witch eyes' rowing with a broom, and with a black cat perched on her shoulder. 'Jump in,' she called to the girl, and rowed her to dry land. Then she said: 'Turn three times to the right and look each time at the boat.' The girl did as she was told, and every time she looked the boat was smaller, until it was like an egg. Her rescuer sang:

> *'That is the shell you threw to me,*
> *Even a witch can grateful be.'*

Then she vanished, shell and all.[1]

As a rule, people were terrified of witches, because of the immense powers for harm which they were said to possess, and that was why they smashed the egg-shells. Sometimes this was rationalized: in north Germany, Belgium and England, for instance, you would hear people saying that if an egg-shell was left whole it would cause ague and epilepsy.[2] This was only a step away from saying that the spells of the witches brought on these dread diseases. In coastal areas they were accused of using egg-shells to bewitch men at sea and wreck their boats. The Faroese say, 'Crush your egg-shells or a ship will be lost.'[3] Perhaps that is why Scottish fishermen attribute bad luck to eggs brought on to a ship. They are said to provoke quarrelling and bad temper. English sailors will not even use the word and talk of 'round-abouts' instead.[4]

Elves and sprites often hatch out from eggs, and in Germany they say you can actually see the pixie inside an egg laid before sunrise. But if he breaks the egg the person who sees it happen is doomed to die.[5] That is in Brunswick. In Schleswig-Holstein the witches hide in eggs, and set up house inside the shells.[6] Generally, however, in Germany, as elsewhere, the shells were smashed to prevent the witches making boats, not houses.

[1] *Ibid.*, 72-3.
[2] Thorpe, Benjamin, *Northern Mythology*, London, 1851, iii.174. Bonnerjea, Biren, *A Dictionary of Superstitions and Mythology*, London, 1927, 87.
[3] Williamson, Kenneth, *The Atlantic Islands*, London, 1948, 84.
[4] Hole, *Encyclopaedia*, 149.
[5] Bächtold-Stäubli, ii.597. [6] *Ibid.*, 688.

In Britain the idea still lingers on. My husband, born in 1930, remembers being taught as a child to put his spoon through an empty egg-shell. No one ever told him why, and he went on doing it, from force of habit, until he was a grown man.

It could have been British influence which carried the custom to the Southern States of America, where local Negroes burn shells and mix the ashes with seed corn.[1] Of course, besides the British, there were many French settlers in the area, and it is equally possible that the habit came from France, since it is known there as well. Shortly after his Accession, Napoleon III consulted a high authority on etiquette to know if he had committed any *faux pas*. There were several: one was that he had not broken the shell after eating a boiled egg![2] French peasants struck their shells three times with something hard, to break the witches' power, just as the Germans smashed them to avoid fever.[3]

Despite the experience of Napoleon III, British etiquette books have long condemned the custom as boorish peasant behaviour. It is all the more surprising, then, to find that it was a cherished habit of Miss Mellon, Duchess of St Albans. Mrs C. B. Wilson, in her *Life*, describes how the Duchess faithfully observed the ritual – to let the fairies out and stop the evil spirits from coming in. She was said to have acquired it from an Irish grandmother.[4]

Earlier and more distinguished authors have written on the subject. Here is Sir Thomas Browne:

> To prevent house spirits from using the shell for their mischievous pranks . . . to breake an egg shell after ye meat is out we are taught in our childhood . . . and the intent thereof was to prevent witchcraft; lest witches should draw or prick their names therein and veneficiously mischiefe ye persons, they broke ye shell. . . . This custome of breaking the bottom of the Eggeshell is [yet] commonly used in the countrey.[5]

There is no mention of a voyage here. But Reginald Scot refers to it in his *Discoverie of Witchcraft*: 'They [witches] can go in and

---

[1] Puckett, 155.

[2] *Notes and Queries*, 21 January 1888, 7th Series, v, 48.

[3] Bächtold-Stäubli, ii.688.

[4] *Notes and Queries*, 11 February 1888, 7th Series, v, 113.

[5] Browne, Sir Thomas, *Pseudodoxia Epidemica*, London, 1686, v.xxii, para 4.

out at awger-holes, and saile in an egge-shell ... through and under the tempestuous seas.'[1]

The witches sail to different places and at different times of year. Montenegran witches, the *vjeshtitza*, ride in the shell of an egg eaten on 1 March, though some peasants smash any egg-shells as soon as they finish eating, to make quite sure.[2] And the Dutch aim to stop witches from crossing the Channel to England[3] – a kindly thought.

The tradition is common to many countries. Possibly it reached us from the Romans, who believed, according to Pliny, that egg-shells might be used for practising harmful magic: '*Huc pertinet ovorum, quae exorbuerit quisque, calices coclearumque protinus frangi aut isdem coclearibus perforari.*'[4]

In Haitian folk belief the dried-out yolk of an egg, left on an iron roof and moistened with morning dew, changes to a deadly poison.[5] Are we to see in this another adaptation of European lore? If so, perhaps there are racialist undertones – poignant in these days when Europeans are ogres in so many parts of the world. Agoué, the Haitian god of the sea, is credited with helping drive out the whites after the 1791 Negro revolution. They escaped into the sea, floating with calabashes at their navels, or in egg-shells transformed into little ships by lighting a candle inside.[6] The association of ideas here is quite logical. Nations dominated by rulers of a different colour often considered their overlords as in some way connected with evil magic: the pink devils in Chinese history – white men, as we would say – share their colour with the symbolic mask for evil in many Chinese operas. Here, in the rich variety of Haitian lore, nationalism and magic may be blended.

But in most of these accounts it is the magical element that is uppermost, and the puzzle remains: What could have been the

---

[1] Scot, Reginald, *The Discoverie of Witchcraft*, London, 1654, 1.iv.7. First published 1584.

[2] Durham, M. E., *Some Tribal Origins, Laws and Customs of the Balkans*, London, 1928, 258.

[3] Information kindly supplied by Henk Arends of Amsterdam.

[4] Bostock, John, ed., *Pliny's 'Natural History'*, London, 1856, v.282, and note 36. Aubrey, 110, 193. Brand, John, *Observations on Popular Antiquities*, London, 1810, 353; see note.

[5] Huxley, 43.

[6] *Ibid.*, 194.

significance of such a fragile, unlikely vessel? An analogy with Chinese lore suggests a possible answer. After death the soul travelled in an egg-shell boat. On the sixtieth day food offerings are laid out for the deceased on a table, together with a bowlful of water. Floating on this is an egg-shell. Standing near it in the water is the image of a duck carrying a seated human figure. This represents the dead man, and the shell is his boat.[1]

There is an old idea, common among seafaring peoples, but found among others too, that after death the soul sets out on a journey for a land across the seas. The poet Tennyson in his old age employed a sentimental treatment of this theme:

> *Sunset and evening star*
> *And one clear call for me!*
> *And may there be no moaning of the bar*
> *When I put out to sea,*
>
> *But such a tide as moving seems asleep,*
> *Too full for sound and foam,*
> *When that which drew from out the boundless deep*
> *Turns again home.*
>
> *Twilight and evening bell*
> *And after that the dark!*
> *And may there be no sadness of farewell*
> *When I embark;*
>
> *For tho' from out our bourne of Time and Place*
> *The flood may bear me far,*
> *I hope to see my Pilot face to face*
> *When I have crost the bar.*[2]

A Dutch friend writes that this was a Continental idea, and the mysterious country beyond the water is England – Brittia. A certain scholar from the Dutch province of Friesland, called Halbertsma, told the famous German folklorist Jacob Grimm that in his country people believe the souls of the dead make use of egg-shells to cross the sea to 'the other side', so people de-

[1] Bächtold-Stäubli, ii.689, note 32. Doolittle, Justus, *Social Life of the Chinese*, London, 1866, i.188.

[2] Tennyson, Lord Alfred, *Works*, London, 1894, 894.

stroyed their egg-shells after a meal, in case witches got inside who might vex the departing souls.[1]

The seafaring Vikings prepared great ship burials. Graves in Gotland and elsewhere were made in the shape of a boat, and in England we have the magnificent seventh-century grave at Sutton Hoo – a ship containing the treasures of a king. The poem *Beowulf* gives a full description of a boat filled with riches, in which the corpse is laid and sent out across the sea.

Dr H. R. Ellis Davidson, in her *Gods and Myths of Northern Europe*, describes these customs in full, and stresses the antiquity of the ship as a funeral symbol. In Egypt, she says, where ships were placed in graves beside some of the pyramids, it was natural to link the ship with the departure of the divine Pharaoh to the realm of the gods and with the journey of the sun across the heavens; the ship therefore, came to represent the gifts of warmth and fertility to man.[2]

Of course, in Egyptian belief the life-giving sun was an egg, which came from the water and returned to it in the evening. Does not the soul in its small egg-shell boat – a frail craft to be tackling the stormy seas – carry with it a suggestion of the breath of life returning back across the limitless waters of creation, the source from which it arose, long ago before time began? The most powerful sorcery involves the misuse of something good and meaningful – the Black Mass is a parody of a sacred rite – and the witch in her boat, utilizing the fount of life and creation, possessed a peculiarly potent magic weapon.

THE CASTING OF SPELLS

Evil influences were supposed to strengthen with the waxing sun, and so it was that witches increased the power and scope of their activities at the beginning of the summer. On no account, warn the Faroese, ought one to eat eggs on 14 April, the day which marks the end of their winter. Anyone who does will suffer from boils for the rest of the year.[3] This belief held good in the mid-twentieth century. Further south, May was the proper witching

---

[1] Information kindly supplied by Henk Arends.

[2] Ellis Davidson, H. R., *Gods and Myths of Northern Europe*, London, 1964, 133–7.

[3] Williamson, 238.

time. According to an English superstition transported to America, if a broody hen is set then, all her chicks will be sure to die.[1]

Until the eighteenth century both Scots and Irish celebrated the Beltane Festival on May Day. This, among other things, was an attempt to prevent the spread of witchcraft. A cake was shared out during the rites, and whoever received the piece marked specially with charcoal served as a scapegoat for the witches. He became a figure of terror and the assembly pelted him with egg-shells.[2] It is worth comparing this with the German custom of casting shell fragments after a disagreeable stranger.[3] As with the witches' boats, the destruction of the shells probably minimized the power of doing harm. Although the full Beltane ceremonies were discarded over two centuries ago, certain elements remained until more recently – on 1 May 1893 bannock and hard-boiled-egg rolling took place around Kingussie in the Highlands.[4]

Walpurgis Night, on the Eve of May Day, was when witches held their mountain revels with the Devil. The Brocken peak in Germany, now in the closed border zone between East and West and hence as mysterious and inaccessible as ever, was a favourite rendezvous. Walpurgis, whose name is associated with these gatherings, was in fact a Christian saint, protectress against witchcraft, and a niece of St Boniface, who helped to introduce Christianity into Germany.[5] In his *Faust* Goethe describes the festival of witches and spirits upon the Brocken. Mephistopheles says to the Witch:

> *And if you have a favour to request,*
> *Upon Walpurgis Night just mention it.*[6]

In England and Scotland at Walpurgis branches of rowan were fastened on houses and cattle-stalls to keep the witches at bay. Rowan, or mountain ash, is often called the witch-tree because of

---

[1] *Dictionary of Folklore, Mythology and Legend*, New York, 1949, i.341.

[2] James, E. O., *Seasonal Feasts and Festivals*, London, 1961, 313.

[3] Bächtold-Stäubli, ii.643.

[4] Mackinlay, James M., *Folklore of Scottish Lochs and Springs*, Glasgow, 1893, 298.

[5] *Encyclopaedia Britannica*, 14th Ed., London, 1929, xxiii.313.

[6] Goethe, Johann Wolfgang, *Faust*, tr. Philip Wayne, London, 1949, i.8, 120.

its power against witchcraft, and on May Day in Westphalia cowherds drove the cattle by slapping them with switches from this
same tree. They were given eggs to eat while they did so and the
shells were later used to adorn the fronds.[1] Here the egg is a protective symbol, and there is a parallel in Brandenburg, where a
fresh one carefully buried beneath the threshold of a house on
May Day will ward off evil influences.[2]

1 May is an ill-omened day for Polish farmers too. Hens are not
set, since any eggs which hatched would yield misshapen chickens.
In certain districts this belief is so strongly held that no broodies
are subsequently set on the day of the week on which May Day
fell.[3]

Witches often cast their spells on humans with the aid of an
egg. To discover if a child is bewitched, throw an egg into the
water, and if he is it will sink[4] – a perverse variant on the old
method of unmasking a witch. The suspect was thrown into
water and, if she sank and presumably drowned, her innocence
was established. But if she did not, it meant she was guilty and
would be burnt to death.

Albanians use garlic to protect their children against witches.[5]
The herb, which must be eaten before Lent, is widespread as a
charm, probably because of its pungent odour. But the protective will not take effect if there is an egg in the house,[6]
which presumably could be used to cast a spell. There were
various ways in which this might be done. Sometimes the unsuspecting victim ate an egg with a hex upon it. Scot describes
how an Englishman was changed into a donkey:

It happened in the city of Salamin, in the kingdom of Cyprus . . .
that a ship laden with merchandise stayed there for a short space. In
the meantime many of the soldiers and mariners went to shore, to
provide fresh victuals. Among which number a certain Englishman,
being a sturdy young fellow, went to a woman's house a little way
out of the city and not far from the sea side to see whether she had
any eggs to sell. Who perceiving him to be a lusty young stranger
and far from his country (so as upon the loss of him there would be
the less miss or enquiry) she considered with herself how to destroy

[1] Bächtold-Stäubli, ii.611.   [2] *Ibid.*
[3] Benet, Sula, *Song, Dance and Customs of Peasant Poland*, London, 1951, 65.
[4] Bächtold-Stäubli, ii.609.
[5] Durham, 244.   [6] Bächtold-Stäubli, ii.609.

him. .... After some detracting of time, she brought him a few eggs, willing him to return to her, if his ship were gone when he came. The young fellow returned towards his ship: but before he went aboard, he would needs eat an egg or twain to satisfy his hunger, and within short space he became dumb and out of his wits. .... When he would have entered into the ship the mariners beat him back with a cudgel saying: 'What a murrain lacks the ass? Whither the devil will this ass?' ... Being many times repelled, and understanding their words that called him ass, considering that he could speak never a word, and yet could understand everybody: he thought that he was bewitched by the woman at whose house he was.[1]

Witches, according to a 1540 handbook, could cast spells upon cattle by burying an egg in their pasture. The serving-maid of Gockelius found an egg, wrapped in green leaves and tied with green thread, hidden beneath the threshold. This was interpreted as an attempt to cast a spell on the daughter of the house and also on their billy-goat.[2] Since this measure was sometimes taken to protect a possible victim, it again shows how in witchcraft a symbol of good is turned to ill use.

Ceremonial burial of an egg is quite common in the Middle East. In Morocco, if you want to make a person go insane, empty an egg and write the name of a *djinn* around the shell. Use the white, saffron, and unripe fig juice in place of ink. Then mix the contents of the egg with gunpowder and replace them. Bury it where the victim is certain to walk and he will go mad. For even if the gunpowder is damp, the power of a terrifying *djinn*, who originates from an egg and regards it as his emblem, will be present.[3]

Again in Morocco, when parents of a new-born child omit to give the schoolmaster money so that his pupils can enjoy a holiday, the boys take their revenge. They steal an egg from the parents' chickens, and secretly dig a little grave outside their door. In it they bury the egg and then recite a chapter from the Koran, as is the custom at a funeral. When the unsuspecting mother walks over this, her child is doomed to die and she herself will be permanently afflicted with an issue of blood. Presumably this

[1] Scot, v.iii.72–3.
[2] Bächtold-Stäubli, ii.629.
[3] Westermarck, i.361.

means a continuous menstruation, so that she will be unable to bear other children.[1]

In Egypt a divorced wife inscribes a spell upon an egg. Then she gives it to a male relative for burial. Provided that the new wife does not find the egg, she will be unable to bear a child.[2] The idea behind these charms seems to be that burial of the life symbol places an embargo on the reproductive organs.

In the same country, if a man wants his wife to hate him, so that he will be able to divorce her, he engages a sorcerer to write magic letters on a Wednesday egg. The inscription must be part of the name of the King of the Tombs. Then it is buried secretly in a Christian or Moslem grave, according to the religion of the family. The spell will start to take effect at once, but the egg must never be moved from its place; and if it were found the magic would depart.[3]

The ritual to obtain a death is more elaborate. The egg must be laid by a black hen, and the inscription written in its blood. Incense is burnt and, with the egg held over it, inscription face downwards, the following incantation is spoken before the egg is placed in a tomb:

> In the Name of God, the Compassionate, the Merciful. By the name of God, the Mighty King and Majesty. Possessor of Possessions, the Throne and Seat, the Heavens and Earth. Blessèd be God, Lord of the World, Lord of all power and transcendant might. Light of Light and spirit of Spirits. All Glorious, Holy Lord of Angels and the Spirit, praise Him, the Highest. Take charge, Angel Gabraïl, of the illness of – the Son of – . Quickly now![4]

European witches were often accused of murder. In 1583 a certain Mother Gabley of King's Lynn was condemned to death for drowning fourteen men. She had boiled some eggs in a pail of water and this was accepted as proof of her guilt.[5] At Ramsey (Isle of Man) in 1665 a witch told one of her clients to bury a goose egg in the name of the person to be affected in a dung-hill. As the egg rotted, so the victim too would decay and die.[6] As recently as 1904 a mother who had lost her child accused her

---

[1] *Ibid.*, 601.
[2] Blackman, Winifred, *The Fellahin of Upper Egypt*, London, 1927, 108.
[3] *Ibid.*, 190.   [4] *Ibid.*, 190–1.
[5] *Norfolk Archaeology*, London, 1859, v.87.
[6] Craine, David, *Manannan's Isle*, Douglas, 1955, 16.

neighbour of murdering him by witchcraft: the other woman had boiled some eggs and mashed them up.[1]

The Swiss, on the other hand, believed that a spell cast with an egg would be ineffective if the egg could be crushed, but the victim had to do it. A German pamphlet, published in 1627, even goes so far as to say that anyone leaving an uncrushed egg-shell may be responsible for the death of another human being.[2] Witches sometimes wrote their victim's name inside a shell, which was then conjured into the stomach, inflicting severe wounds.[3] They were used in Scotland, however, as an effective counter-charm. If a cow had been bewitched, and was yielding no milk, a little was poured in an egg-shell and secretly carried to the house of the suspect, in the Devil's name. If the guess was correct, and the milk curdled, the stricken cow would be healed.[4] On the Isle of Man they obtain the right herbs from someone who knows about these, together with nine eggs from a long way off, so that they will be clean of *buitcheragh*. At midnight, with the doors bolted, a third of the herbs and three of the eggs are boiled in a pot of well water for three minutes. This is done three nights running. The source says nothing about giving this mess to the cow, but presumably this was done.[5]

To strip an evil-doer of his harmful power, runs a German counter-charm, fill an egg-shell with his urine and hang it sealed inside the chimney. His strength will wither as the contents evaporate.[6] This practice hinges on an ancient and common belief that witchcraft can be practised on excreta from the human body. In Haiti, too, an egg is used to exorcize the power of a voodoo *houngan*, or rather to prevent its being used after his death by a magician. An egg and seven fathoms of white cotton thread tied with seven knots – a magic number – are placed under the *houngan*'s death-bed pillow, to prevent his conversion to a zombie.[7]

Black magic is very much alive in the Caribbean, though in Jamaica *obeah*, as they call it, is in fact illegal. According to an Act passed in 1781:

[1] *The Lindsey and Lincolnshire Star*, 1 October 1904.
[2] Bächtold-Stäubli, ii.688.   [3] Aubrey, 110.
[4] Polson, Alexander, *Scottish Witchcraft Lore*, London, 1932, 138.
[5] Gill, W. Walter, *A Third Manx Scrapbook*, London, 1963, 332.
[6] Bächtold-Stäubli, ii.630.   [7] Huxley, 87.

And in order to prevent the many mischiefs that may hereafter arise from the wicked art of Negroes going under the appellation of *obeah* men and women, pretending to have communication with the devil and other evil spirits, whereby the weak and superstitious are deluded into a belief of their having full power to exempt them whilst under protection from any evils that might otherwise happen: Be it therefore enacted by the authority, aforesaid, any Negro or other slave who shall pretend to any supernatural power, and be detected in making use of any blood, feathers, parrots-beaks, dogs-teeth, alligators-teeth, broken bottles, grave dirt, rum, egg shells, or any other materials relative to the practice of *obeah* or witchcraft, in order to delude and impose on the minds of others, shall upon conviction before two magistrates and three freeholders, suffer death or transportation; anything in this or any other act to the contrary in any wise notwithstanding.[1]

Despite this, *obeah* flourishes. The sorcerer prefers an egg laid by the night-hawk, known locally as *gi-me-me-bit*, in imitation of the bird's cry. A piece of local lore warns: 'Tek up *gi-me-me-bit* egg you tek up trouble.'[2] An egg 'set' for anyone by the spirit doctor is the cause of considerable terror. An egg on the road, or indeed anywhere, wrapped in string and supposedly put there for that purpose, would be left untouched, although many people are poor and food is precious. No one would go near such a thing or step over it. Emerick, in his book on Jamaican magic, writes: 'Of all things, an egg is perhaps the most dreaded.'[3] The same is true of Haiti. Recently a man found an egg by his front door, 'set' by the *houngan*, or voodoo priest. The victim at once took it back to the *houngan*'s home and broke it to ensure that the evil would go back there. But he kept the shell himself and told a friendly voodoo priestess to prepare a ritual bath with the crumbled fragments.[4] The Sicilian death charm *fattura della morte* is an object of similar awe. Shells filled with wax and stuck with a nail and pins – one was used as late as 1903 – they are reminiscent of the wax images pierced in England at an earlier date.[5]

[1] *Acts of Assembly*, Kingston, 1786, 277.

[2] Beckwith, Martha, *Jamaica Folklore*, New York, 1928, xxi.108. *Ibid., Black Roadways*, 120–1.

[3] Emerick, Abraham J., *Obeah and Duppyism in Jamaica*, Woodstock, 1915, 190. [4] Huxley, 119.

[5] Hastings, James, ed., *Encyclopaedia of Religion and Ethics*, Edinburgh, 1912, v.614.

There was a case in Scotland in 1696 which suggested, at first glance, that an egg had been 'set' in the same fashion. A child named Christian Shaw claimed to have been bewitched by the family maid, who had caught her stealing milk. She became ill and vomited a number of unusual items, including egg-shells. Attributing these symptoms to a charm beneath her bed, she had a look and brought out an egg-shell. When thrown on the fire, it apparently melted away, instead of crackling loudly, as though it were made of wax.[1] It seems likely that she had put the shell there herself, so it is interesting to see how prominently it figures in what one assumes to be the hoax of a spiteful child, determined to have her revenge. Presumably she chose what was most likely to be accepted as genuine.

A peculiarly unpleasant egg was 'set' by a Hungarian girl for her faithless lover. The girl was not a witch and the story ends sadly. In the Kalotaszeger district a man can make a *szerencse tojás*, or 'good-luck' egg, by removing the white through a small hole and replacing it with some of his sperm. The opening is sealed with wax or gypsum, and the egg placed beneath a black broody hen. In three weeks' time the egg will be really hard, and anything it touches will bring good luck to the owner. But there is one thing: on no account ought the egg to be dropped in water at night. If it is, the owner will die or go insane. Márisko Györgyi, the prettiest girl in Jegenye village, doted on a man who had been her lover, but he grew bored. Realizing this, she managed to prepare a 'good luck' egg, intending to throw it in the water in front of him, so that a spectre would leap out and strangle him to death. She carried the egg about for a long time, concealed in her bosom, watching for a chance to use it. One night, as she did her washing, it fell from the front of her dress into the tub of water and broke open. The girl was found lying unconscious on the ground: she said a black spirit came out of the egg and struck her on the head. Not so long after she became deranged, and the village boys jeered, calling her 'Egg Mary' – *Tojásos Márisko*.[2]

This pathetic, ludicrous tale, which is a true account, is only too plausible in the light of modern psychology. Distressed, first by the loss of her lover and then her precious egg, the jilted girl could easily have pictured an evil spirit in her mind. All these

[1] *A History of the Witches of Renfrewshire*, Paisley, 1877, 76, 96. No author.
[2] Wlislocki, 144–5.

spells and charms in which eggs were used inevitably tended to give them a sinister aura. Camden, in *Ancient and Modern Manners of the Irish*, notes that horse-owners make sure of eating an even number, otherwise some ill will befall the animals. Grooms should avoid them at all costs and riders must wash their hands after handling any.[1]

Here is an analogy of sorts with an old Cornish superstition, that egg white spilt upon the hands produces warts. Even washing in water used for boiling eggs brought about the same nasty effect,[2] a belief which was common in Cheshire too.[3] Germans pour egg water carefully away where sunlight and moonshine cannot reach it. Failure to do this could bring on an attack of fever.[4] In England people were afraid to have strings of egg-shells inside the house. They had to be left in a shed.[5] This is not an exclusively European idea: in Guinea and Senegal the Agni tribe associate egg-shells with Sakarabu, the demon of darkness.[6]

Sometimes magic spells got a little out of hand. It was evidently, for instance, possible to bewitch one's own eggs, or those of other people, quite by accident. Should someone sitting at table happen to mention the name of a bird, the cuckoo would come and suck the contents from all the eggs that any of his hens might lay.[7] This superstition is rooted in the idea that a man's name is sacrosanct, and a living part of his being. Unsophisticated people and, in our own folklore, fairies, are very unwilling to let anyone know their name, for knowledge of names gives power. So many objects, often without any apparent reason – for the reason has been forgotten – become taboo and may not be mentioned.

Sometimes the idea behind the magic is almost impossible to guess. In France, only in 1960, Joisten collected a story from an old countryman in Montferrand. A man made a peasant woman give him an egg, and told her husband to put his foot on top of his own. The egg immediately rushed inside the house, emitting peals of thunder and lightning flashes, and causing the

---

[1] Jones, *Credulities*, 464.
[2] *Notes and Queries*, 10 September 1887, 7th Series, iv, 212.
[3] Information kindly supplied by Miss E. M. Loughran.
[4] Bächtold-Stäubli, ii.634.   [5] Hole, *Encyclopaedia*, 151.
[6] *Larousse Encyclopaedia of Mythology*, London, 1959, 489–90.
[7] Bächtold-Stäubli, ii.643.

building to burst into flames. Terrified, the couple begged the sorcerer to stop, and he obliged.[1] Here the magic of the egg has degenerated into a *tour de force*, displaying the sorcerer's skill. But probably in an earlier version it possessed some greater significance.

Pedemontanus also gives us an egg conjuring trick. This is a recipe for causing an egg to rise up in the air: coat it with wax and place it below a lance stuck in the ground when the sun is overhead. The egg will then run up the lance.[2] The point of this is not clear, but it must have some meaning, for, in an account from Bächtold-Stäubli, a witch used the same method to escape burning at the stake. It was in the Upper Palatinate towards the end of the eighteenth century; just before the fires were lighted she complained of thirst and asked for an egg. One was brought and she sucked it. But to everyone's amazement she disappeared completely and the empty shell rolled up the stake. Since witches often travelled in this way, she was presumed to be inside.[3]

Another story describes an even stranger transformation. In a legend from the Minyong tribe on the North-East Frontier of India, a girl takes an egg, breaks it, smears the yolk on her head and body, puts a knife into her mouth and changes into a tigress;[4] while in the Kaffir *Story of Sikulume* the egg throws up a protective mist. This enables a girl eloping with her lover to escape from her father, who is pursuing them.[5]

On journeys it was often felt that the traveller might contract some alien influence from the strangers he went among. Frazer mentions various precautions taken to overcome this.[6] In Dauphiné (France), if someone pays a visit after a long absence, it was the custom to cook an egg. They say, 'I must give you an egg,' without actually doing so, though no doubt it was really given in earlier times. Joisten, who collected this information, was told by one woman that she had received an egg on one of these occasions and held it in her hand.[7] At Prélenfrey (Isère), they say, 'We must cook a few eggs,' and the visitor replies, 'Cook

---

[1] Joisten, 60.   [2] Bächtold-Stäubli, ii.627.   [3] *Ibid.*, 687.

[4] Elwin, Verrier, *Myths of the North-East Frontier of India*, Shillong, 1958, 364–5.

[5] Theal, George McCall, *Kaffir Folklore*, London, 1886, 87.

[6] Frazer, Sir James G., *The Golden Bough*, London, 1911, iii.194–198.

[7] Joisten, 58.

them quickly.'[1] Again the exchange is generally only verbal and an egg is not produced. In Germany a stranger visiting the house for the first time, and rare visitors too, were given a 'chatter egg' to loosen their tongues.[2]

Jewish custom is the exact opposite: visitors are not given eggs. The source of this is a Talmudic saying that 'A guest should not eat eggs'.[3] Jewish traditions reach back to ancient times, when every man feared the hostile magic of unknown strangers. Life was passed in small, closed communities, with no knowledge of the world beyond, and the arrival of an outsider was regarded with fear and suspicion. A threatening figure, he could so easily appear to cast the evil eye or exert a malign influence. If offered eggs in one's home, he might use them to disadvantage. Hence perhaps the later custom that it would be discourteous of the guest to ask for such a thing, implying that the use of eggs as witching objects might go back to the very dawn of history.

[1] *Ibid.*, 59.   [2] Bächtold-Stäubli, ii.643.
[3] Hershon, Paul Isaac, *Treasures of the Talmud*, London, 1882, 146.

Chapter 4
Bird and Egg

die Sophisten und die Pfaffen
stritten sich mit viel Geschrei :
was hat Gott zuerst erschaffen,
wohl die Henne, wohl das Ei?
Eduard Morike

FARMYARD SUPERSTITIONS

Because they supply eggs, meat and feathers, domestic fowl are immensely important to the life of any peasant community and their well-being is a natural cause for concern. In the past, when people's lives were ruled by magical beliefs – as they still are to some extent – great pains were taken to see that everything was done in the proper way at the correct time. When, how many, by whom and under what conditions to set the eggs – these things, which now seem so absurd, all had to be taken into consideration. If any were overlooked, a blight of some sort would fall on the poultry and a source of food dry up; the same applied to cows and other farm animals.

First of all, certain general conditions had to be observed. For instance, in Brunswick it was the custom to go begging for eggs at Whitsun. If any refused to give, their hens would cease to lay.[1] Perhaps the appeal here is to sympathetic magic: give, and the hen gives too. To guard against adverse contingencies, one needs some kind of powerful protective. Bächtold-Stäubli mentions iron and straw gathered at Christmas – a pagan and a Christian charm combined. This strikes us as quaint, but two traditions are often confused, and not only by peasants. Just as the sacred season guards the bird from harm, a piece of magic iron laid in the nest will stimulate and encourage her to lay.[2]

Iron is commonly regarded, in folk-tales and in folk-lore, as a metal with miraculous powers. Man did not use it until a com-

---

[1] *Dictionary of Folklore, Mythology and Legend*, New York, 1949, i.341.

[2] Bächtold-Stäubli, Hanns, ed., *Handwörterbuch des deutschen Aberglaubens*, Berlin, 1929–30, ii.641.

paratively late period of development and, because it was so much more useful – especially for making weapons – than either bronze or stone, it was supposed to be supernatural, and the belief persisted into modern times. Frazer attributed this partly to traditional awe at anything new or unusual, so typical of unsophisticated people and indeed of the vast majority, even today.[1] This may sound rather sweeping, but one only has to think of how very conservative many people are – merely about their food, for example. I remember a man with a university training who would eat nothing but fruit, meat and potatoes prepared in a certain way, not for any reasons of health, but because this was what he was used to. An extreme case, perhaps, but most of us know people like this.

Our ancestors, apart from the importance of routine, were also slaves to time – not in the sense that we know it today, when everything moves at such speed, but to the appropriateness of the occasion: there was a right and a wrong time for doing things. Anyone who broke the rules could bring about terrible disasters. Time of day, conjunction of planets and positioning of the stars – all these had to be taken into account. The day of the week governed the character of a child, as the old rhyme tells us:

> *Monday's child is fair of face,*
> *Tuesday's child is full of grace,*
> *Wednesday's child is full of woe,*
> *Thursday's child has far to go,*
> *Friday's child is loving and giving,*
> *Saturday's child works hard for a living,*
> *But the child that is born on the Sabbath Day*
> *Is blithe and bonny, good and gay.*

As with a child, so with a chicken. The day on which the eggs were set was very important, and the ancient Romans selected it with great care. In modern Germany, Friday is a bad day: the hen will eat her clutch.[2] Of course, as the day of the Crucifixion, Friday is usually unlucky in Christian countries. The pagan Romans called it *nefastus*, because their armies were badly defeated then at Gallia Narbonensis,[3] and in medieval romance

---

[1] Frazer, Sir James G., *The Golden Bough*, London, 1911, iii.230–2.
[2] Bächtold-Stäubli, ii.641.
[3] Brewer, E. Cobham, *Dictionary of Phrase and Fable*, London, 1896, 489.

elves and fairies changed into monsters on a Friday and remained in that state until the Monday following.

Why Sunday should be an unpropitious day in England – eggs set then will never hatch[1] – is hard to say; perhaps because of a shift in emphasis. Since witches used eggs for sorcery, they may have become identified with evil and supposedly not prospered on the holy day of the week. A Scottish belief that they only hatch if set after sundown, when the powers of darkness are strongest, may spring from the same source.[2] The idea that eggs set in daylight produce only blind chicks is probably related too, but influenced by association of ideas – the bright sunlight which might dazzle the eyes of a newly hatched brood.

The strange power which the moon appeared to exert over tides and the physiological cycle of women was noticed from earliest times along with its mysterious rhythms of waxing and waning, something absent from the course of the sun. Inevitably comparisons were drawn and the cycle of the moon became equated with the life of man. And so the different lunar phases had to be taken into account. Some of these beliefs conflict. German peasants say that eggs set at the new moon will hatch blind birds, but if set in the moon's increase produce only cockerels;[3] in England they never go bad.[4]

Gennep collected contradictory lunar beliefs in France. Eggs must not be set at new moon, for the baby chickens will be weak – this from St Romain de Jalionas. But in Sillans eggs set then will definitely prove more fertile.[5] Probably both are different interpretations of the same idea, that the waxing and waning of the moon affect husbandry and human life. To some the new moon in its insignificance represents the lowest point of influence. To others it is the initial moment of growth, and a time when its power strikes out anew.

The moon, of course, also affects the tide and, especially in a seafaring land like Great Britain, it was thought that its ebb and flow exert a control upon human life. People could only die at the ebb or turn of the tide, and Mistress Quickly, describing Falstaff's last moments, says: 'A' made a finer end and went away

---

[1] Hole, Christina, ed., *Encyclopaedia of Superstitions*, London, 1961, 149.
[2] Gregor, W., *Notes on the Folklore of North-East Scotland*, London, 1881, 141.
[3] Bächtold-Stäubli, ii.641.   [4] Hole, *Encyclopaedia*, 238.
[5] Van Gennep, Arnold, *Le Folklore du Dauphiné*, Paris, 1932, ii.437.

an it had been any christom child; a' parted even just between twelve and one, even at the turning o' the tide.'[1]

At one time the state of the tide used to be entered in parish registers, together with the details of death. Dickens, in *David Copperfield*, writes:

> He was as mute and senseless as the box, from which his form derived the only expression it had.
>
> 'He's agoing out with the tide,' said Mr Peggotty to me, behind his hand.
>
> My eyes were dim and so were Mr Peggotty's; but I repeated in a whisper, 'With the tide?'
>
> 'People can't die, along the coast,' said Mr Peggotty, 'except when the tide's pretty nigh out. They can't be born, unless it's pretty nigh in – not properly born, till flood. He's agoing out with the tide. It's ebb at half-arter three, slack water half-an-hour. If he lives 'till it turns, he'll hold his own till past the flood, and go out with the next tide.' . . .
>
> He tried to stretch out his arm, and said to me distinctly, with a pleasant smile:
>
> 'Barkis is willin'!'
>
> And, it being low water, he went out with the tide. [2]

Farmers near the coast in England and Scotland, if they wanted hens, were careful to set their eggs at ebb tide and at the flood for cockerels.[3] The usual practice of equating the strong, vigorous element with the male, the weak with the female, was here a means of influencing the sex of the unborn chicks. The connection with the tide is correspondingly less as one moves inland, where the hen-wife carries the eggs to the bird wrapped in her blouse if she wants pullets; there will be a brood of roosters if she wears her husband's hat.[4] In Switzerland she puts the eggs in her corset and shakes them down into the nest[5] – an unappealing idea, and probably not very safe. German farmers who require cockerels wrap the eggs in a pair of trousers.[6]

Ebb and flow, masculine and feminine, even life and death: all these were thought to play their part in the hatching process. For if a corpse is merely in the same room as a hen, her eggs will never

[1] *Henry V*, ii.iii.
[2] Dickens, Charles, *David Copperfield*, London, 1870, ii.8–9.
[3] Gregor, 141.   [4] *Ibid.*
[5] Bächtold-Stäubli, ii.641.   [6] *Ibid.*

hatch, or so they said in Poland.[1] More baffling is the belief, shared by us with the French, that a pregnant woman can spoil the eggs if she sets the hen – sometimes by her presence. Either the eggs will not hatch or the foetus will die.[2] In Germany, if she steps over them, they become diseased; a Japanese woman, on the other hand, in this way increases the difficulties of her labour.[3] The idea behind this would seem to be a confused thought that two life principles cannot coexist.

In poultry-farming the number of eggs set under a hen was also of vital importance. We may laugh, but it is amazing how strong a hold the magic of numbers still retains over our daily lives. Today in various homes – I have come across this in Northumberland, but it is probably widespread – it is the height of ill manners to seat thirteen at table. Many avenues of houses, and even modern blocks of flats, are without the number 13; one finds 12A and 12B instead. This is because it would be difficult to find a tenant for No. 13. Among older people the stigma of Friday the 13th remains. Perhaps in the case of a dinner party – a clear parallel with the Last Supper in popular lore – it was supposed that ill would befall a member of the group identified with Judas. Certainly in France they set thirteen eggs to ensure that twelve will hatch.[4]

As a rule, people preferred to set an uneven number.[5] A Lincolnshire woman remarked to Ethel Rudkin: 'It's a straange queer thing, but a' eaven number o' eggs niver hatches nowt but stags [cockerels].'[6]

Much the same is true in the Tyrol.[7] Like so many beliefs, this probably reached us from the Romans: '*Numero Deus impare gaudet*,' says Virgil[8] – the gods rejoice in uneven numbers.

Individual eggs are occasionally singled out, not because they

[1] Benet, Sula, *Song, Dance and Customs of Peasant Poland*, London, 1951, 241.

[2] Fowler, Alice, 'Note', *Folk-Lore*, xxviii (London, September 1917), 322–3.

[3] Bächtold-Stäubli, ii.689.

[4] Joisten, Charles, 'Le Folklore de L'Œuf en Dauphiné', *Arts et Traditions Populaires* (Paris, January–March 1961), 60.

[5] Aubrey, John, *The Remaines of Gentilisme and Judaisme* (1686-87), London, 1881, 178, 183. Briggs, K. M. and Tongue, R. L., *Somerset Folklore*, London, 1965, 145.

[6] Rudkin, Ethel, *Lincolnshire Folklore*, Gainsborough, 1936, 21.

[7] Bächtold-Stäubli, ii.641.   [8] *Eclogues*, viii.75.

look strange or freakish in any respect, but because of the circumstances in which they are laid. Why, for instance, should the tenth egg be the largest – an English superstition?[1] Perhaps because illiterate people reckon on their fingers, and therefore count in tens, they regard it as the number which clinches all the rest. Our own word 'ten', the German *zehn*, goes back through Old German *ze-hen* to Gothic *tai-hun*, which means 'two hands'.

If the eggs safely survive all these hazards and calculations and hatch into little chickens, the next problem is how to get rid of the debris. Disposal of shells was just as important as the actual hatching process. Because they were used by witches for magic rites, people generally smashed them – though some Germans thought the shell of an egg which had hatched possessed peculiar powers, and in Central America the Miskito carefully keep them to protect the poultry from harm.[2] The Southern Slavs avoid walking on egg-shells, which they regard as a cause of disease.[3]

Whatever one did to get rid of the shells, it was generally a bad idea to burn them. Germans, in some parts, considered that shells or salt were the only way to stop wood from crackling in the grate – an unlucky sign[4] – and in Yorkshire they thought that egg-shells thrown on the fire will 'come again'. But in England as a whole, if they are burnt, it affects the hens. They all stop laying and something serious could happen.[5] In Holland shells on the fire cause physical and spiritual pain: they burn the chicken's rump and harm the suffering souls of the damned.[6]

THE SOUL EGG

There are two sides to most myths and popular beliefs. The everyday, practical aspect is what strikes one at first. Often this is confused with an attempt, unconscious and incoherent, to come to terms with an immeasurable world of spiritual concepts. What, for

---

[1] Bonnerjea, Biren, *A Dictionary of Superstitions and Mythology*, London, 1927, 87.

[2] *Dictionary of Folklore*, i.341.

[3] Kemp, P., *Healing Ritual: Studies in the Technique and Tradition of the Southern Slavs*, London, 1935, 45.

[4] Bächtold-Stäubli, ii.689.

[5] Salisbury, Jesse, *A Glossary of Words and Phrases Used in S.E. Worcestershire*, London, 1893, 72. Udal, J. S., *Dorsetshire Folklore*, Hertford, 1922, 276.

[6] Bächtold-Stäubli, ii.688.

instance, can be meant by saying that burning egg-shells will injure the souls of the damned? One thinks of the flames of Hell and the association of ideas. But perhaps, too, there is a connection with the missing source of the changeling tale,[1] and the imagined cry of pain which involuntarily breaks from the creature when the housewife burns egg-shells or heats them. And we must not forget the egg-shell boat of the soul, a frail craft apparently returning back across the waters of creation to the place from which it came. In the Dutch belief above, the curious association of soul and egg reasserts itself. How might it have arisen in the first place?

The creation myths provide a clue. Time and again the universe egg appears from the waters of creation at the beginning of the world, preceding matter and existence. It contains all being, all life, and the creator god who is the soul of the world. The evolution of the universe serves as a pattern for the evolution of man, and a large group of myths also describe how the first ancestor appeared from an egg of this kind. If it is from this that life derived originally, in turn the egg appears to have become recognized as a possible seat of the soul.

The idea that the soul could be separated from the body was in fact quite common. Sometimes it took the form of an animal or creature, which led an independent existence, but was none the less closely associated with the body. This soul could be immortal, like the Egyptian *ka*, but if it was not its death might well presage the doom of its owner. In the famous Icelandic *Saga*, his *fylga* or fetch appeared to Thorð, the friend of Njal, as a goat covered with blood, shortly before his murder.[2]

This is in effect a simple formulation of an esoteric concept. Man, groping for a means of expressing the inexpressible, hits on the idea of the spirit, his *alter ego*, as a thing quite separate from himself, with a life of its own. The *fylga* served as an omen of death, but sometimes the life of an individual was even more closely linked with the well-being of his external soul: if the soul was injured, its owner died. So precious a thing needed careful guarding, and certain traditional stories describe magicians and sprites who had the power to enclose their soul within an egg.

[1] See ch. 3, p. 80.
[2] Magnusson, Magnus, and Pálsson, Hermann, *Njal's Saga*, London, 1960, xli.109–10.

Here the folk-tale seems to parallel the ancient myth, its significance and source forgotten, in the guise of a story for children.

The soul egg could be inside a number of other objects, much like a Russian *matrioska* doll: open the first and you find another, and so forth. Frazer mentions several of these tales. Koschey the Deathless, an alarming magician in Russian lore, is one of the best known.[1] Iceland has the *fjor* egg, or life egg of the ogres, and an old Norse tale, 'The Giant Who had no Heart in His Body', describes a giant who will never die because his heart is hidden inside an egg; when the hero crushes it, the giant dies.[2] Since these events are exactly paralleled in a Celtic tale from the island of Islay,[3] it would be tempting to posit a common Norse source, and to say that the theme was carried with Viking influence from Scandinavia to the Hebrides and Russia. Perhaps in a limited sense, this could be true. The same motif appears in Ireland, Lapland[4] and Brittany, but also in Italy, Bohemia and elsewhere, and Frazer gives a version from the Kabyle.[5] There are besides a number in the Cape Verde Islands off Portuguese Guinea: 'The Three Brothers-in-Law: His Life in an Egg',[6] 'The Two Friends: His Life in an Egg',[7] 'The Division: His Life in an Egg',[8] and 'The Magic Sword'.[9]

In the first of these a devil keeps his life inside an egg. It is broken against his forehead and he dies – a common theme. In a variant of the Koschey tale, which is reminiscent of the same, a magician is killed when the life egg is smashed against his forehead. The significance of this gesture probably stems from the fact that the head, with the eyes as its windows, was often believed to be the soul-seat within the body.

'The Division' tells how the heroine's wicked father keeps his soul inside an egg. He dies when it is crushed by her lover and the young couple are free to marry. 'The Magic Sword' describes how a key required by the hero is concealed inside an egg, and 'The Two Friends' relates the villain's life to a light inside an egg. 'Light of my life' is a popular expression, and Othello exclaims,

[1] Frazer, xi.108ff.   [2] *Ibid.*, 119–20.
[3] *Ibid.*, 126–7.   [4] *Dictionary of Folklore*, i.341.
[5] Frazer, xi.139.
[6] Parsons, Elsie Clews, *Folklore from the Cape Verde Islands*, Cambridge, Mass., 1923, i.208.   [7] *Ibid.*, 211ff.
[8] *Ibid.*, 220–3.   [9] *Ibid.*, 355.

Colour Plate VII Middle Eastern eggs. Those hanging are
Armenian, made at Kutahya in Asia Minor. Eggs showing this angel
design were made from the early eighteenth century. The engraved
ostrich egg made into a rose-water sprinkler dates from about 1900,
and the large egg, lower left, from approximately the same period.
The design shows Central Asian influence, and includes a circular
panel of Arabic script at each end.

Colour Plate VIII Toys and special eggs.

Top shelf: Japanese lacquer egg, based on a *Kogo* (incense box), but possibly made for the European market. The eggs surmounted by wooden birds are from Lithuania. The design on the green egg shows birds' feet, and on the red egg (but invisible in the picture) is a cross. The eggs are wooden.

Middle shelf: German (Erzgebirge) Easter toy, showing a decorated egg beneath a fir-tree; the egg, which is wooden, is surmounted by a bird, and is hatching an Easter rabbit at each end. The style of carving is traditional. The six shell eggs, given the appearance of jugs by the addition of cardboard trimmings, are Polish. The designs on these are paper-cuts, a traditional craft in Poland.

Bottom shelf: Traditional Bavarian Easter Lamb made of iced cake (see the Easter Lamb as an egg-motif, colour plate X). The egg-shaped wooden *Matrioska*, which is hollow and opens, is from Russia. The leather-decorated ostrich egg, provided with a loop for hanging up, was made in Timbuktu. Two female figurines in the foreground are Moravian, and carry baskets of coloured eggs; one is receiving an Easter whipping from a young boy. All three are made of maize leaves, a typical local handicraft.

'Put out the light, and then put out the light',[1] snuffing the lamp and preparing to murder his wife. In this it is used as an image of the life essence and other legends refer to it. The Saxons of Transylvania tell of a witch whose life is a flame inside an egg within a duck.[2] A German egg talisman contained a pixie's flame of life,[3] and the hair which another German elf bewitched and enclosed inside an egg may also refer to this idea.[4]

In Hungarian legend the devil's egg determines the life of its owner. Inside a ruined castle in a secret cupboard sits a black hen with an egg inside her. This contains the life of the devil. If it is smashed, he dies and a flash of fire shoots through the air, falling to earth as a black stone – presumably a meteor.[5] A black hen's egg also houses the soul of the *pchuvuschi*, earth fairies who are ancestors of the Transylvanian gipsies. If the hen is killed and the egg thrown into a running stream, they will all die.[6]

'Danilo the Unfortunate', a Russian folk-tale, uses the gold egg as a mystic image of the soul. The hero is given three eggs by his bride, the Snow Maiden – two of silver and one of gold. The two silver eggs are an Easter offering for his Prince and Princess, but the gold he must guard carefully. For his life is measured by it, and if he gives it up he is doomed to die.[7]

The function of the soul egg is sometimes more subtle. If maltreated in any way, it can be the cause of considerable pain. Among the Hausa of west Africa a lonely wife can summon her husband by leaving an egg all night on the roof. His heart will be affected, and he will have to return.[8] A Pomeranian method of punishing a thief is to wrap an egg in green silk and bury it in hot ash in the culprit's name. The result is to cause him so much torment that he will return the stolen goods.[9] Jamaicans punish an egg-thief by throwing an egg into the sea: then his stomach will heave like the waves.[10]

[1] *Othello*, v.ii.7. [2] Frazer, xi.116.
[3] Bächtold-Stäubli, ii.597. [4] *Ibid.*, 628.
[5] Wlislocki, Heinrich von, *Volksglaube und religiöser Brauch der Magyaren*, Münster, 1893, 161.
[6] Leland, C. G., *Gypsy Sorcery and Fortune Telling*, London, 1891, 70.
[7] Magnus, Leonard A., *Russian Folk Tales*, London, 1916, 22.
[8] Tremearne, A. J. N., 'Bori Beliefs and Ceremonies', *Journal of the Royal Anthropological Institute*, xlv (London, 1915), 102.
[9] Kittredge, G. L., *Witchcraft in Old and New England*, Cambridge, Mass., 1928, 102.
[10] Williams, Joseph, *Voodoos and Obeahs*, New York, 1932, 205.

Sometimes the separated soul is broken up into sections. 'Juggin Straw Blue', also from Jamaica, is about an old witch-man who steals away a young girl. Fortunately, however, her sweetheart's mother is a witch and she gives her son a powerful charm to help him in the rescue – eight eggs, this because the witch-man has seven heads and seven corresponding eggs. The young man goes in pursuit, mashes an egg, and cuts off one of the heads at the same time. Each time he does this, it becomes light. Then the old witch-man mashes one of his seven eggs and it grows dark again. Finally, because he has an extra egg, the young man wins and the girl is saved.[1]

In Western belief it is not usual for a man to possess more than one soul. But in the summer of 1965 an American working in northern Thailand saw a member of the Karen tribe cured of a fever when one of his thirty-two souls – which had escaped and so caused the illness – was recaptured inside a hard-boiled egg. Friends called to the soul repeatedly and, when they were able to balance the egg on a small stick stuck in the ground, they knew it had heard and gone inside. The sick man was then given this to eat and made a good recovery.[2]

A final echo of the soul egg comes into the tales of talking eggs. '*Dézef Ki Parlé*', as it becomes in Creole, is a story common to the Negroes of both Jamaica and Louisiana, and tells how two girls, one good and one bad, meet an amiable witch. The first is rewarded for doing as she is told, the second punished for disobedience.[3] In a version from Dominica – a Catholic country – the old lady is the Blessed Virgin in disguise.[4] The theme is of virtue rewarded and the eggs act as her magic agents, providing treasure and clothes for the good girl, snakes and toads for the bad. Her supernatural powers inside the eggs are only made known to the girls when their different characters emerge. Here the soul has dwindled into a helper, part of the witch's stock-in-trade.

[1] Beckwith, Martha, *Jamaica Anansi Stories*, New York, 1924, 92–3.

[2] Kunstader, Peter, 'Living with Thailand's Gentle Lua', *National Geographic* (Washington, July 1966), 151–2.

[3] Fortier, Alcée, *Louisianian Nursery Tales, Journal of American Folklore* (Boston, 1888), i.142–5. Beckwith, *Anansi Stories*, 94–6.

[4] Hansen, T. L., *The Types of the Folk Tale in Cuba, Puerto Rico, the Dominican Republic and Spanish South America*, Berkeley, 1957, 95.

THE BIRD OF THE SPIRIT

The close metaphysical link between bird and egg is underlined by an extraordinary cult practised within the memory of Easter Islanders living in the 1920s, when it was recorded. The greatest event each year was the arrival of *manu tara*, a migratory tern which came in September – spring in the Southern Hemisphere. It nested at the top of a steep cliff on which there were figures of a man carved with the head of a bird and the remains of a village composed of stone huts. Every year a group of men gathered there to take part in a competition, each specially selected by someone with supernatural gifts who declared that his protégé had found favour with the gods. Curiously, it was not the competitors themselves, but their servants who took part in the contest on their behalf. At the appointed time these servants ran to get the first egg of the season. While the others slashed themselves with knives as a mark of sorrow, the master of the winner shaved his head and was called 'bird man'. He enjoyed great prestige for the rest of the year, changing his name and living apart in strict taboo. Food which had been prepared separately was brought to him by the servant, who was himself prohibited from eating with his right hand because it had held the sacred egg.[1] The carvings on the mountain perhaps represent successful competitors – like the example in the British Museum, which shows a bird-headed man clutching an egg.[2]

Folk-tales usually locate the soul egg inside a bird, and in myth this is often the form assumed by the creator god: Thoth the ibis, the Egyptian goose which is mate of Seb, the Finnish duck that lays its eggs on the knee of the Daughter of Nature, and the Spirit of God in the form of a dove – there are many. The Mbaya in the Gran Chaco, South America, have the following tale: long ago there were no Mbaya, but one day a great bird nested in a cave and laid two eggs. These hatched and out came the Mbaya, who populated the earth.[3] This type of myth, common among primitive peoples, which represents man's birth or that of his environment from an egg, must invariably pose the old question:

[1] Routledge, Mrs Scoresby, 'The Mysterious Images of Easter Island', *Wonders of the Past*, ed. J. A. Hammerton, London, 1922, iii.922.

[2] See plate I.

[3] Hellbom, Anna-Britta, 'The Creation Egg', *Ethnos*, i (Stockholm, 1963), 78.

Bird and Egg

Which came first, the egg or its creator? A magical procreative cycle is implied and the future, like the past, stretches into eternity:

> Men's curiosity searches past and future
> And clings to that dimension. But to apprehend
> The point of intersection of the timeless
> With time, is an occupation for the saint.[1]

According to the Giliaks, a primitive race on the Sea of Okhotsk, each person possesses two souls: one big and one little. The big soul contains the little one, which is in the form of an egg. At death the big soul dies and the little one takes its place.[2] This suggests an unending process: a combination of the separable soul, whose existence is bound up with the body, and which perishes with it, and the more nebulous immortal soul, which survives after the death of the flesh.

Why should immortality be represented by an egg? Perhaps because it hatches a bird. For it was a commonplace idea that the soul resembled a bird.[3] At death it left the body, and flew up to the heavens. To earth-bound man a winged creature, like an angel, hovered above – an emblem of the indescribable divine. In Hindu tradition birds represent the higher states of being, and some of the earliest examples known to man are the Egyptian hieroglyphs, where the *ka* is represented as a bird with a human head. A butterfly over a corpse also signified to the Egyptians that the soul was leaving the body; later the Scots and Irish thought the same. Birds were often taken for shades of the dead. In Ireland black or grey fly-by-nights are souls doing penance for their sins. The spirits of dead sailors change to stormy petrels, and in Yorkshire nightjars are babies who died before their baptism. The Cornish say that the spirit of King Arthur inhabits a chough and in Islam the souls of the faithful are snow-white birds, seated beneath the throne of Allah, awaiting the Resurrection.[4] In the *Mirach* Mahommed goes to heaven and finds the Tree of Life surrounded by shady groves in which beautiful birds are

[1] Eliot, T. S., *Four Quartets*, London, 1944, 32.

[2] Wildhaber, Robert, 'Zum Symbolgehalt und zur Ikonographie des Eies', *Deutsches Jahrbuch für Volkskunde* (Berlin, 1960), vi.81. Bächtold-Stäubli, ii.597.

[3] Kelly, Walter, *Curiosities of Indo-European Tradition and Folklore*, London, 1863, 103–5.

[4] Brewer, 137, 1,295. Hole, *Encyclopaedia*, 50–1.

singing. These are the faithful, but those who sinned during their lives on earth are transformed into birds of prey.[1]

The soul returning to its source is embodied in the flight of a bird. But the soul before death is stored up in an egg, before the bird has flown. Hence the two souls of the Giliaks symbolize a continuous process: the cycle of bird and egg, which is unending. Christian Slavs believe that at death the soul changed to a dove,[2] perhaps because the Holy Ghost assumed this form. Picasso's dove is a creature of the materialist imagination, and modern Soviet lore stresses the importance of a dove as the 'bird of peace'. But the severe penalties imposed in Russia for killing one, even by accident, are a direct relic from the old days.

[1] Cirlot, J. E., *A Dictionary of Symbols*, London, 1962, 27.
[2] *Ibid.*, 81.

Chapter 5
Fertility

The egg, the egg is round,
And the belly is round;
Come child in good health!
God, God, calls thee!
Song of the south Hungarian gipsies

THE SOURCE OF LIFE

The enchanter's soul egg, which ended his life when it was broken, is a curious theme; but the practice of the Karens in Thailand, also described earlier, of capturing a wandering soul inside an egg, helps to show how such an idea might have gradually evolved. The Karens are a Tibeto-Burman people, and a not dissimilar method for ascertaining whether the soul has left a corpse is found among their neighbours.

The Burmese believe that if his *ka-lá*, or spirit, has been destroyed, there will be no happiness in store for a dead man. So to find out if it still exists, a rod, touching the corpse, is pushed through a hole in the coffin. A thread dangles from the upper end, which is fastened to a ring, and beneath the spot where this hangs down is a cup containing a hard-boiled egg. If the *ka-lá* is present, the ring will sway on the end of its thread and droop down towards the cup. This implies that the soul leaves the body by travelling up the rod and down the thread and ring into the egg.[1]

These examples – and it is unimportant here whether the spirit lives on or dies with its owner – illustrate in simple terms the universal significance of an egg as an image of the life force. This is why, in certain cultures, people avoided destroying one if they possibly could. The Romans said, *'Ovum ruptum est'* – 'The egg is smashed' – to describe a catastrophe,[2] and in Germany, even in modern times, if an egg broke accidentally it meant good fortune vanished; to trample on one meant trampling on your luck.[3] The

---

[1] Jones, William, *Credulities Past and Present*, London, 1880, 471–2.
[2] Leland, C. G., *Gypsy Sorcery and Fortune Telling*, London, 1891, 77.
[3] Bächtold-Stäubli, Hanns, ed., *Handwörterbuch des deutschen Aberglaubens*,

time of year could also be significant. Since New Year's Eve was popular for predicting the future, anybody who smashed one then would probably die in the course of the year.[1] The same omen also meant doom for an animal. Estonian farmers used to put an egg in front of the byre door and the cow which stepped on it was led away for slaughter.[2]

Naturally, though, the shell must be broken before you can eat the contents. Moroccans resolved this problem by saying first, '*Bismillah*' – 'In the name of God' – to ward off potential evil.[3] But some racial groups eschewed eggs altogether. Stefánsson, investigating Eskimos in the Mackenzie Delta, found that most people, regardless of age or sex, preferred not to eat them, the overt reason being that they were known to cause disease.[4] Certain religions – the Orphic and Pythagorean, for instance – excluded them from their list of permitted foods, and aborigines of central Australia avoid eggs laid by their tribal totem. The People of the Emu observe this even when very short of food; *in extremis* they compromise, distributing a nest among the tribe so that each family can have one to cook, and that serves as their ration.[5] The eggs appear to be more taboo than the flesh of the bird itself, implying that they suppose the life of the totem to reside in them, rather than in the creature. Another primitive people, the Herero of South West Africa, have a clan of the Ostrich Egg Girdle, who regard it as an honour to wear a belt of these huge shells: here the eggs have clearly become the tribal totem.[6]

Prohibitions on eggs as food extend to many parts of Africa – central, south and west. In northern Nigeria, for example, the Keffi Yegomawa forbid young women to eat eggs, because this would render them barren[7] – a belief which they share with the

Berlin, 1929–30, ii.643. Kemp, P., *Healing Ritual: Studies in the Technique and Tradition of the Southern Slavs*, London, 1935, 45.

[1] Bächtold-Stäubli, ii.619.   [2] *Ibid.*, 611–12.
[3] Westermarck, Edward, *Ritual and Belief in Morocco*, London, 1926, i.206.
[4] Stefánsson, Vilhjálmur, 'The Stefánsson–Anderson Arctic Expedition', *Anthropological Papers of the American Museum of Natural History*, New York, 1919, xiv.136.
[5] Frazer, Sir James G., *Totemism and Exogamy*, London, 1910, i.102.
[6] *Ibid.*, ii.362.
[7] Wilson-Haffenden, J. R., 'Ethnological Notes on the Shuwalbe Group of the Borroro Fulani in the Kurafi District of Keffi Emirate of Northern Nigeria', *Journal of the Royal Anthropological Institute*, lvii (London, 1927), 279.

Konde of Tanganyika, who say that hard-boiled they form a snake in the stomach, causing infertility.[1] In this case a common phallic symbol seems to have instead a neutralizing effect, rather in the manner of a male hormone. But, either way, sterility appears to be the penalty for destroying a symbol of life.

INCREASING THE CROPS

One important function of the egg in folk-belief is bringing life to the fields and assisting crops to grow. In many countries peasants carry it out into the meadows and byres as a magic charm for increasing stock and doubling the yield of grain. A farmer's work is governed by the rhythm of the seasons, the 'turning year', and agricultural rituals reflect this sense of pattern.

There are ceremonies for opening and closing the season of growth. Scots laid a nail and an egg in the bottom of the *sgeap a' chuire* (sowing basket), with the seed-corn resting on top. This egg symbolized corn 'as full of substance as an egg is full of meat'.[2] Eliade notes that Finnish peasants kept one in their pockets during sowing, or placed it in the ploughed ground.[3] Estonians ate an egg while ploughing and the Swedes threw them over the fields.[4] The Cheremiss and Votyaks buried them in the furrows, or hurled them in the air before sowing began,[5] and Germans did this to ensure that the grain would grow as high.[6] They also buried shells in the fields before seedtime, or mixed chopped eggs in with the wheat itself. Sometimes, at first ploughing, an egg on a dish with meal and bread was placed between the team and ploughshare. The animals were then driven forward, and if the tokens remained untouched it was a good omen: the food was afterwards given away to the poor. Bavarians buried an egg beneath the farmyard gate before performing the same ritual;[7] and Slavs and Germans share a common custom of smearing the plough with bread, flour and eggs.[8]

The ceremonies of harvest are not dissimilar. Certain peoples

---

[1] Mackenzie, D. R., *The Spirit-Ridden Konde*, London, 1925, 127.

[2] Banks, M. Macleod, *British Calendar Customs: Scotland*, London, 1939, ii.12–13.

[3] Eliade, Mircea, *Patterns in Comparative Religion*, London, 1958, 415.

[4] *Ibid.*   [5] *Ibid.*

[6] Bächtold-Stäubli, ii.611.   [7] *Ibid.*, 613, notes 167, 168.

[8] *Dictionary of Folklore, Mythology and Legend*, New York, 1949, i.341.

of India, the Marāthā, Bhils and Konkanis, place an egg in the pit of the threshing-floor to increase the gathered grain.[1] But in Germany, if it had been bewitched, the yield became unfruitful.[2] Another German custom was the placing of an egg together with a loaf, inside the first sheaf gathered.[3] The importance of this ritual derives from the idea that the strength of the crop lay in the first or last sheaf, and it was vital that this should not be exhausted.

The magical first or last sheaf was often credited with wonderful powers: the gift of prophecy, rendering barren women fruitful, and ensuring an abundant harvest. Sometimes the power of the grain, which it contained, was personified as an animal or a human being. In Westphalia they nail egg-shells to the Harvest Cock, a piece of wood shaped like a cockerel[4] and Malayan farmers engage a magician to secure 'the souls of the rice' before harvesting by cutting seven swaths of grain and fashioning a kind of rice baby from them. This is laid in a basket along with seven more swaths, a banana, and an egg to feed 'the baby rice soul'. When the ceremonies are over, the magician takes the egg and breaks it open. An empty space at the top of the shell is a bad sign, but a space at the side is good, and a full egg better still. Then the farmer and his family eat both the egg and the banana.[5]

Such rituals mark the opening and close of the agricultural cycle, but in parts of Germany local people favour a charm which covers a longer period. Some villages hang a great cascade of eggs up in the street at midsummer, where it remains until the crop is in. A huge egg bell was used at a recent church dedication in Bendorf. But the Christian association is misleading, and it is worth comparing the ceremony with a similar secular affair in a village near Bonn.[6] On both occasions the eggs were collected by bachelors, and the dedication was performed at midsummer, too.

These festivals, common throughout the Rhineland, are called *Kirmis* in the north, deriving from *Kirchen-Messe*; and *Kerwe* fur-

---

[1] Abbott, J., *The Keys of Power: a Study of Indian Ritual and Belief*, London, 1932, 371.

[2] Bächtold-Stäubli, ii.613, note 165.

[3] *Ibid.*, 611.

[4] Bächtold-Stäubli, ii.611.

[5] Winstedt, Richard O., *Shaman, Saiva and Sufi*, London, 1925, 83–7.

[6] *The Times*, 22 June 1962, photograph. See plate 17.

ther south, from *Kirchweih*.[1] As these names imply, the origin is supposed to be the annual commemoration of the dedication of the local church or chapel, beginning on the Sunday nearest the patron saint's day – if it is a suitable summer saint, and they make sure that it is. The cascade of eggs takes different forms, but generally it is shaped as a crown. The hoisting of this *Eierkrone* by two *Kirmis* youths dressed in white is quite an occasion, and the village band meantime plays some suitable music, such as '*Es liegt eine Krone*'. Today there are *Kirmis* societies which vie to see who can produce the finest egg crown. Bendorf men hold the record for the largest in central Rhineland. In 1955, the twenty-fifth anniversary of the local *Kirmis* society, their bell was made up of 25,000 eggs.[2]

Shapes like this developed from the earlier egg crown, also associated with Whitsun and St John's Day. Specially beautiful ones are used in Flanders. They hang over the street, elaborately decorated, and young people perform dances beneath them; in the Netherlands one called '*onder der kronen*' is known to have existed in 1453. These festivals are rather earlier in the year. Mössinger, who believes they descend from the crown of the May, considers that they were connected with spring fertility originally and then shifted to other times of year.[3]

In Poland it was customary to crown the harvest, though not with eggs. This idea of conferring a royal status on the occasion finds an echo in the ancient Jewish tradition of crowning the Torah – the scrolls of the law – with beautiful silver regalia, to stress the importance of God's teaching. Farmers crowned the corn as a king because it provides the main source of food. God's word brings life to the spirit, the corn life to the flesh.

In Germany, when *Kirmis* ended, participants, accompanied by funeral music and lamentations, performed a symbolic burial of the festival, and the following year whatever was buried is disinterred. If it had been a bottle of wine, all drink to the health of the new *Kirmis*.[4] And so the cycle continues from year to year. The *Kirmis* died, and to early man it seemed that the crops died

---

[1] Scheidt-Lämke, Dora, 'Kirmesbräuche im Regierungsbezirk Montabaur', *Rhein-Lahn-Freund* (Niederlahnstein, 1956), 112.

[2] *Ibid.*, 50–1.

[3] Mössinger, Friedrich, 'Eierkronen und Eierketten', *Volk und Scholle*, xvi (Darmstadt, 1938), 147.   [4] Scheidt-Lämke, 117.

too. The Romans expressed this poetically in the myth of Proserpina, daughter of Ceres, goddess of agriculture, who was abducted by Pluto and forced to dwell underground for six months of the year. This linking of the goddess of agriculture with the god of death is not accidental. One finds it in other cultures: the Norse god Odin and Toci of the Aztecs fulfil the same dual function.[1]

The cult of the dead was closely linked with agriculture. They lie in the earth guarding the seeds, enabling them to germinate and helping the crops to grow. This is so even when the dead are believed to inhabit another region. The Bantu of north Kavirondo, for example, use an egg in much the same way as the tribes of Thailand and Burma described earlier. The evening before planting begins, a seed-basket is put into the middle of the hut, below the central post, which is where their ancestral spirits live. The basket is filled with seeds, and a raw egg, together with other items, is placed on top. During the night the spirits enter the egg, and it is left in the basket throughout the next day's planting. When evening comes, it is thrown away, for it has served its purpose in temporarily housing the spirits. Now they are all in the newly planted field.[2]

It is only with the help of the *sairem*, soul of the dead man, that our crops thrive; without his blessing the young blades would wither, say the Bondos of India.[3] Eliade provides some interesting material on this theme. The soil is a sphere under the jurisdiction of the dead: black is the colour of mourning and of the earth in which they are interred. When the Bambaras bury a corpse they pray for good winds, rain, and an abundant harvest. Conversely, some people, like the Finns, carry bones or soil from the cemetery and bury them at the time of sowing; Germans scattered earth from a fresh grave among the seeds.[4]

At harvest, Arabs ceremonially inter the last sheaf in a tomb, praying that the wheat may be reborn from death to life, and a burial stele in the British Museum shows a dead man praying to Râ that his body 'may grow as a seed'.[5] The idea behind this is most beautifully expressed in one of the parables of Our Lord,

[1] Eliade, 344.
[2] Wagner, Günter, *The Bantu of North Kavirondo*, Oxford, 1949, i.98.
[3] Quaritch Wales, H. G., *The Mountain of God*, London, 1953, 82.
[4] Eliade, 351.   [5] *Ibid.*, 199, 351.

when He compared a spiritual concept to the budding grain: 'Verily, verily, I say unto you, Except a corn of wheat fall into the ground and die, it abideth alone: but if it die, it bringeth forth much fruit. He that loveth his life shall lose it; and he that hateth his life in this world shall keep it unto life eternal.'[1]

Milton, brooding over the irreparable tragedy of his blindness, expressed a sense of loss of the pattern of existence:

> *Thus with the year*
> *Seasons return, but not to me returns*
> *Day, or the sweet approach of Ev'n or Morn.*[2]

Not so primitive man, to whom the revolving year was inextricably bound up with the cycle of human life. Instead of rigid divisions, all was envisaged as part of a continuous chain of existence, and life and death were only different aspects of the same phenomenon. Even on the most physical level it is undoubtedly true that death and new growth are closely linked. We know that crops grow well on a battlefield, and the lament for Ophelia in *Hamlet* is not idle fancy, but a poetic statement of fact:

> *Lay her i' the earth;*
> *And from her fair and unpolluted flesh*
> *May violets spring!*[3]

The nitrogen cycle, part of any school's scientific syllabus, explains in prosaic terms that we return to the earth what we took out of it.

The Vietnamese put ancestor shrines in their gardens and fields, out among the growing things,[4] and in other countries rituals for the dead and for agriculture are associated. Indian commemoration of the departed forms the main festival of harvest, like our own All Souls' Day. In early Greece both the dead and the grain were put into pots,[5] and the connection is even more apparent in Russian lore, where spirits of the dead inhabited the trees; spring festivals, at which young girls offered eggs to the birches, were closely related to the cult of ancestor-worship.[6]

---

[1] John, xii.24–5.
[2] Beeching, H. C., ed., 'Paradise Lost', *The Poetical Works of John Milton*, Oxford, 1922, III.228.xl–xlii.   [3] *Hamlet*, v.i.
[4] Personal observation near Hué, South Vietnam, winter 1963.
[5] Eliade, 352.
[6] See the section dealing with 'Tree Spirits', ch. 2.

Grains cast over the left shoulder are an offering to the dead, and Russians threw fried eggs backwards for the same purpose. According to Eliade, animal forms, such as the cock, used to represent spirits of vegetation, are associated with the souls of the dead.[1] Shelley fuses these two conceptions in his great elegiac poem, *Adonais*. Lamenting the death of Keats, he writes:

> *He is made one with Nature: there is heard*
> *His voice in all her music.*[2]

Delatte in his *Herbarius* notes that, when they pick a herb, some people lay an egg on the spot to ensure that another will grow in its place.[3] The plant, the crop, will return again. Japanese express this idea of constant renewal in the form of the *toyo-oka-daruma*, the egg-shaped figure, intended in this case to ensure successful silk-culture and an abundant harvest of the five cereals. Its eye-balls are white and without pupils. If the spring silk-raising has been without mishap a pupil is painted on the right eye, and if the autumn crop is also successful the left one is drawn in as a celebration of the good fortune. This toy is also called *huto*, literally 'the non-falling Old Man', and *okiagara kobosi*, 'the little priest who rises up'. Weighted heavily at the bottom, it rights itself immediately if knocked down. While the smaller examples serve as children's playthings, bigger ones over 1 foot in height have their place on the shelf for the family gods.[4]

RAIN-MAKING

The cycle of plant life mirrors the cycle of human reproduction and Eliade notes how closely ancestors, death and sexual life are linked with the harvest. In China the marriage-bed used to be placed in the darkest corner of the room, where the seeds were kept and the dead were buried.[5] The seeds of plants and those of man are sometimes indistinguishable: in India grains of rice represent the spermatozoa of the male. Various myths identify rain with semen. The Pima Indians of New Mexico have a legend about a beautiful woman (the earth) who became pregnant after

---

[1] Eliade, 353.
[2] Glover, A. S. B., ed., 'Adonais', *Shelley*, London, 1951, 559. xlii.1-2.
[3] Delatte, *Herbarius*, Paris, 1938, 120. Referred to by Eliade, 416.
[4] Nisizawa, Tekiho, *Japanese Folk Toys*, Tokyo, 1939, 33.
[5] Cirlot, J. E., *A Dictionary of Symbols*, London, 1962, 98.

a drop of water fell from a cloud.[1] In the stories of some people far from the sea the fertility of water, that elemental creative force, becomes centred in the clouds; the Chinese dragon, a water emblem, possesses more sky powers than in the myths of other nations.[2]

Rain fertilizes the soil, like semen in animal reproduction. If crops are to prosper, they must be kept moist, so rain charms are a popular part of agricultural ceremonies. In Rumania the *scaloian,* a kind of doll, is placed in the water on St George's Day, enclosed in a small wooden box. This figure, sometimes referred to as 'Mother of Rain', is surrounded with flowers, shells, candles and red eggs. Rain is supposed to fall after the ritual, just as it fell 'after the burial of Jesus'.[3]

In another part of the Balkans, Albania, the *dordolec,* or rain-maker, was a young person of either sex, who went around the village in times of drought singing:

> Dordolec, dordolec, *bring the rain*
> *For our corn up on the plain.*
> *Three ears on every stalk!*
>
> > *Rain in May*
> > *A golden tray.*
> >
> > *Rain in June*
> > *A pretty tune.*
> >
> > *July rain*
> > *A brimful wain.*
> >
> > *August rain*
> > *Bushels of grain.*

Housewives offered a gift of money or eggs and threw water over the *dordolec,* who is also found in Yugoslavia.[4] Rather similarly, at Navpaktos, Greece, the May Boy dances in the midst of the old men and is offered gifts which imply increase: cotton, wheat, money and eggs.[5]

[1] Eliade, 190.
[2] *Ibid.,* 208.
[3] Liungman, Waldemar, 'Das Mardukneujahrsfest', *F. F. Communications,* xlviii–xlix (Helsinki, 1937–8), 308.
[4] *Albanian Notes,* Ilford, November 1965, iii.22.
[5] Megas, George A., *Greek Calendar Customs,* Athens, 1958, 118.

Too much rain, on the other hand, can destroy a crop. In Morocco a counter rain-charm consists in placing a carefully drained egg-shell under a leak in the roof. After it has filled with rain-water, it is sealed and interred in the threshing floor, where it remains until more rain is needed.[1] If, in spite of everything, the crop is bad, one can always transfer the ill luck to someone else by burying an egg in his fields – this in Ireland.[2]

THE CATTLE

Cattle are as important to the livelihood in a simple economy as the crops, and farmers as anxiously guard the well-being of their livestock as they do the other features of their rural existence. Since evil powers are supposed to be stronger in the spring at the waxing sun, the Bulgarians hide an egg in a hole on *Tschiporofszki*, St George's Day, which marks the official opening of the season, to protect the sheep from witches.[3] Again, in early spring East Prussians draw a circle round their herds with the contents of an egg. Another custom was to visit the crossroads at dawn before the cattle were brought out, and cast three eggs across them.[4]

Hungarians express a wish that their beasts will grow fat and round, like an egg. Sometimes they are driven along a board across a ditch on which an egg has been placed; sometimes one is put out for every head of cattle. In Baranya-Ozd district the shepherds used to hold the egg in their hands when the animals were driven out, saying: 'God save the master and his cattle, and may they come home as round as this egg.'[5]

Around Vép in the west they hang a chain of eggs in front of the stalls, so that the feet of the animals will be strong like the chain and the poor, who are given the eggs, shall pray for them.[6] Germans share many of these customs. In Minden eggs are sometimes used to clean the mouths of new-born calves, and at

[1] Westermarck, *Ritual and Belief*, ii.278.
[2] Evans, E. Estyn, *Irish Folk Ways*, London, 1957, 150.
[3] Roheim, G., 'Hungarian Pageant: Hungarian Calendar Customs', *Journal of the Royal Anthropological Institute*, lvi (London, 1926), 370–1.
[4] Bächtold-Stäubli, ii.612.
[5] Roheim, 366. Károlyi, Alexander, *Hungarian Pageant*, Budapest, 1939, 78. See Somsich, S., 'Baranyai Népszokások', *Ethnographia*, ix.378.
[6] Roheim, 366. See Varga, J., 'Vépi Népszokások, Babonâk', *Ethnographia*, xxxi.100.

Landshut shells are hung up in the stables as a charm. In both Altmark and Westphalia eggs are thrown beneath the animals' feet when they first go out to pasture.[1]

A ritual observed in Bengal during the *Sohrae* festival of the Santals bears some resemblance to these European customs. A circle of rice is spread over the village street. An egg is laid in the centre of this and the village cattle are then driven down it. Most of the animals try to avoid the rice, but eventually one of them accidentally crushes the egg. Her owner will have good luck for the remainder of the year. The smashing of an egg does not normally bring good luck, and this custom presents an interesting contrast to that which we noted among Estonian farmers, where the cow which succeeds in doing this is marked for slaughter.[2]

LOVE

As with agriculture, so with human life. If mankind is to continue, the reproductive cycle must be acted out. The fulfilment of marriage begins with love, and eggs figure in many aphrodisiac recipes. The Moslems and ancient Romans used them for this purpose. Hungarians take the first laid by a black hen at the new moon and blow the contents. The shell is then dried on the hearth and filled with hair, blood and nail-parings from the person whose love is desired. The charm is completed by placing it on the grave of an unbaptized child[3] – presumably a demand for a profane form of love, fitting the general character of the ritual. In Swabia the girl writes 'Esa + His + Masmo + Caldi + Male + On + He' on an egg-shell before putting it into the fireplace. Her young man will have no peace from then on until he has submitted to her. He will burn, like the egg on the fire. On the other hand if a cow has spurned the bull the farmer will feed her with crushed shells taken from eggs which have hatched out chickens.[4]

Perhaps the use of an egg here involved a subconscious desire to link an extra life force to one's own. An English shepherd would give his sweetheart the luckiest gift he could find – the first

[1] Bächtold-Stäubli, ii.611, 635, 687.
[2] Hutchinson, Walter, ed., *Customs of the World*, London, n.d., i.544.
[3] Wlislocki, Heinrich von, *Volksglaube und religiöser Brauch der Magyaren*, Münster, 1893, 50.
[4] Bächtold-Stäubli, ii.629, 634.

egg laid by a young hen. In Hungary, on the Monday following Easter, an interesting love ritual used to be acted out. Called *Husvét Hetföje* or *Vizbeveto*, it translates into English as 'Water Plunge Monday'. That was the day when young men went and splashed all the unmarried girls with water in nearby fountains and streams. In return, as a ransom, the girls gave them coloured Easter eggs.[1] Sometimes things were more decorous. A tale from the Great Hungarian Plain describes how all the special Easter foods – breads, cakes and baskets of coloured eggs – were laid out on the family table. At some stage during the day a wagon called, bringing men from the village. Holding small flasks of water, they stood and chanted:

> *Glory be to the Holy Father*
> *Who gave us food and pure water.*
> *As we water the rose to make it bloom*
> *We sprinkle the rosebud in this room.*
> *May you live long,*
> *Old and young.*
> *Peace be with you on this holy day of Easter.*

When this was over, the boys threw water over the girls, saying: 'We want eggs! Give us some eggs. We'll stop sprinkling if you do.'[2] The day following it was the turn of the men to be drenched. The symbolism of wetting the girls, so that 'Like the flowers, they may not wither away',[3] is, on this level, easy to understand, though a complex symbolism underlies it. Now the custom is dying out, but a Hungarian friend from a well-to-do urban environment recollects observing it as late as 1945. It was, he says, usual to sprinkle a special girl-friend with a few drops of cologne and she gave a small gift in return.[4] Quite often this consisted of decorated eggs. The Banat is another area where the custom was known.[5]

In Poland during *Zapusty*, the last days before Lent, girl-auctioning was popular. A young man bargained for his sweet-

---

[1] Viski, Károly, *Volksbrauch der Ungarn*, Budapest, 1932, 46. Károlyi, 79–80.

[2] Hazeltine, Alice, and Smith, Elva, ed., *The Easter Book of Legends and Stories*, New York, 1947, 241–2.

[3] Spicer, Dorothy, *The Book of Festivals*, New York, 1937, 168.

[4] Information kindly supplied by Edmund de Unger, formerly of Budapest.

[5] Bächtold-Stäubli, ii.625.

heart much as one might purchase a cow or horse. She was taken to the byre, set in a manger full of hay, and all her points, including teeth, were carefully examined. The successful bidder was rewarded at Easter with a gift of coloured eggs.[1] Indeed, until the Second World War a Polish girl presented her lover with numbers of exquisite decorated eggs, sometimes as many as 100, wrapped in a fine linen handkerchief, hand-embroidered with his initials.[2]

In Germany, too, a young girl would give her sweetheart a gift of eggs when Easter approached. Around Baden, if she gave him an egg cake, it usually meant he had been accepted; but Württemburg girls hung egg-shell strands around the window of a faithless lover – tokens of broken trust. At Innviertel an engagement was usually clinched at the Egg Fair and, if there had been a marriage broker, Austrians gave him an egg to show that the bargain was sealed.[3] In Macedonia, too, the betrothal was finalized with eggs. Among the Orthodox, especially at Easter, the man presented gifts to his fiancée. On the day preceding, he sent her red eggs, and she was expected to reciprocate.[4] If a girl is engaged in nearby Albania, and Easter falls reasonably near to the wedding, when she goes to the Easter service her future mother-in-law presents her with an egg and a candle.[5] This custom comes from Elbasan, where it is practised by the Orthodox, and was no doubt intended to promote fecundity.

REPRODUCTION

Eggs being such powerful fertility charms, the Byzantine Bogomils were forbidden to eat them. They abhorred anything connected with the reproductive cycle, and since the material world and flesh are both of the devil, they shunned marriage and the sexual act, even spitting contemptuously whenever they saw a child.[6]

Others less extreme used eggs to cure different forms of sterility and impotence. Staricius describes such a spell used in ancient

[1] Benet, Sula, *Song, Dance and Customs of Peasant Poland*, London, 1951, 46–7.
[2] Hole, Christina, *Easter and Its Customs*, London, 1961, 44.
[3] Bächtold-Stäubli, ii.639–40, 694.
[4] Abbott, G. F., *Macedonian Folklore*, Cambridge, 1903, 154.
[5] Information kindly supplied by Dr Ihsan Toptani, formerly of Tirana.
[6] Obolensky, Dmitri, *The Bogomils*, Cambridge, 1948, 214.

times. In present-day Peć, a mainly Albanian town in Serbia, pain
in the testicles is cured by an application of fried eggs sprinkled
with sal ammoniac.[1] This also restores lost virility. A Moroccan,
who wants to increase his sexual capacity, eats the yolk of an egg
every morning for forty days. Then he fills a shell with oil and
drinks that too.[2] A Hungarian woman mixes an egg white and the
white speck from the yolk with her spouse's blood, stuffs the
mixture inside a dead man's bone, and buries it where the husband
generally urinates. If all this is faithfully done, the woman will
conceive. They say of a man with a large family, '*Véréval tojást
kevertek neki*' – he has mixed his blood with eggs.[3]

Barrenness in a Jewish woman is cured by eating a double-
yolked egg,[4] and in circumcision rites among certain peoples
an egg is used, probably to ensure the sexual capacity of the
boy. The Moroccan Ait Neder tie a raw egg with a hole in its
shell around the penis of the boy immediately after the ceremony.
It is only removed, briefly, when he needs to urinate and must
otherwise stay in position until the following morning.[5] The Ait
Waryager dip the wounded area of the penis into an egg yolk, which
is then thrown away.[6] Moslems in Malaya hold a great feast to
honour the boy, and every guest receives the *bunga telor*, a ceremonial egg dyed red and set on a stick decorated with paper
flowers.[7]

A German picture sheet dated 1617 shows a bridegroom receiving an egg, and in Danish folk-humour the 'slipper hero' is
teasingly told to take one.[8] The reference is obviously to his
virility, and even to the more sophisticated this joke has not
grown stale. A recent Danish film, described as Rabelaisian, is set
on an island, where the local eggs give the men a virility and
appeal which the ladies are unable to resist.

Ghanaians are said to regard eggs, sexual organs and all parts
of the body involved in procreation with a feeling of religious
awe.[9] The implied connection here is quite explicit in some

[1] Kemp, 248–9.   [2] Westermarck, *Ritual and Belief*, i.581.
[3] Wlislocki, 140.
[4] *The Jewish Encyclopaedia*, New York, 1903, v.54.
[5] Westermarck, *Ritual and Belief*, ii.428.
[6] *Ibid.*, 429.
[7] Alhady, Alwi bin Sheikh, *Malay Customs and Traditions*, Singapore, 1962, 9.
[8] Bächtold-Stäubli, ii.640.
[9] Antubam, Kofi, *Ghana's Heritage of Culture*, Leipzig, 1963, 35.

countries, where eggs are specifically associated with testicles. Dutch and German workmen say *Eier* when they mean testicles,[1] and the answer to a German riddle: 'How can you divide five eggs between two men and one woman?' is: 'Give three to the woman and one each to the men, because they already have two.'[2] Russians use the same expression. Stalin, who was an earthy man, once declared that you could not make omelettes without breaking eggs. Later, at a student reunion, Radek said he could see plenty of 'eggs' broken by Stalin, but not the socialist omelette they had been promised. Here the broken eggs were testicles – standing for the lives taken by Stalin.[3]

Julius Streicher, condemned at the Nuremburg trials, referred to the semen of non-Aryan men as 'the alien egg-white'. Absurd though it may sound, such ideas played their part in Nazi racialist ideology and were accepted by many apparently sophisticated people within our lifetime. According to this, a man's semen during intercourse is absorbed by the woman's womb and enters her blood, one intercourse between an Aryan woman and a Jew being sufficient to poison her blood forever. With 'the alien egg-white' she took the foreign soul into her body, and so became incapable of bearing pure Aryan children, even if she later married an Aryan man.[4] This does not seem so fantastic when one still hears English country people say of dogs that, once a pedigree bitch has borne mongrels, she will never produce a pure litter again.

Traditions in other countries imply that eggs are a symbol for testicles. In the Southern States of America parents quarrel if eggs are put into their bed.[5] A Nigerian Hausa wife will be divorced if she dreams of eggs, though for a girl it represents marriage.[6] And if a Moroccan woman finds partridge eggs her husband knows that she is desired by another man.[7]

[1] Information kindly supplied by Silvio van Rooy of Amsterdam.

[2] See Fischer, H., and Bolte, *Die Reise der Söhne Giaffers*, Bibliothek des Litterarischen Vereins in Stuttgart, Tübingen, 1895, No. 208.

[3] Alexandrov, Victor, *The Tukhachevsky Affair*, London, 1963, 28.

[4] Maser, Werner, *Die Frühgeschichte der NSDAP*, Frankfurt-am-Main, 1965, 230.

[5] *Dictionary of Folklore*, i.341.

[6] Tremearne, A. J. N., 'Bori Beliefs and Ceremonies', *Journal of the Royal Anthropological Institute*, xlv (London, 1915), 41.

[7] Westermarck, *Ritual and Belief*, ii.336.

CONCEPTION AND CHILDBIRTH

Women are condemned to child-bearing, according to the Guiana Indians, because they broke the original egg, a story bearing comparison to Genesis. Uraima, one of their gods, once had in his possession a bird's egg which he kept in a calabash. He guarded it with great care, so that it should hatch out. But one day he met two girls on the road. They saw the egg, and asked him to let them have it. 'No,' he said. 'I cannot.' They followed him, but, despite their persistence he still refused, so they tried to seize it, and in the struggle it broke. Then Uraima said: 'Since you have done this, trouble will follow you from now onward. Up till now the egg has belonged to man. For the future, it will belong to woman, and she will have to hatch it.' The account concludes: 'It is only the female that lays eggs nowadays.'[1] There seem to be elements in this legend of a struggle at some stage between the sexes, and perhaps the idea is not too improbable. Guiana, after all, is a northwards extension of Brazil, whose great river gave its name to the Amazons. It is likely that in various cultures there have from time to time been disputes of this kind, though, of course, it is impossible to agree with the Marxist concept that the original social organization was inevitably matriarchal.

A custom of Keisar, an island in the East Indies, probably exhibits features of this conflict. A childless woman brings the first egg laid by the hen to a 'Wise Man'. He lays it on a *nunu* leaf, presses it against her breast, boils it and makes her eat some. The remainder, also wrapped in a *nunu* leaf, is kept in the branches of the tallest tree nearby.[2] This suggests a division of effort between the 'Wise Man', perhaps the symbol of a male-dominated society, and the woman.

Remembering the frequent association of eggs with testicles, it is often difficult to separate demonstrations of male superiority from forms of crude phallicism. For instance, in Ruthenia a barren woman's husband will sometimes blow the contents of an egg into her mouth, and she must swallow it. In Transylvania, when difficulties of conception arise the woman gives her husband a black hen's egg to eat by the light of the full moon, a rather

[1] Roth, Walter, 'An Enquiry into the Animism and Folklore of the Guiana Indians', *Thirtieth Annual Report of the Bureau of American Ethnology*, Washington, 1915, 323.

[2] Hartland, E. S., *Primitive Paternity*, London, 1909, i.60.

unusual custom, implying that the man may be responsible.[1] In contrast with this is a French Canadian tale of a man who will only marry a girl able to lay eggs. The story ends pleasantly, for the chosen girl pretends on her wedding night that she fell downstairs and broke her egg-laying mechanism.[2]

Very often the egg is used in aiding conception as an apparent fertility symbol, sometimes with the added intercession of a child-bearing woman. This happens at Aglu in Morocco. On a very windy day a woman nursing a baby takes an egg and wraps it in a cloth which the child has touched. Then it is given to the barren woman so that she can bury it.[3] Among the Hungarian Schokaz of the Banat around Temesvar, a childless woman must eat the egg. It is administered by one who is fertile, in a glass of water.[4] Galicians used the final egg of an old hen for the same purpose. Credited with wonderful powers, it should have two yolks, and whoever ate it, whether human or beast, would be certain to conceive.[5] South of the Tatras in Ruthenia the small, unformed eggs, taken from a chicken killed specially, had to be placed in the woman's vagina.[6]

A Chinese legend sets the same idea more attractively. T'ung, the mythical founder of the Shang Dynasty, was born from an egg. His mother, the Empress Kien Tieh, prayed for a son and bathed in the river. While she was washing a dark swallow flew overhead and dropped a speckled egg down from its mouth. The Empress swallowed this and became pregnant.[7] In Japan, however, as mentioned earlier, a woman who treads on egg-shells will have illness and difficulties in childbirth, though nothing is said about swallowing eggs whole. Oriental Jewish girls step over fish-roe to increase fecundity,[8] a practice which is worth mentioning because, according to Christian usage, fish-roe is egg,

---

[1] *Ibid.*, 57.

[2] Aarne, Antti and Thompson, Stith, *The Types of the Folk-tale*, Helsinki, 1964, 427.

[3] Westermarck, *Ritual and Belief*, ii.281.

[4] Hartland, i.60.

[5] *Ibid.*, 61.

[6] *Ibid.*, 57.

[7] Granet, Marcel, *Festivals and Songs of Ancient China*, London, 1932, 157, 188.

[8] *The Jewish Encyclopaedia*, v.54. Westermarck, Edward, *Early Beliefs and Their Social Influence*, London, 1932, 136.

not fish.[1] Nowadays caviar is held to be an aphrodisiac – an expensive idea. It would hardly do for Moroccan women, who may not eat eggs in front of their husbands.[2] This carries overtones of indecency, as well as apparent fears of destroying the life symbol. These inhibitions are absent in Chetim Tess Baba, whose holy grave lies near Monastir in Moslem Macedonia. Barren women must pass two eggs through holes bored in his head and foot stones, and then eat them.[3]

Eggs also played their part in sex-divination. Pliny describes the pregnancy of Livia Augusta, Nero's wife. At that time she always carried an egg about with her in her bosom. The egg hatched a cock and she gave birth to a son, Tiberius.[4] Moroccan women divined in the same way. But the egg, after lengthy inspection in a bowl of rain-water by the would-be mother, was given to a broody hen for hatching. The same technique was recommended for sterility, in which case the mother not only gazed, but also drank the rain-water.[5] English gipsies expect to conceive if they see an egg upon the road; but if it is broken, the child will die.[6]

After birth, according to Van Gennep, a Frenchwoman is required to walk between two eggs without breaking them, and also to jump over others in a basket.[7] The custom could refer, as he suggests, to the idea of eggs as testicles. But it may simply represent a ceremony of renewal. Indeed, if the Germans are right, a speedier renewal than the woman might desire. According to their beliefs, if she happens to step on an egg-shell she will conceive.[8] But the intended symbolism is probably that of the life emblem giving new reproductive strength to the exhausted mother, enabling her to conceive again at a future date.

[1] Hartley, Dorothy, *Food in England*, London, 1954, 208.

[2] Westermarck, *Ritual and Belief*, ii.364.

[3] Hasluck, F. W., *Christianity and Islam under the Sultans*, Oxford, 1929, i.359.

[4] Needham, Joseph, *A History of Embryology*, Cambridge, 1934, 4–5.

[5] Westermarck, Edward, *The History of Human Marriage*, London, 1921, ii.485–6.

[6] Payne, Charles F., 'Some Romani Superstitions', *Journal of the Gypsy Lore Society*, xxxvi (Edinburgh, 1957), 112.

[7] Van Gennep, Arnold, *Le Folklore du Dauphiné*, Paris, 1932, i.36–7. Joisten, Charles, 'Le Folklore de l'Œuf en Dauphiné', *Arts et Traditions Populaires* (Paris, January–March 1961), 57.

[8] Hartland, i.112.

Once a woman has become pregnant and is ready to give birth, the egg becomes a protective against evil influence, increasing her strength by its power and easing her pain. Indians, using it for transference, wave one above her head before throwing it into the road.[1] In Hungary the magic is stronger still: an egg, boiled in a skull and mixed with oil and human grease, is rubbed on the woman's breast. It will heal her soreness and strengthen the child.[2] The skull would be seen as considerably increasing the power of the charm, because of the old idea that it was the soul seat. By drinking or eating out of one, people supposed that they gained the dead man's strength.

In south Hungary, when a gipsy is enduring painful labour, her relations come and one of them drops an egg. They sing:

The egg, the egg is round,
And the belly is round.
Come child in good health!
God, God calls thee!

If she dies they place two eggs under her arms, perhaps an offering to her life-giving milk, and say:

When this egg shall be decayed
Here will be no milk![3]

Serbian women screaming in labour have an egg dropped in the front of their nightgowns, which are then ripped in half, and Germans also believe that an egg lessens the agony of child-bearing.[4] Immediately before birth the Ait Yusi of Morocco warm an egg and pour the contents into the woman's mouth, to ease her pains and speed the baby on its way.

In Tangier, when birth is difficult, the children take one of the mother's garments, place an egg on it and carry it round the houses, saying: 'This lying-in woman is in the throes of childbirth, O God give her delivery.' People then lay eggs upon the garment in the hope that she will bear as easily as a hen.[5] Sometimes one of them is rolled over her abdomen. If it is then thrown in the nearest holy well, the child will be born in the time that it

[1] Abbott, *Keys of Power*, 131, 431.
[2] Wlislocki, 139.   [3] Leland, 49.
[4] Bächtold-Stäubli, ii.640.
[5] Westermarck, *Ritual and Belief*, ii.371.

takes to reach the bottom.[1] The Ait Waryager give the mother eggs to eat as soon as she is delivered.[2] And in Andjara the infant is held over a boiled egg upon a sieve.[3] Forty days later the mother will have a ritual bath, when she and her friends eat eggs.[4] In France, according to Joisten, a lying-in mother receives six dozen eggs from the godparents, and she may not get up until she has eaten them all.[5] This would certainly provide a much-needed rest – something peasant mothers seldom enjoy – but make her liverish too.

THE NEW BABY

The Monumbo of New Guinea use the same word for 'egg' and for 'family'.[6] They are linked in our culture too. Lithuanians offer an egg to the Tree of Life, a favourite symbol, when a baby arrives,[7] and in the north of England, as indeed in other parts of the country, an egg was often given along with other items as a present to a new-born child.[8] In Leicestershire and elsewhere he received these gifts on his first visit.[9] The egg was kept and brought good luck in later life.[10] Derbyshire folk insisted that it be new-laid on the day that it was given.[11] Jews in St Louis, Missouri, hand a baby eggs when he is brought to their house for the first time: one for a girl and two for a boy.[12]

French families have a ceremony similar to that in England. The child is presented with bread, salt, a match and an egg, with the greeting: 'May your house be full like an egg, may you be

[1] Legey, F., *Folklore of Morocco*, London, 1935, 123.

[2] Westermarck, *Ritual and Belief*, ii.376–7.

[3] *Ibid.*, 360.

[4] *Ibid.*, 398.

[5] Joisten, 58.

[6] Weinhold, Gertrud, *Das schöne Osterei in Europa*, Kassel, 1965, 8.

[7] Bächtold-Stäubli, ii.638, note 482.

[8] *Notes and Queries*, 4 December 1880, 6th Series, ii.443–4. *Ibid.* 22 January 1881, 6th Series, iii.73. Hole, Christina, ed., *Encyclopaedia of Superstitions*, London, 1961, 97. Gutch, Mrs, and Peacock, Mabel, ed., *Examples of Printed Folk-Lore concerning Lincolnshire*, London, 1908, 229–30.

[9] Thiselton-Dyer, T. F., *English Folk-Lore*, London, 1884, 176.

[10] Hardy, James, ed., *The Denham Tracts*, London, 1895, ii.48.

[11] Jones, 469.

[12] Yoffie, Leah R., 'Popular Beliefs and Customs Among the Yiddish-speaking Jews of St Louis, Missouri', *Journal of American Folklore*, xxxviii (Boston, 1925), 391.

good like bread, may you be pure like salt, and here is the support of your old age.'[1] Bad luck came if this egg was eaten or broken. The Faroese proffer one of these ceremonial eggs at the christening. In the old days there were no less than four. It was customary to set these under a broody hen and, if they all hatched, the omens were excellent. Föhr islanders gave one or two, intending them as symbols of strength and as lucky auguries for the child's development.[2]

In the French High Alps an older child, visiting a house for the first time, was also given an egg.[3] The reasons offered for these gifts vary: to bring good luck, to launch him in life with something useful, and a symbol that he will lack for nothing in the future. The commemorative burial of an egg in a wall by New Mexican Spaniards on 2 February, to recall the cutting of a baby's umbilical cord, derives from these ideas.[4] But since eggs figure so prominently throughout the reproductive cycle, it seems just as likely that the practices ensure the fertility of the child. In due course he or she, too, will sire or bear children.

Sometimes the ceremony is more immediate. In Germany a baby's eyes were anointed with liquid from a new-laid egg.[5] Women neighbours in northern Albania call upon the mother, bringing a gift of eggs: an even number if it is a boy – two, four, six or eight – and an odd number if it is a girl – one, three, five or seven. One of them is broken across the baby's face, to protect him from the evil eye.[6] In southern Macedonia the same custom is observed, though in a less unpleasant manner for the baby. Forty days after the birth a mother takes her infant to be churched. On the way home she calls at the house of the sponsor and nearest relatives. If the baby is a boy, the woman of the house takes an egg and, passing it over the infant's face, she blesses him: 'Mayest thou live, my little one. Mayest thou grow old, with hoary hair and eyebrows, with a hoary beard and moustache.'[7]

[1] Joisten, 58. Van Gennep, i.56.

[2] Jensen, Christian, *Die nordfriesischen Inseln*, Lübeck, 1927, 305.

[3] Joisten, 58.

[4] Espinosa, Aurelio M., 'New-Mexican Spanish Folk-Lore', *Journal of American Folklore*, xxiii (Boston, October–December, 1910), 411.

[5] Bächtold-Stäubli, ii.634.

[6] Durham, M. E., *Some Tribal Origins, Laws and Customs of the Balkans*, London, 1928, 191.

[7] Abbott, *Macedonian Folklore*, 137.

Eggs are often used when the child is bathed for the first time. Germans put one in the water so that he will grow up with a good, clear voice, and in Bosnia they add a yolk. Friar Rudolphus notes: '*Ovum in primo balneo ponunt quod patri dant cibum.*'[1]

The Chinese have a similar custom. When a baby is born, each guest at the celebration party receives a bowl of noodles and an egg. The noodles signify long life, the eggs, which are dyed red, peace and happiness. On the morning of the third day following the birth, the baby is ritually bathed. His grandmother performs the ceremony and, passing a red egg three times over his head, prays that it shall become just as round.[2] The mother puts eggs in the bath-water – one for a boy, two for a girl – and stands nearby a plate of mixed eggs, some red and some white. Each guest must place one in the water with the appropriate good wishes: white for long life and a hoary old age, red for good luck. The mother herself is also given both raw and cooked red eggs.[3]

If a Chinese baby falls ill, his grandmother takes a bowl of raw rice containing an upended egg, and goes to a nearby street-corner. Here, sticking two incense sticks in the ground and burning some paper money, she makes a ritual offering of the food and calls the child's name repeatedly. This done, she returns home with the rice and egg.[4] The ceremony was probably common, since the Chinese had an uncomfortable habit of feeding a baby with a boiled egg on the occasion of his first birthday.

Similar German customs seem more overtly practical. Though Rottenburg children usually take one when they go upstairs to bed, and innumerable other egg customs for German children are in existence, there was none the less a peculiar old folk-belief that eggs are dangerous food for any child, and if a young baby was fed them it could not survive the year.[5] On the face of it, this is just a sensible prohibition. Egg is much too rich for a baby. But, since it is perfectly suitable food for older children, the meaning becomes less clear. Perhaps it refers to the sexual significance of an egg, inappropriate for a child.

---

[1] Bächtold-Stäubli, ii.637.
[2] Yueh-Hwa, Lin, *The Golden Wing*, London, 1947, 20.
[3] Cormack, J., *Everyday Customs in China*, Edinburgh, 1935, 33.
[4] Hsu, Francis L. K., *Under the Ancestors' Shadow*, London, 1949, 203.
[5] Bächtold-Stäubli, ii.637–8.

Egg charms, whatever their purpose may be, continue to be given to a child at different stages of its growth. In France the shells facilitate teething.[1] German children who visit relatives are given a 'talking egg', and told: 'Learn to teach yourself to talk, as the hens begin to squawk.'[2] This is said three times. Meanwhile, the child must eat a piece of the boiled egg. In Baden they say: 'Mumble is out, ask if in doubt,'[3] and in Egerland they make a cross over the child's mouth with the egg, saying: 'Children learn to chatter as the chickens natter.'[4] In Saxon Switzerland the talking egg is baked into a cake, which mother and child immediately eat.[5] Schwarzenburg children are given larks' eggs to make them sing, and in other regions they keep twenty-one eggs in the house to make sure of this. In Baden chopped eggs facilitate learning to read, and a boy attending school for the first time in Bavaria was always given one to eat.[6] These must be intended to stimulate the brain, just as it is a common fallacy in England that fish increases intellectual capacity.

The south Hungarian tent gipsies observe a curious ritual when a child first has his hair cut. Three eggs laid by a black hen are mixed with salt water and massaged into the scalp.[7] In many races hair-cutting is an important occasion, for it was once supposed that a person's strength lay partly in his hair. Eggs were perhaps to counteract this loss and also to guard the child against malignant influence, which he would be specially prone to on the first occasion.

Chinese babies are shaved at the age of one month and red eggs are sent, not to the child, but by his parents to friends and relations. These are invitations to a feast and they must accept, bringing a gift for the child. In the south this custom was observed for a girl or boy. But the people of the north were more particular. Girls were not honoured at all and for boys it was restricted to the first-born alone.[8]

[1] Van Gennep, *Dauphiné*, i.56.
[2] Bächtold-Stäubli, ii.637.
[3] *Ibid.*, 638.
[4] *Ibid.*
[5] *Ibid.*, 639, note 507.
[6] *Ibid.*, 637, 638, 639, note 494.
[7] Winstedt, E. O., 'Forms and Ceremonies', *Journal of the Gypsy Lore Society*, ii (Edinburgh, July 1908–April 1909), 341.
[8] Ball, J. Dyer, *Things Chinese*, London, 1926, 77.

MARRIAGE

Eventually, of course, as the child becomes an adult, he wants to marry and raise a family himself. And just as egg charms featured prominently in other phases of the human reproductive cycle, so they are often used in the marriage rites of widely differing cultures. Jews attached a special importance to the symbol of fertility. It was customary, writes a correspondent from Greece, to fix one on to the veil of a bride, representing the abundance of the hen, and as a token of good luck and many children.[1] At a fifteenth-century Jewish wedding in Mainz the happy pair broke their fast after the ceremony by eating an egg and a hen.[2] Seventeenth-century English Jews laid both items in front of the woman as a sign that she would bear a large family.[3] The egg represented an easy and painless labour, as effortless as the pullet's production of her young; afterwards it was apparently thrown into someone's face! A Moroccan Jewish bridegroom casts it at his wife, expressing good wishes for a speedy childbirth,[4] and in Russia she carried one in her bosom on the journey to the ceremony.[5] Orthodox Christians fed the couple with eggs once they had been united, scrambled for the bride, because this meant that she would bear sons.[6] Later, at his mother-in-law's house, the groom was given an omelette.[7] The Mordvins on the Volga also fed the woman with eggs, but before the wedding took place. Armenian Moslems and Kurds insisted that the couple share one inscribed with the 112th chapter of the Koran:[8] 'In the Name of Allah, the Compassionate, the Merciful say: "Allah is One, the Eternal God. He begot none, nor was He begotten. None is equal to Him."'[9]

French couples ate an egg and a piece of rabbit – also standing for fertility – in full view of all the guests, to make sure that it was done.[10] Sometimes this sharing of food was purely symbolic. The

---

[1] Information kindly supplied by Mr Asher Moisis, Chairman of Athens B'nai B'rith, in a letter to me, published in the *Jewish Chronicle*, 18 March 1966.

[2] Schauss, Hayyim, *The Lifetime of a Jew*, New York, 1950, 173.

[3] Wood, Edward J., *The Wedding Day*, London, 1869, i.21.

[4] Westermarck, *Early Beliefs*, 137.   [5] *The Jewish Encyclopaedia*, v.54.

[6] Sokolov, Y. M., *Russian Folklore*, New York, 1950, 206.

[7] Jones, 470.   [8] Hartland, i.58–9.

[9] Dawood, N. J., tr., *The Koran*, London, 1964, 257.

[10] Čerbulenas, K., 'Margučiu Menas Lietuvoje', *Mokslas Ir Gyvenimas* (Vilnius, March 1967), 27.

Champas of Thailand put brass plates between bride and groom
on which they stand a jar of wine, a chicken, and two eggs. A
sorcerer offers the right egg to the groom, seated on his left, and
the left egg to the bride, seated on his right, reflecting their
union.[1]

The Tsul in Morocco share a raw egg, so that their future will
be bright, but on the second night of the marriage. They also mix
one with grit from the wedding corn and throw it into a well,
to bring happiness for the new couple and rain for the crops. Here
fertility rites for people and for the harvest have merged. In
Andjara, when corn is prepared for a wedding, a bowl with a raw
egg is put on one of the piles of grain, 'So that the life of the
bridegroom shall be white'.[2] Japanese *darumas* are also connected
with the success of agriculture, so it is of particular interest that a
special kind, the *hatiman-okiagari*, painted with a design of plants,
is laid in the drawer at a marriage.[3]

Similar customs existed in western Europe too. A Tyrolese
couple would generally provide the woman with a large boiled
egg when arranging the wedding feast, which she had to eat
alone,[4] and German brides liked to stitch one into the folds of
their wedding gowns.[5] In some areas guests are expected to play
their part. After the wedding feast in Gasselte (Netherlands), they
search the hen-houses belonging to the couple's relations, to see
if the hens have laid. This is called Egg-threshing.[6]

Sometimes an egg is smashed, apparently symbolizing rupture
of the hymen during intercourse. The custom is quite commonplace. Serbs in Syrmia try to break an egg in a sack during horse-
play among the guests, while bride and groom retire to bed.[7] In
Indonesia the man must crush it with his foot on the flight of
steps leading to the marriage hall,[8] and the bride may smear this
mess on her own feet. The Moroccan Ait Waryager place one on
top of a mug in the courtyard of the bridal home and the groom

[1] Urlin, Ethel L., *A Short History of Marriage*, London, 1913, 151.
[2] Westermarck, *Ritual and Belief*, 19–20.
[3] Nisizawa, 36.
[4] Hartland, i.58.
[5] Bächtold-Stäubli, ii.640.
[6] Information kindly supplied by Henk Arends of Amsterdam, from the *Folkloristisch Woordenboek*.
[7] Westermarck, Edward, *A Short History of Marriage*, London, 1926, 191–2.
[8] Lewis, Reba, *Indonesia, Troubled Paradise*, London, 1962, 55.

Colour Plate IX A German egg-tree, with small wooden eggs. Beneath it is a Moravian egg whip or switch (*Dynovacka*); see also plate 15 and colour plate VIII. The two central eggs suspended above the tree are also Moravian, threaded with ribbon. Hanging to the left are two eggs from a Serbian Convent, covered with wool and sequins. On the far right is a Polish paper-appliqué decorated egg, strung within a straw cage. The gold-coloured egg, made of metal and covered with filigree, is Russian.

Colour Plate X Painted eggs. The five upper eggs are Russian and show, left to right, the Cathedral of the Archangel and the Belfry of Peter the Great (Moscow); bell ringing at an Orthodox Church; St Basil's Cathedral (Moscow); a pair of peacocks (one only visible in the picture: between them appear the letters XB — for meaning see caption to colour plate V (a); St Nicholas. The eggs are wooden, painted in oils. The remaining six eggs are all Bavarian, from the Convent of Eichstätt. They are painted in water colours, the designs being largely self-explanatory. The top left egg of this group illustrates the miracle of the loaves and the fishes.

must destroy it with a single blow of his foot.[1] Moslems in Deccan, India, put one beneath the hooves of the man's horse and crush another on the door of the bride's house.[2]

This custom, in fact, is popular in several continents. A bride in seventeenth-century France broke an egg before entering her new home,[3] and one finds the same thing done elsewhere by relations and friends. In Africa after a Hausa wedding guests throw an egg at the doorway of the new house.[4] Indonesian Dyaks smash one against the teeth of the bridal pair.[5] This is also common among Moslems of Morocco and varies according to the tribe. Ait Yusi tie a scarf around the forehead of the bride. It contains an egg which is crushed and which she must leave in place until the following morning.[6] Elsewhere in Morocco egg is smeared on the groom's forehead and he may receive one as a gift.[7] Chieftains of the Olon Lavangan in Borneo smear egg on the foreheads of the couple.[8]

Some people simply put one in front of the door of the new home – for example, in western Java.[9] Moroccans bury one under the threshold so that the couple will step over it many times and be happy,[10] while Sindi Moslems go one better and bury it in the bridal chamber.[11] Some Moroccan women put a raw egg in a bowl outside their house just before the wedding. This is greatly coveted by unmarried girl friends, so that they can eat it to help them find a husband.[12] When the bride arrives at her mother-in-law's riding on a mule, the older woman throws an egg at the animal's forehead.[13] Perhaps this is to avert anything unpropitious which may have been brought by the stranger – for in such primitive communities the bride is in effect a stranger. When purchasing

[1] Westermarck, *Ritual and Belief*, i.581.

[2] Abbott, *Keys of Power*, 416.

[3] *Dictionary of Folklore*, i.341. Hartland, i.58.

[4] Tremearne, A. J. N., 'Bori Beliefs and Ceremonies', *Journal of the Royal Anthropological Institute*, xlv (London, 1915), 37.

[5] Hartland, i.59.

[6] Westermarck, *Ritual and Belief*, i.581–2.

[7] *Ibid.*, *Marriage Ceremonies in Morocco*, London, 1914, 348.

[8] Hartland, i.59.

[9] *Ibid.*, 58.

[10] Westermarck, *Ritual and Belief*, ii.19.

[11] Abbott, *Keys of Power*, 234.

[12] Westermarck, *Marriage Ceremonies in Morocco*, 363.

[13] *Ibid.*, *Ritual and Belief*, ii.296.

an animal in Morocco it was in any case customary to safeguard it with an egg in this way, as a protective against the evil eye.[1]

A present of eggs can mean an offer of marriage, as in Sikkim,[2] or they might be included among the wedding gifts. In the southern Celebes this signified a desire that there should be children.[3] A Shan bridegroom gives his wife a present of eggs,[4] and in Malaya coloured ones are always given to the guests as wedding favours: to refuse would cause a fight.[5]

Elsewhere in the East Indies an account of a wedding ceremony in eighteenth-century Amboina says it mainly consisted in tossing an egg to and fro between the wide sleeves of the bride and groom's wedding garments, evidently trying not to break it.[6] Risky though this may sound, it pales beside the dreadful scene described by George Borrow, writing about a Spanish gipsy wedding in 1841:

> Sweetmeats of all kinds, and of all forms, but principally *yémas* or yolks of eggs prepared with a crust of sugar were strewn on the floor of a large room, at least to the depth of three inches. Into this room, at a given signal, tripped the bride and bridegroom ... to convey a slight idea of the scene is almost beyond the power of words. In a few minutes the sweetmeats were reduced to a powder, or rather to a mud, the dancers were soiled to the knees with sugar, fruits and yolks of eggs.[7]

---

[1] *Ibid.*, 285.
[2] Hartland, i.59.
[3] *Ibid.*, 59–60.
[4] *Ibid.*, 59.
[5] Hutchinson, i.321.
[6] Jones, 470. Wood, 153.
[7] Borrow, George, *An Account of the Gypsies of Spain*, London, 1893, 190–1.

Chapter 6
Purity

O Lady Egg, Egg, make white for me my writing board!
Moroccan schoolboy song

Notions about disease have varied throughout the centuries, but the idea of something portable which could be taken and moved elsewhere was evidently popular; and even in developed communities anyone afflicted with an illness or blemish might attempt to wish the disagreeable condition on to another person. Equally unpleasant was the habit of trying to foist it on an animal, as in the French cure for a sick child: giving an egg, filled with its urine, to a dog.[1] In the same way Germans healed jaundice by feeding one containing the patient's blood to a hen.[2] Here the egg only serves as agent of the transfer, but sometimes it is used as a substitute for the person or animal. Jaundice was a common scourge, and Rhineland Germans got rid of it by placing a thread across the patient's stomach and then wrapping it round a fresh egg, which was laid in hot ashes. If the egg jumped out of the grate, the jaundice would leap out with it, and so depart.[3]

Hungarians supposed that this disease was caused by looking through a window at a corpse, and to cure it one obtained nine lice from the head of a person sharing the same Christian name. These were baked in an apple-pie and eaten. Next, faeces from the same person were inserted in a hard-boiled egg, from which the yolk had first been removed; the charm was sewn into a bag and laid under the altar, where it remained secretly until three Masses had been said. The patient, who then had to wear it for nine days, was obliged to repeat the whole process nine times.[4] Probably, by the time all this had been done the jaundice had a good chance of clearing up on its own. Ingredients must have been difficult to

---

[1] Bächtold-Stäubli, Hanns, ed., *Handwörterbuch des deutschen Aberglaubens*, Berlin, 1929–30, ii.632.

[2] *Ibid.*, 631.

[3] *Ibid.*, 632, note 399.

[4] Jones, W. H., *The Folk Tales of the Magyars*, London, 1889, xlvi–xlvii.

obtain for this disgusting charm, which is none the less full of interesting folk-ideas: the importance of names, a Christian gloss, and the use of excreta and blood in obtaining power over anybody. Lice, which live by sucking blood, would be thought to contain something of the essence of a healthy person. As for the magic number 9, uneven digits are popular, and often 9 is best of all: the trinity of trinities and multiple of three. Man, said Pythagoras, is a full chord – eight notes – and deity comes next.

The same important number figures in an American Negro cure for goitre: the place is rubbed on nine consecutive mornings with an egg, which is buried, when this has been done, under the doorstep. A baby's birthmark is given similar treatment.[1] Paracelsus has a more elaborate version of this: an egg, filled with the sick man's blood, is baked in the oven and laid on his stomach, the strength of its attraction drawing out the disease. Then it is interred.[2]

Burial of an egg is a popular feature in this kind of folk-cure. In Mecklenburg, when epidemics were raging, people dug a hole for one in the graveyard.[3] Presumably by burying the egg they hoped to bury the disease. Another German technique, wrapping a length of cotton – three times the length of the patient's arm – around an egg, and giving it to him to hold before throwing it away, is more explicable: the trouble leaves with the discarded object.[4]

Some cures which helped to alleviate more elusive ailments, such as sorrow and sickness of the mind, were based on sound psychology. Mourning widows, for instance, took comfort in their grief by giving four eggs to the first stranger they encountered, hoping in this way to transfer their misfortunes – an unappealing idea from Tripoli.[5] Mecklenburg children suffering from fright were more agreeably cured by an egg rubbed three times all over the skin and then thrown over the hedge.[6] The psychological effect on the child was probably considerable; even

---

[1] Puckett, N., *Folk Beliefs of the Southern Negro*, Chapel Hill, 1926, 340–1, 374.
[2] Bächtold-Stäubli, ii.631.
[3] *Ibid.*, 632.   [4] *Ibid.*, 631.
[5] Dalyell, John Graham, *The Darker Superstitions of Scotland*, Edinburgh, 1834, 110. Quoted by Dalyell from *Letters from Tripoli*, ii.271.
[6] Bächtold-Stäubli, ii.632.

more so on Spanish New Mexican children, whose mothers cured their constipation by smashing an egg right on the stomach.[1]

DISPERSION

It was not always enough just to throw away an egg or bury it. The unwelcome ailment had also to be dispersed. And so in Germany, for instance, people cured bed-wetting by filling an egg-shell with the culprit's urine and hanging it up in the chimney. As its contents evaporated, so the trouble disappeared,[2] an idea which colours a seventeenth-century English remedy for fever. Here the egg, boiled in the patient's morning urine, is pricked all over and buried in an ant's nest. The illness diminishes as it decays, for myriads of tiny insects carry away the evil influence and scatter it in all directions.[3] Much the same was done in Germany.[4]

Another favourite remedy for disease involved burying an egg at the crossroads. Yugoslav fever patients washed there before dawn, placed their egg beneath a stake in the nearest fence and went quickly home;[5] a similar ritual, observed in total silence, was recorded from England in 1787.[6] Crossroads were popular for magical rites. For they pointed north, south, east, west, and the influence of anything interred there would spread in all directions. By breaking it up, the original process was radically weakened. Westermarck thought this accounted for the custom of burying suicides at the crossroads – unfortunate people, once greatly feared, for it was supposed that after death they transformed into vampires.[7]

---

[1] Espinosa, Aurelio M., 'New-Mexican Spanish Folk-Lore', *Journal of American Folklore*, xxiii (Boston, October–December 1910), 410.

[2] Bächtold-Stäubli, ii.634.

[3] Aubrey, John, *The Remaines of Gentilisme and Judaisme* (1686–87), London, 1881, 256–7.

[4] Bächtold-Stäubli, ii.631–2.

[5] Kemp, P., *Healing Ritual: Studies in the Technique and Tradition of the Southern Slavs*, London, 1935, 106.

[6] Jones, William, *Credulities Past and Present*, London, 1880, 463. Pettigrew, T. G., *Superstitions Connected with the History and Practice of Medicine and Surgery*, London, 1894, 70.

[7] Westermarck, Edward, *Origin and Development of the Moral Ideas*, London, 1917, ii.256–7, 256, note 1. Owen, Elias, *Old Stone Crosses of the Vale of Clwyd*, London, 1886, 74–5.

A buried egg might also represent an offering to the deity who ruled there. Cicero refers to the Feast of the Compitalia when woollen figures – presumably relics of earlier sacrifice – were hung up at the crossroads.[1] But there is yet a third possibility: emanation – the exertion of a universal influence. Mystic Christian literature describes Our Lord's Cross radiating out from the heart of the world to the four corners of the earth.[2] A Sindi charm, unconnected with disease, illustrates this reverse process. A shopkeeper who wants more customers goes early to the crossroads with an egg and a little salt. Waving them above his head, he breaks the egg open and throws the contents down; shell and salt are brought home for burning on the fire.[3]

THE EVIL EYE

A Moslem custom, again from Sind, employs the same technique for curing someone bewitched by the evil eye: egg, salt and turmeric are waved over the victim and thrown down at the crossroads.[4] A story from the Scottish Highlands, collected at the beginning of this century, describes how a servant-girl fetched home some eggs. A neighbour, who happened to be in the house, looked at them. Later, during cooking, one cracked and hot water splashed up in the girl's face. The others, which broke as well, were not fit to use. Everyone blamed the neighbour, who must have 'overlooked' them.[5]

This was rather unusual. As a rule eggs were considered effective in curing, or helping to cure, illness produced by the evil eye. *El ojo*, the eye, is a serious fever in New Mexico, supposed to be caused by an excess of affection towards a child – a woman making much of a child can bring on an attack. The superstition itself is known as *hacer ojo*, 'to make the eye', and it must in fact mean the evil eye, since the Spanish for this is *hacer mal de ojo*.[6]

It was not unique to New Mexico. In many countries, England

---

[1] See Cicero, *Orations*, London, 1852, iii.346–7, note 1.
[2] Dickens, Bruce, and Ross, Alan S. C., ed., *The Dream of the Rood*, London, 1964, 21.vii–viii. See also note 8.
[3] Abbott, J., *The Keys of Power: a Study of Indian Ritual and Belief*, London, 1932, 234.
[4] *Ibid.*, 234.
[5] Maclagan, R., *The Evil Eye in the Western Highlands*, London, 1902, 66.
[6] Espinosa, 409. See also note 1.

included, people avoided commenting too favourably on another's good fortune, for fear it would bring disaster, and praise of children was specially frowned on. A child suffering from *el ojo* is put to bed with the contents of an egg on a plate beside his head. Soon an eye appears on the egg and the child recovers.[1] This fanciful idea – that the evil eye is something tangible – is no doubt given substance by the little speck one occasionally sees in a raw yolk. The Moroccans have a cure on similar lines, for the Ait Warain believe that sleeping under stars produces a white spot in the eye, and subsequent blindness. To heal it, a scribe must write an inscription from the Koran upon an egg, which he then touches against the eye, before breaking it open and pouring the liquid into his hand. If a white spot is there, the patient will recover.[2]

Other people see a diagnostic significance in this spot. American Indians rub a sick man's body with an uncooked egg. Then it is broken open and the contents carefully examined. If there is a spot inside, or any other unusual feature, it will throw light upon the nature of the illness. In cases of fever the egg is buried in a stream to draw away excess heat from the patient's body. Sickness arising from the evil eye is often treated in this way.[3]

EXORCISM

Disease-transference involves shifting a tiresome ailment from one object to another. On a more esoteric level this appears in the tradition of the scapegoat, on to whom were transferred all the evils of the community where he lived. Complex ideas of sin and guilt, crime and expiation, were involved. A tale from the North-East Frontier of India illustrates the point – it describes an egg sacrificed by the Idu Mishmis to ensure peace:

> In the old days, when Mishmis were always fighting one another, a man called Alyomi was born to bring peace. When he was old enough to do anything, there were two men, Yutute and Potonye, fighting each other. Alyomi went and made peace between them. He gave an egg to the priest to sacrifice, to ensure lasting peace.

[1] *Ibid.*, 410.
[2] Westermarck, Edward, *Ritual and Belief in Morocco*, London, 1926, i.130.
[3] *Dictionary of Folklore, Mythology and Legend*, New York, 1949, i.341.

The priest cried: 'Let the man who brought peace live well and be in health.' He put the egg on the ground, and Alyomi broke it with his foot and went home. Ever since we have sacrificed an egg whenever there is a meeting of the tribe, in order to free the chief man present of any blame.[1]

Before modern knowledge could provide explanations of disaster and disease, primitive man attributed these ills to the work of malevolent spirits. They also brought mental disorders, and had to be driven out into a suitable animal scapegoat: the Gadarene swine ran down into the river and so drowned.[2] Shakespeare refers to this:

> *I charge thee, Satan, hous'd within this man,*
> *To yield possession to my holy prayers,*
> *And to thy state of darkness hie me straight:*
> *I conjure thee by all the saints in heaven.*[3]

Just as eggs were substitutes for human sacrifice, so they are used in exorcism in lieu of a human being. A child possessed by devils is placed in front of the altar, according to Taoist rites, with five eggs near his feet, and priests command the devils to enter them.[4] In pre-revolution China eggs were widely used in exorcism, and on the first day of the first month everybody ate one. Many evil influences which could strike a man down and instantly kill him were abroad during the year. But an egg, which holds the concentrated vitality of the bird who laid it, gave protection against this and also a little of the 'soul' or creative force of the universe.[5] This last must owe something to the Chinese world creation myth, where the egg plays a prominent part.

The idea that devils could be exorcized into one may lie behind a quaint German notion that a red-yolked egg draws out the sulphur from home-made wine.[6] In medieval Europe sulphur was closely associated with the Devil. Besides, an egg was sometimes taken to be an image of the sun, and it was once a popular belief that the sun absorbed disagreeable odours: 'This majestical roof

[1] Elwin, Verrier, *Myths of the North-East Frontier of India*, Shillong, 1958, 239.

[2] Luke, viii.26–33.   [3] *The Comedy of Errors*, iv.iv.62–4.

[4] Gray, J. H., *China*, London, 1878, i.101–2.

[5] Groot, J. J. M. de, *The Religious System of China*, Leiden, 1910, VI.2, iv.1,076–7.

[6] Bächtold-Stäubli, ii.643.

fretted with golden fire, why, it appears no other thing to me than a foul and pestilent congregation of vapours,'[1] cried Hamlet in his disillusionment with life. That old kitchen favourite, clarifying soup with egg-shells, which still appears in many recipe books, seems intended as a practical application of the superstition – particularly since it does not work.

INVIOLABILITY

If there is a link with the sun in Europe, Arab countries tend to stress instead the whiteness of an egg. For white has always been a colour denoting purity and goodness. Persian divinities, Roman priests of Jupiter[2] and newly baptized Christians in the early Church all wore it.

In Tangier, on the seventh evening in her new home, a bride is belted by two boys, who are each given a raw egg, so that their future will be white[3] – a propitious colour in that part of the world. Moroccans in general emphasize this aspect: 'May your life be white like an egg' is a common wish. In Europe the Croats put an egg into the new baby's cradle 'so that he shall become as white',[4] and in Germany eggs were one of the Three White Offerings which fulfilled every wish.[5] These were bread, salt and eggs – hence, perhaps, an old German superstition that eggs must be eaten with bread and salt if one is to avoid catching a fever.[6]

Romans, in their expression *ab ovo ad malum*, equated an egg with special merit. The idea that something is pure and good invests it with a certain inviolability. It would be quite wrong to steal such a thing, and indeed the egg-thief of folklore suffers for his crime in abusing so worthy an object. They say in Germany – and also in Jamaica – that anybody stealing one will be launched on a life of theft.[7] Among the Jews it brings seven years' bad luck, and not only that: after death the body of the thief rolls around in the grave and is never still.[8]

[1] *Hamlet*, II.ii.314–17.
[2] Brewer, E. Cobham, *Dictionary of Phrase and Fable*, London, 1896, I,295.
[3] Westermarck, *Ritual and Belief*, ii.20.
[4] Weinhold, Gertrud, *Das schöne Osterei in Europa*, Kassel, 1965, 5.
[5] *Ibid.*, 6. Bächtold-Stäubli, ii.617.   [6] *Ibid.*, 643.
[7] Beckwith, Martha, *Black Roadways: a Study of Jamaican Folk Life*, Chapel Hill, 1929, 60. Bächtold-Stäubli, ii.643.
[8] *The Jewish Encyclopaedia*, New York, 1903, v.54. Bonnerjea, Biren, *A Dictionary of Superstitions and Mythology*, London, 1927, 87.

If virtue is a form of spiritual cleanliness, it is not too long a jump from spiritual to physical purity, and so quite often an egg is used as a cleansing agent. In Mecklenburg the year's first goose egg is rubbed three times on the face, in order to whiten the skin.[1] This shows that the purity and goodness of the symbol can simply wipe off on to the body: a primitive idea, but there are traces of it in the concoctions of modern beauticians, who recommend eggs for similar purposes with apparently as little justification. Egg shampoos are supposed to improve the hair, while, according to an improbable German tradition, the yolks will make it curl.[2]

VOTIVE OSTRICH EGGS

What is pure and good must be inviolable, with power to ward off evil, and the Moroccans believe that a snake can be rendered harmless by giving it eggs to eat.[3] Such ideas are especially common in the Middle East, for the egg symbolizes perfection, not only esoterically, but in the most literal sense. Its shell forms a complete, though fragile, sphere and there are none of the pits and perforations which mar the surface of a fruit. As such, it is specially suited to ward off the evil eye, despite the Scottish story mentioned earlier, and eggs are in fact widely used for this purpose. A Tunisian woman in childbirth keeps evil spirits away with a chain of shells hung above her head,[4] and sick people in Morocco eat one hard-boiled, with a charm inscribed upon it.[5] Negroes in the southern United States avoid bad luck by breaking one before speaking to certain people.[6]

But perhaps the most interesting examples of this are the ostrich eggs that hang in churches, monasteries and mosques all over the Middle East and also in Africa: some have been stuck sideways to ornament the minarets of the mud mosque at Mopti (Mali).[7] They also appear in Spain – perhaps relics of the Moorish Conquest – and can be seen in the Cathedral Church at Burgos, and in the

---

[1] Bächtold-Stäubli, ii.632.   [2] *Ibid.*, 634.

[3] Westermarck, *Ritual and Belief*, ii.354.

[4] Wildhaber, Robert, 'Zum Symbolgehalt und zur Ikonographie des Eies', *Deutsches Jahrbuch für Volkskunde*, vi (Berlin, 1960), 81.

[5] Westermarck, *Ritual and Belief*, i.211.

[6] Compare with this the Moroccan custom of always breaking open an egg 'in the name of God', Westermarck, *Ritual and Belief*, i.206.

[7] Information kindly supplied by Dr Wolfhilde von König of Munich.

Franciscan Convent at Sasiola, where they dangle beside the images of St Francis and Diego de Alcalá.[1]

Moslems rationalize this custom by saying that these eggs are symbols of God's watchful care. Traditionally the ostrich hatched her eggs by looking at them:

> *Oh! even with such a look, as fables say,*
> *The mother ostrich fixes on her eggs,*
> *Till that intense affection*
> *Kindle its light of life.*[2]

If she turned away, even for a moment, the eggs would addle, and thus shall God deal with all wicked men.[3] Durandus, Bishop of Mende, refers to this belief in his treatise, *Rationale Divinorum Officiorum*, published in 1286:

In some churches two eggs of ostriches and other things which cause admiration and which are rarely seen, are accustomed to be suspended, that by their means the people may be drawn to Church, and have their minds the more affected. Again, some say, that the ostrich, as being a forgetful bird 'leaveth her eggs in the dust' and at length, when she beholdeth a certain star, returneth unto them, and cheereth them by her presence ... therefore be the aforesaid eggs suspended in churches, this signifying that man easily forgetteth God, unless being illuminated by a star, that is, by the influence of the Holy Spirit, he is reminded to return to Him by good works.[4]

An account written by nineteenth-century travellers in Greece describes the conversion in 1863 of the cathedral in Salonika to a mosque. Candles and ikons were replaced by ostrich eggs on strings.[5] They are much in evidence in Egypt, too, and appear in the religious buildings of Copts, Greeks and Moslems. I myself saw them in the Greek monastery church at Sinai. Since the charm should not be pierced, they are usually mounted in a metal frame, which then hangs by a single wire from the roof. Sometimes instead of real eggs they use imitations of fine Damascus porcelain,

[1] *Notes and Queries*, 15 September 1906, 10th Series, vi.206.

[2] Southey, Robert, 'Thalaba', iii, *Poetical Works*, London, 1849, IV.95.xxiv.

[3] Brewer, 925–6. Hasluck, F. W., *Christianity and Islam under the Sultans*, Oxford, 1929, i.233.

[4] *Notes and Queries*, 5 May 1894, 8th Series, v.348.

[5] Mackenzie, G. Muir and Irby, A. P., *Travels in the Slavonic Provinces of Turkey in Europe*, London, 1867, i.57.

coloured with signs in blue and purple – these being specially popular in the Middle East for averting the evil eye.[1]

Real eggs are also quite usual in Cairo as protectives for houses and shops. They seem to have been used as *ex votos* at a very early date. Hasluck refers to a tree worshipped at Mecca in pre-Islamic days, which had ostrich eggs suspended from it.[2] Still earlier examples have been found: the coloured shells in Punic tombs near Carthage and others at Mycenae, Greece. Five more examples, decorated with figures of animals, are painted and engraved, the incised lines filled with gold. These were imported into ancient Egypt and Phoenicia from the land of Punt (Somaliland), and their shells have been excavated from early tombs. Sometimes there were clay models of them. Petrie discovered an example at Hu, decorated with an imitated network of carrying cords. They are similar to those adapted by modern Africans as water-bottles, transported in a netting bag:[3] the modern Tuareg adorn these with leather, and I have seen examples of this work in Timbuktu.[4]

Coptic churches in Ethiopia also use quantities of votive ostrich eggs, which are fixed outside the churches and on top as a charm to ward off lightning and absorb all evil influence.[5] The cross in the Holy of Holies is often decorated with them.[6] In Greece and Turkey such eggs – presumably rather rare – must have been brought as curiosities by pilgrims from the Holy Land; this would also have invested them with an added religious significance. Other Orthodox churches acquired this custom from the Greeks. In Rumania ostrich eggs hang in numerous monastery churches of the Bukowina. I have seen them in the monastery at Putna, in Sucevita Monastery, in the church at Voronets, and also in the little mountain chapels of Sinaia. Saborna Crka, the Serbian Orthodox Cathedral in Peć, said to be almost 800 years old, contained in 1902 glass chandeliers from which ostrich eggs

---

[1] Bassili, William, *Sinai and the Monastery of St Catherine*, Cairo, 1962, 139, note 1, 140.

[2] Hasluck, i.232.

[3] Ingersoll, Ernest, *Birds in Legend, Fable and Folklore*, London, 1923, 54.

[4] See colour plate VIII.

[5] Information kindly supplied by Mr Haile of Addis Ababa, April 1966.

[6] Dalton, O. M., *A Guide to the Early Christian and Byzantine Antiquities*, London, 1903, 96.

were dangling.[1] Londoners can see them in the Greek Church of St Sophia, where they hang beneath the lamps. The priest-in-charge asserts that this is to prevent rats from running up to drink the oil.

These votive offerings are invariably suspended high up in the air, and an egg charm is often placed over an entrance, as at the Mar Behnam Syrian Monastery, Mosul.[2] Here the importance of the keystone in an archway probably originally gave its significance to the charm. Possibly two separate ideas are involved: the protection of an arch against collapse and good fortune for those who pass beneath.

While visiting Leeuwarden, Friesland, in the spring of 1965, I noticed an interesting ostrich egg inside the local museum. It hangs in a reconstructed apothecary's shop, suspended on a cord, and carved scenes represent people gathering medicinal herbs. Since this seems to be an isolated example, it was perhaps a curiosity, brought back and decorated by some traveller from the Middle East. But equally it may have served as an emblem of the early chemist's healing art.

LIGHTNING TALISMANS

If an egg was popular as a protective against the evil eye, it was also used as a talisman for many other purposes. In France and Tunis it wards off hail and unpleasant vermin;[3] Germans hung it up to repel mice, keep witches at bay and deflect the lightning flash.[4] For the last it was kept in the hole of a tree trunk or under the roof and only had an effect if it had first been flung over the house.[5] This is quite common, presumably because the house is enclosed within the sphere of the egg's protection. But then why not carry it round the walls instead of hurling it over the roof? Probably because lightning always strikes down from the sky. In north Europe, spared such terrible phenomena as earthquakes, but battered by violent electric storms, lightning is an aspect of nature unpredictable and feared. Thor, one of the prominent gods of northern mythology, is associated with thunder, and hence with lightning.

[1] Durham, M. E., *Through the Lands of the Serb*, London, 1904, 307.
[2] Information kindly supplied by Edmund de Unger.
[3] Bächtold-Stäubli, ii.687.
[4] *Ibid.*, 611, 687.   [5] *Ibid.*, 601, 609.

Schaudel mentions an old lady from Haut-Rhin (Alsace) who wore a small stone egg around her neck. She believed it would protect her against lightning,[1] and in Switzerland young girls used to wear a perfume-container which resembled the shape of an egg.[2] But in this case the purpose of the custom is not recorded.

The African Bantu possess a curious reversal of these lightning beliefs, imagining that the element actually appears in the form of a bird: the *hammerkop*, or 'tufted amber', seems to be connected with lightning, and to destroy one means causing a storm. The Xosas, on the other hand, blame a mythical bird, the *impundulu*, which means 'electric tram-car' – presumably a new tag to an old idea. When it darts down, lightning flashes and bad luck strikes the whole surrounding region. It lays a great egg, which the local doctor must destroy. If he does the lightning will stay away; otherwise it returns to find its property.[3]

REPELLING EVIL SPIRITS

A person struck by lightning becomes severely ill, even if he survives; so the importance of an egg as a protective overlaps into the field of preventative medicine. Though more recently, as life symbols, they have been used to cure disease, early man supposed sickness to be the work of malignant spirits: keep them away and you would be healthy. The Megrians of Georgia, whose cult resembles the Mithraic, touch their eyes with eggs, asking their god Mirsa to protect them from eye disease; and Germans bury one containing thirteen grains of salt and thirteen peppercorns in the garden as a charm against fever.[4]

When illness has set in, it can be healed with an egg, which repels evil spirits and strengthens the sufferer with its magic life-giving power. St Augustine refers to such beliefs in one of his sermons: 'Behold a neighbour, a friend, a maid or an old witch is

---

[1] Schaudel, L., 'Œufs Talismans dans les Murs des Maisons', *Revue de Folklore Français et de Folklore Colonial*, iii (Paris, March–April 1932), ii.88–9.

[2] *Ibid.*

[3] Werner, Alice, *Myths and Legends of the Bantu*, London, 1933, 223–4.

[4] Tseretheli, M., 'The Asianic (Asia Minor) Elements in National Georgian Paganism', *Georgica* (London, October 1935), I, 42. Bächtold-Stäubli, ii.632.

standing by your side carrying wax or an egg and saying, "Do this and you will be cured."[1]

Remedies of this kind are legion, especially in Germany, where they restore lost strength, alleviate fever, prevent horses coughing, and heal any number of miscellaneous ills. They also cure sores, so midwives in Schleswig-Holstein heal the navel of a new-born baby by hanging an egg up in the chimney. Epileptics derive great benefit from one placed in their bath, but it must have been laid by a chicken clucking for the first time,[2] and Swan, in his *Speculum Mundi* (1635), recommends owl eggs for drunkenness: 'The egges of an owle broken and put into the cup of an drunkard or one desirous to follow drinking, will so work with him that he will suddenly loathe his good liquor and be displeased with drinking.'[3]

A report from Spain, dated 1874, claims that storks eggs are just as effective.[4] The ancient Romans sprinkled cattle with raw egg as a salve for insect bites,[5] and short-sighted people touched their lids with the eye of a frog; it was then inserted in an egg and hung around the neck at full moon.[6] More practical, and less disagreeable, a German cure for the stiff joints of a horse suggested massage with an egg white.[7]

Childish ailments are cured by similar methods; on the Island of Dama, between New Guinea and the Celebes, a doll is laid on the sufferer's head, together with a betel-nut and half an egg-shell.[8] Evil spirits could make a child restive at night, so the Germans put an egg yolk in his evening soup and hung shells in a chain on the corner of the bed. This amuses the demons and prevents them molesting the child; French mothers used the same trick to outwit the spirit horse.[9]

---

[1] Wildhaber, 'Zum Symbolgehalt', 80. See Dölger, Franz Joseph, 'Das Ei im Heilzauber nach einer Predigt des Hl. Augustinus', *Antike und Christentum*, vi (1940), 57–60.

[2] Bächtold-Stäubli, ii.632, 634.

[3] Jones, *Credulities*, 462–3.   [4] *Ibid.*, 463.

[5] Vegetius, Renatus Publius, *Artis Veterinariae sive Mulomedicinae*, Republished (Leipzig, 1797) as Vol. IV, i–ii. of Schneider's Collection of Early Veterinary Works (See p. 48ff). The first printed edition was in 1528; Vegetius fl. in A.D. 450.

[6] Bostock, John, ed., *Pliny's 'Natural History'*, London, 1857, VI.32, xxiv.32.   [7] Bächtold-Stäubli, ii.635.

[8] *Ibid.*, 693.   [9] *Ibid.*, 692.

Indeed, the strength of an egg as a power of good was highly esteemed in many countries. Silesians said it was lucky to find the shells[1] and English farmers kept the last from an old hen as a talisman.[2] Germans used one to swear an oath, and the farm of a Mecklenburg peasant was actually destroyed because his wife refused to give evidence holding an egg, and told a lie.[3]

But it is a ceremony from Ghana which perhaps sums up more completely this aspect of an egg. The Nyanku-Sai Festival, celebrated in spring on 'New Year's Day', confirms the king in his position as ruler of the land by rejuvenating his divine powers. At a suitable moment the chief blacksmith puts an egg, a gift from the king, on top of his pile of tools. He prays to the royal ancestors, asking them to bless the State and crops. Next tools and egg are thrown into the river and everyone jumps in to search for them. If the egg is whole, omens are good for the coming year. But if it has broken the outlook is bad. Three eggs are then put on the bank – an offering to the god of the river, and part of the special food brought along for purification. After the ritual what remains – and this will include five eggs – is cooked; yams are mashed and hard-boiled eggs chopped and sprinkled over them. The ceremonial figure, who impersonates the king, is obliged to eat at least three mouthfuls of this dish. Through this elaborate festival, using eggs in a number of different ways, the king's magic strength is perpetuated.[4]

[1] Bonnerjea, 87.

[2] Hole, Christina, ed., *Encyclopaedia of Superstitions*, London, 1961, 150.

[3] Bächtold-Stäubli, ii.596.

[4] Meyerowitz, E., *The Divine Kingship in Ghana and Ancient Egypt*, London, 1960, 143, 173.

Chapter 7
Resurrection

wie die Vogel aus dem Nest gekrochen
hat Jesus Christus das Grab zerbrochen.
German saying

Touch me not, my name's Temptation,
My owd soul has gained damnation;
Season's come for your salvation,
For Egg's the life o' Resurrection.
Lancashire Pace-eggers Play: *Owd Nick*

REBIRTH

In early mythology the god who created the world egg often emerged from it himself in a different form. For the cosmic egg, according to Vedic writings, has a spirit dwelling within it which will be born, die and be born yet again. Certain versions of the complicated Hindu mythology describe Prajapati as forming the egg and then appearing from it himself. Brahma does likewise, and we find parallels in the ancient legends of Thoth and Râ. Egyptian pictures of Osiris, the resurrected corn god, show him returning to life once again, rising up from the shell of a broken egg.

In ancient Egypt the scarab's egg was also a resurrection symbol. But legends of another creature – the fabulous phoenix, mentioned by Herodotus – have become more widely known. This lovely mythical bird, which lived for hundreds of years, was consumed in flames when it died, rising again newly formed from the egg it had laid itself. Perhaps we see a trace of this idea in the old Yorkshire custom of burning egg-shells, so that they may 'come again'.

Red Bird, the Chinese phoenix – symbol of Yang, which represents masculinity – presides over the south and brings prosperity. It hatches from the sun egg and, like its Western counterpart, consumes itself and recreates from its own ashes; when it leaves, a curse falls on the land.[1] D'Alviella believed that the

---

[1] Newberry, J. S., *The Rainbow Bridge*, London, 1934, 52.

phoenix became confused with the eagle and, as such, was adopted by the Romans as an emblem of imperial power.[1] There is a delightful, rather garbled account given in Mandeville's *Travels*:

> In Egipt is the citee of Elyople that is to seyne the cytee of the sonne. In that cytee there is a temple made round after the schapp of the temple of Ierusalem. The prestes of that temple han all here wrytynges under the date of the foul that is clept Fenix. There is non but on in all the world. And he cometh to brenne himself upon the awtere of that temple at the ende of v. hundred yeer for so longe he lyueth. And at the v.c. yeres ende the prestes arrayen here awtere honestly and putten there upon spices and sulphur vif other thinges that wolen brennen lightly. And than the brid Fenix cometh and brenneth himself to askes. And the first day next after men fynden in the askes a worm. And the seconde day next after he fleeth his wey. And so there is no mo briddes of that kynde in all the world but it allone and treuly that is a gret myracle of god. And men may wel lykne that bryd unto god because that there nys no god but on. And also that oure Lord aroos from deth to lyue the thridde day.[2]

Here and in other accounts the phoenix is likened to Christ, ideal example of the firebird and of the old creator gods who rose with the universe from primeval darkness, as Christ rose from the darkness of death 'with healing in His wings';[3] a carved stone font in Alsleben bei Zerbst actually shows Our Lord at the Resurrection, appearing from the shell of an egg.[4]

Already by the first century A.D. the phoenix had become a Christian symbol; St Clement mentions the legend in his first Epistle to the Corinthians.[5] It is inscribed on funeral stones in early Christian art, and often appears in churches, religious paintings, ecclesiastical embroidery and stonework. I have in my possession a carving from Lithuania: a phoenix with outspread wings stands on the egg from which it has risen. The bird, with a broad span of feathers and three head-plumes, closely resembles the traditional Russian firebird, *tzarpitza*, immortalized in

---

[1] D'Alviella, Goblet, *The Migration of Symbols*, London, 1894, 95.

[2] Hamelius, P., *Mandeville's Travels*, London, 1919, ed. from MS. Cotton Titus C.XVI, 30–1.

[3] Mal. iv.2.

[4] Weinhold, Gertrud, *Das schöne Osterei in Europa*, Kassel, 1965, 14.

[5] Ferguson, George, *Signs and Symbols in Christian Art*, New York, 1961, 23.

Yershov's story.[1] The egg, evidently an Easter egg, is coloured red and marked with a cross. Taken together they represent the Resurrection, the triumph of eternal life over death, which Christian writers sometimes visualized as a spiritual rebirth for mankind through fire:

> *Enough the Resurrection,*
> *A heart's clarion! Away grief's gasping, joyless days, dejection.*
> *Across my foundering deck shone*
> *A beacon, an eternal beam. Flesh fade, and mortal trash*
> *Fall to the residuary worm; world's wildfire leave but ash:*
> *In a flash, at a trumpet crash,*
> *I am all at once what Christ is, since he was what I am, and*
> *This Jack, joke, poor potsherd, patch, matchwood, immortal diamond,*
> *Is immortal diamond.*[2]

As a vehicle of miraculous rebirth, the egg became an emblem of resurrection, and the Church incorporated it into the ceremonies of Easter. According to a German belief, to fulfil this ritual function the shell must first be shattered – by breaking it the blessing of Easter will enter in.[3] There is a related tradition, quoted by Brewer, that the world was hatched at Eastertide:[4] a broken egg provides food – just so Our Lord's body was broken to provide spiritual food. Certain liturgists even saw the egg as an emblem of the Eucharist, and maintained that it was every Christian's duty to eat one at Easter for that reason.[5] The Armenian Church has *ova de crucibus*, eggs of the Cross, since they say that both are symbols of eternal life. These special eggs are large and made of white glass.[6] Some European Easter egg designs elaborate these ideas: one I have seen, from the Salzkammergut, contains the image of Our Lord arising from the tomb with an

---

[1] Yershov, P. P., *Конёк–Горбунок*, St Petersburg, 1834, 54. See also Azadofskij, M. K., *Lines of Pushkin on the Humpback Horse* (periodical of the Pushkin Commission, 1936), 315–16, and colour plate VIII (this volume).

[2] Gardner, W. H., ed., 'That Nature is a Heraclitean Fire and of the Comfort of the Resurrection', *Poems of Gerard Manley Hopkins*, Oxford, 1950, 112. xxiii–xxxii.

[3] Bächtold-Stäubli, Hanns, ed., *Handwörterbuch des deutschen Aberglaubens*, Berlin, 1934–5, vi.1,327.

[4] Brewer, E. Cobham, *Dictionary of Phrase and Fable*, London, 1896, 402.

[5] Wildhaber, Robert, 'Zum Symbolgehalt und zur Ikonographie des Eies', *Deutsches Jahrbuch für Volkskunde* (Berlin, 1960), vi.78–9.

[6] Leland, C. G., *Gypsy Sorcery and Fortune Telling*, London, 1891, 78.

Easter banner. Another, from Oberammergau, shows the Paschal Lamb surmounting a red egg.

JEWISH PRACTICE

In the early days of the Church Christians observed all the traditional Jewish festivals, and up to the time of the Nicene Council in A.D. 325 the Church celebrated Easter at the same time as the Passover. *Pasch*, from which many words for the Christian Easter derive, originates from the Hebrew *Pesach*, meaning Passover. Thus in Europe there is the Dutch *Pasen*, Swedish *Påsk*, Albanian *Pashkë*, Spanish *Pasqua*, French *Paques*, Italian *Pasqua*, Welsh *Pasg*, English *Paschal* and the north English *Pace*.

The proximity of the two festivals is stressed in a piece of traditional weather-lore from Strasbourg, 'When *matza* [unleavened] bread and Easter eggs coincide, the sun shines through the wintry mist',[1] and in an anecdote from the early life of Karl Marx at Trier, whose immediate family were converts from Judaism:

> On the eve of Easter Karl would make his way to the ghetto of Trier. The Jewish Passover preceded the Christian Easter. The members of his Uncle Jacob's house would be busy baking *matza* and preparing stuffed fish for the Seder . . . in Brueckengasse [outside the ghetto] they were colouring eggs and roasting a piglet. Karl used to bring some *matza* home and eat it with thin slices of Paschal pork. We all have the same God, his aunts would say indulgently. Sacrilege! Henrietta [his mother] would storm indignantly, trembling in expectation of God's wrath.[2]

Young Karl Marx, brought up as a Christian, would eat what food he liked. But, of course, pork would be forbidden for a practising Jew, and eggs at Easter would have no significance for anyone brought up in the Jewish tradition. In 1919, when the Bolshevik Government in Hungary collapsed, Bela Kun fled to Vienna, where he was interned in a lunatic asylum. An attempt was made to assassinate him with a gift of poisoned Easter eggs. Being Jewish, he did not eat them, and this saved his life.[3]

[1] Pfleger, Alfred, 'Osterei und Ostergebäck im Elsass', *Schweizerisches Archiv für Volkskunde*, LIII (Basle, 1957), ii–iii.118.

[2] Ainsztein, Reuben, 'The Jewish Background of Karl Marx', *Jewish Observer and Middle East Review*, London, 23 October 1964.

[3] Romanelli, Guido, 'Bela Kun', *Encyclopaedia Britannica*, London, 1929, 14th Ed., xiii.517.

Eggs have long figured prominently in Jewish tradition, and it is conceivable that the Christian *pasche* egg has its origins in the Passover. The Jews use eggs on many important occasions. At Lag B'Omer, a festival of joy celebrated on the thirty-third day between Passover and Pentecost, children are taken by their parents into the countryside to picnic with coloured eggs. This feast honours the memory of a pious rabbi, Simeon ben Jachai. As long as he lived, it was said, the world existed by virtue of his piety. God's symbolic rainbow, signifying that He would not destroy the world, was no longer necessary. But after the Rabbi's death mankind again needed a token that the world would be preserved. They waited for a rainbow, and hastened its coming by staining eggs in rainbow colours.[1]

In some areas coloured eggs are also used for the Passover celebrations. Onion-peel is wrapped round the eggs, which are boiled and turn a rich golden hue. Jews in Greece eat numerous coloured eggs at this time of year. They are baked in the oven or hard-boiled. During the boiling coffee powder, onions and salt are added to turn the eggs dark brown. These are called *haminados* or *chamin* throughout the Middle East.[2] In Sislevitsh, near Grodno on the present Byelorussian-Polish border, Jewish children at the beginning of this century were given coloured hard-boiled eggs by their parents and relatives. These were called *valétshovnes*. They were not coloured with paint, since this would have made them ritually impure according to Jewish teaching. Instead, they were cooked with onion peel, or with hay, which turned them green.[3] Correspondents of the *Jewish Chronicle* wrote me their recollections of the custom from Smolensk (Russia), and Bialystok, Warsaw and Lodz (Poland), but it was unfamiliar to many.[4]

In these countries colouring Easter eggs was a particularly important Christian folk-tradition. The fact that many Jews from other nations did not know the custom implies that it was

---

[1] Information kindly supplied by Dr H. Abt of Johannesburg, South Africa.

[2] Information kindly supplied by Asher Moisis, Chairman of Athens B'nai B'rith, in a letter to me, published in the *Jewish Chronicle*, 18 March 1966.

[3] Patai, Raphael, ed., *Studies in Biblical and Jewish Folklore*, Bloomington, 1960, 341.

[4] I received many interesting letters in reply to my 'Coloured Passover Eggs', which was published in the *Jewish Chronicle*, 4 February 1966.

borrowed from the Christians. Passover lasts for eight days, and coloured eggs, when used, are restricted to the final seven. On the first evening, which is the most important, only white eggs appear.[1] Jews with Gentile friends and neighbours often gave them wine and *matza* at this time of year and received sometimes a gift of eggs called *hostinets* in exchange.[2] Perhaps it was through contacts like this that the custom of colouring eggs spread to the Jews.

The central feature of the traditional Jewish festival is the Seder meal, consumed at home in the evening. Passover commemorates the exodus of the Jews from bondage in Egypt, and the various foods prepared at this time all have a symbolic meaning. It is customary to drink four cups of wine during the meal to recall the four expressions of redemption, when God spoke to Moses: 'Wherefore say unto the children of Israel, I am the Lord, and I will bring you out from under the burdens of the Egyptians, and I will rid you out of their bondage, and I will redeem you with a stretched out arm, and with great judgments: and I will take you to me for a people.'[3]

A special platter contains the six ritual foods: a shankbone represents the Paschal lamb; *maror*, bitter herbs, recall the bitter slavery in Egypt; *karpas*, or greens – generally parsley – symbolize the bad food the Jews were given in captivity, and the salt water they are dipped in represents the tears which were shed; *haroset*, a mixture of apple, almond and cinnamon, stands for the mortar used by the Israelites in their Egyptian bondage; *matza* is the unleavened bread without which no Passover celebration can be complete.[4] God told the Israelites to prepare for a hasty departure from Egypt. There would be no time to bake proper bread: it would have to be unleavened, and the command has always been scrupulously observed to this day.

Always included among these foods is a roasted egg, the *betzah*. The meanings attached to this are various.[5] The most usual is that it represents the *hagigah*, or burnt offering, brought to the Temple

---

[1] Information kindly supplied by Mrs Joseph Lefkevitch of London.
[2] Patai, 340.   [3] Exod. vi.6–7.
[4] Idelsohn, Abraham Z., *The Ceremonies of Judaism*, New York, 1930, 41–2.
[5] Fishman, Isidore, *Introduction to Judaism*, London, 1962, 67. Levy, Isaac, *A Guide to Passover*, London, 1958, 57. Gaster, Theodor H., *Passover: Its History and Traditions*, New York, 1958, 54.

at major festivals. Brasch calls the egg a symbol of hope in the midst of persecution.[1] Since the Jews regarded it as an emblem of life in any case, it may here have represented, in part, the new life begun after release from captivity in Egypt.

As well as the ritual egg, which always appeared on the cere-monial platter, hard-boiled eggs in fish sauce or in salt water are a popular dish, as part of the main Seder meal.[2] This custom could originate from the Romans, who habitually began their meals with eggs. Just as the Romans reclined when they ate, so Jews de-liberately adopt a relaxed posture at the Passover meal; and, equally, eggs were considered symbolic of the freeman's food.[3] Statues of the gods were often adorned with egg-shaped caps,[4] as an emblem of this. Romans usually ended their meals with apples, hence the Latin saying, *ab ovo ad malum*,[5] which means from good to evil, but which translates literally 'from egg to apple'.

It was propitious to begin with an egg, since it was representa-tive of good. Romans also used *ab ovo* to mean 'at the beginning', with the double significance of the 'first course' and the source of life. Horace says he will not begin his description of the Trojan War with the twin eggs, i.e. at the beginning. This refers to the eggs of Leda, one of which hatched Helen of Troy: '*Nec gemino bellum Trojanum orditur ab ovo.*'[6]

The ritual Passover egg must always be roasted, a method not often used in this country in ordinary cookery, though Pope observes, 'The vulgar boil, the learned roast an egg', and there is a reference in Shakespeare: 'Truly, thou art damned like an ill-roasted egg, all on one side.'[7] It is known that the ancient Romans prepared eggs in this way. Martial writes, '*Et sua non emptus praeparat ova cinis*',[8] which suggests a further connection.

In western Jewish communities the roasted egg is a ceremonial item, not meant for eating. But in fact anyone who gets hold of

[1] Brasch, R., *The Star of David*, London, 1955, 44.

[2] Gaster, 64. Patai, 339.

[3] Gaster, 55. Fishman, 65.

[4] O'Neill, John, *The Night of the Gods*, London, 1897, ii.924–5. Payne Knight, Richard. *The Symbolical Language of Ancient Art and Mythology*, New York, 1876, 96. See ch. 1, note 108.

[5] Horace, *Satires*, i.3.

[6] Gubernatis, Angelo de, *Zoological Mythology*, London, 1872, ii.292–3.

[7] *As You Like It*, iii.ii.

[8] Martial, i, *Ep.* 56.

it the day after the festival will have good luck and see his wish come true.[1] Oriental Jews present it to the eldest son as an emblem of life, hope and protection for Israel's firstborn. Others feed it to the girls, for it will help them to a good marriage and plenty of children.[2]

The *betzah* arrived late in the Passover ceremony. Originally, in biblical times, during the exodus from Egypt, roasted lamb, un-leavened bread and bitter herbs were eaten. Later people came to the Temple in Jerusalem and offered Paschal lambs, which were roasted and eaten in family groups. Roughly when Our Lord was born, worshippers were bringing a *hagigah* – the burnt offering – for the festival, as well as a lamb. After the Temple was destroyed in A.D. 70 no further sacrifices could be made and the celebration took place at home, with symbolic foods. A shank-bone repre-sented the Paschal lamb; it was called *zeroa*, meaning 'the arm', and signified the outstretched arm which brought vengeance on the Egyptians. A roasted egg, replacing the *hagigah*, was laid beside it.[3]

The *betzah*, then, stands out as a comparative newcomer to the Passover, of puzzling origin. Though possibly a borrowed Roman dish, Jewish scholars seem agreed that it has acquired a significance similar in spirit to that of the Christian Easter egg, standing for resurrection.[4] Here the word is understood loosely in the sense of spiritual rebirth – to a new life after bondage in Egypt and to the hope of redemption after persecution.

Both Christians and Jews regard death as a temporary state. Judaism believes that there is a world to come and that the soul, deathless and immortal, will return to the Maker who created it:[5] 'And I will dwell in the house of the Lord for ever.'[6] The resurrec-tion symbolism of the egg is underlined by its important role in death ceremonies. Eggs are the first food given to Jewish

---

[1] *The Jewish Encyclopaedia*, New York, 1903, v.54.

[2] Levy, 58.

[3] Fishman, 67. Levy, 57. Gaster, 54.

[4] Newman, Louis, *The Jewish People, Faith and Life*, New York, 1965, 182. Brasch, 44. Gaster, 54. See also Simpson, William, *Jewish Prayer and Worship*, London, 1965, 47.

[5] Joseph, Morris, *Judaism as Creed and Life*, London, 1920, 143. Newman, 90–4.

[6] Ps. xxiii.6.

mourners.[1] They are served with salt because these two foods represent resurrection and incorruptibility, and every Jewish child is taught what these things mean.

An account of Jewish funeral customs in Turkey, from eighty years ago, tells how the Rabbi and a few friends returned after the service to eat supper with the family: seven different kinds of food, including hard-boiled eggs, were served.[2] There must surely be a connection between this and the seven full days of mourning observed by Jews. This period is called the *shiva*. Greek Jews say that eggs served at this time symbolize life, which 'rolls like an egg'.[3] The custom is comparatively recent. For in the centuries immediately following the death of Our Lord a dish of lentils was served to mourners, and it was only in the Middle Ages that this was replaced by a dish of eggs.[4]

In Jewish belief, some commentators say, joyful occasions must be touched with sorrow – a glass is always shattered at weddings and 'mourning eggs', if that is what they are, appear on the Passover table.[5] Libyans lay an egg on the Seder platter for each member of the family, and others are put out for relatives who have died.[6] Eggs are also eaten on another sad occasion, the Eve of the Ninth of Ab, when they are sprinkled with ashes.[7] This was the day when the first Temple was destroyed by Nebuchadnezzar, and the second by Titus. Just as Passover eggs, whatever their first origin, express a sense of spiritual rebirth after bondage in Egypt, and 'mourning eggs' a belief in the resurrection of the body, so eggs on this occasion could signify a desire that the Temple be resurrected – that is, rebuilt. The sprinkling of ashes will represent sorrow for its original destruction.

FUNERAL RITES

The practice of food-offerings to the dead within the Christian

---

[1] *Jewish Encyclopaedia*, v.54. Brasch, 221. Wagner, Leopold, *Manners, Customs and Observances*, London, 1894, 122–3.

[2] Garnett, Lucy M. J., and Stuart Glennie, J. S., *The Women of Turkey and Their Folk-Lore*, London, 1891, ii.33.

[3] Information kindly supplied by Asher Moisis.

[4] Schauss, Hayyim, *The Lifetime of a Jew*, New York, 1950, 252.

[5] *Jewish Encyclopaedia*, v.54.

[6] Information kindly supplied by the Rev. Vassily James.

[7] *Jewish Encyclopaedia*, v.54. Levy, 57.

era is recorded of no less a person than St Monica, mother of St Augustine, who wrote in his *Confessions*:

> Whenas my mother therefore had one time brought unto the oratories erected in memory of the saints, as she was wont to do in Africa, certain cheesecakes, and bread and wine . . . so soon therefore as she found this custom to be countermanded by that most famous preacher, and the most pious prelate Ambrose . . . and for that these funeral anniversary feasts, as it were, in honour of our dead fathers, did too nearly resemble the superstition of the Gentiles, she most willingly forbare it ever after: and instead of a basket filled with the fruits of the earth, she now had learned to present a breast replenished with purer petitions, at the oratories of the Martyrs.[1]

Such habits, strange though they may seem to Western Christians, have flourished among the Orthodox down into modern times. In some areas of Russia, for instance, relatives offered a corpse money, butter and eggs, saying: 'Here is something for you; Marfa has brought you this. Watch over her corn and cattle, and when I gather the harvest do thou feed the chickens and look after the house.'[2]

The family of anyone strangled or drowned took pancakes, alcohol and red eggs to the grave, where they poured out the alcohol, broke open the eggs and offered these with the pancakes to the *Rusalkas*, female water sprites. Meanwhile this rhyme was said:

> *Queen Rusalka*
> *Maiden fair*
> *Do not destroy the soul*
> *Do not cause it to be choked*
> *And we will pay homage to thee.*[3]

This ritual might be connected with the idea of the egg as a life sacrifice,[4] although even here the alcohol and pancakes could be intended for the sprites and the eggs as symbols of resurrection. The plea 'do not destroy the soul' bears this out, and so – as we shall see later – does the colour of the eggs.

Orthodox Christians in Russia celebrate the memory of the

[1] Watts, William, ed., *St Augustine's Confessions*, London, 1919, 1.6.ii.269.
[2] Jones, William, *Credulities Past and Present*, London, 1880, 472.
[3] *Ibid.*, 470.
[4] See ch. 2.

dead on the Ancestor Days, which are particularly associated with the week after Easter – St Thomas's week – and the week preceding Trinity, the seventh week after Easter, which is called *Rusalia*. The Monday of St Thomas's week was called *Radunitsa*, or 'Ancestors' Day', and the Tuesday 'Day of the Dead'.

The congregation assembles and names are handed in of those for whom memorial prayers are to be said.[1] In the church at Kolomenskoye, near Moscow, I saw innumerable eggs, with some other foodstuffs, heaped in dishes on special tables during one of the festivals in 1963. In the seventeenth century ancestor wakes were held on those dates by the whole parish. A dish of porridge and honey was placed on the lectern, pancakes brought by the congregation were set around it on the floor, and coloured eggs were offered. At one time these were placed upon the graves.

Such feasts of the dead are often associated with nature. Moroccan Jews eat 'mourning eggs', coloured with onion peel or coffee, at the Feast of Tabernacles[2] – Succoth, which is, in part, a harvest festival. The Hindu vegetation feast, Holi, is also a feast of the dead; some people kindle fires and throw two statues of a man and a woman – Kāmadeva and Rati – into the flames: an egg and a hen are flung in with them. The occasion commemorates the death of these two and their subsequent resurrection, assisted by the egg.[3]

And so in old Russia, at the spring Shrovetide festival, when plants grow again after the winter, simple people thought that their dead would come to life, or at least that they would be easier to communicate with. They took eggs to the cemeteries, some of them fried, as these were thought to be particularly effective, broke them on the graves and flung them over their shoulders. This was because a ghost would never speak to one face-to-face.[4]

The tomb is more a symbol of resurrection in the Orthodox Church than it is in other branches of Christendom. At the most important feast of the dead, Vespers are sung on Easter Day in the four corners of the graveyard and painted wooden Easter eggs are laid on the graves. Each year the previous batch are taken away and fresh ones substituted. This custom is still observed by

---

[1] Sokolov, Y. M., *Russian Folklore*, New York, 1950, 188, 190–2.
[2] Information kindly supplied by Edgar Samuel of London.
[3] Eliade, Mircea, *Patterns in Comparative Religion*, London, 1958, 414.
[4] Sokolov, 188.

Russian Orthodox communities in the West,[1] and probably in Russia itself.

Feasts of the dead are held in Bulgaria too, and on Easter Monday an egg is placed on every grave.[2] In Montenegro black mourning eggs, called *korotna jaja*, are dyed in boiling alum and laid on family tombs.[3] The Hutzuls, Orthodox Ukrainian mountaineers in the eastern Tatras and Bukowina, perform these rituals, elsewhere associated with Easter, on St George's Day.[4]

Jon Visensky, a Galician monk, writing in 1597 about 'the horrors of Russian folklore', mentions cakes and eggs carried to graves on St George's Day.[5] Serbs lay red eggs on the graves of their dead;[6] and the Setukese of old Estonia, evangelized by the large Orthodox monastery at Petseri, still take coloured eggs to the graveyard on Easter Day and bury them – calling to the dead, 'Christ is Risen.'[7]

Ukrainians buried eggs in their family graves on St Thomas's Day, one of the Ancestor Festivals.[8] In Bosnia and Herzegovina a plate of *žito* – sweet boiled wheat with an egg in the centre – is at once laid on the spot where there has been a death. When the corpse is removed from the house, the *žito* is thrown after it. Sometimes an egg is broken on the same spot.[9] In Poland, not, of course, predominantly Orthodox, but formerly part of Tsarist Russia, coloured eggs used to be laid on the graves at carnival time, and afterwards were given away to beggars.[10]

Travellers in Greek Macedonia in 1919 saw many village graves enclosed by a wooden fence. Attached to this was a glass case

---

[1] Information kindly supplied by Archbishop Alexis of Meudon, Administrator of the Russian Orthodox Exarchate in Paris.

[2] St Clair, S. G. B., *A Residence in Bulgaria*, London, 1869, 77.

[3] Spicer, Dorothy, *The Book of Festivals*, New York, 1937, 338.

[4] Roheim, G., 'Hungarian Pageant: Hungarian Calendar Customs', *Journal of the Royal Anthropological Institute*, lvi (London, 1926), 235.

[5] *Ibid.*, 369. Mansikka, V., *Religion der Ostslaven*, Helsinki, 1922, 235.

[6] Bächtold-Stäubli, ii.615.

[7] Ränk, Gustav, 'Ostereier in Estland', *Schweizerisches Archiv für Volkskunde*, LIII (Basle, 1957), ii–iii, 142.

[8] Bächtold-Stäubli, ii.615.

[9] Wenzel, Marian, 'Graveside Feasts and Dances in Yugoslavia', *Folklore*, lxxiii (London, Spring 1962), 3.

[10] Seweryn, Tadeusz, 'Les Œufs de Pâques Polonais et Hutsules', *Schweizerisches Archiv für Volkskunde*, LIII (Basle, 1957), ii–iii.173.

containing dried fruit, flowers or coloured eggs. Sometimes it hung from the burial cross itself.[1] In Greece on Holy Saturday many families go with the priest to the cemetery, where a service is held beside the graves of their dead relatives. Children who come are rewarded with eggs and buns. At Kastania, in Lacedaemon, many families take Easter food – red eggs, cheese and bread – to the cemetery, after the Easter Resurrection service, and lay these on relatives' graves.[2] After a funeral in Greece, guests used to eat a frugal meal of fish, vegetables, eggs and nothing else. Since eggs are not a fast food, the Greeks presumably eat them, like the Jews, as resurrection symbols.

In Metaxades, western Thrace, when anyone has died in the previous year, the family paints eggs dark blue or black, and takes them to the cemetery on Easter Monday. Several are laid on the grave; the rest are given to the poor.[3] Greek families in Asia Minor (Bithnyia), who had lost a son or daughter during the year, used at one time to distribute Easter buns, with a red egg embedded in the centre, to those who had attended the funeral. This was done on White Friday – the Friday after Easter – and each bun also had a flower stuck into it.[4] The Sunday following, known as Little Easter, a funeral egg was eaten among the Wallachians.[5] The time was highly appropriate for such observances, since Easter, the time of agricultural and spiritual renewal, stands at the beginning of the Christian year.

These widespread customs among the different rites of the Orthodox Church may have their origin in early Greek votive offerings for the departed. The Greek Church – the original church of Constantinople, from which the other branches grew – must have adopted certain customs from pre-Christian times; statues of Dionysus in Boetian tombs, for example, all clasp an egg.[6] Early funeral rites included a yearly, or more frequent, feast held at the tomb with the idea of perpetual renewal. This 'never-ending meal', known as the Death Feast, was carved on a

---

[1] Goff, A., and Fawcett, H. A., *Macedonia*, London, 1921, 169.

[2] Megas, George A., *Greek Calendar Customs*, Athens, 1958, 110.

[3] Arnott, Margaret, 'Die Ostereier in Griechenland', *Schweizerisches Archiv für Volkskunde*, LIII (Basle, 1957), ii–iii, 192–3.

[4] Megas, 111–12.

[5] Wildhaber, Robert, *Wir färben Ostereier*, Bern, 1957, 1.

[6] Eliade, 415.

stone set up on the grave. A series of early Spartan reliefs, dated seventh to sixth centuries B.C., show two seated figures being offered a cock and an egg;[1] and scenes on Athenian vases show that baskets of eggs were left on graves.[2] A cup containing five hen's eggs, dated late fifth century B.C., was found in a tomb on Rhodes, and a grave in the Acropolis of Mycenae contains an ostrich egg.[3] Nilsson has collected many similar examples.

Such offerings could have been connected with the Orphic mysteries, where eggs were regarded as sacred objects.[4] Plutarch, after a dream, would not for a long time eat them.[5] He was thought to be 'infected by Orphic and Pythagorean notions, and to be refusing eggs just as certain people refuse the heart and brains, because he held an egg to be taboo as being the principle of life'. Alexander, discussing this with him, says that 'in the orgiastic ceremonies in honour of Dionysus an egg is among the sacred offerings as a symbol which gives birth to all things, and in itself contains all things'.[6] Macrobius, in the *Saturnalia*, says: 'Ask those initiated in the rites of Father Liber, in which an egg is the object of reverence on the supposition that it is in its spherical form the image of the universe.'[7] Achilles Tatius notes: 'Some assert that the universe is egg-shaped and this opinion is held by those who perform the Orphic mysteries'.

These quotations are from Harrison's *Prolegomena to the Study of Greek Religion*,[8] in which the author believes – I think wrongly – that the egg in these rites has a purificatory significance. She cites Lucian, who mentions eggs, together with Hecate's suppers, as the refuse of purification, and also quotes Ovid:

> *Then too the aged hag must come,*
> *And purify both bed and home,*
> *And bid her, for lustration, proffer*
> *With palsied hands both eggs and sulphur.*[9]

[1] Rouse, W. H. D., *Greek Votive Offerings*, Cambridge, 1902, 5–7.

[2] Harrison, J. E., *Prolegomena to the Study of Greek Religion*, Cambridge, 1903, 630.

[3] Wildhaber, 'Zum Symbolgehalt', 78. Nilsson, Martin P., 'Das Ei im Totenkult der Alten', *Archiv für Religionswissenschaft*, ii (Leipzig, 1908), 532.

[4] See ch. 1.

[5] Plutarch, *Symposiacs*, ii.3.

[6] Guthrie, W. K. C., *Orpheus and Greek Religion*, London, 1935, 254.

[7] *Saturnalia*, vii.16.691.   [8] 628–30.

[9] *Ars Am.*, ii.330.

Colour Plate XI Ukrainian eggs, decorated by the batik (wax-resist) technique; the work of refugees living in England and the United States. Particularly noteworthy are the designs showing Christian symbols: the cross, a church, fishes; symbols of fertility: ears of wheat, the rake, the tree of life with two deer, other representations of animals (deer, horses), emblems of the sun; Ukrainian regional designs, mostly non-geometrical in form. The design top centre, showing a quatrefoil-like motif, is called 'The Forty Days of Lent'. Like many of these eggs, this is the work of Mrs Olena Jenkala (London).

Colour Plate XII Wooden eggs. The eggs in the centre (6) are Polish, the remainder Ukrainian. The Polish eggs are painted, certain of the traditional designs bearing comparison with motifs used in the Ukraine, Slovakia, Rumania and elsewhere. See colour plates XI, XIV, and XV. Designs based on the fir tree, ear of corn, sun, tree of life and swastika are worth noting. Bottom left of the Polish group is an egg resembling some of the 14 Ukrainian examples. Many designs of this type are found in the Carpatho-Ukraine and Bukowina. The Ukrainian eggs are polished, then engraved, the incisions being filled with colour.

Ovid's view, however, is late and is not proof, since it may well be a misinterpretation of earlier practices. Harrison draws the conclusion that from being propitiatory offerings to the dead, and hence purificatory, eggs acquired a general use for this purpose.[1] It would be rash to claim that this was never at any stage the case, but it seems to ignore the point that they are an almost universal – and rather obvious – symbol of resurrection, and were probably used by the Greeks in this connection. Orphic beliefs, after all, contained this idea. While her theory – that association with the dead explained the food taboo – could hold good, the sacred integrity of a resurrection symbol would fit better.

Old Syrian burial memorials show eggs as part of a funeral feast.[2] Barondes, describing the Michaux Stone, an egg-shaped rock covered with Assyrian writing, says the idea of this derives from decorated ostrich eggs, which have been found in ancient Assyrian and Egyptian tombs.[3] Certainly egg-shells, the significance of which we can only guess, have been found in very early tombs. For instance, in excavations at Los Millares, southern Spain, ostrich egg-shell bowls, probably of ritual significance, have been found and dated 2,400–1,400 B.C.[4]

Wildhaber believes that such offerings were sacrificial and, noting that the placing of eggs in graves is of prehistoric origin, refers to finds from Telod, Eleusis, Corinth, and from Etruscan graves; to early artificial eggs of limestone, aragonite, marble and clay found in Egyptian, Punic, Greek, Roman, Etruscan, Gallo-Roman, and Christian graves, and notes that marble eggs were placed with the relics of St Balbina and St Theodora.[5]

Despite the undoubted importance of such practices in Greece and the influence of later Greek culture through the medium of the Orthodox Church, these death ceremonies appear in a far wider area. The Maoris of New Zealand put an egg into the hand of a dead person before burial.[6] In India the Khasis of Assam place an egg in the navel of a corpse;[7] the Hill Savaras in the south

---

[1] Harrison, 630.

[2] Wildhaber, 'Zum Symbolgehalt', 78.

[3] Barondes, R. de Rohan, *China, Lore and Legend and Lyrics*, London, 1960, 7–8, pl. 2.

[4] Cles-Reden, S. V., *The Realm of the Great Goddess*, London, 1961, 198.

[5] Wildhaber, 'Zum Symbolgehalt', 77.

[6] *Dictionary of Folklore, Mythology and Legend*, New York, 1949, i.341.

[7] *Ibid.*

buried cremated human remains with a broken egg;[1] and a Hindu custom, if a man dies under an inauspicious star, is to throw a piece of iron and an egg on to the pyre during cremation.[2] The Lepchas, Tibetans living in Sikkim, scatter eggs upon their friends' graves.[3] In China, 100 days after a death, a banquet is prepared and dishes of hard-boiled eggs are served.[4]

Further west, the Yezidi Kurds celebrate their spring festival in mid-April by placing boiled wheat and eggs on family graves. They also exchange coloured eggs at this time of year and take a holiday from work.[5] These people – their name means 'angel-worshippers' – believe that God retired when He created the world, giving it into the keeping of Malak Ta'us, the peacock angel; their ideas are a blend of Christian, Jewish, Moslem, Zoroastrian and pagan elements.[6]

Even in England duck eggs have been found in a jar inside a child's grave in East Anglia,[7] and in Switzerland an egg painted gold was hung on the lid of a dead child's coffin.[8] Enamelled eggs were excavated from a fourth-century grave at Worms,[9] and, more recently, at an Allgau funeral in 1700 three eggs and three little lights were set out on a loaf of bread.[10] Indeed, within the last sixty years, at Beihingen in Ludwigsburg, an egg was actually buried with the corpse.[11] All these grave ceremonies are much too scattered for it to be feasible – or even necessary – to track each one to an original source.

[1] Hutchinson, Walter, ed., *Customs of the World*, London, n.d., i.481.

[2] Abbott, J., *The Keys of Power: a Study of Indian Ritual and Belief*, London, 1932, 221.

[3] Arundell of Wardour, Lord, *Tradition, Principally with Reference to Mythology and the Law of Nations*, London, 1872, 307.

[4] Gray, J. H., *China*, London, 1878, i.306.

[5] Drower, E. S., *Water into Wine*, London, 1956, 8, 25–6, 38.

[6] Glasenapp, Helmuth von, *Non-Christian Religions*, New York, 1963, 231–2.

[7] Lethbridge, T. C., *Recent Excavations in Anglo-Saxon Cemeteries in Cambridgeshire and Suffolk*, Cambridge Antiquarian Society, 1931, Quarto Publications, N.S., iii.33–4, 85. I am indebted to Dr H. R. Ellis Davidson for this reference.

[8] Bächtold-Stäubli, ii.615.

[9] Wildhaber, *Wir färben*, 2. I wrote to the Worms Museum, and the Director, who was unable to say whether the eggs were from a Christian burial or not, mentioned several similar finds in the area.

[10] Bächtold-Stäubli, ii.616.

[11] *Ibid.*, 615.

An Egg at Easter

SPIRITUAL PERPETUITY

Customs of the Orthodox countries can be traced back to a probable root in the Church of Constantinople, and hence to early pre-Christian Greek rites, such as the Orphic, in which the egg played so important a role. But the custom is, as we have seen, exceedingly far-flung and examples occur among the most disparate cultures, both in Europe and elsewhere. Even if one tried to put forward the rather unlikely answer of a common Indo-European source, this would not solve the problem. The Jewish custom, since it is comparatively recent, might – as already suggested – derive from the Romans; and thence, perhaps, via the Etruscans, in whose burial paintings eggs appear, from the Greeks.

But this still leaves other cultures unaccounted for. Are we not therefore obliged to turn back still further for an explanation, and to seek it in the ancient recurring myth of a world egg, from which a living creator god is born, dies and is born again? The association of the egg with funeral rites in all these scattered regions is consistent enough to imply some obvious solution. Purification, propitiation and sacrificial food offerings – the alternative explanations usually offered – though they may sometimes be valid, do not sufficiently account for the universality of the belief. Eggs are easily destructible and putrefy quickly, so that they would not be natural purificatory objects. Nor are they rich or rare enough to be the first choice for propitiation. The same might be said to apply to sacrifice, but where they are chosen for this particular purpose it is precisely as life substitutes or life symbols that they are being used.[1] It seems then that burial, graveyard, funeral and remembrance eggs are being used in identically the same manner as symbols of resurrection.

The desire for immortality is a basic human need. We are unwilling to believe that life ends in death, either for ourselves or for our family and friends. Most religions encompass in one form or another ideas of resurrection, reanimation or spiritual perpetuity. Even primitive thought patterns, which have evolved nothing as elaborate as the world egg idea or anything approaching it, contain an element of this belief.

For Christians the egg must mean hope and resurrection.

[1] See ch. 2.

Melito, a second-century bishop of Sardes, refers to *ovum spes*,[1] and St Augustine compares it to hope of eternal life – both as yet unrealized and awaiting fulfilment. In medieval Germany a death in the house was indicated by eggs and wax laid in front of the main entrance, no doubt for the same reason – the wax possibly being the antithesis of decay.[2]

Ostrich eggs found in early Christian graves stress the idea of resurrection. According to ancient custom, each member of the congregation in Angers (Anjou) Cathedral takes one as a gift for the Bishop, who is seated there on Easter morning,[3] perhaps because they performed a Passion play there in which the Mary's took two ostrich eggs out of the Holy Sepulchre.[4] In the Middle Ages it was quite usual to place a coloured egg in the representation of Our Lord's tomb during the Easter liturgy.[5] Sometimes the three officiating priests took up the eggs, usually ostrich eggs, and laid them on the altar as they exchanged the traditional greeting, 'Christ is Risen.' This custom was observed in Reims and Rouen until the eighteenth century.[6] Often the eggs were adorned with silver, and there are records of others enriched with gold, pearls and precious gems. One, mentioned in the inventory of Mainz Cathedral, came from a sixteenth-century church in Halle.[7] A traveller to the Holy Land in 1662 noticed ostrich eggs hanging directly above the Sepulchre of Our Lord,[8] and in Rumania they are traditionally placed in any church which is a necropolis; at Sucevita Monastery one hangs from a chandelier close to the founder's tomb.[9]

Christian resurrection beliefs which collected around eggs sometimes took elaborate and complex forms, as in the following legend from Pomerania: A village woman threw away two bad

[1] Kraus, F. X., *Real-Encyklopädie der christlichen Alterthümer*, Freiburg -im-Breisgau, 1880, 394–5. Wildhaber, 'Zum Symbolgehalt', 78.

[2] Bächtold-Stäubli, ii.615.

[3] Van Gennep, Arnold, *Manuel de Folklore Français Contemporain*, Paris, 1947, I.iii.1,325.

[4] Chambers, E. K., *The Mediaeval Stage*, Oxford, 1903, ii.36. This was still being performed in the eighteenth century.

[5] Wildhaber,'Zum Symbolgehalt', 78.

[6] Weinhold, 17.

[7] *Ibid.*, 18.

[8] *Ibid.*, 17.

[9] Personal observation, October 1963.

eggs, but when they touched the ground gold coins rolled out. The inscription on them said that they were made by a man who was in her kitchen. She went and found the man, but he immediately died.[1]

A possible explanation of this baffling tale is that it had been used to explain the doctrine of the Resurrection in language that a peasant could understand, but that the original meaning had subsequently been forgotten and omitted. In this interpretation the eggs which have gone bad represent the human body decayed in death. Man, in his ignorance, would see no further than this were it not for the intercession of Our Lord, who redeemed him by ransoming his immortal soul, symbolized here by the golden coins.

Gold was often taken as an emblem of immortality – as in early medieval art – since it never tarnished or decayed, and coins also underline the idea of ransom. Christ brought us the message of salvation, the inscription on the coins, but man who 'sees through a glass darkly' could not fully comprehend it and, without true understanding of what he was doing, killed the Saviour. Hence the woman, by going into the kitchen, unwittingly causes the death of the man who is there: 'Father, forgive them, for they know not what they do.' Why is he in the kitchen? This must be the hearth, centre of home life, stressing the doctrine that Christ came down on earth, to be with mankind and live in a humble way. Such a story, told in familiar idiom, would make the doctrine easier for the simple mind to grasp. The focal point is the egg, which, as it 'dies' or decays, brings forth the golden coins of the soul, which never fade, and represent life everlasting.

[1] Bächtold-Stäubli, ii.628.

Chapter 8
Christian Eggs

When Yule comes, dule comes,
Cauld feet and legs;
When Pasch comes, grace comes,
Butter, milk and eggs.

Harings Harings white and red
Ten a penny Lent's dead
Rise dame and give a Negg
Or else a piece of Bacon
One for Peter two for Paul
Three for Jack a Lents all,
Away Lent away.
Traditional Easter Rhymes

CATHOLIC AND PROTESTANT

Curiously enough, in spite of the considerable significance attached to eggs in many world religions, some Scottish Presbyterians will not touch Easter eggs, which they regard as examples of 'Popish idolatry'. In 1914 a visitor to Galloway found that local people had never heard of them. A woman living at Isle of Whithorn said her grandfather would not even allow her to cook eggs for breakfast on Easter Day, 'lest she be doing something that savoured of Popery'. In such areas, where the spirit of the Covenanters is strong, Easter was never kept at all. The same writer was told by a leading Dumfries solicitor that he only knew Easter eggs from seeing them in shop-windows, and was not aware of any customs attached to them.[1] I myself was told much the same in Orkney as recently as 1966.

Early British settlers in the Pennsylvania Dutch (German) area of America were mostly Quakers and Presbyterians from Scotland and Ireland, who did not celebrate either Christmas or Easter. This would have been 'Dutch Popery';[2] not that everyone was prepared to accept such a state of affairs with a good grace.

---

[1] Banks, M. Macleod, *British Calendar Customs: Scotland*, London, 1937, i.41.
[2] Shoemaker, Alfred L., *Eastertide in Pennsylvania*, Kutztown, 1960, 4.

An 'Old Presbyterian', writing to a local Pennsylvania newspaper in 1882,[1] disparages the '"Anti-Easter dogma" of the Presbyterian Church. Not even a word, or prayer, or any blessed and glorious resurrection hymns were even alluded to in all of the services of yesterday [Easter] morning.'[2]

That Christians should completely ignore the commemoration of Our Lord's Resurrection will strike many people as strange. But even the less severe within the Puritan tradition looked on the pleasures of Easter with a jaundiced eye. Brand, writing in 1777, sternly remarked that:

> Eggs stained with various colours in boiling, and sometimes covered with leaf gold, are at Easter presented to children at Newcastle, and other places in the North – they ask for their Paste Eggs, as for a fairing, at this season. This custom, which had its beginning in childish superstition, seems to be ending in a way not unsuitable to its origin. This is also a relique of popish superstition which, for whatever cause, had made eggs emblematic of the resurrection.[3]

Swift, satirizing contemporary squabbles between Protestant and Catholic, evidently thought them equally childish and used eggs to illustrate his point:

> ... the two great empires of Lilliput and Blefuscu. Which two mighty powers have, as I was going to tell you, been engaged in a most obstinate war for six and thirty moons past. It began upon the following occasion. It is allowed on all hands, that the primitive way of breaking eggs before we eat them, was upon the larger end: but his present Majesty's grandfather, while he was a boy, going to eat an egg, and breaking it according to the ancient practice, happened to cut one of his fingers. Whereupon the Emperor his father published an edict, commanding all his subjects, upon great penalties, to break the smaller end of their eggs. The people so highly resented this law, that our histories tell us there have been six rebellions raised on that account; wherein one Emperor lost his life, and another his crown. . . . It is computed, that eleven thousand persons have, at several times, suffered death, rather than submit to break their eggs at the smaller end. Many hundred large volumes have been published upon this controversy: but the books of the Big-Endians

---

[1] *The Easton Daily Argus*, 10 April 1882.

[2] Shoemaker, 47–8.

[3] Brand, John, *Observations on Popular Antiquities*, Newcastle, 1777; 343 (in the 1810 edition).

have been long forbidden, and the whole party rendered incapable by law of holding employments. During the course of these troubles, the Emperors of Blefuscu did frequently expostulate by their ambassadors, accusing us of making a schism in religion, by offending against a fundamental doctrine of our great prophet Lustrog . . . for the words are these: 'That all true believers shall break their eggs at the convenient end', and which is the convenient end, seems, in my humble opinion, to be left to every man's conscience . . . to determine.[1]

Here, big and small ends are used to represent major doctrinal differences. But Swift's metaphor was not as improbable as he supposed. In ancient times Aristotle believed that the small end, if unusually pointed, would hatch out a cockerel. This was because the principle of life was supposedly located in that particular part of the egg.[2] Swift's account embraces much the same idea, the major Christian doctrines representing life in the spiritual sense. The debate has continued; in England—Lincolnshire for example—to break an egg at the small end was, even comparatively recently, thought unlucky.[3] The Danes used to make a three-way egg-cup – one angle for Germans, who used to eat eggs sideways; another for French and Italians, who preferred them broad end up; and a third for Jews, who placed the tip uppermost.[4]

LENTEN RULES

Whatever certain Protestants may have felt about eggs at Easter, the Roman Catholic Church had long since rationalized their use in such ceremonies. To appreciate the part they played, we must go back to the third and fourth centuries, when a Lenten fast was first adopted – a period of forty days to imitate the time which Our Lord spent fasting in the wilderness. During the reign of Pope Gregory the Great it was agreed to abstain from meat and all dairy products such as milk, cheese, butter and eggs.[5] For this purpose fish eggs, such as cod's roe or the 'wombe of a luce',

[1] Swift, Jonathan, *Gulliver's Travels*, Oxford, 1954, 53–4.

[2] Bächtold-Stäubli, Hanns, ed., *Handwörterbuch des deutschen Aberglaubens*, Berlin, 1929–30, ii.641.

[3] *The Gentleman's Magazine*, London, 1833, i.590–3.

[4] Wollin, Nils G., *Äggkopar, Äggstallase och Äggställ*, Stockholm, 1962; pamphlet.

[5] Whittick, Arnold, *Symbols, Signs and Their Meaning*, London, 1960, 180.

counted as eggs and not fish.[1] These rules became law, though they were never strictly enforced in the case of milk products in either Britain or Scandinavia, due to the lack of oil and other foods which could be satisfactorily substituted. Perhaps this was why the Celtic church of Iona was so strikingly different. We are told that, in the time of St Columba, Lent was carefully observed, but in a distinct way. Throughout the entire period, Sundays only excepted, no food might be taken until the evening, when supper consisted of bread, milk and eggs.[2]

In the early days of the Church Lent was a sterner period than it is today; indeed, in Germany not only might eggs not be eaten, they could not even be offered for sale.[3] Various foods were progressively given up in the preceding period until the complete fast began on Ash Wednesday. Those who broke the rule and ate milk products in countries where this was not permitted, donated alms to atone for their fault. A steeple of Rouen Cathedral, France, was called the Butter Tower because the money to build it was given for this reason.[4]

Offenders were not always so lightly dealt with: a man who ate meat on a fast day in March 1629 was beheaded the following July.[5] This happened in England. So did the case of a certain Thomas Freburn, who lived in Paternoster Row. His wife longed for pork one Lent, and her devoted husband duly obtained a pig for her. Unfortunately, this was found out and the offender summoned by his landlord, who was Garter King-at-Arms. Next he was brought before the Bishop, and finally to the Lord Mayor, who put him in the stocks, the flesh of the whole pig loaded on his shoulders. Eventually he was freed through Cromwell's personal intercession, but a fine of £20, a lot of money in those days, was imposed. The unfortunate man was then turned out of his house and could not obtain another within four years, so infamous had he become. The pig which caused all the trouble was confiscated and duly buried.[6]

In Spain the law was also severe. At the Eighth Council of

[1] Hartley, Dorothy, *Food in England*, London, 1954, 208.
[2] Bullock, James, *The Life of the Celtic Church*, Edinburgh, 1963, 178.
[3] Becker, Albert, *Brauchtum der deutschen Osterzeit*, Jena, 1937, 43.
[4] Weiser, Francis X., *The Easter Book*, London, 1955, 61.
[5] Brady, John, *Clavis Calendaria*, London, 1815, i.231.
[6] *Ibid.*, 231–2.

Toledo it was decreed that anyone eating meat during Lent would be officially denied it for the rest of the year.[1] From the same rule the Hungarians derive their word for Easter – *Húsvét* – meaning 'The Festival of Meat'.[2] Further east the Orthodox Church also observes strict Lent restrictions. All dairy products are forbidden and additionally, in Greece, wine and olives are not allowed on Wednesdays or Fridays, nor during the whole of Holy Week. In 1958 there were still many, especially in the villages, who faithfully kept to this depressing diet. The first three days of Lent are the worst, when even water and bread are not allowed, though generally this is only observed by women, who can stay in the house. The men, as a token of respect, bring them special dishes, such as bean soup and walnut cakes.[3]

Other Orthodox countries were equally strict. Before the revolution Russians ate only vegetables, honey, fruit and bread. Hakluyt published details of sixteenth-century observances:

> They have foure Lents in the yeere, and the weeke before Shrofetide, they call the Butter Weeke. . . .
>
> The Russes begin their Lent alwaies 8 weekes before Easter: the first weeke they eate egs, milke, cheese and butter, and make great cheare with pancakes and such other things, one friend visiting another, and from the same Sunday until our Shrofesunday ther are but few Russes sober, but they are drunke day by day, and it is accompted for no reproch or shame among them.
>
> The next weeke being our first weeke of Lent, or our clensing weeke, beginning our Shrofesunday, they make and keepe a great fast. It is reported, and the people do verily beleeve that the Metropolitan neither eateth nor drinketh any manner of thing for the space of seven dayes, and they say that there are many religious men which doe the like.
>
> The Emperors Majestie eateth but one morsel of bread, and drinketh but one draught of drinke once in the day during that weeke, and all men that are of any reputation come not out of their houses during that time, so that the streetes are almost void of company, saving a few poore folkes which wander to and fro. The other six weekes they keepe as we do ours, but not one of them will eat either butter, cheese, egs or milke.[4]

[1] *Ibid.*, 239–40.
[2] Károlyi, Alexander, *Hungarian Pageant*, Budapest, 1939, 79.
[3] Megas, George A., *Greek Calendar Customs*, Athens, 1958, 75.
[4] Hakluyt, Richard, *The Principal Navigations, Voyages, Traffiques and Discoveries of the English Nation*, Glasgow, 1903, ii.423, 433–4. Voyages, 1557–8.

Until recently Rumanians existed on Indian corn and beans,[1] and during Passion Week the Bulgarians ate only black foods as a token of mourning: black bread, black olives, prunes and beans cooked in olive oil. [2] Even today Christian Albanians in Massachusetts, where their largest American community is located, abstain from dairy products and meat in Lent, and often fish and oil as well. The full fast may be limited to the first and last weeks of the period.[3]

It was not only the Catholics and Orthodox who observed such self-denial. In Lent, and on all fast days, Copts are not permitted dairy products or meat; and until noon nothing – not even water – is consumed. Clergy, heads of families and other people who are very devout take no food or drink of any kind for forty-eight hours before Easter.[4]

Naturally, Lent does not concern practising Jews. But one can compare the Christian prohibition against eggs, which were included among the dairy products, with that of Orthodox Jews on eggs laid during Sabbath. This was the traditional holy day of rest and, by rights, the hen too should be on holiday. Hence eggs laid then or on other feast days may not be consumed until the day following. If Sabbath-laid eggs are, through some oversight – perhaps on the part of a Gentile servant – muddled with those to be used that day, then all must be put aside until the Sabbath is over. Obviously it would be impossible to sort them apart.[5]

For Christians, until more recent times, Lent meant a very lean diet. But even so there were certain occasions when special foods were eaten. In central Europe on the Friday before Palm Sunday – the Feast of the Seven Sorrows of the Blessed Virgin Mary – a special soup containing seven bitter herbs is served at dinner. This *Siebenkräutersuppe*, recalling the bitter herbs of the Passover, contains *Brunnkress* (watercress), *Petersilie* (parsley), *Lauch* (leek), *Nessel* (nettle), *Sauerklee* (sour clover), *Schlüsselblume* (primrose) and *Spinat* (spinach).[6]

---

[1] Murgoçi, Agnes, 'Rumanian Easter Eggs', *Folk-Lore*, xx (London, September 1909), 296.

[2] Spicer, Dorothy, *The Book of Festivals*, New York, 1937, 69.

[3] Information kindly supplied by Joseph Chiaffitelle of San Costantino Albanese, formerly resident in America.

[4] Information kindly supplied by Mrs Jean Jenkins of the Horniman Museum.

[5] Garnett, Lucy M. J. and Stuart Glennie, J. S., *The Women of Turkey and their Folk-Lore*, London, 1891, ii.51–2.   [6] Weiser, 83.

The English call the fourth Sunday in Lent Refreshment Sunday, because it provided a welcome rest from the rigours of the fasting period, an idea which derives from the Gospel for the day, describing the feeding of the 5,000 by Our Lord. Known also as *Laetare* and Mothering Sunday, these different names come from the appointed psalm, which begins, 'Rejoice [*laetare*] ye with Jerusalem, and be ye glad with her',[1] and from the Epistle, which speaks of Jerusalem as 'the mother of us all'.[2] Servants and children living away from home used to return for a visit to their 'mother' church and to their actual parent. Maids in domestic service took a gift of flowers and a rich cake, baked by the mistress of the house and called, after an old French word, a 'simnel'. This was made with fruit and marzipan and decorated on top with a sugar bird's nest and eleven eggs – one for each month the girl had been away from her mother. Now that Lenten fasting is no longer so rigorously observed, the cake is often not presented on the traditional day, but prepared as part of Easter celebrations.[3]

EGG TITHES

Hungarians in some regions traditionally ate a special soup prepared with eggs on Good Friday. But these Lenten treats were rather exceptional. Certainly elsewhere in Hungary the most solemn day of Lent was spent in total fasting – not unusual in a traditionally Catholic country. It is more striking to see this observed by certain Puritan sects. Thus the Amish, the 'Plain Folk' of Pennsylvania, abstain entirely from food and drink till sundown on Good Friday.[4] Deriving their doctrine from the sixteenth-century Frisian Anabaptist, Menno Simons, the Amish are a dissident sect who began their emigration from the Rhineland in the early eighteenth century.

Catholic practice during Mass on the day of the Crucifixion is to approach the altar rails and render homage to the cross. In Europe, as late as the sixteenth century, this ancient custom – known as 'creeping to the cross' – was accompanied by an offering of eggs and other foodstuffs.[5] A certain William Keltie, preaching

[1] Isa. lxvi.10.
[2] Gal. iv.26.
[3] Wright, A. R., *British Calendar Customs: England*, London, 1936, i.42–3.
[4] Shoemaker, 21.
[5] Jones, William, *Credulities Past and Present*, London, 1880, 457.

in Dorset in 1570, alludes to it: 'The Roman Catholics offered
unto Christe eggs and bacon to be in his favour till Easter Day
was past.'[1]

The Bishop of Ossory (Ireland), in 1553, called it 'holding
forth the Crosse for egges on Good Friday', and Thomas
Kirchmeyer (1511–63) wrote:

> *Two priestes, the next day following, upon their shoulders beare*
> *The image of the crucifix about the altar neare . . .*
> *And after them the simple souls, the common people come,*
> *And worship him with divers giftes, as gold and silver some*
> *And others corne or egges againe, to poulshorne persons sweete.*[2]

Corn and eggs were similarly offered in some Italian churches. In
Bavaria touching and stroking the cross with eggs was also customary.[3] It was prevented by an edict against 'superstition and
false beliefs' in 1611. Even up to the Second World War in
Limousin, Van Gennep tells us that children came to kiss the
cross and gave an egg gift to the Vicar; but this was actually on
Easter Day or on the Monday following.[4]

This curious custom of offering eggs to the crucifix must have
an ancient history. Václavík traces it back to the grave feasts discussed in the previous chapter.[5] But probably it arises from the
egg-tithe formerly levied at Lent and at Easter in certain Western
European countries. These were part of the rent due from tenants
to their landlords. We are told that the Dean and other clerics of
St Paul's received a huge number of eggs,[6] and monks at
Worcester Priory ate them for supper at Easter.[7] Thirteenth-
century tenants and cottagers of Saperton, Gloucester, gave their
lord five eggs apiece, and he received 120 altogether.[8]

That was in 1262. During the fourteenth century egg-rents are
recorded from Droitwich and Chaddesley Corbett. The parish

---

[1] *Ibid.*

[2] Tyack, George S., *The Cross in Ritual, Architecture and Art*, Edinburgh,
1900, 58–9. Tyack quotes translation by Barnabe Googe in *The Popish
Kingdom* (reprinted London, 1880).

[3] Bächtold-Stäubli, ii.617.

[4] Van Gennep, Arnold, *Manuel de Folklore Français Contemporain*, Paris,
1947, I, iii.1,241.

[5] Václavík, Antonín, *Výroční Obyčeje a Lidové Umění*, Prague, 1959, 522.

[6] *Notes and Queries*, 15 May 1915, 11th Series, ii. 382.

[7] *Ibid.*, 22 April 1905, 10th Series, iii.303–4.

[8] *Ibid.*, 15 May 1915, 11th Series, ii.382.

register of St Michael le Belfrey, York, refers in an entry dated 1587 to 'certayne egges at East'r, due to the clarke by anncyent custome', and a record from 1726 of North Burton, also in Yorkshire, mentions the 'tythe of eggs on Good Friday', which belonged to the curate.[1] A rent of 140 hens and 1,300 eggs used to be paid to the Bishop of Lincoln, but this was abolished at the Reformation.[2] However, as late as 1829 villagers of Clee in Lincolnshire were still presenting their vicar with a tithe of Easter eggs collected in the parish.[3]

Sometimes other goods were offered. The Almoner of Worcester Priory paid one pair of gloves as rent for a house, and another for hiring a meadow, while pepper, cummin, cinnamon and other spices are mentioned as payments in the same county.[4] Occasionally eggs were merely a portion of such a tithe 'in kind'. A history of Leicestershire, dated 1795, describes how 'The Vicar of Garthorpe hath also tithe pigs, geese, ducks, chickens, apples, pears, and eggs, as usual in other places on Good Friday: two eggs for a hen and three for a cock'.[5]

In eighteenth-century Wales, the expected quota from tenants was two eggs per cock and one per hen – not quite such a heavy expense. An old farmer from Denbighshire, interviewed in 1894, remembered the custom as a child. He said the parish clerk collected the eggs, which were called *Wyau Pasc*.[6] In Ireland they became *tulken* eggs, and a correspondent of *Notes and Queries* recalled that as a boy in 1838 he had seen them levied from tenants for their landlords.[7]

These customs were not confined to Britain. In Limburg, Netherlands, the sexton collected eggs on behalf of the clergy and before the First World War Dutch Protestants gave coloured ones as a present to their minister.[8] In Germany early records from the

[1] Wright, i.95. *Notes and Queries*, 14 April 1906, 10th Series, v.285.
[2] Drake-Carnell, F. J., *Old English Customs and Ceremonies*, London, 1938, 92.
[3] Gutch, Mrs, and Peacock, Mabel, ed.; *Examples of Printed Folk-Lore Concerning Lincolnshire*, London, 1908, 193. *The Gentleman's Magazine Library: Manners and Customs*, London, 1883, 37–9.   [4] Wright, i.95.
[5] Billson, Charles J., *County Folk-Lore: Leicestershire and Rutland*, London, 1895, 75.
[6] Owen, Elias, *Old Stone Crosses of the Vale of Clwyd*, London, 1886, 192.
[7] Jones, 455–6.
[8] Meertens, P. J., 'Ostereier und Ostergebäcke in den Niederlanden', *Schweizerisches Archiv für Volkskunde*, LIII (Basle, 1957), ii–iii.126.

twelfth century refer to a tithe of eggs, called *Zinseier*. Thus the *Codex Falkensteiniensis* stipulates that certain estates of Upper Bavaria should supply 100 eggs, *'centum ova ad Pascha'*.[1] The custom evidently survived from the days of genuine barter. Farms in Württemberg made similar contributions in the thirteenth and fourteenth centuries, and payments of eggs and chickens were made by Estonian peasants to their landlord – generally a German Balt – or to the Lutheran Church.[2]

In the late Middle Ages this levy, known as the *Osterrecht*, or Easter tribute, extended into a general collection of eggs: 'as many as shall be available'.[3] An entry from the annals of a Diessen monastery dated 1506 notes the expenses of the egg-collectors – *'collectoribus ovorum'*.[4] Sometimes each household was required to provide a loaf and two eggs, or every peasant five eggs apiece for the Mayor.

These levies were not popular, as one can imagine. Carvings on choir-stalls in many Rhineland churches show a man threshing eggs with a flail.[5] This *Eier dreschen* – 'egg-threshing', as the people scathingly called it – referred to the gusto with which the tithe was imposed and gathered in. Later, when the original purpose had been forgotten, it became a tradition instead of a right. Legal action was brought in 1843 to determine whether the Vicar of Melton, Leicestershire, was entitled to tithe in kind from part of his parish. A witness was called to say that, according to ancient custom, the Vicar was paid eggs on Good Friday – two for a hen and three for a cock – but denied that it had ever been a tithe.[6]

In recent times Hungarians offered a few eggs to their local priest,[7] and French congregations often put baskets of eggs beside the steps of their church on Easter Day. Mothers, bringing their children to be blessed during Holy Week, walked round the altar

---

[1] Moser, Hans, 'Brauchgeschichtliches zu Osterei und Osterbrot in Bayern', *Schweizerisches Archiv für Volkskunde*, LIII (Basle, 1957), ii–iii.78–9.

[2] Ränk, Gustav, 'Ostereier in Estland', *Schweizerisches Archiv für Volkskunde*, LIII (Basle, 1957), ii–iii.140.

[3] Moser, 79.

[4] *Ibid.*, 79–80.

[5] Evans, E. P., *Animal Symbolism in Ecclesiastical Architecture*, London, 1896, 239–41.

[6] *Leicestershire Chronicle and Mercury*, 5 August 1843.

[7] Sándor, István, 'Ostereier in Ungarn', *Schweizerisches Archiv für Volkskunde*, LIII (Basle, 1957), ii–iii.179.

5a (above)　An egg in conjunction
with symbols of virility and reproduction: a detail from *The Garden of
Earthly Delights* by Hieronymus Bosch
(c. 1462–1516)
5b (right)　Death and birth: a detail from
The Temptation of St Anthony by Hieronymus Bosch (c. 1462–1516)

6 Sixteenth-century Flemish Egg Dance (1557); by Pieter Aertsz
(c. 1500–75)

7   Egg Dance after Pieter Bruegel (c. 1525–69); engraved (1558) by
Frans Huys (1522–62)

8 Egg Dance in the Netherlands; engraving by Hieronymus Cock
(c. 1510–70)

9   Seventeenth-century engraving of the Egg Dance; Joan Galle
(1600–72), after M. de Vos. The scene portrayed is from the sixteenth century

10 Egg Running in Switzerland (nineteenth century)

11   Indian Egg Dance (nineteenth century)

12   Moravian figure, standing about 5 feet, symbolizing the end of
winter. It is known as *Smrt* (Death), and is drowned in a river on
Palm Sunday

and laid a few eggs in a basket put there to receive them.[1] Houses
in the parish were also blessed by the priest, who arrived with
holy water, accompanied by a choir-boy. Sometimes – for example,
at Lugrin in Savoy – the eggs actually constituted his salary. Elsewhere, in the week following Easter he called and collected a gift
of eggs, money, sausages and salt. In Roussilon this *sal i ous* (*sel et
œufs*) still existed in 1945.[2] In the valley of the Frick (Aargau) the
sacristan used to receive a loaf and two eggs for performing the
same ceremony.[3]

Swedish farm-workers, too, were often paid with a set quantity
of eggs; maids, considered inferior, received only half the number.
Children also sometimes brought them for their teachers.[4] In 1956
a German postwoman in Slamen (Lausitz) was given some
coloured eggs as a kind of Easter box.[5] When the gift was made
to a priest or pastor it was, if not at Easter, on a suitable religious
occasion, such as confirmation; French children brought them
before making their first Communion.[6]

In England this ancient feudal relic was modernized at the close
of the nineteenth century. The *Church Times* of 1894 reported a
children's 'egg service' in Hambridge, celebrated on the Sunday
after Easter. The children, singing hymns, processed down the
aisle to the chancel steps, where two huge flower-decorated
baskets were waiting to receive their egg gifts. Next day these
were sent to the local hospital.[7] Today in the Church of St Mary
the Virgin, Westwell, an Oxfordshire village, each member of the
congregation contributes an egg. These, nicely sorted into brown
and white, are also donated to a hospital. The custom here is not
ancient but harks back to earlier practice.[8]

CARNIVAL TIME

Such offerings underline the important part which eggs played,

[1] Van Gennep, *Manuel*, I, iii.1,240.
[2] *Ibid.*, 1,252.   [3] Bächtold-Stäubli, ii.620–1.
[4] Eskeröd, Albert, 'Ostereier in Schweden', *Schweizerisches Archiv für
Volkskunde*, LIV (Basle, 1958), 11.
[5] Nickel, Johanna, 'Lausitzer Ostereier', *Schweizerisches Archiv für Volkskunde*, LIII (Basle, 1957), ii–iii.88.
[6] Van Gennep, *Manuel*, I, iii.1,242.
[7] *Notes and Queries*, 2 June 1894, 8th Series, v.429.
[8] Hole, Christina, ed., *Oxford and District Folklore Society Annual Record*,
Oxford, 1962, 8.

not only at Easter, but also at the pre-Lenten Carnival – a traditional period of rejoicing before the onset of the fast. The word
itself, which comes from Latin, means 'bidding farewell to meat',
and Carnival customs have this origin – the necessity for using up
all forbidden food. Hence the orgy of rich dishes on the days
immediately preceding Lent.

Mardi Gras (Fat Tuesday) the French call the day before Ash
Wednesday. To the Germans it is *fetter Dienstag*, which has a
similar meaning.[1] On our own Shrove Tuesday, the day for eating
pancakes, young people in Stirling, Scotland, presumably not
Presbyterians, enjoyed eggs which 'in the morning they dis-
coloured with various devices and in the evening boiled and ate
out in the field'.[2] The previous day was Collop Monday for people
in the north of England.[3] Again the meaning comes from Latin:
colpones are 'cut pieces', in this case slices of meat or bacon eaten
with eggs and butter. Langland, in *Piers Ploughman*, says:

> *And yet I say by my soule, I have no salt bacoun*
> *Ne no kokenayes, bi Cryst, coloppes for to maken.*[4]

Carnival fare can be unbelievably rich in Europe. Ponti, an
Italian town of Alessandria, prepares a gigantic omelette containing as many as 1,000 eggs, on the final Friday before Lent.[5] Pre-
revolution Poland and Russia named the concluding Carnival
week *Tluste Dni* and *Sedmica Syrnaja* – the Fat Days and Butter
Week. Russian peasants drove *Masslianitsa*, the Butter Goddess,
around on a sledge to the accompaniment of songs and fun, and
everyone enjoyed *blinni*, the traditional Russian pancake. Before
the fast began, the decorated figure was burnt.[6]

The last Saturday before Lent, Egg Saturday, was called Egg
Feast Day in Oxford because they were given to the students.[7]
Children called round the houses begging for gifts of eggs. If any-
one refused, broken crockery was thrown at their windows.
Aubrey says this custom was observed on the Saturday just before

---

[1] Weiser, 37.
[2] Reference kindly supplied by the late Kenneth Moss, London.
[3] Wright, i.3.
[4] *Piers Ploughman*, vi.284–7.
[5] Spicer, 180.
[6] Weiser, 38.
[7] Wright, i.1. Thiselton-Dyer, T. F., *British Popular Customs*, London,
1876, 52.

Easter. Youngsters in Oxfordshire went round with wooden clappers and small baskets, singing and demanding eggs. A householder who ignored them might find his latch wrenched off, or possibly worse damage.[1]

Greece celebrates Cheese Sunday, the last before Lent, as a day of merry-making. As one might imagine, cheese figures prominently in the dishes traditionally offered at supper. Besides cheese-pies and *tyrozonmi*, a blend of stewed herbs and cheese, milk-pies and macaroni are eaten. The meal is completed with eggs, hence the saying, 'With an egg I close my mouth, with an egg I shall open it again', alluding to the red hard-boiled egg with which the Lenten fast is broken.[2]

There were various ways of ritually 'closing one's mouth with an egg'. On the island of Skyros they suspend one left over after the meal from the ceiling with a piece of string. Everyone bumps this egg with his forehead, to make it swing about before catching it between his lips. In eastern Rumelia it is rolled across the table and you say, 'May Lent roll by, like this egg', before using it to 'stop your mouth'.[3]

Spanish-speaking countries do not generally stress eggs at Easter; but in Mexico empty egg-shells are an important feature of Carnival. These *cascarones*, whether coloured or gilded – the one in my collection is painted with green stripes – are filled with scraps of coloured paper, ashes or eau-de-Cologne, and broken against the heads of women and children. Sometimes sweets called *colacion* are mixed up with the paper. These are sold in all the markets. Women bring them in great baskets and sit, colouring the shells with paint daubed on from rags, or sometimes just from their fingers. Elaborate creations, covered with tin-foil, wax or coloured tissue, are more costly and presented as gifts to friends. This custom is not confined to Carnival. *Cascarones* appear at weddings, and indeed at any major festival. They resemble miniature versions of the great clay pot, traditionally broken at Christmas, emitting a stream of gifts and sweets.[4]

[1] Aubrey, John, *The Remaines of Gentilisme and Judaisme* (1686–87), London, 1881, 162.   [2] Spicer, 146. Megas, 70, 109.

[3] Wildhaber, Robert, 'Zum Symbolgehalt und zur Ikonographie des Eies', *Deutsches Jahrbuch für Volkskunde*, vi (Berlin, 1960), 83. Megas, 71.

[4] Starr, F., *Catalogue of a Collection of Objects Illustrating the Folklore of Mexico*, London, 1899, 77–9. See colour plate VI.

THE EGG FEAST

Easter was known as *Munadepühad*, the Egg Feast, in old Estonia, and in their folk-songs children ask about 'Easter, the lovely egg time'.[1] The Dutch always enjoyed an egg meal on the first day of Easter;[2] so did the Swedes, washing it down with a special 'Easter dram'.[3] French people served an omelette, or perhaps stuffed eggs, depending on local custom.[4]

Certainly it is not surprising that eggs figured so prominently in the joyful Easter fare which followed such a long and dreary fast. In England at least eight different kinds were eaten. Peacock eggs were set under broody hens as early as the eleventh century, but were perhaps too precious to eat, and we hear of turkey eggs similarly brooded in the sixteenth century, though they must surely have provided food too. The many varieties enjoyed included those laid by duck, plover, goose, sea-gull and guinea-fowl. Some people certainly did not eat them in large quantities, for 'One egg is gentility, two sufficient and more excess'. But both this and another old saying that 'All eggs hard roasted be grosse meat' are contradicted by the vast numbers prepared and eaten at Easter-time.[5]

In those parts of Scotland where the custom was observed, Easter was *Bas nan vibhean* – 'death day of the eggs' – because so many of them were devoured.[6] Boys and girls made oatmeal and egg cakes with some, boiled the remainder and ate them together as a little feast. Sometimes the boys stole and hid them until Easter, when they met secretly with their friends to have a pancake meal. Where this was the case – and stealing was sometimes an important part of the ritual – the feast took place in a cave or some other remote spot.

That eggs were so plentiful in Scotland is exceptional among northern countries. In Norway, much of which stretches up beyond the Arctic Circle, they were eaten as part of the normal diet, but by the wealthy upper classes rather than the population as a

[1] Ränk, 140.
[2] Meertens, 125.
[3] Eskeröd, 10.
[4] Joisten, Charles, 'Le Folklore de l'Œuf en Dauphiné', *Arts et Traditions Populaires* (Paris, January–March 1961), 60.
[5] Hartley, 208.
[6] Banks, i.38.

whole.[1] Production of eggs was presumably low, so they were only available to a small and favoured section of the community.

Easter eggs, however, are not unknown, especially in the milder south, for there is a saying, 'The hen which does not lay at Easter loses its head', and Norwegian children, like the young Scots, hide in the forest and prepare a meal of boiled eggs – either hens' eggs or wild birds' eggs. But very often the custom was introduced within living memory, perhaps as recently as the last twenty years, and was unlikely to have spread north without foreign influence – chiefly from travellers and sailors visiting their ports. The Gregorian Calendar, which permits of Easter falling between 22 March and 25 April, was not introduced into Norway until 1700; and the Julian Calendar, used until that date, caused it to fall some eleven days earlier. In such a chilly climate the prospect of finding wild birds' eggs so early in the year would not have been good.[2]

At Easter-time in Finland the birds of passage are still to come and local varieties have not yet begun to lay; so, as in parts of Norway, the egg feast is enjoyed at Whitsun, when eggs are more readily available. This is the case even today, when local conditions have altered.[3]

Similar geographical influence on local folk-custom seems to be common to much of the Baltic – for example, in Estonia they prepare coloured eggs, and this too is at Whitsun, no doubt for like reasons. But here the problem cannot have been so acute, for we read of boys and girls collecting Easter eggs from the woodland and water birds. Sometimes girls performed this task and presented the findings to their sweethearts. In any case domestic poultry was not a modern innovation in Estonia; there are records of a medieval tithe of eggs and chickens, paid by the peasant to his feudal lord.[4]

In Denmark, another northern Protestant land, Easter eggs have been a tradition of special importance. Now, especially since emphasis in the religious year has shifted from Easter to

---

[1] Weiser-Aall, Lily, 'Osterspeisen und Osterei in Norwegen', *Schweizerisches Archiv für Volkskunde*, LIII (Basle, 1957), ii–iii.131.

[2] *Ibid.*, 132.

[3] Vilkuna, Kustaa, 'Osterfeiern und Vogeleiersuchen in Finnland', *Schweizerisches Archiv für Volkskunde*, LIII (Basle, 1957), ii–iii.136.

[4] Ränk, 140.

Christmas, they do little more than provide an amusement for the children. All the same, no Danish Easter would be complete without hard-boiled eggs and mustard sauce, sometimes enjoyed with a drink of hot beer.[1]

In many countries eggs, so essential to Easter feasting, were given precedence over the Paschal lamb. Lewis Morris, who lived in Anglesey in the early eighteenth century, described the 'decent celebrations of Easter with dinner, eggs, Lamb or Kidd, even ye poorest family'. Every Easter dish prepared in the Welsh border country contained eggs as the principal ingredient, and they were also served at every meal.[2] The same was true of France, where, in addition to the usual omelette, egg salad and cake of eggs flavoured with rum were very popular; the cake was called a *pogne*.[3]

Easter foods in central and eastern Europe were prepared in advance and blessed by the priest before anyone thought of tasting them. In Hungary, by the time Good Friday had arrived the house was clean, the baking completed, and the eggs all decorated. Usually they were carried carefully to church.[4] Photographs of the Russian Orthodox church, St Peter and St Paul, in New York, show the local gipsy community surrounded by heaped baskets of Easter eggs, brought to receive the priest's special blessing.[5] Exiled Ukrainians living in Leicester also do this. The people of northern Bohemia arrived with eggs, bread and wine. Afterwards every member of the family ate some of this food at home; the animals too received a share to make sure that they would still be loyal to the house and bring good luck.[6] This custom was mostly observed in Catholic and Orthodox countries. Even the Orthodox Setukese Estonians took their particular Easter foods – eggs, cheese, butter and bread – to church on Holy Saturday to be blessed.[7]

[1] Cruickshank, Constance, *Lenten Fare and Food for Fridays*, London, 1959, 80. Uldall, Kai, 'Les Œufs de Pâques au Danemark', *Schweizerisches Archiv für Volkskunde*, LIV (Basle, 1958), 1–2.

[2] Owen, Trefor M., *Welsh Folk Customs*, Cardiff, 1959, 85.

[3] Van Gennep, Arnold, *Le Folklore du Dauphiné*, Paris, 1932, i.290.

[4] Spicer, 167–8. Károlyi, 79.

[5] Wright, Richardson, 'Easter Celebrations of the Gypsy Coppersmiths in New York', *The Journal of the Gypsy Lore Society*, xxvi (Edinburgh, 1947), 132–3.

[6] Information kindly supplied by Herr Hans Zühlke, of Stralsund.

[7] Ränk, 141.

Often the Easter lamb lay in a bed of green branches, surrounded by coloured eggs, the other food heaped round about,
and the whole ensemble prettily garnished with flowers and garlands.[1] The *Sarum Manual* contains two blessings: '*Ben. Carnis
Casei Butyri Ovorum Sive Pastillarum in Pascha*' and '*Ben. Agni
Paschalis Ovorum et Herbarum in Die Paschae*'.[2] Nicholas Dorcastor
(1554) refers to these forms for 'halowing of the Pascal Lambe,
egges and herbes on Easter Daye'.[3] So does the following passage
from a book curiously entitled *Frauds of Romish Priests and Monks*,
which also describes an Italian Easter table, groaning with good
things:

> On Easter Eve and Easter Day all the heads of families send great
> chargers full of hard eggs to the church to get them blessed, which
> the priests perform by saying several appointed prayers, and making
> great signs of the Cross over them, and sprinkling them with holy
> water ... These blest eggs have the virtue of sanctifying the entrails
> of the body, and are to be the first fat or fleshy nourishment they
> take after the abstinence of Lent. The Italians do not only abstain
> from flesh during Lent, but also from eggs, cheese, butter, and all
> white meats. As soon as the eggs are blessed, everyone carries his
> portion home, and causeth a large table to be set in the best room of
> the house, which they cover with their best linen, all bestrewed with
> flowers, and place round about it a dozen dishes of meat, and the
> great charger of eggs in the midst. 'Tis a very pleasant sight to see
> these tables set forth in the houses of great persons, when they ex-
> pose on side tables (round about the chamber) all the plate they have
> in the house, and whatever else they have that is rich and curious, in
> honour of their Easter eggs, which of themselves yield a very fair
> show, for the shells of them are all painted with divers colours and
> gilt. Sometimes they are no less than twenty dozen in the same
> charger, neatly laid together in the form of a pyramid. The table
> continues, in the same posture, covered all the Easter week, and all
> those who come to visit them at that time, are invited to eat an
> Easter egg with them, which they must not refuse.[4]

Today Italians still eat eggs with salad and lamb, a custom
which can be traced back to 1578.[5] Sometimes pastries called
corona di nove are baked; these are circular and decorated with

[1] Weiser, 190–1.
[2] Chambers, E. K., *The Mediaeval Stage*, Oxford, 1903, i.128.
[3] Jones, 451.   [4] *Ibid.*, 451–2.
[5] Perusini, Gaetano, 'Uova e Pani di Pasqua in Friuli', *Schweizerisches
Archiv für Volkskunde*, LIII (Basle, 1957), ii–iii.144.

Easter eggs. Children are given a *ciambella*, a cake made of flour, sugar and olive oil. For boys it is shaped like a horse with a handle of twisted dough to carry it by. Little girls get a dove stuck full of real feathers, which are attached to the mixture before the cake is baked. These *ciambella*, which are blessed on Holy Saturday and eaten on Easter Sunday, always have a coloured egg cooked in the centre;[1] in Calabria they are shaped like a man. Italian Albanians in the province of Potenza do not use whole eggs, but colour the outside of their cake with yolk, an old custom which they believe was brought across the water to Italy by their ancestors 500 years ago.[2] In Albania itself Orthodox Christian families prepare Easter bread which has whole coloured eggs embedded in it. The dough is marked with a cross.[3]

Václavík sees in such ceremonial pastries the remnants of an old magic rite, where ritual offerings of bread assured prosperity to family and community.[4] Certainly all over Europe eggs and cake are closely associated at this time of year. Generally speaking, in Orthodox countries and in the German areas Easter cake or bread is baked with eggs. Perhaps this custom too derives from the ancient tithes, when bread, as well as eggs, was often supplied to the feudal lord. Indeed, the Tithe Order of the Augsburg Hospital stipulates that the Easter bread must always be baked with Easter eggs.[5] Presumably beaten egg stirred in the mixture is what was meant. But it is not such a far cry from this to the pretty coloured egg inserted whole as a decoration.

Though it is more usual to find them cooked together, children in Hessen are given separately Easter eggs and a large pastry in different shapes: girls get a doll and boys a hare.[6] German settlers in the American 'Pennsylvania Dutch' country recreated their *Oschter Haws* – the *Oster Hase*, our Easter Hare – in the form of a cake.[7] This transplanted custom seems to have made its appear-

---

[1] Hazeltine, Alice, and Smith, Elva, ed., *The Easter Book of Legends and Stories*, New York, 1947, 228.

[2] Information kindly supplied by Joseph Chiaffitelle, of San Costantino Albanese.

[3] Information kindly supplied by Mrs Valeria Vrioni, formerly of Tirana.

[4] Václavík, 524.   [5] Moser, 81.

[6] Hain, Mathilde, 'Bemalte Ostereier in Hessen', *Schweizerisches Archiv für Volkskunde*, LIII (Basle, 1957), ii–iii.73.

[7] Shoemaker, 47, 49. Lichten, Francis, *Folk Art of Rural Pennsylvania*, New York, 1946, 231–2.

ance towards the end of the last century. Local bakers shaped the hare as though it were laying an egg – which was realistically placed below the tail. When customers objected, the egg was transferred to the stomach, but even this offended some people, and in the end the cake was baked without its egg. The Amish and other stern sects reject this custom outright, because the Easter Hare does not exist, and to say otherwise would mean telling a lie.[1]

In Germany proper the Schirgiswald cake manikin cradles a baked white egg inside its arms.[2] Silesian Easter bread men sport an egg face or stomach – in which case the hands are clasped across it.[3] One sees these still in Holland, with pink egg stomachs – or with an egg tucked under each arm.[4]

Elsewhere one finds a great variety of birds and curious animals. Spartans make a dolphin, and the dragon cake from Simi in the Dodecanese represents the mythical beast of old Greek legend. It has a red egg baked into its middle. Plainer, round pastries are suspended from the ceiling after baking, until Easter Day arrives, all sporting red eggs.[5] Another circular sweet cake from the island of Hydra – actually an Albanian community – off the Morean coast, contains no less than three, presumably emblems of the Trinity.[6]

Such cakes, which are baked all over Greece, are called *christópsomon*, the bread of Christ.[7] Often they are shiny on top and marked with a cross or with a contracted form of the Easter greeting, '*Christos Anesti*', meaning 'Christ is risen'. Both egg and cake should be baked on Maundy Thursday. Usually they are made with yeast left over from the day before – possibly this was thought to affect their potency – and contain all sorts of good things: dried fruit, spices, almonds, bay leaves. Those intended for children are doll-shaped, with a red egg in the middle or one at either end. Each woman bakes a large cake for her household, and a smaller doll-cake for every child, including nephews, nieces

---

[1] Shoemaker, 48. See plate 13.
[2] Weinhold, 38.
[3] Hahn, Konrad, *Deutsche Volkskunst*, Berlin, 1928, pl. 74.
[4] Meertens, 129.
[5] Wildhaber, Robert, *Wir färben Ostereier*, Berne, 1957, 28.
[6] Personal observation, Easter 1962. See plate 13.
[7] Spicer, 148.

and godchildren. Newly wedded girls must make one and present it to their mothers-in-law.[1]

Austrian children are given a nest-shaped cake, filled with eggs, as an Easter gift,[2] and in Slovenia – part of old Austria – delicious traditional breads and pastries are prepared. The basis is generally an excellent egg dough, spread with cream and filled with nuts, currants and dried pears. *Monih* – the monk – is for children: a plaited bread, about 1 foot long, shaped like a man and with an egg embedded in the mixture. Before baking, it is coated with yolk to make it nice and shiny. Istrians prepare a bird, with an egg serving as the head.[3]

In eighteenth-century Belgium, where toxophily was a national tradition, an egg-cake was the prize offered; the occasion was a guild sporting competition. A contemporary brotherhood of archers organized a shoot of their own, and carefully marked out the target with the stakes offered for each particular section. These were eggs, beer, custard and, farthest from the bull's-eye, water.[4]

French children are sometimes given a basket-shaped bread containing a red egg.[5] Armenians, less inventively, just plait the dough around it. Their *cheorig* mixture, which is used throughout the year, requires vegetable or dairy fat at Easter, instead of the usual mutton-grease.[6]

The flavour probably resembles a certain type of Portuguese Easter cake. These *folares*, some heart-shaped with eggs baked into the dough, some actually egg-shaped, and some just round, are made with eggs, flour, milk, yeast and olive oil. The variety popular in the north is filled with a mixture of small pieces of meat – veal, chicken, ham, pork and slices of sausage. These are all baked together, and the fat from the meat oozes out into the dough, making the texture softer. The sugar-cake is topped with hard-boiled eggs, but not the savoury one. There is also a sweet variety, flavoured with cinnamon or perhaps herbs, and this is a

[1] Megas, 96.

[2] Layard, John, *The Lady of the Hare*, London, 1944, 172.

[3] Jagodic, Maria, 'Über Ostereier und Ostergebäck in Slowenien', *Schweizerisches Archiv für Volkskunde*, LIII (Basle, 1957), ii–iii.159.

[4] Pieters, Jules, 'Œufs de Pâques en Belgique', *Schweizerisches Archiv für Volkskunde*, LIII (Basle, 1957), ii–iii.124.

[5] Van Gennep, *Dauphiné*, 290.

[6] Information kindly supplied by Dr Wolfhilde von König from an article by Mrs Margaret Arnott.

southern favourite. Yet a third type of Portuguese Easter sweet-meat is made entirely from sugared egg yolks. What little flour is used is only there to give the required consistency. These are called *pain-de-lo*. When the priest makes his Easter visit, he is given a gift of eggs, and this, like the cake, is called a *folar*. Some-times, when all the houses had been called at, an Egg Procession followed.[1]

Godparents are supposed to give their godchildren an Easter *folar* – a real egg-cake, shaped like a star or a bird.[2] This obliga-tion, variations of which one finds in other countries, stresses the Christian significance of eggs at the Easter festival. In Germany an egg used to be put in the cushion on which a baby was carried for christening, and the godfather also brought an egg when first he visited the infant. This egg was especially lucky if it had been laid between the days of the Blessed Virgin's birth and her Assumption into Heaven.[3]

Sorb children from the Lausitz received a handsome gift: Easter bread, a large cake, three pretzels and three coloured hard-boiled eggs. Traditionally these were yellow, red and violet. How-ever, if the godparent was mourning a recent bereavement, he or she gave only white eggs. If the death was some time past, dark eggs were given instead, but never red. The godparents bring these eggs in person at the first Easter after the child's birth, except where they live at a distance, when the eggs are fetched for the child on 'Young Easter' – the Sunday before Easter Day. From then on he is taken to fetch them himself and the custom continues until Confirmation.[4] In Hungary such egg gifts from godparent to child were given in front of the church, which suggests that it derived in some way from the *agape* – the love-feast of the early Christians.[5]

EASTER EGGS OF OLD RUSSIA

Polish Catholics in times past always halved a hard-boiled egg with an Easter visitor, the host consuming his share in the

[1] Spicer, 268. Oliveira, Ernesto Veiga de, 'Folares et Œufs de Pâques au Portugal', *Schweizerisches Archiv für Volkskunde*, LIII (Basle, 1957), ii–iii.152.
[2] Oliveira, 154.
[3] Bächtold-Stäubli, ii.637.
[4] Nickel, 86–7.
[5] Sándor, 179.

presence of his guest. But it was in pre-revolutionary Russia that the tradition of proffering Easter eggs assumed such immense importance. According to local hagiography, the custom comes down from Mary Magdalene, who was arrested by a centurion in Alexandria. She offered him an egg and he allowed her to pass.[1]

Another version says that she gave one to the Roman Emperor as a token of Christ's Resurrection.[2] Easter, the festival which commemorates it, is the focal point in the calendar of the Orthodox Church. Russian monasteries presented all visitors from Easter until Ascension Day with an egg, and this custom is still observed in expatriate establishments of Western Europe. At home the Lenten fast was broken at a family ceremony when the head of the household shared out an egg, distributing a piece to everyone present.[3] *Kulice*, the traditional sweet bread signed 'XB' – *Christos Voskrese* – was always surrounded with coloured eggs.[4]

When wishing a friend the compliments of Easter, an egg was pressed into his hand, and Brand, writing in 1777, quotes the Abbé d'Auteroche from his *Journey to Siberia*:

> Easter Day is set apart for visiting in Russia. A Russian came into my room, offered me his hand, and gave me at the same time an egg. Another succeeded, he embraced me, and also gave me an egg. I gave him in return the egg I had just received. The men go to each other's houses in the morning and introduce themselves into the houses by saying, 'Jesus Christ is risen.' The answer is: 'Yes, He is risen!' The people then embrace, give each other eggs, and drink a great deal of brandy.[5]

A more privileged nineteenth-century traveller in Russia wrote:

> Scarcely any material is to be named that is not made into Easter eggs. At the imperial glass-cutting manufactory we saw two halls filled with workmen employed on nothing else, but in cutting flowers and figures on eggs of crystal. Part of them were for the Emperor and Empress to give away as presents to the courtiers. The wax-fruit-makers and confectioners produce some pretty pieces of

---

[1] Information kindly supplied by Archbishop Alexis de Meudon.
[2] Information kindly supplied by Archbishop Alexis de Meudon.
[3] Cruickshank, 83.
[4] Information kindly supplied by Mrs Marina Bowater, London.
[5] Brand, 347–8.

workmanship, in elegant boxes filled with eggs of all sizes, in regular order, from the mighty ostrich egg down to the nightingale's, and all in wax and sugar. Very costly presents are also offered in egg-shells. Some are transparent, and in place of the yolk contain little fairy bouquets, and some have a magnifying glass neatly fitted in, and displaying pictures of saints and tiny angels couched in roses.[1]

It is well known that members of the Tsar's family once presented each other with elaborate eggs, designed by the court jeweller, Carl Fabergé, which were executed in gold and encrusted with precious jewels. The House of Fabergé was founded in St Petersburg, now Leningrad, in 1842, by Gustav, a descendant of Huguenot refugees who had settled on the Baltic.[2] When he retired, his son Carl took over the business and, through him, an old Russian folk-tradition was raised to the level of exquisite and expensive *objets d'art*.

His finest works were the eggs made for Tsar Alexander III and Tsar Nicholas II. The very first, a gift to the Tsarina from Alexander III, was of gold and white enamel. Inside, a gold yolk contained a golden hen with eyes of ruby, which in turn concealed a miniature crown. At the very centre hung a tiny ruby egg. The Tsar loved this so much that he arranged for Fabergé to create an egg every Easter as his gift to his wife. The whole conception closely resembled an egg in the collection of the Danish kings. This was probably quite deliberate, for the Tsarina had been a Danish princess, and the Tsar at that time was especially anxious to give her pleasure to help her forget the dreadful murder of his predecessor, Alexander II.[3]

The last ill-fated Tsarina received as her first Easter gift from her husband a strawberry pink egg, decorated with Cupid's arrows. Inside was a golden rosebud, which contained a tiny crown of diamond and ruby. Other royal eggs were of practical interest. The opening of the Trans-Siberian Railway was com-memorated by a silver egg engraved with a map of the route. A jewel marked every station. Inside was a gold clockwork train with crystal windows. A white-and-gold egg, honouring 300

[1] Dixon, J. H., 'The Paschal Egg: an Enquiry into Its Origin', *Northumber-land Legendary Tracts* (Newcastle, 1844), 3–4.

[2] Snowman, A. Kenneth, *The Art of Carl Fabergé* (London, 1953), 31–2.

[3] Snowman, 76, 78, pls. 313–16. Bainbridge, H. C., *Peter Carl Fabergé* (London, 1949), 71, 74.

years of the Romanov Dynasty, contained a steel globe showing how the Empire had been extended during that period. That was in 1913. Another egg contained a ship from the Baltic Fleet. One, made to commemorate the bicentenary of the founding of St Petersburg in 1703, was worked in pure gold and set with diamonds and rubies. When opened, the mechanism raised up a tiny gold model of Peter the Great's famous statue by the Neva, mounted on a sapphire pedestal.[1]

Most of these eggs are so rich and exquisite that ordinary people today cannot afford them, and they are in the collections of kings and queens. Our own Royal Family possesses a beauty, fashioned in a network of platinum and set with square-cut precious stones – rubies, emeralds and others – and encircled with pearls and scrolls of diamonds. It opens, revealing a cameo of the five Russian royal children.[2] This is typical of how they were always made, for the Tsar insisted that each egg must contain a surprise. The design, within and without, was left to the craftsman's discretion, so greatly did Alexander value his taste and workmanship.

The winter egg, one of Fabergé's loveliest creations, charmingly portrays the changing of the seasons. Carved from a single block of crystal and resting on another representing ice, this Easter egg is adorned with a frost of diamonds. Inside a diamond-and-platinum basket filled with snowdrops, executed in white quartz, gold and nephrite, depicts the promise of spring with its earliest blossoms.[3]

The last known to be exchanged, in 1916, was made of steel, decorated only with the date and the Tsarina's initials in gold – a wartime egg. Another, symbolic of the times, but rather less austere, was made for the Dowager Empress Marie, mother of the Tsar, in 1915. Embossed with two emblems of the Red Cross, it is not inlaid with precious stones and is finished in single, white enamel. The inscription reads: 'Greater love hath no man than this, that a man lay down his life for friends.' Today this egg is in the Virginia Museum of Fine Arts, U.S.A. Another in the same collection, presented by Tsar Nicholas II to his mother, is of gold, surmounted by a pelican in diamond and enamel feeding her

[1] Snowman, 34–5, pl. 325; 91, pl. 336; 93–4, pl. 341; 104, pl. 373; pls. 359–60. Bainbridge, 72, pl. 50; 82, pls. 321–3.

[2] Bainbridge, 73, pls. 51–2.

[3] *Ibid.*, pl. 60. Snowman, 104–5, pl. 374.

babies – the emblem of motherly love. It is inscribed: 'Visit our vineyards, O Lord, and we shall live in Thee.'[1]

A fine example, once in the collection of the late King Farouk of Egypt, is of mauve enamel, latticed with diamond ribbons. The surprise inside is a tiny golden swan, which swims in a lake made of a single aquamarine.[2] Fortunately for the ordinary collector, apart from such splendid ceremonial examples, the Russian Royal Family also presented more modest eggs to members of the court. These, usually of white porcelain, were stamped in gilt with the royal cipher and initials of the donor. During the war they were marked with a red cross on the back, no doubt because the Tsarina was President of the Russian branch. Since these eggs were intended to hang above the ikons, they are pierced and a ribbon is slotted through. Generally this is yellow, the royal colour, but wartime eggs have black. The same custom of presenting eggs to members of the Court spread to Bulgaria, a country greatly influenced by Russian culture. In pre-revolution days, the Bulgarian King and Queen gave each one of their courtiers an egg stamped with the royal crown and monogram.[3]

This ceremony was performed immediately after the midnight Resurrection service on Easter morning. Although it was late, presumably no one was ready for bed. In Russia the bells were rung all through the night – a practice, of course, no longer permitted in present atheistic times. This, and another particular Russian custom, do not seem to have reached to other countries. For forty days after Easter – that is, until Ascension Day – members of the aristocracy wore a necklace of tiny eggs, which traditionally had to include two eggs of Tula silver.

A woman was given an additional miniature egg each Easter by her husband and father. The whole strand was put on for the midnight service, and removed as soon as the forty days were over.[4] Many, made by Fabergé and other jewellers, were of precious stones. But some, like the one in my own collection, are quite simple. Mine contains nine miniature eggs, worked in traditional Russian style with stones from the Urals, enamel and

[1] *Ibid.*, 87–8, pls. 330–1; 108, pls. 382–4. Bainbridge, 73, pls. 56, 66.
[2] *Ibid.*, pl. 59. Snowman, 97, pls. 348–50.
[3] Urlin, Ethel L., *Festivals, Holy Days and Saints' Days*, London, 1915, 83.
[4] Information kindly supplied by Mrs Marina Bowater and Dr Wolfhilde von König. See colour plate VI.

Colour Plate XIII (a) Appliqué techniques. Top centre is an egg decorated with appliqué beads; this is Rumanian work. The remaining five eggs are Moravian, the shells being reddened by boiling with onion peel, or sometimes basil wood; paint was used for the black shell, bottom centre. The designs are achieved by attaching to the shells cut-out straw pieces, either dyed or natural colour.

(b) Slovak scratch-technique eggs. On these, shallow engraved designs are produced by scraping the surface colour. A notable motif is strawberries, and otherwise flowers, fruit and birds are common. Multi-coloured scratch eggs of this type are unusual.

Colour Plate XIV Sixteen Slovak and four Ukrainian batik (wax-resist) eggs. Various of the motifs symbolize the sun, birds' feet, the fir tree and ears of corn. The Ukrainian eggs, which form the bottom row and are all the work of Miss Marta Jenkala (see plate 19), show the similarity between certain Ukrainian and Slovak motifs. For comparison see also colour plate XX.

niello, a craft well known in Caucasia. Several are marked with the usual 'XB', standing for *Christos Voskrese* – Christ is risen.

It was not, of course, only the aristocracy who exchanged Easter eggs. The custom was widespread throughout the country and all classes of society. An old Russian folk-tale, 'The Brother of Christ', describes how a young man is told by his dying father to care for the poor. He sets out for church on Easter Sunday, taking with him many eggs to distribute. By the time he reaches the church, all the eggs but one are gone. This he gives to a dirty old man. 'You shall become my brother by the Cross,' he says to the youth, and the young man sees that it is Our Lord Himself.[1]

THE EGG AND THE EUCHARIST

Henry VIII received from the Pope an Easter egg enclosed in a silver case,[2] an instance of the extreme importance of the symbol as a ceremonial gift, but the Russian folk-tale above shows a still deeper significance. Ostrich egg-shells were thought worthy to house the relics of SS Benoit, Thierry, Aman, Crespin and Crespianin, and St Rupertus, Bishop of Salzburg, who died in 718, has a basket of eggs as his emblem.[3]

Hieronymus Bosch, in the central panel of the 'Garden of Delights', places a symbolic egg beneath the Tree of Life, but Christian art more usually associates this emblem with the Blessed Virgin Mary – one hangs suspended above the holy pair in Piero della Francesca's painting of the Madonna and Child; and in a fifteenth-century Valence painting a basket of eggs is placed at the feet of the Virgin of Enguera.[4] Art critics who have made a study of such symbolism believe that an egg represented the Immaculate Conception. According to Descargues, the central panel of the 'Millennium', another work by Bosch, represents the perfection of the unspotted Virgin, and this is borne out by Albertus Magnus: '*Si ovo struthionis sol excubare valet, cur veri solis ope virgo non generaret?*'[5] (If the sun can hatch the eggs of the

---

[1] Magnus, Leonard A., *Russian Folk Tales*, London, 1916, 162.

[2] Cox, Marian Roalfe, *An Introduction to Folklore*, London, 1895, 31.

[3] Descargues, Pierre, 'Chefs d'Œuvre à Partir d'un Œuf', *Connaissance des Arts*, clxxxii (Paris, April 1967), 94.   [4] Descargues, 96. See plate 3.

[5] Quoted by Meiss, Millard, 'Ovum Struthionis, Symbol and Allusion in Piero della Francesca's Montefeltro Altarpiece', *Studies in Art and Literature for Belle da Costa Greene*, Princeton, 1954, 95.

ostrich, why cannot a virgin conceive with the aid of the true sun?)

Certainly this emblem lay at the very heart of the Easter story. In the tale, 'The Brother of Christ', Our Lord reveals Himself when given an Easter egg; and the seventeenth-century writer, Georg Stengel (1635), tortuously likens an egg to the virtues of Our Lord – His humanity, for example, and to the Sacraments He instituted, such as baptism and the Eucharist.[1]

The sixteenth-century *Codex Sandor* makes the comparison more direct: the white is Christ's pure soul, the golden yolk His godliness.[2] A Fabergé egg, designed for Alexander III, stresses this idea by enclosing the Resurrection scene within a crystal globe, as though it were in a monstrance.[3] Another piece of his work, a golden chalice, has an egg of lapis lazuli inserted into the stem.[4] An analogy with Francesca's egg can be found in the huge cathedral-size eggs hung in Russian churches – though Francesca's egg is of normal size.

According to an unusual local custom at Barcelona Cathedral, on the Feast of Corpus Christi an egg dances all day long in the water-jets of a fountain.[5] This important Catholic festival, which falls on the Thursday after Trinity, has a close link with Easter, for it commemorates the institution of the Eucharist, an essentially joyful event, which cannot be suitably celebrated on Maundy Thursday, a time of sorrow and fasting.

The symbolism of this dancing egg is curious, but rather apt; for Our Lord is the 'Sun of Righteousness',[6] and the real sun was supposed to dance in the sky on Easter Day, the time of the Resurrection.[7] Brand notes sourly: 'It is a common Custom among the vulgar and uneducated Part of the World, to rise before the Sun on Easter-Day, and walk into the Fields. The Reason of which is to see the Sun Dance.'[8]

Similarly, at Corpus Christi it is said to shine more brightly. A Lithuanian song describes how 'The sun dances over a mountain of silver; he is wearing silver boots upon his feet'.[9]

[1] Wildhaber, 'Zum Symbolgehalt', 78.
[2] Sándor, 178.   [3] Snowman, 79, pl. 317.
[4] Bainbridge, pl. 23.
[5] Alford, Violet, *Pyrenean Festivals*, London, 1937, 42.
[6] Mal. iv.2.   [7] Banks, i.43.   [8] Brand, 267.
[9] Cirlot, J. E., *A Dictionary of Symbols*, London, 1962, 90.

The dance of the egg in silvery water-jets must be symbolic of joy on this happy occasion. But, according to a metaphor much loved in the Middle Ages, the dance was a means of portraying life and even death; the whole of Our Lord's life on earth, and His Passion, have been described in the form of a dance:

> *Tomorrow shall be my dancing day:*
> *I would my true love did so chance*
> *To see the legend of my play,*
> *To call my true love to my dance:*
> *Sing O my love, O my love, my love, my love;*
> *This have I done for my true love.*
> *Then was I born of a virgin pure,*
> *Of her I took fleshly substance;*
> *Thus was I knit to man's nature,*
> *To call my true love to my dance:*
> *Sing O my love, O my love, my love, my love;*
> *This have I done for my true love.*[1]

When the egg can so obviously be taken as a symbol of the Eucharist, it is logical enough that it was once the Christian duty of Catholics to eat one at Easter-time. The people of west Eifel in the Rhineland said it should be consumed either first thing in the morning or in the evening,[2] and the Slavs have a pleasant variant of this. In Russia, for example, red Easter eggs are sometimes served embedded in salt on a wooden dish, and the Croatians have a specially constructed platter with sockets to hold the eggs. Known as the credence dish, this sometimes contains four eggs, emblematic of the four Apostles, or, far more often, twelve, carrying out the idea of the twelve disciples at the Last Supper.[3] A pile of salt heaped in the middle echoes the words of Our Lord: 'Ye are the salt of the earth: but if the salt have lost his savour, wherewith shall it be salted?'[4]

---

[1] Dearmer, Percy, ed., *The Oxford Book of Carols*, Oxford, 1928, 154.
[2] Bächtold-Stäubli, vi.1,327.
[3] There is an example of this in the Belgrade Ethnographic Museum.
[4] Matt. v.13.

Chapter 9

Red Eggs

And moreover the common people use to carry in their hands one of these red eggs, not only upon Easter day but also three or four days after.

Hakluyt

der Himmel ist blau,
die Eier sind rot
ich will dich lieben
bis in den Tod.

Traditional German

MAGICAL RED

Throughout Europe one finds that, while all colours of the rainbow appear, red is by far the most usual for egg-dyeing, especially in countries of the Orthodox faith. 'Oh, when will Easter come', runs a Macedonian children's rhyme, 'bringing with her red eggs?'[1]

The colour is credited with wonderful powers; according to a Roman legend, a hen laid a red egg when Alexander Severus was born, and a seer who was consulted foretold that the child would become a mighty emperor.[2] In Ireland we find Yeats writing in his *Fairy and Folk Tales of the Irish Peasantry* that 'Red is the colour of magic in every country, and has been so from the very earliest times. The caps of fairies and musicians are well-nigh always red.'[3] This is borne out by archaeology – red chalk and other red colouring matter is a fairly constant feature of early burials, dating from the Stone Age and later.

In modern times, too, the colour has been thought propitious, ensuring protection against malevolent powers. It is apotropaic throughout Europe, much like blue in the areas of Moslem tradition. In Scotland it kept the witches at a distance.

[1] Abbott, G. F., *Macedonian Folklore*, Cambridge, 1903, 26.
[2] Čerbulenas, K., 'Marguču Menas Lietuvoje', *Mokslas ir Gyvenimas*, Vilnius, March 1967, 27.
[3] 61.

Cows, especially prone to their influence, had red thread and a rowan cross tied around their tails:

> Ran *tree and red threed*
> *Pits the witches to their speed.*[1]

Red-furred animals, such as the fox, were often thought blessed: in parts of Germany they even bring Easter eggs. But plainer-coloured cows needed protection from *ran* – the rowan tree, whose power lies in its brilliant red berries, as, of course, with that other magical plant, the holly.

A red substance, coral, guarded children against the evil eye.[2] The ancient Romans used it, and today their descendants all over Italy wear a small, red, pendant object – resembling a pimento. Variants of this custom are common to both northern and southern Europe. But the idea that the red hair of Thor – god of thunder and hence of lightning – shields one from this particular hazard, is peculiar to the north.[3]

RENEWAL OF LIFE

In Rumania years ago red eggs were known as love apples – they symbolized the longings of young girls.[4] For Slovenians they were emblems of fervent passion, an idea perhaps exchanged with Austria in the days of the Empire, since a Tyrolese girl traditionally secured a young man's love with a present of red eggs.[5] They say in Freithof that these eggs must be boiled in dye on Good Friday over a fire blessed by the priest. Alternatively, the girl should have found her eggs in the graveyard on Easter Saturday, and sent them to her lover without revealing her name. If this is faithfully observed, the young man's heart will burn with desire for her.[6]

More is implied here than just the traditional colours of passion. The red egg is an aphrodisiac, and the love which it represents

---

[1] McPherson, J. M., *Primitive Beliefs in the North-East of Scotland*, London, 1929, 219.

[2] Hole, Christina, ed., *Encyclopaedia of Superstitions*, London, 1961, 112.

[3] McPherson, 220. See Ellis Davidson, H. R., *Gods and Myths of Northern Europe*, London, 1964, 85.

[4] Wildhaber, Robert, *Wir färben Ostereier*, Berne, 1957, 6.

[5] Leland, C. G., *Gypsy Sorcery and Fortune Telling*, London, 1891, 78.

[6] Bächtold-Stäubli, Hanns, ed., *Handwörterbuch des deutschen Aberglaubens*, Berlin, 1934–5, vi.1,329.

suggests renewal of life. For it will lead, if nature follows its course, to marriage and a family. In China the birth of a male child used to be hailed by red eggs.[1]

Red has always been a propitious colour in China, and this was a normal part of the celebration party organized by the mother. But sometimes such eggs were specially offered in fulfilment of a vow. Traditionally, this was done at the Festival of the Goddess Tin Hau, the Heavenly Queen,[2] and the eggs were laid on tables covered with red paper. A woman who had prayed to the goddess for a son, and then borne one, might bring as many as 500 eggs. Similar offerings are made to Tam Kung. These celebrations are especially popular in Hong Kong, where both deities are patrons of the boat people: a considerable percentage of the population lives in junks and sampans.

An old folk-tale from the same part of the world, describing the miraculous birth of a male child in Korea, features a red egg as more than just the emblem of renewed life, which a new-born child represents. It is the actual vehicle. According to the story, the people of Chinhan saw a white horse bowing to an object on the ground. When they drew near, the horse flew up to Heaven, neighing loudly. On the ground lay a beautiful red egg. They broke it open and out came a boy child who shone so brightly that the birds and beasts danced around him, the sun and moon increased their brilliance, and the earth shook. They called him Hyokkose, which means brightness, and he became the first King of Silla.[3] The homage of the animals, the wonderful birth, and the brightness of the new-born child – these details of the story point to yet another version of the sun myth, and all that it implies of life-renewal.

In France an offering of red eggs ensured the continuance of the crops. At the Church of St Andrew, Grenoble, on St Jacques' day (25 July) the statue of this saint, which normally decorates the portal, is removed and carried in procession through the streets. Then it is laid on napkins filled with little pieces of bread and taken to the fountain, where the bread is distributed. Everyone eats a piece and drinks several cups of water, in honour of the

[1] Ball, J. Dyer, *Things Chinese*, London, 1926, 77. Cormack, J. G., *Everyday Customs in China*, Edinburgh, 1925, 30–1.

[2] *The Birthday of Tin Hau*, Hong Kong, 1960, no author; pamphlet.

[3] *Korea, Its Land, People and Culture of All Ages*, Seoul, 1963; no author, 651.

saint and to ensure a bountiful harvest. When these ceremonies are completed, red eggs are offered up in church.[1]

This was in summer. But springtime, when the sun gathered strength again after winter, was the usual period of regeneration; an obscure belief, attributed to the Egyptians, relates how the world was all on fire at this time.[2] It was the season when the ancient Persians stained eggs red, and even today in the remote north-west of the country Moslems exchange scarlet ones during the days of Ali in Ramadan.[3] A visitor to Abbasabad on the Khorassan frontier in 1885 saw boys playing with red hard-boiled eggs.[4] It was the time of the Persian New Year – 20 March – which is still called 'The Festival of Red Eggs'.[5] Conceivably this custom derives from the world egg of the Persian creation myth, over which the spirits of good and evil fought until the end of time.

St George's Day (*Gurgovden*) has always been an important festival of spring and new life among the Serbs. A popular custom was to wash with water in which a red egg – and herbs to ensure good health – had been placed.[6] The Greeks followed the same custom and so did the Russians, who omitted the herbs.[7]

Serbian gipsies of Kopljari hold a festive picnic at 3 p.m. on *Gurgovden*. The various families gather, and each group sticks a pear-tree branch into the ground. An Easter egg is suspended from it, and a wax candle placed nearby. This is lit during the meal, and must burn until everyone has finished.[8] Around Arandjelovac on the same occasion they serve a roasted lamb. The head is cut off, and a red egg left over from Easter inserted in the mouth after several gold coins have been pushed into the shell.

[1] Van Gennep, Arnold, *Le Folklore du Dauphiné*, Paris, 1932, ii.349.

[2] Howitt, William, *A Country Book*, London, 1859, 97–100.

[3] Personal observation in the town of Tabriz, March, 1963.

[4] Simpson, William, *The Buddhist Praying Wheel*, London, 1896, 285.

[5] Liungman, Waldemar, 'Das Mardukneujahrsfest', *F.F. Communications*, xlviii–xlix (Helsinki, 1937–8), 118, i.20.

[6] Information kindly supplied by Captain Miodrag Jovanovič, formerly of Kragujevač. See also Eterovich, F. H., and Spalatin, Christopher, *Croatia: Land, People and Culture*, Toronto, 1964, i.239.

[7] Wildhaber, *Wir färben*, 6.

[8] Petrović, Alexander, 'Contributions to the Study of the Serbian Gypsies', *Journal of the Gypsy Lore Society*, xvii (Edinburgh, 1938), 66.

A member of the company reputed to be good in business then ceremonially purchases the head. It is turned towards him, and he says: 'Is this a good horse? Will you sell him to me?' His host replies: 'Let me sell it to you.' The buyer continues, 'What a fine horse you have. Fire is coming from his mouth. His bridle is of pure gold. What do you want for him?' He is asked for 100 ducats. They agree on this and kiss. The buyer then shells the egg and shares it out among the family – one piece for each member present, so that they will always be ruddy and healthy. He takes the coins which were in the egg, and puts them on the table, together with some of his own money, then carves the head, sharing out the brains, so that they will all be clever.[1]

This interesting ritual seems based on the idea of the luck of the head and its oracular powers. Warriors once drank potions from a skull to gain the dead man's strength – *skaal* in Danish and *Schale* in German are both words used to mean a drinking vessel[2] – and here a red egg is first inserted into the lamb's mouth to heighten its magic powers before sharing it out among the company. Gold coins were often placed under the tongue of a corpse for magical purposes.

The more obvious significance of the red egg is to ensure rosy cheeks and the good health that goes with them – an example of association of ideas. It is no coincidence, however, that magical red eggs, which renew health and life, are also the colour of blood. For, according to an ancient folk-belief, blood is the seat of life itself and a life-giving vital force.[3]

One finds this idea occurring quite recently in political writing of the more florid kind. Patrick Pearse, leader of the 1916 Irish rebellion, said of the First World War that 'The old heart of the earth needed to be warmed with the red wine of the battlefields'.[4] The symbolism of his uprising at Easter – Ireland's rebirth – was not accidental, and something of the same notion in traditional form occurs in a custom from Sierck (Alsace). Fathers there used to give their children a red egg on Easter morning to ensure long lives for them.[5] In ancient times the theory behind this was more

---

[1] *Ibid.*, 70.
[2] Brewer, E. Cobham, *Dictionary of Phrase and Fable*, London, 1896, I, 149.
[3] Hole, *Encyclopaedia*, 57–8.
[4] Holt, Edgar, *Protest in Arms*, London, 1960, 82.
[5] Bächtold-Stäubli, vi.1,328.

clearly stated: 'the life of all flesh is the blood thereof',[1] according to Leviticus. Jewish observance of *kosher*, the correct slaughter and preparation of meat to ensure that all blood is removed, is based upon this passage.

In northern Europe centuries ago, and even today in parts of the south, a dispute over murder was described as a 'blood feud'; money paid to rectify it was known as 'blood money'. Among Albanian mountain tribesmen, where such customs still persist, the blood of a murdered man is drawn and placed in a tiny bottle. This is put aside until it begins to ferment, when the relatives say: 'His blood is boiling! It is time.' Then they go out and exact revenge.[2] Friends who wish never to be parted become true brothers by mingling their blood. In Albania the blood is actually consumed on a lump of sugar – or in a glass of wine. This way they are irrevocably bound together.[3]

Belief in the renewing qualities of life-giving blood occurs in both ancient and modern cults. To take a single example from many: the *Taurobolium*, or Bull Festival, was celebrated at one time in Rome. Initiates during the ceremony were stood inside a pit, the opening protected by a grill. A bull was then ritually slaughtered in such a way that its blood ran down on to them. Thus they were cleansed from all impurities and reborn.[4]

More recently, though the origin of the new red flag at the time of the French Revolution was purely practical, the mystique of blood has occupied a central position in communist mythology. Red symbolizes the blood of the people, shed for the revolution and for the new communist citizen, a revitalized perfect being, who will build the new society. Red is displayed everywhere, and is used copiously in decoration of streets, buildings and interiors, not only on public occasions, but at all times.

During a visit to communist China (1964) I met the chief surgeon in a Hankow hospital, who became very eloquent on the subject of blood-transfusions. With considerable emotion, he told me the following story: There had been a serious accident, and a manual worker was badly injured. He urgently needed a

---

[1] Lev. xvii.14.

[2] Durham, M. E., *Some Tribal Origins, Laws and Customs of the Balkans*, London, 1928, 164.

[3] *Ibid.*, 153–5.

[4] James, E. O., *Seasonal Feasts and Festivals*, London, 1961, 191–2.

blood-transfusion, and this blood was donated by a professor on the staff of the hospital. The man eventually recovered and, when he was discharged, made a little speech:

> The Communist Party of China has given me this second life. A worker could not have had treatment at such a hospital in the past. In the old society it was the workers who gave their blood for the rich. Never before has the blood of a professor flowed into the body of a worker.

The partisan views expressed in no way detract from the interest of this extraordinary piece of modern folk-lore. The worker, the new communist citizen, has been born again through the revitalizing blood given in the revolution, and the new *élite* is now empowered to draw the life-blood from that of the past.

CHRIST'S SAVING BLOOD

For Christians, especially in the revivalist sects, it is an article of faith that one can only be reborn into eternal life through the cleansing blood of the Saviour. This idea, in its simplest form, is expressed in the motto of the Salvation Army – 'Blood and Fire' – an organization which, according to its magazine, *War Cry*, was organized 'to carry the Blood of Christ and the Fire of the Holy Ghost into every part of the World'.[1] Vachel Lindsay, in his poem about the founder, 'General William Booth enters into Heaven', wrote:

> *Then in an instant all that blear review*
> *Marched on spotless clad in raiment new . . .*
> *Are you washed in the blood of the Lamb?*[2]

stirring lines which echo the Book of Revelation: 'These are they which came out of great tribulation, and have washed their robes, and made them white in the blood of the Lamb.'[3]

The striking metaphor underlines the point and gives it emphasis: that true purity, whiteness of soul, can only be obtained through the red of the Saving Blood, as in the words of a well-known hymn:

[1] Kellett, E. E., *A Short History of Religions*, London, 1962, 527.
[2] Lindsay, Vachel, 'General William Booth enters into Heaven', *The Faber Book of Modern Verse*, London, 1936, 159.
[3] Rev. vii.14.

Rock of ages, cleft for me,
Let me hide myself in Thee;
Let the Water and the Blood,
From Thy riven Side which flowed,
Be of sin the double cure,
Cleanse me from its guilt and power. . . .
Foul, I to the Fountain fly;
Wash me, Saviour, or I die.[1]

We have already seen how an egg is sometimes used as an emblem of the Eucharist. In similar context, women of eastern Thrace put the first red egg prepared on Maundy Thursday in the garden under a rose-bush before placing it in front of the ikons on Easter Day. This action was intended to symbolize the laying out of Christ's body in the grave.[2]

More often the red eggs of Easter represent, in a form that the simplest peasant can understand, the mystery of the Saving Blood of Christ. Hyde in *De Ludis Orientalibus* (1694) describes how Christians of Mesopotamia dyed Easter eggs red, just as the Christian Chaldeans and Syrians do today: *'In memoriam effusi sanguinis Salvatoris eo tempore crucifixi.'*[3]

They are indeed of supreme importance in many countries where no Easter celebrations would be complete without them. The Alsatian Thomas Kirchmeyer, better known as Naogeorgus, refers to red Easter eggs as early as 1553.[4] Macedonian peasants will tell you that in 'the old days' eggs were always coloured red, as they still are today, and in Hungary eggs decorated with patterns of red flowers have long been usual. Indeed, the traditional name for Easter eggs is *piros tojas* – red eggs:[5] a gift the girls used to present to the boys on Easter Monday, called in Hungary 'Water Plunge Monday', because of the splashing with water which always took place then.[6] Czechs often coloured their Easter eggs red or purple, and in parts of Austria they say that, while the Easter hare produces a variety of coloured eggs on

[1] Toplady, A. M., 'Rock of Ages', *The English Hymnal*, Oxford, 1906, 378.
[2] Weinhold, Gertrud, *Das schöne Osterei in Europa*, Kassel, 1965, 27.
[3] Hyde, Thomas, *De Ludis Orientalibus*, London, 1694, 7.
[4] Wildhaber, *Wir färben*, 3.
[5] Károlyi, Alexander, *Hungarian Pageant*, Budapest, 1939, 80. Viski, Károly, *Volksbrauch der Ungarn*, Budapest, 1932, 51.
[6] Spicer, Dorothy, *The Book of Festivals*, New York, 1937, 168.

Easter Sunday, it lays only red on Maundy Thursday, in token of the Passion of Christ.[1]

How clearly they represent the Saving Blood of Christ is brought out by legends from many lands. Miraculous tales of all the stones in the world becoming red at the Resurrection have been handed down by the Orthodox Setukese of Estonia.[2] The Yugoslavs restrict this to the stones at the foot of the Cross, which were stained by the blood of Our Lord.[3] But most of these wonderful events relate to eggs, rather than stones, which they slightly resemble in shape and with which they are occasionally confused. Sometimes this change is attributed to stones which were thrown at Our Lord, and there is a Rumanian apocryphal story of red eggs used as missiles by the guardians of the Sepulchre.[4]

Other legends from the same country centre about the Blessed Virgin Mary, chief mediator between God and sinful man. One recounts how she made up a basket of eggs and took it to the soldiers sitting at the foot of the Cross, in the hopes that it would rouse in them some pity for the sufferings of Our Lord. But they ignored her, and the basket remained beneath the Cross, where she had left it. After a time, the blood of Our Lord flowed down – as, in early art, it does over Adam's skull, in token of man's redemption – and stained the eggs their characteristic colour.[5] The mystic price of blood money has been paid:

> *The Royal Banners forward go,*
> *The Cross shines forth in mystic glow;*
> *Where He in Flesh, our flesh Who made,*
> *Our sentence bore, our ransom paid.*[6]

In a Yugoslav legend the eggs which Our Lady brings to distribute on Easter Sunday are already coloured by her to commemorate the blood shed by Christ. Hearing of His Resurrection on the

[1] Kretzenbacher, Leopold, 'Vom roten Osterei in der grünen Steiermark', *Schweizerisches Archiv für Volkskunde*, LIII (Basle, 1957), ii–iii.107.

[2] Ränk, Gustav, 'Ostereier in Estland', *Schweizerisches Archiv für Volkskunde*, LIII (Basle, 1957), ii–iii, 142.

[3] Georgieva, Milica, Бојадисување и шарање на Велигденски Јајца Во Скопје и Околијата, Skopje, 1960, 179.

[4] Murgoçi, Agnes, 'Rumanian Easter Eggs', *Folk-Lore*, xx (London, September 1909), 297. [5] *Ibid.*, 298.

[6] Fortunatus, Venantius, '*Vexilla Regis Prodeunt*', *The English Hymnal*, Oxford, 1906, 77.

way, she gave them to the children to play with and that – so they say – is how the custom first arose of presenting them at Easter.[1]

Here it is as though the Blessed Virgin intercedes on mankind's behalf. Other miraculous tales involve St Mary Magdalene, proto-type of the redeemed sinner, a courtesan cleansed from what was a woman's blackest sin by the grace of Our Lord. In Russian tra-dition an egg, which she held in her hand, turned red, as a proof of the Resurrection. Sometimes she is credited with offering it to the Roman Emperor, Tiberius;[2] Estonians say that she gave it to Pontius Pilate, beseeching him not to condemn Our Lord.[3]

Certain Rumanian legends in this tradition are distastefully anti-Semitic, but should be mentioned none the less, on account of their intrinsic interest. Rumania, especially in the early years of this century, when these stories were recorded, was notorious for anti-Semitism, a phenomenon which is to a certain extent religious in origin.

History has long slanted the account of Christ's death so that the Jews bear sole responsibility, and they are cast into the role of scapegoats, bearing the sins of the whole of mankind, which was actually culpable. References to their 'wickedness' add a highly coloured emotional touch. According to one version, the Blessed Virgin Mary coloured the first red eggs after Our Lord was born, and saved them to throw at the Jews, so that she and her Son could escape.[4]

Another rabble-rousing Passiontide legend makes one realize why the most appalling Christian massacres of the Jews generally occurred in Holy Week. It is related in a story – which suggests a garbled version of the Passover – that, after Christ was buried, several Jews, glad to be rid of Him, met to have a feast and to make merry. Among the dishes served was a cock, boiled whole, and various platters of hard-boiled eggs. In the course of the meal, someone recalled Our Lord's saying that He would rise again on the third day. The host laughed, and said: 'When this cock, which we are eating now, rises from the dead, and when all these clean, whole eggs turn red, then Christ will also rise from

---

[1] Georgieva, 179–80.
[2] Information kindly supplied by the Rev. Vassily James, London. Zernov, Nicholas, *Eastern Christendom*, London, 1961, 268.
[3] Ränk, 142.
[4] Murgoçi, 297.

the dead.' At once the eggs changed colour and the cock rose up, crowing and sprinkling the company with sauce. This sprinkling, so they say, caused skin diseases, absurdly said to afflict the Jews, and the event itself is supposed to explain why eggs are coloured red for Easter in Rumania.[1]

This disagreeable tale has certain interesting features. The feast itself is a distorted account of the Jewish Passover Seder – a ritual meal, noted for merry-making and congeniality – when hard-boiled eggs are invariably eaten. In fact, the legend obliquely acknowledges the debt, already mentioned, which our own Easter egg owes to the egg of the Passover. The cock must be borrowed from the Gospel narrative of St Peter's betrayal, the dramatic point of the story in each case being marked by the crowing of the cock.

There are also echoes of such apocryphal themes as the blood slander, with which the Jewish people were burdened for so many centuries. This false belief, that Jews consumed the blood of Christian children at their feasts, no doubt arose from the fact that cups of red wine are drunk, not only at the Passover, but also on the occasion of the weekly Sabbath blessing – the source, incidentally, of our own Eucharistic chalice. Such confused thinking may have derived from the shouts of the crowd witnessing Our Lord's appearance before Pilate: 'His blood be on us, and on our children.'[2] The foolishness of attributing this single cry to a whole race throughout the world and for all perpetuity need not be dwelt on here. Yet the particular manner in which the white eggs changed to red in the story just related seems to be linked with the same idea. The prejudice is endorsed by the old belief that Easter should not coincide with the Passover. In fact, an Orthodox acquaintance recently remarked that their basis for calculating Easter was preferable to that used by the Western Church, for the very reason that it avoided this. His comment underlines the irrational nature of such thinking, since the events of the Christian Easter, of course, centre around the Jewish Passover, which Our Lord Himself was observing with His Jewish disciples on Maundy Thursday; and since they were celebrating it in exactly the same way as all Jews, whether friendly or hostile

[1] *Ibid.*, 297–8.
[2] Matt. xxvii.25.

to Our Lord, the Passover should by rights be an occasion for Christians' rejoicing.

These virulent, miraculous legends are regrettably abundant in Rumania. A more elaborate, violently racialist account of the eggs at the foot of the crucifix has also been collected, using stronger and more highly-coloured, emotive language than has so far been described. Once again Our Lady is carrying eggs to Calvary, but instead of offering them to the soldiers she takes them to the Jews. They, instead of pitying Him, torment Him more, offering vinegar and nettles. Since the gift of eggs apparently makes no difference, Our Lady starts to weep. Suddenly streams of blood from the wounds of Christ flow down over the eggs, staining some of them entirely, splashing others. Our Lord Himself then speaks from the Cross, declaring that henceforth eggs must be coloured red for Easter, either wholly or in part, in memory of His Crucifixion: 'For thus have I done today.' After the Resurrection, Our Lady was the first to make red eggs. Full of joy that her Son was alive, she greeted everyone with 'Christ is risen', and proffered them a red egg.[1]

This distasteful piece of hagiography is, as we know, wildly inaccurate. In the Gospel narrative it is the Roman soldiers, and not the Jews, who offer Our Lord vinegar to drink; the nettles are pure invention. The reasons for the change are not hard to find. Rumanians have always looked back with pride to their Roman past. The Dacians of the Danube, as they were, are relics of Roman settlements, established in the Balkans during the Empire, and their Rumanian language is related to the others of the Romance group. Hence chauvinism, by a process parallel to that of the Nazis, who claimed Our Lord as an Aryan, has absolved the Romans of all blame for the Crucifixion, and foisted it instead upon the Jews.

Sometimes these miraculous tales have a pagan tinge, like the Transylvanian legend which describes Antichrist gnawing through a thick iron chain; when it snaps, the end of the world will come. He chews and chews until Easter, and it is almost worn right through. But then he sees the red coloured eggs and is momentarily distracted. The chain magically reforms and the world is saved for another year.[2]

[1] Murgoçi, 298.
[2] Wildhaber, *Wir färben*, 7.

This legend owes a considerable debt to Scandinavian myth. There are echoes of Loki, the mysterious evil god who was bound in chains, and of his child, the wolf Fenrir, demon of death and destruction, who lies in wait, ready to destroy all in the *Ragnarök* – even Odin himself. Fenrir was fettered by the gods, and broke two chains. But the third, a magic one, was made by dwarfs from the noise of a cat, a woman's beard, the breath of a fish and spittle from a bird. It held and will not break till *Ragnarök* – doom of the gods.[1]

The material form of Antichrist in the Rumanian tale must be that of a monster, and there is a suggestion, too, that the world is fastened by a chain, the red eggs acting as a charm which will mislead the forces of evil; hence a local saying that when Christians stop dyeing eggs red for Easter the end of the world will come. Again, the Saving Blood of Christ, of which the red eggs are the emblem, preserves the world against the forces of evil.

A custom observed by the Greek Patriarch, and said to date back to Byzantine days, reflects not only the Trinity, but also the dual nature of Christ, human and divine. As a man, His blood, symbolized by the red eggs, was shed for us. But, on Easter morning, visitors to the Patriarch are presented not only with two red eggs, but also with a gold one, all three wrapped up together in a silken handkerchief; in Turkish times, when Islam was in the ascendant, the gold egg was omitted.[2]

In early Christian art gold represents eternity, and it is also a colour associated with kings, and so it may portray the divine aspect of Christ as the eternal king. One of the earliest known records of colouring Easter eggs comes from the household accounts of Edward I, dated 1290, which show an entry of 18*d.*, spent on purchasing 450 eggs, to be coloured or covered with gold leaf and distributed to members of the royal household.[3]

These may, of course, have been coloured gold, not for religious reasons, but simply as the gift of a king. An Englishman writing during the reign of Tsar Alexander II notes that it was customary for members of the royal family to be presented with

---

[1] Ellis Davidson, 31.

[2] Arnott, Margaret, 'Die Ostereier in Griechenland', *Schweizerisches Archiv für Volkskunde*, LIII (Basle, 1957), ii–iii.192.

[3] Hone, William, *The Every-Day Book*, London, 1837, i.429.

red or gilded eggs on Easter Day by their own Patriarch – three, two, or one, according to their rank.[1]

Perhaps this custom came from the Greeks, through the close relationship of the Churches. But it is interesting that much earlier (1557–8) Anthony Jenkinson observed that while the ordinary people of Russia carried red eggs at Easter, the gentry had theirs gilded.[2] The red and yellow eggs sold in eighteenth-century French markets may be a different survival of a similar custom,[3] and so could be the golden eggs coloured with onion peel, and popular in many European countries – though perhaps this is just due to the cheapness and availability of onions.

RED EGGS OF THE RESURRECTION: THE EASTER CYCLE

In Rumania 'red eggs at Easter' was a way of saying that something was inevitable,[4] for Easter without red eggs was quite unheard of. Indeed, the red eggs of the Resurrection are accepted practice in all Orthodox countries. In Greece, where they are sometimes known as 'the eggs of the Good Word', they are believed to possess miraculous qualities.[5] In Athens one sees them made of wood, hanging suspended from ribbons.[6]

A lesser resurrection festival characterized by red eggs is the Feast of the Raising of St Lazarus, celebrated on the Saturday preceding Palm Sunday. Syrians of the Greek faith call it *Sabt al-Azar* and the local teacher, accompanied by his pupils, calls round the houses singing songs of Lazarus' miracle. They are given eggs in return.[7] Greek children of Chios were sent by the priest to perform this same task, and one of their songs describes what Lazarus saw in the other world:

> *I saw fears, I saw tremblings,*
> *I saw great torments,*
> *I saw demons and pains.*

[1] Cremer, William Henry, *Easter Eggs: a Sketch of a Good Old Custom*, Ipswich, 1870, 10.

[2] Hakluyt, Richard, *The Principal Navigations, Voyages, Traffiques and Discoveries of the English Nation*, Glasgow, 1903, ii.436.

[3] Wildhaber, *Wir färben*, 7.

[4] Murgoçi, 296.

[5] Megas, George A., *Greek Calendar Customs*, Athens, 1958, 107.

[6] Personal observation, Easter, 1961.

[7] Spicer, 329.

Give me a little drop of water,
To wash away the poison
From my heart and lips,
And ask me no more:
But give me an egg
That I may go hence,
And may also wish you
Health, grace and a good heart
To have at Easter.[1]

Bulgarians celebrate the festival by sending parties of girls, six to a group, from house to house to sing and dance in honour of the occasion. They are thought to bring good luck and are given coins and red eggs by the peasants.

In Greek Kydoniae preparation for Easter and the red eggs used to begin as early as Palm Sunday. The verger put *vaya*, a bundle of green branches,[2] over his shoulder and toured the parish with a group of children singing:

Vaya, vaya! On Palm Sunday
We eat fish and mackerel
And next Sunday
We shall eat red eggs.[3]

Children of Greek Macedonia sang an almost identical verse:

Palm, Palm, Palm Sunday
Kolio fish we eat today.
And when next Sunday comes
We eat red eggs.[4]

On Palm Sunday in the Ukraine not a bundle, but a single willow branch is carried, and friends who meet by chance tap one another with it, saying: 'Not I that strike thou, but the willow. In a week the great day comes. The red egg is not far.'[5]

In Holy Week itself, sometimes on the Wednesday, it was usual

---

[1] Argenti, Philip, and Rose, H. J., *The Folklore of Chios*, Cambridge, 1949, i.364–5.

[2] *Vaya* consists of a branch of bay or myrtle and a palm cross.

[3] Megas, 91.

[4] Garnett, Lucy M. J., and Stuart, Glennie, J. S., *The Women of Turkey and Their Folk-Lore*, London, 1890, i.115.

[5] Zmigrodzki, Michel de, 'The History of the Swastika', *Archives of the International Folklore Association*, I (Chicago, 1898), 364.

for Greek priests to anoint the people, not only in church, but also with private ceremonies at home. In Kotyora each family received the priest with a tray containing certain items – raw eggs, flour and salt – and these were anointed. On the following day, Maundy Thursday, they were taken to church, together with a number of red coloured eggs, in little baskets covered with red cloth.[1]

Similar offerings including red eggs are to be found elsewhere. In Slovenia, usually nearer to Easter Day, a girl from every household takes special Easter food to church, for blessing, in a basket. This is hand-made, large and round, and is carried by a handle on either side. It is kept for this one occasion, and otherwise is never used. There is a decorative edging of dark green and purple rushes, to stress the beauty of the occasion. At one time these baskets were balanced on the head.

The food they contain varies slightly according to local custom, but there is always a clear symbolism. Generally it would consist of smoked ham (Christ's body), lamb (the Lamb of God), white bread (Christ's tomb), a big nut or plum cake baked in the form of a wreath (the crown of thorns), a string of small sausages (the ropes which bound Christ), some roots of horseradish (the nails which fastened Him to the Cross), oranges (the sponge soaked in vinegar which was offered to Christ), and always five red eggs which represent the five wounds of the Saviour.

All these things are carefully covered with a fine white cloth, embroidered with the picture of a lamb, representing the shroud in which the body of the Lord was wrapped. The children also carry little baskets with the same contents, but on a smaller scale. After blessing they are brought home and placed under the family crucifix until Easter morning; no one may eat any of this food until after Easter Sunday Mass.[2]

Dyeing red eggs for Easter is an important ritual usually reserved for Maundy Thursday, though a girl from Ljubljana remembered doing it with her mother on the Saturday. In Yugoslav Macedonia it must be done during Holy Week. Even washing the eggs, so that the dye will take nicely, is a special ceremony, performed as a rule on the Wednesday. The eggs to be used are

[1] Megas, 94.
[2] Information kindly obtained by Miss Jacqueline Simpson from Marija Rak and Eryanec Lucka of Ljubljana, Slovenia.

saved and put aside during Lent – two for each member of the family, and one apiece for relatives and friends. In general, this is a woman's task, as they have preserved and handed on the tradition, though the Mijaci monks also prepared eggs for Easter in the same way.[1]

The red eggs are coloured with Brazil wood which has been soaked in tepid water on Holy Wednesday. Many stories and customs surround the first egg, which is not dyed with the others, but placed in the water at the same time as the wood. It is then regarded as specially significant. Sometimes referred to as the Egg of Our Lady, or Our Lord's Egg, and in Gorno Lisichi as 'the Prophet', it is never eaten or given away.[2]

Further south, in Greek Macedonia, a mother takes this first egg and makes the sign of the cross with it over the neck and face of her child, saying: 'May thou grow as red as this egg, and strong as a stone.'[3] In Yugoslav Macedonia she will go to the children when it is early, and they are still asleep. Then lightly she touches their cheeks with the warm red egg, not long from the pan, and says 'Red-white', to ensure their health for the coming year.[4] Next, as in the Thracian custom already mentioned, the egg is taken into the garden and laid under a rose bush or a cherry tree, in token of the laying of Christ's body in the grave – a Eucharistic gesture, which is completed on Easter Day, when the egg is put before the family ikons. The Panaghia, or Madonna, is the ikon usually chosen by the Greeks, and its power is said to prevent the egg from going bad. There it remains until the following Easter,[5] when it is carefully burnt like the crosses from Palm Sunday, and replaced by a fresh one.

Often this first egg is a charm against hail, and cures the cattle of diseases. Sometimes a little ceremony is performed on Holy Saturday, when the children have their bath. Plants to ensure that they remain plump and healthy are put into the water together with the red egg, so that they will be 'red-white'. The mother touches each child's face and body with it, saying: 'Be red-white, healthy-alive, and meet next Easter healthy.'[6] Since Easter is a movable spring feast, it can happen that it occurs quite close to St George's Day – 6 May in the Orthodox calendar. Due to this,

[1] Georgieva, 179.   [2] *Ibid.*, 180–1.
[3] Abbott, 35.   [4] Georgieva, 181.
[5] Abbott, 35.   [6] Georgieva, 189.

similar rituals are often observed. Some people like to draw water the previous evening from a mill-race or other rapidly flowing stream, and then pour it into a deep container. The first red egg dyed at Easter is placed in the bottom, along with various plants. Afterwards the whole thing is set in the garden under a cherry tree or rose bush, and left to stand all night.

On St George's Day, before dawn, the family all wash their faces with this water, touching their cheeks three times with the red egg, and repeating three times 'Red-white'. Then the water and the herbs are thrown away into the garden, and the special egg is placed before the ikons.[1] This belief in 'red-white' rests on the linking of ideas whereby the egg, once white and now red, will bring these colours to the cheeks of the child, which, magical associations apart, has pleasant echoes of our own 'Cherry Ripe':

> *There is a garden in her face*
> *Where roses and white lilies blow.*[2]

By contrast, oddly enough, red has a distinctly unpleasant connotation for the shepherds of Chios, suggesting the inflamed, diseased udders of their sick sheep. For this reason, by an elaborate process of sympathetic reasoning, they refuse to eat red Easter eggs.[3]

The custom of saving the first egg dyed is also recorded among the Rumanians. But, instead of preserving it whole, they shared it out among the children, who ate it in silence, walking round and round a piece of turf placed in the centre of the room. When they had finished, the shell was filled with some dough from the Easter bread. It was then put on one of the beams of the living-room, where it stayed until the following year to bring good luck.[4]

The first special egg apart, Macedonians do their dyeing on Maundy Thursday. Provided that it is all finished before the church bells ring, it is said that the eggs will not go bad before Ascension Day. If St George's Day falls soon after Easter, the red egg dye is saved and used up then. But if the interval is too long,

[1] *Ibid.*, 189. Information also kindly supplied by Captain Miodrag Jovanovič.

[2] Palgrave, F. T., ed., anonymous poem, 'Cherry Ripe', *The Golden Treasury*, Oxford, 1921, 77.

[3] Argenti and Rose, i.368.

[4] Wildhaber, *Wir färben*, 7.

it is thrown away; carefully, where no one is likely to walk, since it is a sin to step on it. Sometimes it was poured in the hemp fields, to preserve the crop from worms, or in the vineyards to guard against insects and other damage.[1]

Women in Macedonia and in northern Thrace dipped not only eggs but also pieces of cloth in the dye, and these were hung for forty days from the windows or the balconies. Then they were used for various magical purposes, such as exorcism.[2] This custom varies from one area to another. In Kastoria they put out red blankets and kerchiefs; and in Kios, Asia Minor, the women used to rise at dawn on Maundy Thursday and hang cloths from a window facing east, to catch the first rays of the early sun.[3]

The link here, between the magic colour and the life-giving light, again occurs at the climax of Easter, when fire is kindled and red eggs broken. The focal point of Easter Mass in the Orthodox Church comes at midnight, when the priest says: 'Christ is risen.' The congregation reply: 'He is risen indeed', and ignite their candles, so that the church becomes a blaze of light. Everyone goes provided with eggs and, since the Lenten fast officially ends at that moment, it is recorded among Macedonian peasants – and probably elsewhere too – that they broach their eggs at once, in church, the moment the ritual greeting has been given.[4] Bulgarians pass red eggs from one person to another, instead of shaking hands, and the congregation return home to eat Easter cakes, the *kozunatsi*, and red eggs.[5]

In the village of Piano degli Albanese, near Palermo in Sicily, a community of Albanians who have lived there since the fifteenth century celebrate Easter according to the Orthodox rite. When the words 'Christ is risen' have been spoken by the priest, lay workers toss red Easter eggs to the entire congregation.[6] Red eggs also feature in the Easter celebrations at Contessa Entellina, another Albanian community in Sicily. In Orthodox Russian churches red eggs are distributed at the midnight Resurrection service. Greeks take all their red eggs to the church then, irrespective of whether or not they intend to eat them. They call this

---

[1] Georgieva, 182. [2] Megas, 95.
[3] *Ibid.* [4] Abbott, 37.
[5] Vakarelski, Christo, 'Œufs de Pâques chez les Bulgares', *Schweizerisches Archiv für Volkskunde*, LIII (Basle, 1957), ii–iii.185. Spicer, 70–1.
[6] Personal observation, Easter 1961.

'giving the eggs their service', i.e. consecrating them.[1] Sometimes they put them by the sanctuary entrance, near the ikon of Our Lord, sometimes under the tabernacle, so that the words of the priest, 'Christ is risen', are actually spoken over them.[2]

In certain regions the ceremony starts earlier, on Maundy Thursday; the housewife takes to the church one egg for each member of the family, including servants, and an extra one. These are then left inside the church, wrapped carefully in a napkin, until Easter Day arrives. In Chios any one of these blessed eggs – not necessarily the first to have been dyed – is put in front of the family ikons, and in three years they say a pearl will form inside it.[3]

Celebrations varying in intensity follow midnight Easter Mass in most Orthodox countries. At Hassia, in Macedonia, congregants break their eggs against the wooden clapper hanging in the church, which serves as a bell.[4] An eyewitness, describing the 'feast of Paque' celebrated in Moscow in 1702, says that the bells were rung all night, and for the two days following.[5] In modern Athens rockets and fireworks are released[6] as the midnight greeting is exchanged, and a traditional festive meal is often served. Invariably it begins with red eggs, fulfilling the promise made on the last night of Carnival: 'With an egg I close my mouth; with an egg I shall open it again.'[7] At 9 or 10 p.m. that night the shutters had been closed and a hard-boiled egg handed to each person before bed, 'to shut the mouth to flesh', till Easter Sunday. So that the second part of the vow shall be kept – and where propriety forbids an egg being eaten in church – a special breakfast is sometimes served in the early hours of the morning, consisting of red eggs, Easter cake, and coffee.

When Macedonian families go home to bed after the service, mothers slip red eggs beneath the pillows of the younger children. They are told that these were brought by *Paschalia*, the Easter spirit.[8] The Armenians, whose Church is separate from the

---

[1] Argenti and Rose, i.367–8.

[2] Megas, 108. [3] Argenti and Rose, i.368.

[4] Megas, 108.

[5] Cremer, 10.

[6] Megas, 106. [7] *Ibid.*, 109.

[8] Abbott, 37. Wildhaber, Robert, 'Der Osterhase und andere Eierbringer', *Schweizerisches Archiv für Volkskunde*, LIII (Basle, 1957), ii–iii.116.

Orthodox, attend a midday Easter service, after which everyone enjoys the traditional feast of roast lamb and red eggs – an embellishment of two popular Middle Eastern dishes.

Bulgarians say: 'Never omit eggs at Easter, roast lamb on St George's Day, or chicken on the feast day of St Peter.' In their country no one fails to carry a few red eggs about at Easter-time, in case he meets close relatives. If he does, the ritual greeting is exchanged and also the usual red eggs. In the case of highly respected relations – such as godparents or parents – the younger person is obliged to give three eggs, and receives only one in return.[2] Every guest visiting the house on Easter Day is given one. Young men offer one to their sweethearts, wishing that they may be white and rosy like the eggs; the girls reply that they are both these things, and also just as sound.[3]

Ukrainians received their Easter guests with a plate of shelled and sliced red eggs; greetings are exchanged, and some of the egg is eaten.[4] The Orthodox of Montenegro also pay Easter visits to one another's houses, and tables groaning with food, especially red eggs, are laid out for callers.[5] They must kiss their host and hostess three times apiece, in honour of the Trinity,[6] and break eggs with them – these are often inscribed with the ritual greeting. The Russians observe this custom too, laying out on their Easter tables *pashka* and *kulich*, Easter cake and sweet cream-cheese, surrounded by red eggs.[7]

An early eighteenth-century account of Russia describes how eggs were distributed for fifteen days among all sections of the populace; the manner in which this was done varied according to social mores: 'Persons of distinction kept their eggs within doors and made gifts of them to visitors. . . . The ordinary people gave theirs in the streets.'

Servants and employers also exchanged them.[8] Earlier still is the description (1557–8) in Hakluyt's *Voyages* – probably the first lengthy account that we have of these customs:

They [the Russians] have an order at Easter which they alwaies observe, and that is this – every yere against Easter to die, or colour

[1] Spicer, 24.   [2] Vakarelski, 185.
[3] Spicer, 71.   [4] Zmigrodzki, 364.
[5] Wyon, Reginald, *The Balkans from Within*, London, 1904, 302–3.
[6] Durham, M. E., *Through the Lands of the Serb*, London, 1904, 29.
[7] Zernov, 268.   [8] Cremer, 10.

red with Brazell [Brazil wood], a great number of egs, of which every man and woman giveth one unto the priest of their Parish upon Easter day in the morning. And morover the common people use to carie in their hands one of their red egs, not onely upon Easter day, but also three or foure dayes after, and gentlemen and gentlewomen have egs gilded which they cary in like maner. They use it as they say for a great love, and in token of the resurrection, whereof they rejoyce. For when two friends meete during the Easter holy dayes, they come and take one another by the hand: the one of them sayth, the Lord or Christ is risen, the other answereth, it is so of a truth, and then they kisse and exchange their egs both men and women, continuing in kissing 4 dayes together.[1]

The Puritan Brand, commenting on this custom some 200 years later, observes ponderously: 'Our ancient voyage writer means no more, it should seem, than that the ceremony was kept up for four days.'[2]

It is quite usual for festivities to last throughout the week following Easter Sunday. The Greeks have a saying:

> *Three days for His Birth,*
> *Three for Epiphany,*
> *And six for Easter.*[3]

This post-Easter period is called White, or Bright, Week. In some areas – Megara, for example[4] – groups of children or men call round the houses on 'White Sunday', carrying a floral cross attached to a flagstaff, and singing traditional songs – the *Roussalia*; women offer them gifts of red eggs. The time of this particular custom varies considerably, and in Messania[5] the children go about on Good Friday, reciting the Passion. Otherwise the ceremony is similar, and again they are offered red eggs and buns as a reward.

The name White Sunday is apparently peculiar to Greece. Russians called it *Krasnaya Gorka*, Little Red Mountain, and people gathered on a convenient hill to perform the *Khorovod*, a circular dance, to which they sang an accompaniment; the chief

---

[1] Hakluyt, ii.435–6.
[2] Brand, John, *Observations on Popular Antiquities*, Newcastle, 1777; 349 (in the 1810 edition).
[3] Megas, 110.
[4] *Ibid.*, 111.
[5] *Ibid.*, 102.

singer, a woman, held a round loaf and a red egg. This custom has now disappeared, though a friend writes from Russia that egg-rolling is still performed – that was in 1966.

Krasnaya Gorka was the occasion on which Ukrainian widows used to put red eggs on their husbands' graves,[1] and in some villages around Sparta the same is done to family tombs.[2] Bulgarians lay them on the graves on Easter Monday[3] and Yugoslav Macedonians carry them to the churchyard on the Small Day – the third day following Easter – but afterwards distribute them, on behalf of the souls of the dead.[4]

Greek women who have lost their husbands do not dye eggs for some three to five years after their bereavement, and will only accept them as gifts from their more distant relatives.[5] In Yugoslav Macedonia there is a rather similar prohibition, though it occurs at Whitsuntide. The custom of preparing red eggs for that festival, which is usual among the Macedonians, is not observed by mothers whose children died young. They believe that, in the specially blessed period between Easter and Whitsuntide, the souls of all the dead are permitted to wander freely. When that time is ended, an angel comes to collect them and take them back to Heaven.

Some years ago a woman in the village of Bulanchi[6] dreamed that pretty, red-coloured eggs mislead the souls of the little dead children. Instead of returning to Heaven, they wanted to play with the eggs, so that the angels had difficulty in fetching them, and had to beat them with slings. This is why mothers who have lost their children no longer dye red eggs.[7] The rather pathetic account reflects not only the natural fantasies of an era when infant mortality was high, but also an interesting mystical belief regarding the period between Easter and Whitsun.

It is a time when the triumph of the Resurrection is especially stressed, and Catholics sing the Easter Angelus:

> *Joy to thee, O Queen of Heaven; Alleluia!*
> *He whom thou wast meet to bear ; Alleluia!*

[1] Zmigrodzki, 364.
[2] Arnott, 192.
[3] Garnett, 326.
[4] Georgieva, 190.
[5] Arnott, 192.
[6] Named Kipra Grleovski. [7] Georgieva, 191, note 14.

An Egg at Easter

As He promised, hath arisen; Alleluia!
Pour, from us to Him, thy prayer; Alleluia![1]

Whitsun, when the infant souls are summoned back to their Creator – from the Anglo-Saxon *Hwita-Sunnan-Dag* – means White Sunday, and refers to the white robes in which the newly baptized were blessed.[2] Hence it is a festival peculiarly linked, in the popular mind, with children standing before the throne of God, as in the words of a well-known Victorian hymn:

> *We shall see Him; but in Heaven,*
> *Set at God's right hand on high;*
> *When like stars His children crown'd*
> *All in white shall wait around.[3]*

The same curious link between red eggs and the souls of little children who died young runs through the legends of the *Blajini*,[4] said by some to be the meek souls of children who died before their baptism and live in darkness on the edges of the world – a kind of limbo. Their festival, which follows hard on Easter, is celebrated, naturally enough, chiefly by women, who cast red egg-shells for them into the streams, as a sign that Easter has come.[5]

Celebrations involving the traditional red eggs are often continued from Easter until Ascensiontide. Monks at a Russian Orthodox monastery near Paris prepare about 1,500, which are blessed on Easter Day and eaten at all the main meals during that period. Since the monastery is small, they must become rather stale, but a plateful is always on the table for visitors.[6]

Generally speaking, this is typical Orthodox practice. Many Greek women dye as many as 200 eggs, gifts for anyone who calls at their home between Maundy Thursday and Ascension. The eggs are normally plain red, but occasionally are imprinted with the outline of flowers or leaves for heightened effect. This is,

---

[1] *Regina coeli*. See Attwater, Donald, *A Dictionary of Mary*, London, 1957, 240–1.

[2] Caudwell, Irene, *Ceremonies of Holy Church*, London, 1948, 122.

[3] Alexander, Mrs, 'Once in Royal David's City', *The English Hymnal*, Oxford, 1906, 488.

[4] See ch. 2.

[5] Spicer, 277.

[6] Information kindly supplied by Archbishop Alexis de Meudon, Administrator of the Russian Orthodox Exarchate in Paris.

incidentally, an extremely widespread method and will be described in a later chapter. A Greek village recently, in a modern variant on an old custom, erected a huge papier-mâché red egg at its entrance, through which the traffic then passed.[1]

Orthodox Easter and its customs are so important, and so colourful, that some have brushed off on to local non-Christian communities. In Albania, where religious differences became largely blurred, a Moslem acquaintance had Catholic friends who used red eggs at Easter. They not only exchanged these among themselves, but gave them to the Moslem community too. Christians greeted each other by touching their eggs together, and Moslems joined in this ceremony.[2] Similarly, in parts of nearby Bosnia Catholics and Moslems mingle, and while the post-Easter season used to be called *post concussionem ovorum* ('after the egg-breaking') by the Christians, Moslems spoke of *Kyzyl Jumurta* ('the time of red eggs').[3] In Skopje (Yugoslav Macedonia) at Easter, 1962, I noticed local gipsies busy with red eggs. They too were Moslem, but, since gipsies are great hawkers, they may simply have meant to sell them to Christians.

Easter in Macedonia is closely related to the festival of St George on 6 May. On that day the girls get up at dawn, go to the woods, and look for a cherry tree. When they have found one, they touch their faces with a red egg, saying: 'May we be as red as the red egg, and as healthy as the cherry.' Then they rig up a swing on the tree, and rock to and fro with a red egg tucked in each armpit; finally, they break and eat these under the cherry. Later, swings are erected on the village green beneath another leafy tree, and the ancient *hora* – circular dance – is performed while others swing, again with red eggs in the armpits.[4]

Apart from Latvia, where boys even now build Easter swings and give the girls rides,[5] I have not heard of a similar custom still existing elsewhere. But welcoming the spring with swinging was an ancient sport and probably, if one could trace its origin, it was to assist the growth of the crops and help them to sprout just as high.

[1] Bonser, K. J., 'Easter in Greece', *Folklore*, lxxv (London, Winter 1964), 271.

[2] Information kindly supplied by Dr Ihsan Toptani, formerly of Tirana.

[3] Eterovich and Spalatin, i.238.   [4] Georgieva, 190–1.

[5] Information kindly supplied by Mrs Terēza Budiņa Lazdiņa, formerly of Riga.

Chapter 10
Christian Charms

The room contained all those old friends whom it is the lot of everyone to meet in small wooden taverns, of which there are not a few set up along the highways – namely, a frost-rimed samovar, smoothly scraped pine-wood walls, a three-cornered cupboard with teapots and cups in one corner, gilt porcelain eggs dangling on blue and red ribbons in front of the ikons.

Nikolai Gogol: *Dead Souls*

GREEN THURSDAY

Ordinary eggs were endowed with unusual power in popular imagination. How much more so, then, the magic of an Easter egg, when folk-belief is reinforced by religion and former ideas continue, curiously tangled with Christian doctrine and practice – in England a decorated *Pace* egg might be kept the whole year through to bring good luck.[1]

The holy Easter season was especially important. In Berne things would go badly for a farmer if none of his hens were brooding on Good Friday;[2] ideally, so the Germans thought, they should lay between 11 and 12 noon, for this was the time when Our Lord gave up His spirit. But, particularly in Germanic countries, the significance of Good Friday tends to be overshadowed by Maundy, or Green, Thursday.

This name, so popular on the Continent, is not much used in Great Britain, where the colour is thought to be unlucky.[3] People said it was connected with fairies,[4] which is why brides never wear it. In Lowland Scotland this even extends to guests and food at the reception[5] – no one would serve green vegetables or use green table decorations.

[1] Hole, Christina, *Easter and Its Customs*, London, 1961, 44.

[2] Bächtold-Stäubli, Hanns, ed., *Handwörterbuch des deutschen Aberglaubens*, Berlin, 1931–2, iv.1,000.

[3] Bonnerjea, Biren, *A Dictionary of Superstitions and Mythology*, London, 1927, 114.

[4] Brewer, E. Cobham, *A Dictionary of Phrase and Fable*, London, 1896, 442.

[5] Henderson, William, *Notes on the Folk Lore of the Northern Counties of England and the Borders*, London, 1866, 21.

In Ireland, of course, there is a different attitude to green. Indeed the Irish, most rebellious of the British, gave it, instead of red, to these islands as a traditional colour of revolution. There is an Irish Holy Week custom connected with green, but it concerns Good Friday, not Maundy Thursday. It is the time for sowing parsley which, if it grows thick and strong, brings prosperity to the mother of the house.[1]

Green Thursday is the day when it is specially important to have green food in Germanic countries, and plants gathered will have the power to heal; St John's wort and vervain – herb of the cross – protect one from thunder.[2] Peasants ate herb soup, followed by spinach and boiled or fried eggs, meat, and green salad.[3] The 'herbs', usually seven, nine or twelve of them – which were often really vegetables[4] – perhaps derive from the Jewish practice of including green herbs in the Passover meal.

Danes serve green soup at 12 noon.[5] Depending on the district, it is made with split peas or nine varieties of new 'cabbage' – nine representing the nine herbs which are blessed, here a Catholic relic in a Protestant country. Cabbage – Danish *kål* – is used broadly to include nettles, cumin, dandelions, willow leaves, elder and even gooseberry.[6]

Two Englishmen travelling near Weimar in 1911 stopped at a village to try and get lunch on Maundy Thursday. The hospitable farmer who entertained them could offer nothing but green food to eat, and two children in the kitchen were singing:

> *Something green and something holy,*
> *Nine good greens to a Thursday poly.*

The surprised visitors were served an unusual but excellent meal: herb soup, dumplings (polies) speckled with the nine green herbs, and pickled eels in a green sauce.[7]

---

[1] Sheridan, Monica, *My Irish Cook Book*, London, 1965, 118.

[2] Bächtold-Stäubli, iii.1,194.

[3] Cruickshank, Constance, *Lenten Fare and Food for Fridays*, London, 1959, 68.

[4] Bächtold-Stäubli, iii.1,187–8.

[5] Cruickshank, 68.

[6] Uldall, Kai, 'Les Œufs de Pâques au Danemark', *Schweizerisches Archiv für Volkskunde*, LIV (Basle, 1958), 1–2.

[7] *Daily News*, 13 April 1911.

Colour Plate XV Batik (wax-resist) eggs from Rumania, where the local name for this type of work is *incondeiate*. The bottom row (four duck eggs) were given to the Monastery of Putna in 1961–3, by villagers from the vicinity. The same applies to the right-hand vertical row of eggs, except the egg in the second row up. This egg is from Brodina in the same area as Putna, and so is the goose egg on its left (both 1956). The four hens' eggs in the left vertical row are also from the same region, Northern Moldavia, except the blue egg (uppermost) from the Bucharest district. The pair of eggs above the goose egg are again Moldavian, that on the right being another Putna egg. The small, predominantly black and red egg above these two is from Poiana Mâruliu in Brasov Province (district of Tara Bîrsei). The unusual design of the red monochrome egg is based on the *Pristolnic*, an instrument used in the Orthodox and Coptic Churches for preparing the Host.

Colour Plate XVI (a) Hungarian batik (wax-resist) eggs. The upper
row was made by Germans from Hungary (Baranya), but shows
Hungarian designs; see the bottom row (also, for comparison, colour
plates XI, XIV, XV). Note motifs symbolizing the cross, rake, fir
tree and sun. Multi-coloured eggs, such as appear in the middle row,
are confined largely to southern Hungary. At the right of this row
is an egg specially typical of the Ormánység district, near the
Slavonian border. Similar patterns are used for external decoration
of the local cottages. The eggs with a black background are from
Sarköz district, on the western bank of the Danube, east of Pécs.
Hungarian decorated eggs are often blown and filled with wax.

(b) Various traditional techniques. The two centrally placed eggs,
one above the other, are from the Pennsylvania Dutch community,
made by Mrs Huyett (see plate 16). They are decorated with appliqué
fabric cut-outs, mostly taken from old dresses of her mother's. The
lower egg is a duck egg; the upper, with bluish shell, an aracauna.
The mauve and multi-colour batik (wax-resist) eggs are from
Slavonia, the part of Yugoslavia between the Sava and the
Hungarian border. This type of egg is made for presentation to a
Convent, the strawberry design being especially typical. The two
wooden eggs are Ukrainian. That on the left shows a deer, a
Ukrainian symbol of prosperity, in natural surroundings with a
realistic sun. On the second egg the sun appears in stylized form, in
a design common to many egg-decorating peoples.

In Catholic areas Maundy Thursday has a peculiarly mystical significance, because it marks the institution of the Blessed Eucharist by Our Lord; all kinds of beliefs sprang up in connection with the powers of this day. They said in German Bohemia that all water turns to blood during the night,[1] and people round Viersen left their beds unmade because the Saviour did not sleep then.[2] Even the eggs laid transfer a certain sanctity to the household wool and linen if placed in the cupboard: moths and decay will spare the material.[3] This custom from Alsace-Lorraine is scarcely surprising, since Germans even consider a Green Thursday egg blessed while it is still inside the chicken.

Nine in the morning is the most important hour, when church bells ring for the last time before Easter. People say they have gone to Rome, and Styrian farmers, taking an egg from the nest and carefully holding it in a cloth, throw it at that moment over the house. If one of these eggs is placed on the point of the gable, it will prevent the roof from caving in, but on no account ought it to be dyed.[4]

How the name Green Thursday arose is a little obscure. *Dies Viridium*, the Day of the Green Ones, was a time in the early Church set aside for readmission of penitents. These were people, previously declared excommunicate, who throughout Lent had stood in sackcloth at the church door whenever a service began, humbly begging permission to go in. On Green Thursday they were ceremonially welcomed for absolution and readmitted to the sacraments, wearing sprigs of green as an expression of joy.[5]

Conceivably, the term derives from Our Lord's words on the road to Calvary: 'For if they do these things in a green tree, what shall be done in the dry?'[6] Of course, the agony of Our Saviour beneath the olives in Gethsemane is a central feature of the day. Germany commemorates this with a *Baumbeten* (tree prayer),[7] and it has suggested another derivation for 'Green Thursday', from the German word *grunen*, meaning 'to mourn'.

[1] Bächtold-Stäubli, iii.1,195.   [2] *Ibid.*, 1,187.
[3] Van Gennep, Arnold, *Manuel de Folklore Français Contemporain*, Paris, 1947, 1.iii.1,336.   [4] Bächtold-Stäubli, iii.1,191.
[5] Weiser, Francis X., *The Easter Book* (London, 1955), 104. Brewer, 551. Bächtold-Stäubli, iii.1,186. Cruickshank, 68. Urlin, Ethel L., *Festivals, Holy Days and Saints' Days*, London, 1915, 62.
[6] Luke, xxiii.31.   [7] Bächtold-Stäubli, iii.1,196.

But in practice sorrow gives way to rejoicing. At one time the clergy, abandoning Lenten purple, wore vestments of green – an early custom, apparently introduced in the twelfth century, which has not survived today. In the liturgy green is a joyful colour, symbolic of hope, because it reminds us of nature's perpetual renewal after the winter, and of God's generosity in giving us the fruits of the earth.[1]

In French Haut Savoie they used to say that green plants appeared above the snow for the first time on *Jeudi Vert*.[2] So green stands for life and renewal, and herbs eaten on this day are supposed to impart the fresh health of new spring. Ideas of this sort help to explain why Germans called Green Thursday the luckiest day in the year. The significant colour apart, Thursday had been a day sacred to Thor.

Understandably, Green Thursday was an important time for beginning anything new. In fact, among the Eastern Slavs New Year customs seem to have been transferred to that day, perhaps because an earlier New Year originally took place in March.[3] Germans say it is a good time for sowing seed, and planting trees, potted plants and all green things. At Thillot (Vosegen), when the bells stop pealing, they shake fruit trees to get a better crop, and cabbages planted within the sound do well – this last from the Erzegebirge. Farmers in Saxony and Brandenburg liked sowing flax then; the man who did the planting carried two eggs in his pocket, which he left behind in the field to ensure that the crop would prosper.[4]

In Finland, where eggs are scarce, children make little nests, fill them with stones and hide them in the house. Early on Maundy Thursday they search blindfold, and anyone who is successful cries, 'I have found a nest!' and hops up and down. This is a charm to increase the summer's egg yield. Wild birds are the main laying fowl, and fresh moss is put in the nesting-boxes on Green Thursday to encourage them to settle.[5]

[1] Ferguson, G., *Signs and Symbols in Christian Art*, New York, 1961, 151.
[2] Information kindly supplied by Miss Ida-Marie Kaplan, formerly of this area.
[3] Václavík, Antonín, *Výroční Obyčeje A Lidové Umění*, Prague, 1959, 521.
[4] Bächtold-Stäubli, iii.1,193.
[5] Vilkuna, Kustaa, 'Osterfeiern und Vogeleiersuchen in Finnland', *Schweizerisches Archiv für Volkskunde*, LIII (Basle, 1957), ii–iii, 136.

An interesting, not dissimilar, ritual of increase used to be practised by newlyweds in Thuringia. On Green Thursday they hung a pincushion and a ball, attached to strings, out of the bedroom window. Boys tried to jump up and take the ball, girls the pincushion. They sang:

> *Green bush, green tree, green ball for me,*
> *A great wide ball with a silken shirt*
> *And golden lace to hem my skirt.*
> *Fair bride, fair groom, hang cushion and ball*
> *And the God of all green things have mercy on all.*[1]

RITES OF RENEWAL

The Thuringian rhyme must be the relic of some ancient ritual of fertility and renewal, in spite of its connection with one of the Easter holy days. Similarly, consecrated eggs are used to promote increase in man and nature. These customs follow the seasonal round. The Volga Chuvash bury coloured Easter eggs in their fields;[2] Serbians put them in the vineyards on Good Friday to ensure a bountiful crop;[3] in Macedonia they do the same, but carefully mark the places which they choose. Next year the eggs are dug up and eaten – a custom reminiscent of the Chinese eggs, which are buried raw and consumed after six or nine months, when the contents have all changed to black jelly. Indeed, the period of burial can be much longer, as this charming verse shows:

> *I was five years old*
> *When under the tree I buried*
> *Five eggs white as snow . . .*
>
> *I was ten years old*
> *When I felt I should like to see*
> *What had become of them . . .*
>
> *I was fifteen years old*
> *And had forgotten all about the eggs*
> *As I travelled far from my place of birth . . .*
>
> *I was twenty years old*
> *And on my wedding day*

---

[1] *Daily News*, 13 April 1911. [2] Bächtold-Stäubli, ii.613.

[3] Georgieva, Milica, *Бојадисување и шарање на Велигденски Јајца Во Скопјеи Околијата*, Skopje, 1960, 190, note 13.

Remembered about those five eggs
Buried there under the tree

I did as I was advised,
Taking some unslaked lime
Went and sprinkled the spot
And poured water on it

I was twenty five years old,
My first-born son was five,
His brother two years younger
When their little sister was born . . .

Then I dug up those five eggs
Transformed by the years
Into a great delicacy,
And I reflected
On the transformation of the eggs
And on the transformation of my life.[1]

At first glance, the parallel drawn appears to be practical, but there is, I think, a more profound link intended with the fruition of human life. One finds the same idea in Europe, where a connection is often seen between egg and harvest. Swedish farmers say, 'If the eggs are full, the barns will be full too.'[2] Slovakian peasants go out to pray, usually on St George's Day, and roll an Easter egg across the new corn to help it grow. They also crumble one up, and mix it with the seed wheat;[3] Germans prefer one laid on Maundy Thursday. Later, at harvest-time, they take an Easter egg and place it with a loaf inside the first sheaf gathered.[4] These familiar tokens will enrich the crop.

But the term 'harvest' can also be used quite broadly to include other products of the farmer's work. Ukrainian bee-keepers place a coloured Easter egg under each hive to ensure a fine supply of honey,[5] and in France one that has been blessed increases the eggs' fertility; a Green Thursday egg, slipped into a clutch, will help the others to hatch.[6]

[1] Sis, Vladimir, *Chinese Food and Fables*, Prague, 1966, 124–5.

[2] Eskeröd, Albert, 'Ostereier in Schweden', *Schweizerisches Archiv für Volkskunde*, LIV (Basle, 1958), 14.

[3] Pranda, Adam, 'Die slowakischen Ostereier', *Schweizerisches Archiv für Volkskunde*, LIII (Basle, 1957), ii–iii, 170.

[4] Bächtold-Stäubli, ii.611.

[5] Dmytrikw, Olga, *Ukrainian Arts*, New York, 1955, 97.

[6] Van Gennep, *Manuel*, i.iii.1,339.

Animals are not overlooked. In Slovakia, herdsmen receive Easter eggs when they first take cattle out – as many eggs as there are animals. The shells are buried afterwards, so that the herds shall feed well.[1] German cowherds get the same tokens on Whitsun morning, and this should mean a good supply of milk.[2] Swedish children performing this task are given their share on Easter morning, so that the cattle will be easier to control in summer-time.[3] Another rite from Slovakia, when the animals step over an Easter egg at first ploughing, no doubt brings benefit to herd and crop together. The egg, which is put at the entrance to the byre, is afterwards given away to a beggar.[4]

Consecrated eggs were cherished, not only for these pastoral activities, but also to encourage increase in human beings. French and German men used one to promote sexual capacity. Germans preferred an Easter egg; the French one laid on Green Thursday.[5] Good Friday eggs were also popular in Germany with any man who particularly wanted to father a boy. In the Swabian Alps a woman took her husband a boiled goose egg in bed on Good Friday morning; in the evening she baked him an egg cake. Good Friday and Green Thursday eggs were both thought specially good for guarding against the disappointments attendant on too great a sexual indulgence. Indeed, Green Thursday eggs were so powerful that the French believed they even made children virile. German men used the shells as an aphrodisiac, and French couples eat one on Holy Saturday as a protection against impotence.[6]

The connection between eggs and fecundity is made quite clear in a Finnish Easter custom where they are associated with testicles. Anyone proposing to hunt for birds' eggs goes before sunrise to the bull's pen on Easter morning, with eyes shut, walking backwards and wearing a fur put on the wrong way round. Some people wear a blindfold too. The idea is to locate the bull's testicles, simply by sense of touch. Whoever succeeds in doing this first calls out, 'I have found a nest! I have found a nest!' and will collect the greatest number of birds' eggs in the coming

[1] Pranda, 170.
[2] Bächtold-Stäubli, ii.612.
[3] Eskeröd, 10.
[4] Pranda, 169.
[5] Bächtold-Stäubli, vi.1,331. Van Gennep, *Manuel*, 1.iii.1,340.
[6] Bächtold-Stäubli, iii.1,189, iv.1,001. Van Gennep, *Manuel* 1.iii.1,340.

spring and summer; this was specially popular with herd-boys. Elsewhere in Finland it was lucky to touch the testicles of a child.[1]

The same ritual took place, with certain variations, across the Gulf in Estonia. It was not necessary to be blindfold, and touching the bull's penis instead of his testicles ensured a good haul of eggs for that year. In the north they massaged his testicles and recited the following verse:

> *I rub the bull's eggs,*
> *And I get the gulls' eggs,*
> *The eggs of ducks and of kriek ducks,*
> *The eggs of downy geese and the eggs of velvety ducks.*[2]

LUCKY AMULETS

These fertility rites help to show how a pagan symbol, the egg, was gradually included in Christian folk-belief; an Easter egg was a rather special magic amulet, enriched by power from the Christian faith. Greeks say that all Maundy Thursday eggs, especially those from a hen's first clutch, possess miraculous qualities;[3] in Slovenia it is the blessed Easter eggs which bring good luck: whoever eats nine of them will be fortunate for the rest of his life.[4]

In fact, in Yugoslavia the first Easter egg dyed is particularly important; farmers fed it to new-born chicks, and to hens which had just begun to lay.[5] Small babies 'overlooked' by the evil eye recovered if they were washed with water in which the first egg had been placed.[6] Even if children were healthy, their parents thought this would preserve them from harm.

German and French folk-beliefs link a blessed Easter egg with personal well-being: Green Thursday eggs prevent falling off a ladder,[7] and one is concealed in the cushion on which a baby is brought to the font. Thuringian godfathers present their new

---

[1] Vilkuna, 135.

[2] Ränk, Gustav, 'Ostereier in Estland', *Schweizerisches Archiv für Volkskunde*, LIII (Basle, 1957), ii–iii, 140.

[3] Megas, George A., *Greek Calendar Customs*, Athens, 1958, 95.

[4] Jagodic, Maria, 'Über Ostereier und Ostergebäck in Slowenian', *Schweizerisches Archiv für Volkskunde*, LIII (Basle, 1957), ii–iii, 158.

[5] Georgieva, 190.

[6] *Ibid.*, 189.

[7] Van Gennep, *Manuel*, 1.iii.1,337.

charge with an egg decorated with a picture of a stork; it must be carefully put away, for the child would not live to grow old if it got broken.[1]

This is reminiscent of the Sierck custom, when children were given a red egg to prevent an early death. As a protection against the same thing, each member of a French family used to keep a Green Thursday egg that had been cooked on Easter Sunday.[2] Perhaps there are echoes here of the life egg in the old folk-tales, which had to be kept safely hidden if the owner's life was not to be forfeit. Germans used to say that anyone breaking a Good Friday egg would contract consumption[3] – until recently a fatal disease – and in Denmark, if the contents of an Easter egg dried up sooner than expected it was a sign of a coming death.[4] The same belief was popular in Rumania, where women sometimes kept an Easter egg, as a model for the design, fixed below the ikon or else on the joist of a door. Small devils or evil spirits were supposed to come and live inside.[5] The Greeks had a similar omen: if an egg was put on to the fire the Sunday before Lent – Cheese Sunday – and it broke, the owner would not enjoy good health.[6]

The rich symbolism of an Easter egg is even used to suggest the enduring life of the spirit: Tyrolese believe a Good Friday egg not only preserves its freshness all the year – it will not even smash if hurled over the house-top.[7] Wends (Sorbs), Greeks and other races all maintain that an egg boiled at Easter will never go bad; after a few years it changes into a pearl, a common emblem of the soul. In France the yolk of Green Thursday's egg becomes a diamond after 100 years.[8] At home it was Good Friday's egg that never went bad, and kept fresh even for the Christmas pudding;

---

[1] Bächtold-Stäubli, ii.637, vi.1,329.

[2] Van Gennep, *Manuel*, 1.iii.1,337.

[3] Bächtold-Stäubli, iv.1,000.

[4] Uldall, 9.

[5] Slătineanu, Barbu, 'Les Œufs de Pâques en Roumanie', *Schweizerisches Archiv für Volkskunde*, LIII (Basle, 1957), ii–iii, 182.

[6] Megas, 72.

[7] Bächtold-Stäubli, iv.1,000.

[8] *Ibid.*, 1,327. Van Gennep, *Manuel*, 1.iii.1,338. Arnott, Margaret, 'Die Ostereier in Griechenland', *Schweizerisches Archiv für Volkskunde*, LIII (Basle, 1957), ii–iii,193.

Bulgarians guaranteed them until the following Easter.[1] Italians of the Abruzzi stress more the importance of Ascension Day. The evening before, an egg is put out on the window-sill; the Madonna will bless it as she passes, ensuring its freshness for evermore.[2]

All these beliefs in which an egg either stays miraculously fresh or changes to a precious gem suggest eternal life, and hence the Resurrection. A curious perversion of this idea turns up in old Russian folklore; people said that a mouse which had eaten a piece of consecrated Easter egg changed to a bat.[3] More familiar to English minds is the German superstition of sunrise on Easter morning. Anyone who looks at it through a blessed Green Thursday egg, will see the Easter Lamb dancing within.[4]

Since Easter eggs symbolize eternal life, it is not surprising that they are sometimes used in extra-sensory experience. The Saracatsans – probably Hellenized Vlachs, but, according to some sources, Albanians or pure Greeks – send their women to church on Maundy Thursday with two parcels: one for the living and one for the dead. The dead relatives, who are present on that day, receive *kolyvá*, a boiled-wheat funeral cake, and the living get coloured eggs. These are blessed in the course of the service and the eggs should have been laid by a black hen; they are decorated with serpent designs, which probably indicate fertility.[5]

In this curious mixture of black magic and Christianity, Easter eggs bridge the gap between life and death. Sometimes they are used as an aid for seeing the future. They may quite literally assist a child in learning to read, gathering knowledge that lies ahead. Children in Baden were given one, laid on Good Friday, before attending school the first time; letters of the alphabet were stirred into it, and all had to be eaten. Good Friday eggs were also supposed to make adults far-sighted when playing cards.[6]

---

[1] Banks, M. Macleod, *British Calendar Customs: Scotland*, London, 1937, i.36. *Notes and Queries*, 17 December 1921, 12th Series, ix.489. Vakarelski, Christo, 'Œufs de Pâques chez les Bulgares', *Schweizerisches Archiv für Volkskunde*, LIII (Basle, 1957), ii–iii.186.

[2] Canziani, Estella, *Through the Appenines and the Lands of the Abruzzi*, Cambridge, 1928, 328.

[3] Bächtold-Stäubli, vi.1,332.   [4] *Ibid.*, 1,328.

[5] Kavadias, G. B., *Pasteurs-Nomades Méditerranéens: Les Saracatsans de Gréce*, Paris, 1965, 327–8.

[6] Bächtold-Stäubli, iv.1,001.

An egg laid on one of the holy days of Easter helps link the material and non-material worlds in another way. Beaten and poured into a glass of water on the night of Good Friday, it reveals by its shape how the crops will fare in the coming year. Another form of divination uses a Good Friday egg, laid by a black hen, like a divining rod – to find a corpse lost in the water. Girls in Schleswig-Holstein throw egg-shells on the doorstep the evening before Easter, calling out to discover the profession of their future husband; the first man passing by will reveal the secret. Young men throw a Good Friday egg over the shoulder to find a wife. This, too, was a German custom.[1]

From divination it is only a small step to seeing evil spirits. In Messin (France) a Green Thursday egg provided protection against witches. If you offered one to her, the witch would either refuse or smash it, since to accept would mean her death. Anybody who carried one was quite safe, and could then discover which of the local people dabbled in witchcraft.[2] Sometimes one spotted them out of doors; and a Green Thursday egg, carried to the crossroads on May Day, will reveal the witches' dance.[3] In Germany they say you must look through an egg in the sunshine in order to see witches. But a service in church seems to have been the best place of all. Put a black hen's egg in the collection bag on Good Friday and you will see all the evil spirits round about.

In Lower Austria a man with an Easter or Green Thursday egg in his pocket could see any witches who happened to be in church. They might be dancing or sitting with their backs to the altar. It is best to go on one of the holy days, Good Friday or Easter itself, in order to see these sights. But in that case hurry out before the blessing is given or the witches will catch you.[4]

Traditionally, they wear milk pails on their heads in place of bonnets, and carry a slice of pork instead of a prayer book.[5] Pork, which is an odd idea, could possibly link the witches with the Jews, who were much in the popular mind, especially at Easter-time: the story of the Passion aroused annual anti-Semitic outbursts. Here the pork could, by one of those curious processes

---

[1] *Ibid.*, ii.619–20, iv.1,001.   [2] Van Gennep, *Manuel*, 1.iii.1,337.
[3] Leland, C. G., *Gypsy Sorcery and Fortune Telling*, London, 1891, 75.
[4] Bächtold-Stäubli, iii.1,191, 1,192, note 68, iv.1,001.
[5] Kelly, Walter, *Curiosities of Indo-European Tradition and Folklore*, London, 1863, 233. Leland, 77.

common to human nature, link the object which a person shuns all the more closely to him.

The power of a witch over cattle – those staples of peasant existence – was greatly feared. Diseases which affect cows and their capacity for giving milk were blamed on their evil spells. So it was not idle curiosity, but very useful to be able to identify them. The pails or churns – which they wore on their heads – were a symbol of the witches' sway over the milk.

Consecrated eggs, which revealed such sights, were obviously very important. While parents often gave them to children to safeguard health, in Franche-Comté the special Green Thursday eggs were reserved for the head of the household.[1] Such a gift was fitting for a child to offer his parents in days when the younger generation held its elders in considerable awe. In German Bohemia before the war, when father came home from church on Easter Sunday, his children brought hard-boiled Green Thursday eggs, sometimes rolling them towards him. He had to eat these, shell and all, standing in the middle of the road. In other districts they were sometimes offered by women.[2]

In St Moret, France, a Green Thursday egg was shared among the family in a little ceremony – a common practice in many countries. Of course, there would probably be a number of these eggs, so Germans gave everybody one, unless there were not enough to go right round, in which case men were allowed a whole egg but women only half. At least part of the shell had to be eaten too.[3]

In Poland, as in Russia and the Ukraine, a family went home after Easter Sunday Mass and ate a special meal blessed by the priest; he would have done this on Holy Saturday, and been presented with an Easter egg in gratitude. The family stood first in silence while the head of the household distributed shelled eggs – one piece for everyone present. They all exchanged wishes for happiness and long life.[4] In Sweden one should try to sit between brothers and sisters; for anybody who does this while eating Easter eggs, will see his wishes all come true.[5]

---

[1] Van Gennep, *Manuel*, i.iii.1,337.

[2] Bächtold-Stäubli, vi.1,328.

[3] *Ibid.*, iii.1,189, vi.1,328.

[4] Benet, Sula, *Song, Dance and Customs of Peasant Poland*, London, 1951, 55–6. Spicer, 260–1.   [5] Eskeröd, 14.

Jews are very particular about food left over from Passover. The *Afikomen*, a piece of unleavened bread that has not been eaten, is hung by the door for the rest of the year, to protect the household.[1] Christian Poles have a similar regard for scraps from the Easter meal: they are useful charms against evil, and the bones are dropped in the well to prevent worms breeding.[2]

It was specially important to handle egg-shells correctly. Styrians refrained from giving them to the chickens – the usual practice – and burnt them instead.[3] Ukrainians did the same or threw them into fast-flowing water.[4] Slovenians put them in the pond to silence the frogs, though Germans who did this could not be absolved at their next confession.[5]

But as a rule it was general practice to collect the shells and save them for different purposes. In parts of Germany where people ate a boiled goose egg on Easter Day, the shell might afterwards be put up on the door lintel to protect the family from fever.[6] Slovakians hung Easter egg-shells in the trees to increase the size of the fruit, buried them in the garden to support the growing plants, or strewed them on the top-soil to repel caterpillars.[7] In Allgau they prevent damage by worms; if put in ditches around the farm, they keep away insects in summer.[8] Greeks preferred Green Thursday egg-shells, which they laid at the roots of the fruit trees, saying, 'May all the trees bear fruit!'[9]

In Germany people filled them with holy water and placed them, together with a consecrated palm, in a corner of the rye-field to hallow and increase the crop.[10] Poles buried coloured egg-shells in the soil; they also saved some to scatter in the corners of the house for repelling toads and beetles[11] and, in a similar custom, Germans laid them on the window sills to keep

---

[1] Levy, Isaac, *A Guide to Passover*, London, 1958, 57.
[2] Benet, 56.
[3] Kretzenbacher, Leopold, 'Vom roten Osterei in der grünen Steiermark', *Schweizerisches Archiv für Volkskunde*, LIII (Basle, 1957), ii–iii.109.
[4] Dmytrikw, 101.
[5] Jagodic, 158. Bächtold-Stäubli, vi.1,331.
[6] *Ibid.*, ii.633.
[7] Pranda, 170.
[8] Bächtold-Stäubli, ii.1,331–2.
[9] Megas, 95.
[10] Bächtold-Stäubli, iii.1,191.
[11] Benet, 56.

off ants and other insects.[1] Slovenians, who believed that the shell had greater powers than the egg, used it to keep not only vermin, but witches and evil spirits from the house;[2] Rumanians barred them from their farms by burying shells in the dung at the doorways of stables and pigsties,[3] and French farmers similarly hung Green Thursday egg-shells at the entrance to the byre.[4]

If it was important to handle the shells correctly, it was even more essential to treat the Easter egg itself in a proper manner. In Denmark, where at one time the very poor could only afford such luxurious food once a year, eggs being a rarity, it was important to eat your Easter egg on the right day. This might be Good Friday, Easter itself, or the Monday following – it depended on local custom. If one mistook the day illness followed, and a wrong Easter egg gift – an even instead of an odd number – could mean that death was not far away.[5]

The power of Easter eggs extends to things with which they are in contact. Even water used for boiling them is supposed to possess magical powers. Slavs use it to help the complexion,[6] and in some countries it protects the cows from witchcraft: farmers in Poland and Bohemia pour it along the byre, and in Minden the animals are given it to drink.[7]

Such eggs themselves are of apotropaic value. All over Germany they guard family and cattle against any form of harm. Some farmers halved one and threw part in the stable, part in the byre. In Passau they gave animals a whole egg and also two special noodles which they had previously laid on the cross. Bavarians, strangely, buried one under the threshold to keep the family from unchastity.[8]

Such charms are of a general nature, preserving a household from anything untoward, as in France, where a Green Thursday egg prevents one from falling into debt.[9] But in an agricultural community there were many specific hazards from the elements

[1] Bächtold-Stäubli, vi.1,331.
[2] Jagodic, 158.
[3] Slătineanu, 182.
[4] Van Gennep, *Manuel*, i.iii.1,337.
[5] Uldall, 1.
[6] Bächtold-Stäubli, vi.1,332.
[7] Benet, 56. Bächtold-Stäubli, ii.634, vi.1,332.
[8] *Ibid.*, ii.612, 614, notes 185, 192.
[9] Van Gennep, *Manuel*, i.iii.1,337.

to be guarded against. German peasants might enclose a Green Thursday egg in the hearth cavity as a protection against bad weather in general.[1] High winds can be particularly disastrous for farmers, and Ukrainian peasants place coloured egg-shells under their thatched roofs and under the hay-ricks to avert them.[2] Austrians prevent floods by burying a Green Thursday egg at the point of danger – for instance, at the edge of the stream.[3]

Hail can also be an agricultural disaster, and Christian egg charms against it are very common in a number of countries. Styrians blame the witches for throwing hail-stones; this can be prevented with a Green Thursday egg, but its magic must be called on when the church bells ring their final peal.[4] The blend of pagan and Christian here is even more apparent in Macedonia, where the farmers bury red eggs during the thunderstorm to increase their potency still further.[5] Strengthened by this link with the thunder god, their Christian power is redoubled.

In Gottschee, a formerly German area of north Yugoslavia, three consecrated eggs were used as a hail charm. Laid on Good Friday and blessed on Holy Saturday, they were buried in different corners of the field before sunrise on Easter morning.[6] Here the combined influence of three holy days is brought into play, perhaps recalling the Trinity. This ritual might be an attempt to guard the boundaries, as in Rumania, when four eggs were buried at four corners of an estate; the area enclosed was said to be safe from flood and hail.[7]

The time chosen for such ceremonies varies. In Italy Ascension Day is most usual. At Monferrato eggs laid by a white hen are carried to the fields and vineyards.[8] Macedonians favour St George's Day; so do the Ukrainians for their custom of rolling a coloured egg in green oats;[9] then it is buried in the fields. Through all these amulets Our Lord, whom they represent, is believed to protect land and crops from hail and other harm.

[1] Bächtold-Stäubli, iii.1,190.
[2] Dmytrikw, 97.
[3] Bächtold-Stäubli, iii.1,190.
[4] *Ibid.*, 1,191.
[5] *The Times*, 3 April 1958.
[6] Bächtold-Stäubli, ii.610.
[7] Slătineanu, 182.
[8] Gubernatis, Angelo de, *Zoological Mythology*, London, 1872, ii.291.
[9] Dmytrikw, 97.

An especially elaborate ritual is observed in Germany, where a Green Thursday egg is buried in the largest wheatfield, and flanked on either side with a consecrated, burning 'hail Cross'.[1] There is a related hail custom in Czechoslovakia: on Easter Saturday afternoon all the boys collect wood, stack it in a corn-field, and place a tall cross, covered with straw, in the centre. After evening service they light lanterns at the blessed Paschal Candle in church, race to the wood-stack, and the first to arrive sets fire to it. Women are not allowed to take part in this, or to go anywhere within the vicinity of the fire. When the wood flares up, the boys cry, 'We are burning the Judas!' After it has all burnt, watch is kept over the glowing ashes throughout the night to ensure that they are not stolen. Next day at dawn they are thrown into a running stream. The boy who lit the fire is given coloured eggs by women at the church door that morning, the wealthy offering him two, the poor one. This ceremony of the Judas Fire is intended to avert hail from the crops.[2] A straightforward pagan survival, it is given a Christian link by kindling from the Paschal Candle. Especially in the German lands, these fires were wide-spread; people pushed sticks into them, and when these became charred they took them home as a protection, not only against hail, but against fire and lightning too.[3]

Easter eggs, which are prominent in this ritual, can often guard against fire. French peasants in the Vosges and Franche-Comté tossed a Green Thursday egg into the grate.[4] Here the charm has evolved around association of ideas. As a talisman against fire, the Greek Orthodox Setukese in Estonia place an Easter egg in front of the ikon.[5] Germans protect the outside of a house: an egg, laid in Holy Week and blessed at Easter, is put between the front windows.[6]

Another of their customs was to bury the egg – which should be that of a black hen – beneath the threshold, along with the menstrual blood of a virgin.[7] This is plain magic, but Christian

[1] Bächtold-Stäubli, iii.1,191.

[2] Runeberg, Arne, 'Witches, Demons and Fertility Magic', *Commentationes Humanorum Litterarum*, xiv (Helsinki, 1947), Nos. 1–4, 180.

[3] Lehmann, Hedi, *Volksbrauch im Jahreslauf*, Munich, 1964, 34.

[4] Van Gennep, *Manuel*, 1.iii.1,338–9.

[5] Ränk, 142.

[6] Bächtold-Stäubli, ii.609.   [7] *Ibid.*

lore is uppermost in the similar use of Whitsun eggs; these were saved and then, if need arose, thrown into a fire to put it out.[1] Presumably this is a counter-charm, using an egg from the day when the Holy Spirit descended, sitting in tongues of flame on the heads of the Apostles.

In the days before insurance, when houses were often made of wood and water only obtainable slowly in limited amounts from wells and distant streams, the prospect of a fire must have been truly terrifying; peasants lost all their goods. In Slovakia, once a blaze had started, an egg would be carried around it, to enclose the area and stop it spreading further. Then Easter eggs or the shells were thrown into the flames to quench their might. Sometimes a Green Thursday egg was used, and either way it should be thrown from the direction in which the wind was blowing, so that it would not fan the fire.[2]

In Styria eggs which had been doubly blessed, by being laid on Green Thursday or Good Friday and consecrated on Holy Saturday, were used for the same purpose.[3] People of Oberpfalz threw a consecrated Easter egg backwards to stop the blaze.[4] Why backwards does not seem clear: perhaps because a certain secrecy is often maintained in magic rites, even those which are performed with a Christian object. Those who would see a ghost in church must enter backwards, and Russians communing with their dead adopted the same practice.[5] 'Seek to know no more',[6] the witches told Macbeth when he became too inquisitive.

While fire was disastrous, blazing bolts from the sky – lightning – were a danger too. And since it strikes from above, talismans against it are usually placed high up. English farmers hung an Ascension Day egg in the roof, for 'it preserveth the same from all hurts'.[7]

In Slovakia they put an Easter egg in the gables,[8] and Germans wrap a Green Thursday egg in a linen cloth, nailing it to the cross outside the house.[9] It was especially effective if first laid in the sun.

---

[1] Thorpe, Benjamin, *Northern Mythology*, London, 1851, iii.330.

[2] Pranda, 170.   [3] Kretzenbacher, 109.

[4] Bächtold-Stäubli, vi.1,331.

[5] Sokolov, Y. M., *Russian Folklore*, New York, 1950, 188.

[6] *Macbeth*, iv.i.104.

[7] Wright, A. R., *British Calendar Customs: England*, London, 1936, i.147.

[8] Pranda, 170.   [9] Bächtold-Stäubli, ii.1,190.

In German Odenwald, eggs covered with rushes were kept all the year suspended from the ceiling, sometimes as many as three. Catholics put them near the crucifix for good luck, and, since they too hung down from the ceiling, it may be that they had a similar purpose.[1]

German settlers in America took these customs with them. In the Pennsylvania Dutch country a family called Schreiber remember saving two Good Friday eggs and putting them in a can inside a drawer. The Wendts, another family, hid one beneath a crock up in the attic. In doing this each year they hoped that lightning would spare the house.[2]

Sometimes Germans tossed Green Thursday's egg over the roof top, enclosing the house within the magic arc, just as Slovenians scattered shells around it. The egg was buried where it fell, to ward off lightning.[3] Green Thursday eggs were much used for this purpose in both Germany and Holland,[4] no doubt because Thursday is sacred to Thor, the god of thunder and lightning; such an egg was thought especially suitable if it possessed a reddish yolk – a colour associated with the same god.[5]

The all-embracing, blessed egg, preserving everything in its sphere and keeping it safe from harm, is a popular idea. On Easter morning before sunrise, German farmers took a white Easter egg in the mouth and circled the whole of the farm and its adjoining area. This was said to prevent the hens mislaying their eggs, just as an Easter egg was rolled around the flocks to keep them secure.[6]

We meet the same idea in a slightly different form at a popular family occasion in southern Yugoslavia – and, indeed, to some extent elsewhere in the Balkans. For example, in Greece, Cheese Sunday, the last before Lent, is a day when people spread eggshells in the streets and cry, 'Out with fleas and bugs!'[7] It is like a spring-cleaning festival. But in Ohrid (Yugoslav Macedonia) they

---

[1] Mössinger, Friedrich, 'Odenwälder Binseneier', *Schweizerisches Archiv für Volkskunde*, LIII (Basle, 1957), ii–iii.76.

[2] Shoemaker, Alfred L., *Eastertide in Pennsylvania*, Kutztown, 1960, 22.

[3] Jagodic, 158. Bächtold-Stäubli, iii.1,190.

[4] Thorpe, iii.328.

[5] Ellis Davidson, H. R., *Gods and Myths of Northern Europe*, London, 1964, 85.

[6] Bächtold-Stäubli, vi.1,331.

[7] Hamilton, Mary, *Greek Saints and Their Festivals*, London, 1910, 197.

call it Forgiveness Sunday – *Oproštenjedan*. Families first eat a fish supper together. When this is finished, the father chooses a hard-boiled egg from a dishful on the table, and threads it on a piece of string which is fastened to a little stick. He holds this first over his own mouth, and then above the lips of other members of the family. Each person in turn must succeed in getting it into his mouth without using hands. When they have done this, the father cuts the egg carefully in half, and finally into small pieces. Every-one gets a morsel, and also a whole hard-boiled egg from the pile in the dish. Then, using the halves of the shell as cups, he drinks the following toast:

> *Fleas and bugs keep away from our homes*
> *And remain in the mountains afar!*

The shells are refilled and passed round to everyone.[1] Serbo-Croats on the same day suspend an egg from a thread below the ceiling – evidently a variation of the same custom, though the specific purpose here is to protect and increase farm livestock. It is spun with a circular movement above the table, and whoever catches it wins, and is allowed to keep it.[2] The custom has affinities with the Greek method of bumping an egg dangling from a string with the forehead, before catching it between the lips.[3] This ritual, enacted on the island of Skyros, ceremonially closes the mouth to meat before Lent begins.

Just as the encircling egg, in one way or another, was thought to hold the family safe within its sphere, so it served as an amulet, preserving the traveller from harm and enabling him to find his road. It bears comparison with a St Christopher medal, which Catholic travellers carry to guard them on the way, and the re-semblance is borne out by a Pennsylvania Dutch belief that you should not sell Good Friday eggs: *'Du daitsht dei Glick ferkawfa'* – you would sell your luck.[4] For, according to Catholic doctrine, blessed objects do not lose their sanctity by being given away; only through being sold.[5]

[1] Lodge, Oliver, *Peasant Life in Yugoslavia*, London, 1941, 243–4.

[2] Wildhaber, Robert, 'Zum Symbolgehalt und zur Ikonographie des Eies', *Deutsches Jahrbuch für Volkskunde*, vi (Berlin, 1960), 82–3.

[3] Abbott, G. F., *Macedonian Folklore*, Cambridge, 1903, 29–30.

[4] Shoemaker, 22.

[5] Burggraff, Aloysius J., *Handbook for New Catholics*, Glen Rock, N.J., 1960, 135.

In certain areas of Germany, when an Easter egg has been hallowed it is customary to divide it and share it with others. Then, if you are lost during the following year, in order to find the way again, you must remember with whom you ate the egg. Whitsun eggs can serve the same purpose. In Lower Austria, if two people divide one together before witnesses, and one of them goes astray later in the year, he need only remember the face of the other person to get back on to the right road. Similarly, Green Thursday eggs are supposed to be helpful at unfamiliar crossroads.[1]

Besides such workaday benefits, Christian eggs were held to be specially healthy. If you eat a raw egg fasting, on Christmas morning, heavy weights will be no burden. This surprising information appeared in the *Chicago Tribune* as recently as 1921. Easter eggs were a secret source of strength in Oldenburg (Germany). Hence a local saying: '*He mott noch'n paar paaskeier mehr hebben*'[2] – he should eat a few more Easter eggs. Indeed, a lusty man should eat twenty fowl's eggs and a goose egg, or an egg complete with its shell. This is what they say in Butjadingen; and in a seventeenth-century Rhineland source: '*Auf Ostern iss hart gesotene Eyer, dann bist du das gantze Jahr gesundt*'[3] – eat hardboiled eggs at Easter and you'll be healthy all the year round. Farmers in Germany and France thought Green Thursday eggs would keep them fit, though the custom of eating the shell was not shared by the French, who preferred an omelette.[4]

Silesians thought an egg partially brooded at Easter would be better as a cure. Certainly Easter eggs were tremendous aids to health; they were credited with warding off every conceivable type of disease. Years ago, in St Rupert's Church, Gaden, they were offered to avert the plague, and the Germans share with us a folk-belief that a piece of Good Friday egg relieves anyone suffering from colic.[5] In the Dauphiné region of France people ate a morsel on Easter Day for the same complaint.[6] A child with

[1] Bächtold-Stäubli, ii.607, iii.1,191, vi.1,328.

[2] *Ibid.*, vi.1,327.

[3] *Ibid.*

[4] Van Gennep, *Manuel*, 1.iii.1,336. Joisten, Charles, 'Le Folklore de L'Œuf en Dauphiné', *Arts et Traditions Populaires* (Paris, January–March 1961), 60.

[5] Bächtold-Stäubli, vi.617, 633. Henderson, William, *Notes on the Folklore of the Northern Counties of England and the Borders*, London, 1879, 83.

[6] Van Gennep, *Manuel*, 1.iii.1,337–8.

stomach-ache was helped if part of Good Friday's egg was cooked, inserted in an acorn, and hung round his neck. Here even eating the egg was unnecessary: external contact with the patient was enough, as in the most primitive magic charms.[1]

The Pennsylvania Dutch ensured good health by eating Good Friday eggs, either on the day they were laid or for Easter break-fast. A Mrs Cora Snyder, living in York County, suffered from a bad goitre. She rubbed it with a Good Friday egg, which she then put in the attic chimney, claiming that the goitre consequently disappeared. Rubbing was effective in other ways. It prevented babies developing a sore mouth, and removed birthmarks – pro-vided the egg had been laid by a black hen. Again, direct use or consumption of these eggs was not always needed. Simply drink-ing water from the shell on Easter morning ensured good health for the coming year.[2]

These are adaptations of cures found also in Germany itself. Germans say, for example, that an egg eaten on Good Friday morning before sunrise is the answer to all ills. It heals erysipelas and is effective against fever.[3] Dried and powdered, it provides an antidote for heavy menstruation in women – this actually from Franche-Comte. And a huntsman in France who eats one will not be bitten by a snake.[4]

A Green Thursday egg can heal a man's broken limb, though the process is complicated. He must sit in an unweeded corner of the garden, facing the early sun; a young girl should bring him such an egg, placing it as near as possible to the wound and reciting the Lord's Prayer. Removing the top of the egg, she must then give it to the patient, who should eat it, including the shell; then the fracture will mend.[5]

In the Messin area of France, Green Thursday eggs prevent an internal rupture – a hernia – from developing.[6] Germans, too, use an egg – Good Friday's – for the same treatment,[7] and in Slovene Carinthia it has to be an Easter egg laid by a black hen; this last is

[1] Bächtold-Stäubli, ii.631.
[2] Shoemaker, 22–3.
[3] Bächtold-Stäubli, ii.633.
[4] Van Gennep, *Manuel*, 1.iii.1,338.
[5] Bächtold-Stäubli, ii.606–7.
[6] Van Gennep, *Manuel*, 1.iii.1,338.
[7] Bächtold-Stäubli, iv.1,001.

used to make the sign of the cross on the hernia three times before sunset. After the words, 'May Father, Son and Holy Ghost assist', the shell is pierced with a needle and the egg laid in an ant-heap. When the ants have eaten it – the familiar transference ritual – the hernia will be healed.[1]

This type of cure is common in Holland, for instance, where the faeces of a patient were baked in an Easter egg and given to a dog to eat.[2] Ukrainian *krashanka* were also supposed to remove sickness by transference. In serious illness an egg – blessed on Easter Eve – was hung round the neck upon a string, and the disease in due course passed into it. A *krashanka* could also be used to stop blood-poisoning; the patient needed only to be touched with the egg.[3] In such a case one presumes that the egg then lost its beneficial properties. But in Germany even an 'unlucky' Green Thursday egg ought not to be destroyed. Instead, it was set aside, marked with three crosses.[4]

As it turns out, every imaginable complaint is taken care of by an egg from one or other of the holy days: Green Thursday's batch deals with stone and lumbago, Good Friday's prevents ague, so do those from Easter itself, while any produced by a white hen on Ascension Day counteract stomach pains and discomfort in head and ears. In the Hautes Alpes they also use an Ascension Day egg – the yolk only, which never goes bad – mixed with chicken-fat and lemon, as a salve for the skin.

These customs are from Germany, the Netherlands, Italy and France respectively.[5] But it is rather surprising to find a Danish belief that, when eating Easter eggs on Easter Day, you must make sure to remove the small end: it is a seat of disease, and unless it has been discarded you are certain to fall sick.[6] Different reasoning seems to condemn a chicken with the temerity to gobble an egg laid on Good Friday. But, similarly, according to Swiss lore, it will meet a sorry end; it will fall prey to the hawk.[7]

---

[1] Jagodic, 158–9.
[2] Meertens, P. J., 'Ostereier und Ostergebäcke in den Niederlanden', *Schweizerisches Archiv für Volkskunde*, LIII (Basle, 1957), ii–iii.129.
[3] Dmytrikw, 97.
[4] Bächtold-Stäubli, iii.1,189.
[5] *Ibid.*, ii.634, iii.1,189. Leland, 75. Joisten, 60.
[6] Uldall, 1.
[7] Information kindly supplied by Herr Willy Hess of Winterthur.

The consequences of these holy eggs are not in fact uniformly good, and here the elements of earlier magic seem to have triumphed over Christian belief. For instance, a German tradition of considerable charm – that Good Friday's egg, brooded in the armpit for nine days, hatches out a little man who performs all one's wishes – appears in the Sudeten borderlands in a distinctly disagreeable version. In this the egg, now a Green Thursday egg, if brooded by someone unwashed for nine whole days, hatches the Devil.[1] In Normandy they say such eggs contain toads and serpents, and children are forbidden to eat them. Freaks, like a fully-fledged, crowing cock, or a chicken with three feet, might also emerge. The eggs could all produce cockerels or disappear completely.[2]

But elsewhere – in both France and Germany – Green Thursday was a good day for hatching chickens. They would be very pretty and change colour as the bird developed. This could even happen once a year, just as Judas changed colour at the Last Supper when Our Lord looked at him. Flowers cut or planted in window-boxes on Green Thursday are said to bloom in wonderful hues. Surely there must be a connection with Good Friday chicks having variegated feathers – a German belief, which turns up in America, where the Pennsylvania Dutch call them *schechicha* (speckled).[3]

All the major Christian festivals appear to have a magical effect on eggs laid within their octave. Even Ash Wednesday is not excluded: Germans say that all eggs associated with it turn to cinders.[4] But the link with Christianity can be almost negligible. A Baden superstition, that Green Thursday's egg, buried in dung for nine days, helps one find a magic stone, sounds more like a fairy tale. If warmed in the hand, this stone makes the holder invisible.[5] Here nothing remains of Christian faith or doctrine – only the name of the day, which, of course, could itself be pagan.

Among many peoples Christmas has superseded Easter in importance, and it is not surprising to find that certain customs from one festival have spilled over on to the other. Slavs, who give Easter priority, ensure good complexions with an Easter

[1] Bächtold-Stäubli, iii.1,192, iv.1,001.
[2] Van Gennep, *Manuel*, 1.iii.1,336, 1,339. Bächtold-Stäubli, ii.642, note 546.
[3] Shoemaker, 22. Bächtold-Stäubli, ii.641, iii.1,192–3.
[4] *Ibid.*, ii.606.
[5] *Ibid.*, 628.

egg, but in the north of Germany, where the Christmas tradition is strong, the egg – though used in springtime, and for the same purpose – must come from a pullet which started laying immediately before Christmas.[1] The custom is to cross one's face with the egg. The Mordvins, a people related linguistically to the Finns, employ eggs to bring about a whole range of desirable results. Stained a rich golden hue with cloves of garlic, they will stop a fire from spreading if thrown into it; placed in the trees with bee-hives, they will increase productivity; fed to the chickens, they will encourage laying; and the shells, scattered about the byres or burnt with cloves of garlic, will prevent the spread of disease among domestic cattle. The eggs used in these various rites are reserved for the feast day of Semik, the seventh Thursday after Easter, when the Mordvins worship their goddess, Ange Patya. The placing of the festival shows that pagan ritual had become confused with Christian practice. The Mordvins were not converted until the late eighteenth century, and in fact their last sacrifice took place in 1813. It is interesting that these various ceremonies so closely parallel others already described, and also that the same important goddess was honoured on 25 December. Here again the offering of foodstuffs with which she was presented included coloured eggs.[2]

In northern Europe not only Christmas Day eggs, but those laid during the twelve days, will produce fine, handsome chicks[3] – Christmas, the day which commemorates that most Blessed Birth – it is surprising to find that this apt symbolism is not a commonplace.

[1] Jones, William, *Credulities Past and Present*, London, 1880, 458.

[2] Abercromby, John, 'The Beliefs and Religious Ceremonies of the Mordvins', *The Folk-Lore Journal*, vii (London, April–June 1889), 104–5, 120–1.

[3] Thorpe, iii.330.

Chapter 11

Decorated Easter Eggs

And to please the pit laddies at Easter
A dishful of gilty paste eggs.
Traditional Northumbrian song

TOKENS OF LOVE

After breakfast on Easter Sunday Estonian children save the egg-shells and lay them on the doorstep, running up and down the street, looking to see whose is the prettiest: an urban custom, but it shows how popular decorating became, even in the towns.[1] Indeed, it was a highly developed folk-art in many countries, especially those of central and eastern Europe.[2] Lithuanian peasants treasured these eggs, keeping them in winter-time between the glass of the double window-panes as a permanent decoration;[3] and in Bulgaria they say of a man in love, 'He looks after her as carefully as a painted egg'.[4] An old Bohemian folk song tells of a man who wants to present one to his sweetheart:

> *I've got a painted Easter egg.*
> *I've got a painted egg, my dearest.*
> *Hančička, why don't you want it,*
> *Hančička?*[5]

We do not know how the custom first arose, but a very early reference suggests this same connection between painted eggs and the relationship of man and woman: Granet, in his *Festivals and Songs of Ancient China*, refers briefly to eggs decorated with pictures and designs, used at the old spring festival. Young men

---

[1] Information kindly supplied by Miss Salme Pruuden, formerly of Tallinn.
[2] See Newall, Venetia, 'Decorated Eggs', *Folklore*, lxxvi (London, Winter 1965), 266–72.
[3] Čerbulenas, K., 'Margučiu Menas Lietuvoje', *Mokslas ir Gyvenimas* (Vilnius, March 1967), 27.
[4] Vakarelski, Christo, 'Œufs de Pâques chez les Bulgares', *Schweizerisches Archiv für Volkskunde*, LIII (Basle, 1957), ii–iii.189.
[5] Information kindly supplied by Henk Arends of Amsterdam.

and girls took part in the rites, which appeared to have a sexual significance.[1]

The process of evolution has transformed these into courtship rituals which still followed certain patterns even within living memory. Hungarian girls, obliged to colour twenty or even thirty eggs for a special boy-friend, knew that he might be given others by several different sweethearts. The lucky recipient would put them all away for several weeks and then get them out again, to have another look: the girl whose egg had lost most colour was pining for him.[2] In Germany it was an honour for a man to be offered large numbers of eggs, and a girl could save her face – in case she might be rejected – by not giving them all to the same person,[3] a novel way of ensuring that all one's eggs were not in one basket.

Hungarian men often presented eggs themselves – gifts which the girls would treasure for many years to come. In Poland a lover received many dozens with elaborate designs. But in return he bought his sweetheart back during the traditional auction sale of girls on Shrove Tuesday. For anyone without a special boy-friend this was a way of securing a dancing partner. Naturally, it was better to prepare the eggs oneself. But sometimes, especially as Polish designs are very intricate, it was too difficult, and a girl employed a specialist, who was given more eggs as a wage.[4] As a rule, each village in Czechoslovakia and Hungary had its own artist or engraver of eggs – an old woman who had done the work all her life. She would know many designs, perhaps even as many as sixty. Indeed, a Ukrainian woman was said not long ago to know more than 100.

A really skilled expert would be used by many villages besides her own, and even today a few of these women still exist. The regions of Kalocsa and Matyofold in Hungary have several folk-artists who excel in the field,[5] and in Moravia Anna Sterbova, now over eighty, is the senior egg-painter in her town, Ostrozska

[1] Granet, Marcel, *Festivals and Songs of Ancient China*, London, 1932, 191.

[2] Sándor, István, 'Ostereier in Ungarn', *Schweizerisches Archiv für Volkskunde*, LIII (Basle, 1957), ii–iii.179.

[3] Becker, Albert, *Brauchtum der deutschen Osterzeit*, Jena, 1937, 50.

[4] Hole, Christina, *Easter and Its Customs*, London, 1961, 44. Seweryn, Tadeusz, 'Les Œufs de Pâques Polonais et Hutsules', *Schweizerisches Archiv für Volkskunde*, LIII (Basle, 1957), ii–iii.172–3.

[5] *New Hungary* (Budapest, October 1964).

Nova Ves. In sixty years she has decorated over 30,000 eggs. Really beautiful work is often preserved by the family for generations, though traditions vary according to the region. It is surprising, for instance, to find that in certain areas of Czechoslovakia – Kysucia, Oravia, Liptov and Zahori – eggs are just soaked in plain dye, red or brown, without any kind of pattern at all.[1]

Alsatian girls prepared their own eggs on Maundy Thursday and gave them to the boys on Easter Monday, often boldly inscribed with expressions of love, for all the world to see: 'With love and steadfastness, I give you an Easter egg.'[2] A girl whose eggs were not collected by a boy-friend became a laughing-stock. People jeered at her – she would have to hatch them herself.[3] Swedes were more discreet. They painted eggs with patterns of flowers and filled the hollow shell with slips of paper containing verses and messages of love.[4] In Bohemia it was the man who stood to lose face. According to custom, he must knock on his sweetheart's door on Easter morning, and if she gave him some eggs it was a sign that they were engaged.[5] But, of course, there was always the risk that he might be refused.

Occasions for these gifts varied. In Latvia boys built Easter swings for the girls and helped them to take their turns. The reward was a decorated egg, given as a matter of course.[6] Slovenian girls chose a moment during the great circular dance performed on Easter Monday to approach a special boy-friend with eggs, but these were fried – a surprising choice, though Russians offered the same dish to the dead in cemeteries and at their supposed abode in birch trees.[7] Perhaps there is some early common origin from which this curious token derives.

---

[1] Pranda, Adam, *Kraslice v Slovensky' Lejudovej Umeleckej Výrobe*, Bratislava, 1958, 3.

[2] Pfleger, Alfred, 'Osterei und Ostergebäck im Elsass', *Schweizerisches Archiv für Volkskunde*, LIII (Basle, 1957), ii–iii.118.

[3] Pfleger, 117.

[4] Lehmann, Hedi, *Volksbrauch im Jahreslauf*, Munich, 1964, 36.

[5] 'Qui, n'a pas ses Œufs de Paques', *Lectures Pour Tous*, Paris, n.d., no author, 547.

[6] Information kindly supplied by Mrs Terēza Budiņa Lazdiņa, formerly of Riga.

[7] Jagodic, Maria, 'Über Ostereier und Ostergebäck in Slowenien', *Schweizerisches Archiv für Volkskunde*, LIII (Basle, 1957), ii–iii.158. See also ch. 2 and the section entitled 'Tree Spirits'.

Ukrainians intended any gift of decorated eggs, whether large or small, as a sign of fondness for a person,[1] but elsewhere the numbers could have a significance of their own. A Lithuanian girl who presented her lover with two might receive one in return[2] and all would be well. Two eggs meant the same in Switzerland,[3] but in the Bohemian Forest the exact opposite applied: the man had been rejected and a scornful verse like this was often inscribed:

> *You old ass,*
> *Stay at home.*
> *I give you a pair of Easter eggs.*
> *Love is gone.*[4]

Three can be a good number: in Portugal, Belgium and Hessen it gave the man encouragement, and in the Tyrol singled him out from his rivals, who were sent away with one.[5] In the Eifel two meant 'What a pity', and six 'Time to get married'.[6] But, of course, none of these tokens were really binding. A tale from Solothurn dated 1787 observes shrewdly: 'Manzi knew well that it is a long way from Easter eggs to marriage.'[7]

EASTER GIFTS

Any sturgeon caught off our shores – the royal fish – automatically belongs to the Queen; in eighteenth-century France it was the largest egg in the realm, laid during Holy Week, which became the king's prerogative.[8] Other people, royalty included, offered each other decorated Easter eggs as a sign of Christian fellowship without any obvious feudal significance.

The history of this custom in its modern form is lost in obscurity, and authorities disagree in their opinions. Van Gennep

[1] Dmytrikw, Olga, *Ukrainian Arts*, New York, 1955, 101.

[2] *Lietuvin Enciklopediga*, Boston, 1959, xii.309–11.

[3] König, Wolfhilde von, 'Ostereierverse', *Bayerischen Jahrbuch für Volkskunde* (Munich, 1961), 86–7.

[4] *Ibid.*, 'Ostereierverse', 87.

[5] Ilg, Karl, 'Sitte und Brauch um Osterei und Osterbrot in Tirol', *Schweizerisches Archiv für Volkskunde*, LIII (Basle, 1957), ii–iii.94.

[6] Lehmann, 36.

[7] Wildhaber, Robert, *Wir färben Ostereier*, Berne, 1957, 27.

[8] Van Gennep, Arnold, *Manuel de Folklore Français Contemporain*, Paris, 1947, I.iii.1,323.

says it was recorded among the Copts of Egypt in the period spanning the tenth and twelfth centuries, but gives no clear evidence for his statement.[1] Watts maintains that, as there are no records of Easter eggs in Western Europe before the fifteenth century, they may have been introduced by warriors returning from the Crusades.[2] In fact, this is not correct. According to Benet, egg-decorating existed in Poland prior to the eleventh century.[3] She quotes no examples to support her claim, but other sources cite the oldest painted egg in that area from excavations at an early fortified castle in the Opole Wood, Silesia.[4]

The castle itself dates from the eleventh to twelfth centuries, a period which marked the close of a strongly Slav period in Silesia, and after 1200 settlement of Germans became extensive. However, there had been for many centuries colonies of them between Swidnica and Opole, probably relics of a settlement from prior to A.D. 500. There were also many links with German areas, of some interest in view of numerous historic egg finds around Worms – which may or may not be Christian – discussed in the following chapter.

In Poland itself the first written mention of painted eggs occurs in the thirteenth-century *Chronicle* of Archbishop Vincent Kadlubek: 'In distant times the Poles used to amuse themselves at the expense of their lords with coloured eggs [*pictis ovis*].'[5] Professor Watts might say that Poland scarcely counts as Western Europe, but there are thirteenth-century references in both Germany and England. Freidanck, in his poem *'Bescheidenheit'* (Modesty), written in 1216, refers to eggs coloured red and black:

> *ein kint naem ein gewerwet ei*
> *für ander drin oder zwei.*
> (*a child takes a coloured egg,*
> *or perhaps two for those inside.*)[6]

This is the earliest definite clue that we have from Germany, but they were known at the English court too. A record much

---

[1] *Ibid.*, i.iii.1,322, note 6.

[2] Watts, Alan W., *Easter: Its Story and Meaning*, New York, 1958, 29.

[3] Benet, Sula, *Song, Dance and Customs of Peasant Poland*, London, 1951, 50.

[4] Seweryn, 172.

[5] *Ibid.*, 172.

[6] König, Wolfhilde von, 'Kostbare Ostereier', *Die Waage*, iii (Stolberg, June 1964), 206.

later in the same century (1290) from the household accounts of Edward I shows an entry of 18*d*. spent on the purchase of 450 eggs to be coloured or covered with gold leaf and distributed to members of the royal entourage.[1] Perhaps gold signified the gift of a king. French rulers up till the mid-eighteenth century distributed both painted and gilded eggs after Easter Mass, and the archives of a Cistercian monastery in Styria, opened by the Emperor Joseph II in 1601, note proudly that '*Mehr ihr gnaden khaufft guldes ay*' (His Honour buys a gilded egg).[2] Perhaps this was intended as a present for someone else.

Monasteries and other religious houses are, of course, the obvious source for information of this kind, since it was a Christian custom, and they often kept very detailed records. The books of a Dominican convent at Mahrenburg tell us that these eggs were already known in Styria by the fourteenth century. An entry dated 25 November 1393 reads: '*Vnd schol diselben ayer tayln an dem heiligen tefelsampstag vnder di vrawn all di des convents sint.*'[3] (And shall these eggs distribute on Holy Saturday amongst the women present in the cloister.)

Chambers, exploring the Durham Accounts, found similar entries for the fifteenth and sixteenth centuries: '*fratribus et sororibus de Wytton pro eorum Egsilver erga festum pasche*'.[4] Nuns living near Rome were hard at work colouring eggs by the eighteenth century, if not earlier:

> These on Easter day are carried to church to ye parish priests, who bless them and sprinkle ym. w. holy water; on yt day, at dinner, ye cloth is adorned w. sweet herbs and flowers and ye first thing yt is eat are those blessed eggs; wc. are chiefly painted by ye nuns of Amelia, a small city about 30 miles from Rome: ye common sort of these eggs are all of one colour, as yellow, blew, red or purple, wc. are sold in ye streets till Ascension day or Whitsuntide. Anno 1716.[5]

A man with religious connections, Adam Weikand, personal physician to the Bishop of Fulda, described a secular, peculiarly

[1] Hone, William, *The Every-Day Book*, London, 1837, i.429.

[2] Kretzenbacher, Leopold, 'Vom roten Osterei in der grünen Steiermark', *Schweizerisches Archiv für Volkskunde*, LIII (Basle, 1957), ii–iii.105.

[3] *Ibid.*, 105.

[4] *The Durham Accounts*, i.71–174. See Chambers, E. K., *The Mediaeval Stage*, Oxford, 1903, i.128, note 2.

[5] *The Gentleman's Magazine*, ii (London, 1831), 408.

disagreeable ceremony, which he saw in the late eighteenth century. A live donkey walked in the Palm Sunday procession, and women there placed coloured eggs inside its anus, so that they could be blessed.[1]

If customs as horrid as this were at all prevalent, one can understand the numerous Easter egg prohibitions issued by German authorities in the sixteenth and seventeenth centuries. Public collections were forbidden in Strasbourg as early as 1524,[2] and much later, in 1786, the Bishop of Passy restricted them to private preparation in the household for family use.[3] Another reason for this may have been the tendency to overcharge. A Bavarian boy with a keen business sense succeeded in obtaining 4 crowns for a single painted egg, a large sum of money for the day – this was in 1610. Other children just overate and made themselves ill. This, coupled with inflated prices, brought about a ban in Munich as recently as 1802.[4]

Not everyone would have shared this rather Puritan outlook. Elector August the Strong ordered an Easter egg for his mistress costing more than 5,000 thaler;[5] and some of the French kings showered their paramours with gifts not always in the best possible taste. The court jeweller made a special egg containing a cupid for Madame du Barry, but Louis XV ordered others inscribed with bawdy verses and illustrated with obscene pictures – the work of such famous artists as Lancret, Watteau and Boucher.[6]

His successor, Louis XVI, presented Madame Victoire de France with two elaborate eggs commemorating a seventy-year-old hero, Louis Gillet, who rescued a girl from brigands, returned her to her parents and would not accept any reward.[7] Perhaps the old man never saw this gracious tribute, but rulers liked to bestow eggs as a mark of special favour. The Pope gave one to Henry VIII enclosed in a silver case, and Elector Frederick of Saxony

---

[1] Hain, Mathilde, 'Bemalte Ostereier in Hessen', *Schweizerisches Archiv für Volkskunde*, LIII (Basle, 1957), ii–iii.70.

[2] Van Gennep, *Manuel*, 1.iii.1,322.

[3] Moser, Hans, 'Brauchgeschichtliches zu Osterei und Osterbrot in Bayern', *Schweizerisches Archiv für Volkskunde*, LIII (Basle, 1957), ii–iii.84.

[4] *Ibid.*, 83–4.

[5] Von König, 'Kostbare Ostereier', 208.

[6] Snowman, A. Kenneth, *The Art of Carl Fabergé*, London, 1953, 74–5.

[7] *Ibid.*

presented an exquisitely painted example to his court jester. The man, a certain Claus von Rastatt, was equal to the occasion and responded with an elaborate compliment: 'What is beautiful should be praised. But what is good and right should be praised even more.'[1]

Others, less exalted, offered egg gifts as tokens of friendship and esteem. A certain Lithuanian, M. Mazvydas, presumably a nobleman, writes in 1549 that he is sending a new book, *The Song of St Ambrosius*, 'instead of an Easter egg'.[2] Ceremonial presentations were even made by the *bourgeoisie*. In 1635 the Innsberger Hauptgewerkschaft bestowed on one Georg Fronhofer 'for his diligent services to the Company in matters pending at the Court and for his Styrian correspondence, one Easter egg'.[3] A painter, Johann Horstein, offered the Chairman of the same organization an Easter gift of a coat of arms, declaring that he wished '*an statt eines Rotten Ay, weliche ohne das alhir khlem zu bekhomen, hiemit presentiren wollen*'[4] (to present this instead of a red egg, which is very difficult to obtain here).

Indeed, Easter eggs could be gifts from colleagues, lovers, friends and dignitaries, so it is quaint but scarcely surprising to find them in a Polish morality play, since early religious drama drew its strength from the life of the people. The play, *The Glorious Resurrection of Our Lord*, written by Nicholas of Wilkowiecko in 1575, shows an offering to an inferior from his spiritual lord, an angel, who gives them to Lucifer to cheer the pains of Hell.[5]

COLOURING

There are many apocryphal tales of Easter egg decorations, especially in eastern Europe. According to Hungarian tradition, the day when Marcus Aurelius was born a hen belonging to his mother laid an egg spotted with red. This was taken as a sign that

---

[1] Zincgref, J. W., *Teutsche Apophtegmata*, Strasbourg, 1626, 376. Pfleger, Alfred, 'Osterei und Ostergebäck im Elsass', *Schweizerisches Archiv für Volkskunde*, LIII (Basle, 1957), ii–iii.120.

[2] *Lietuvin Enciklopediga*, xii.309–11.

[3] Kretzenbacher, 106.

[4] *Ibid.*

[5] From the text of the play as performed by the Polish National Theatre at the Aldwych Theatre, London, in March 1967.

Colour Plate XVII Moravian batik (wax-resist) eggs. Moravia is an area of especially rich design. Certain types can clearly be picked out, symbols of the sun and cross for example; some motifs are connected with embroidery patterns and designs on early pottery. Among these eggs are examples showing six colours, for instance that with forget-me-nots at the bottom; seven colours are occasionally found.

Colour Plate XVIII Bohemian scratch-technique eggs. The surface colour is scraped with a fine point to produce a shallow engraved design, almost like lace in appearance. The workmanship of these eggs, made by German refugees from Bohemia, is exceptionally beautiful. They mostly have an Easter greeting or rhyme scratched on the reverse.

he would one day become the Emperor, so his mother guarded the secret to protect him from persecution. From A.D. 224, when the omen was fulfilled, it became a custom among the Romans to send one another coloured eggs as tokens of congratulation. The Christians adopted this custom, and transformed it into an expression of their wish for increased spiritual power, to conquer their passions and thereby imitate the life of Christ. The eggs would remind the recipients that, like Marcus Aurelius, they too would become emperors, and must prepare themselves for that time.[1]

An old Polish legend attributes the custom to the Blessed Virgin herself. To please the Infant Jesus, she is said to have taken boiled eggs and painted them different colours, red, yellow and green; so Polish women have done this ever since, but at Easter, not Christmas-time, regarding eggs as symbols of Our Lord's Resurrection.[2]

The saints and holy men who figure in other legends often received the first coloured eggs in the form of a reward. Polish hagiography describes how Mary Magdalene took a basketful of eggs to the Sepulchre, intending them as food while she worked anointing the body of Our Lord. But no sooner had she arrived than they were all miraculously changed, their shells stained with brilliant hues.[3] In the Ukraine it is Simon of Cyrene, transformed by folk imagination into an egg-merchant, who is recompensed for his good deed in carrying the Cross to Calvary. For ever after all his wares were coloured.[4]

Most of these tales link the process of decoration to the story of the Passion, and in recent times Maundy Thursday has been the most usual day for performing this task – throughout central and eastern Europe, even as far north as Latvia.[5] The Swiss think that day's eggs are particularly fresh and good and will take the colouring well.[6]

The Isle of Man – where Easter eggs are 'Good Friday eggs' –

---

[1] *Egyetertes Journal*, 23 March 1883. Quoted by Jones, W. H., 'Magyar Folk-Lore', *The Folk-Lore Journal* (London, November 1883), 359.

[2] Hole, 39. Seweryn, 173.

[3] Hole, 39.

[4] Dmytrikw, 96–7.

[5] Spicer, Dorothy, *The Book of Festivals*, New York, 1937, 210–11.

[6] Wildhaber, *Wir färben*, 27.

is an exception to general practice.[1] Germans, on the contrary, believed that these would not absorb the dye[2] and the Swiss refused to eat them. The eggs would surely bring bad luck because it was then that the 'wicked Jews' had thrown them in the face of Our Lord[3] – one of the many scurrilous anti-Semitic tales which seem to have collected around the central events of the Passion.

Housewives in Styria stained Good Friday eggs black as a sign of mourning,[4] and indeed the colours that were chosen generally had a special significance, which does not vary greatly from one country to another. Green is one exception. In Somerset eggs which were dyed that colour would be unlucky, probably because of the English prejudice that green in general is ill-omened.[5] But in Germany – where blue eggs brought misfortune[6] – and also in Austria green was often preferred,[7] and a style of floral pattern in which it predominates is popular in Czechoslovakia. Here, as in the liturgy, green is the colour of hope and spiritual renewal, reminding us of the fruits of the earth.

In 1906 a traveller in the Holy Land noticed that Moslems had borrowed the custom of Easter eggs from the Christians; and at the feast of Neby Mûsa, which on that occasion fell close to Easter, they were using eggs coloured a brilliant yellow.[8] Perhaps they were imitations of the gold or gilded eggs exchanged by royalty and aristocracy; the Greek Orthodox Patriarch in Istanbul traditionally presents his Easter visitors with one. Equally the custom may have an earlier history. When St Louis (1226–70), who organized several Crusades to the Holy Land, was released from captivity by the Sultan of the Saracens, together with other Christian prisoners, they were given food before they left: 'Little round cheeses baked in the sun to keep the worm out, and hard-boiled eggs, four or five days old: the shells of these they had painted, in our honour, in different colours.'[9]

[1] Gill, W. Walter, *A Third Manx Scrapbook*, London, 1963, 269.

[2] Bächtold-Stäubli, Hanns, ed., *Handwörterbuch des deutschen Aberglaubens*, Berlin, 1931–2, iv.1,002.

[3] Wildhaber, *Wir färben*, 27.   [4] Kretzenbacher, 107.

[5] Briggs, K. M., and Tongue, R. L., *Somerset Folklore*, London, 1965, 150.

[6] Bächtold-Stäubli, vi.1,329.   [7] Kretzenbacher, 107.

[8] Wilson, C. T., *Peasant Life in the Holy Land*, London, 1906, 46–7.

[9] Jourville, John de, *Life of St Louis*, trans. Hague, R., London, 1955, lxxiv.376; 118.

The first reference to coloured eggs in Rumania (1700) from Del Chiaro, Count Brancoveanu's private secretary, is to the colour gold.[1] Indeed, throughout Europe people have dyed yellow eggs with onion peel and still do. It occurs almost everywhere and this list is not exhaustive: England, Isle of Man, Holland, Belgium, Portugal, Italy, Savoy, Alsace, Switzerland, Germany, Styria, Macedonia, Slovenia, Croatia, Hungary, Moravia and in Czechoslovakia generally, among the German Sorbs and the Pennsylvania Dutch, in Denmark, Sweden, Estonia, Latvia, Lithuania, among the Hutzuls, Rumanians and Greeks – also in Russia and Poland, where it was borrowed by the Jews too.

Shades vary from yellow to deep orange and even a reddish brown, according to how long the egg remains in the mixture. Shallots yield a particularly dark, rich hue. In Estonia, where it was the oldest known method, they liked to moisten the shell first, roll it in chopped barley and tie it in a cloth before boiling in onion peel.[2] Latvians did this too, and it produces a pretty effect of white stars on a darker background.[3] The Germans had a not dissimilar method. An eighteenth-century source describes how patterns were made by cutting the onion carefully into shapes and sticking them to the shell with egg-white.[4]

Yugoslav Macedonians call these onion peels *shuski*, and use them for dying wool in weaving and knitting, as well as for colouring eggs. The peel is soaked for several days in tepid water before the eggs are boiled in it. Afterwards whatever is left is thrown out in the garden, but never where the children might walk – it would give them blisters.[5]

Red, a lucky colour in Germany, was probably the earliest to be used. A previous chapter discusses this subject,[6] but it is worth noting that the *Regnum Papisticum* (1553) of Thomas Kirchmeyer mentions a red egg gift,[7] and contemporary records

[1] Slătineanu, Barbu, 'Les Œufs de Pâques en Roumanie', *Schweizerisches Archiv für Volkskunde*, LIII (Basle, 1957), ii–iii.183.

[2] Information kindly supplied by Miss Salme Pruuden.

[3] Information kindly supplied by Mrs Terēza Budiņa-Lazdiņa.

[4] Krünitz, J. G., *Economic Encyclopaedia*, 1777, 47.

[5] Georgieva, Milica, *Бојадисување и шарање на Велигденски Јајца Во Скопје и Околијата*, Skopje, 1960, 182.

[6] See ch. 9.

[7] Wildhaber, *Wir färben*, 3.

from a Styrian convent show that the women bought *Bresilfarbe* – Brazil wood – for egg-dyeing.[1] This is an old method – Hakluyt describes how the Russians use 'Brazzel' – known besides to the Greeks, Bulgarians, Ukrainians, Slovenians, Sorbs, and Swedes. Yugoslavs call it *varsilio*, the Czechs *frizulka*, while Hungarians luxuriously steep it in brandy to extract the dye.[2]

Certain fourteenth-century Magyar documents use the Italian expression *kokonya*, which apparently means simply 'decorated eggs', but modern Hungarians use the same word to indicate 'red egg' and 'Easter egg'.[3] Indeed, the Greeks call Maundy Thursday 'Red Thursday' instead, because of all the dyeing that is done then. They follow a specific ritual. The bowl used must be new, and the dye itself – which should be Brazil wood – has to be carefully handled. It may not be thrown away or taken out of the house once it has been used. In Sinope they customarily stain one egg for each member of the household and one extra for the Blessed Virgin.[4]

Women in Poland, the Ukraine and Rumania prepare two different kinds of eggs. The *krasanki* – *merjsoare* in Rumanian – are edible, dyed one colour only and hard-boiled; *kraska*, the root word, signifies 'colour'.[5] Czechs have a similar expression – *kraslice* – just to mean decorated eggs.[6] The *pysanki* are intended as ornaments, not food, and are never cooked; the root word here, *pysaty*, means 'to write', for highly elaborate designs are literally inscribed on the shell of the egg by a technique similar to wax resist.[7] Rumanians call this sort of egg *impistrite*.[8] Even the Pennsylvania Dutch make a distinction between eggs intended for a meal and those which are 'just for nice'.[9]

Decorating was a job generally reserved for women. Lithuanian Easter eggs, known as *margučiai*, were prepared by young girls, rarely by married women. Coloured on Holy Saturday, the

---

[1] Kretzenbacher, 105.

[2] Sándor, 176.

[3] Károlyi, Alexander, *Hungarian Pageant*, Budapest, 1939, 80. Viski, Károly, *Volksbrauch der Ungarn*, Budapest, 1932, 51. Sándor, 176.

[4] Megas, George A., *Greek Calendar Customs*, Athens, 1958, 94–5.

[5] Seweryn, 173.

[6] Pranda, 1.

[7] Dmytrikw, 95.

[8] Slătineanu, 182.

[9] Shoemaker, Alfred L., *Eastertide in Pennsylvania*, Kutztown, 1960, 26.

designs were scratched on the afternoon of Easter Day. To have done this any earlier would have been a sin.[1] In Poland it was done by young girls during Lent, though recently married women might also help if they had time. It was a great social occasion and all vied with each other to see who could produce the most attractive results.

Each Ukrainian village and family had its own particular techniques, handed down through the generations and executed in secret away from the eyes of inquisitive neighbours. Already by the middle of Lent Hutzul women would be selecting suitable well-shaped eggs with smooth shells. Traditionally six of them had to be the first laid by a young hen, and these were especially important. At sunrise on the Monday of Holy Week they would be cracked against a tree bursting in leaf. The yolks would then be put aside, partly to bind the dyes and partly to polish the finished eggs.[2]

Naturally, much importance is attached to the appearance of the end-product. Yugoslav Macedonians use oil to grease the shells and make them really shiny. Then they can tell how the weather will turn out during the following year. If the dye takes well, they say the year will be fertile and bring good crops. But if the eggs are spotted it means nothing but rain and hail.[3]

Before beginning, a Ukrainian woman would cross herself and say, 'God help me.'[4] Other people might have found this a wise precaution. The Austrians and Pennsylvania Dutch believe that if colour penetrates the shell and stains the white, whoever eats it will be poisoned.[5] In the Tyrol at least, this perhaps arose because colouring eggs was largely unknown before the First World War.[6] Some people, anyway, evidently thought that dyeing them at all meant taking a tremendous risk. A correspondent in the Allentown (Pennsylvania) *Unabhaengiger Republikaner* remarks sourly:

Ostereyer. Wir bemerken mit Vernuegen dass dieses Jahr weniger von diesen Giftballen unter unsern Kindern zu sehen waren als jemals. Die Eltern

---

[1] Jungfer, Victor, *Litauen – Antlitz eines Volkes*, Leipzig, 1938, 135.
[2] Dmytrikw, 98.   [3] Georgieva, 181.
[4] Dmytrikw, 102.
[5] Shoemaker, 26.
[6] Bächtold-Stäubli, vi.1,329. Ilg, Karl, 'Sitte und Brauch um Osterei und Osterbrot in Tirol', *Schweizerisches Archiv für Volkskunde*, LIII (Basle, 1957), ii–iii.93.

verdienen Lob dass sie dem einfaeltigen und gefaehrlichen Gebrauch ein End machen.[1]

(Easter eggs. We note with pleasure that fewer of these poison-balls were then to be seen among our children than ever before. Parents deserve praise that they have put an end to this stupid and dangerous custom.)

This is rather surprising since, originally, at least, only natural dyes were used, the sources varying according to the particular country. As a rule they were linked to local crafts as well as to natural conditions. Hutzul women used various plants, roots, barks and berries which yielded colours for their embroidery,[2] and the Swede, Carl von Linné (Linnaeus), reported that farmers' wives coloured their eggs yellow with birch leaves, a method adopted from dyeing yarn.[3]

Poultry were scarce in Scandinavia, so Easter eggs were not a vital part of Scandinavian folk-lore. But the Danish botanist Simon Paulli wrote in 1648 that people were using not only narcissus leaves and petals for obtaining dye, but beetroot and moss as well.[4] The last seems a curious choice, but what was most readily available was naturally taken – vegetables and flowers which bloomed at the right time of year and moss, which is common in the bleak landscapes of the north.

Faroese children use an infusion of *steinamosi*, a variety which grows profusely among their windswept rocks and yields a shade of brown.[5] *Scriss-ny-greg*, a moss from the Isle of Man, provides crimson, and another, which grows on stone walls, a pleasant silver grey.[6] Estonians take theirs from the logs of country houses to get yet a further colour – green. They also make a good strong yellow by boiling dried birch leaves, saved since autumn from the whisks used in their *sauna* steam bath.[7] There are many similar

[1] *Unabhaengiger Republikaner*, 10 April 1828.

[2] Dmytrikw, 98.

[3] Eskeröd, Albert, 'Ostereier in Schweden', *Schweizerisches Archiv für Volkskunde*, LIV (Basle, 1958), 11.

[4] Uldall, Kai, 'Les Œufs de Pâques au Danemark', *Schweizerisches Archiv für Volkskunde*, LIV (Basle, 1958), 2.

[5] Williamson, Kenneth, *The Atlantic Islands: a Study of the Faroe Life and Scene*, London, 1948, 129–30.

[6] Gill, 269.

[7] Spicer, 103.

methods of obtaining natural dyes and a selection is listed in Appendix I.

DESIGNS

Designs are as varied as the sources for dye and even within small areas there is considerable diversity, but, of course, traditional themes recur. Sorbs use the old familiar emblems – the crown of thorns, chalice and Paschal Lamb; Rumanians the Easter flower and symbols of the Evangelists, while a serpent recalls the events which took place in the Garden of Eden. Russian or Armenian eggs, prepared by Orthodox *émigrés*, often carry ikon portraits of Our Lord and of the saints. Hutzuls use instead the fish symbol – sign of recognition among early Christians, since the letters of the Greek word are the initials of 'Jesus Christ God's Son Saviour'. Little triangles represent the Trinity and there are the obvious Christian signs: the cross and 'XB', the Orthodox Easter greeting, '*Christos Voskrese*'. Rumanians write this out in full, '*Hristos a Inăltat*', and always, on top of the Easter basket, there will be a special egg marked with a cross, which no one is permitted to touch.[1]

Some patterns are more complex, telling a story or containing a hidden significance. Croats prepare an egg representing the passage of time before and after the Resurrection: on one side a crown of thorns, on the other a garland of flowers. Non-representational designs can be meaningful too. The spots which the Hutzuls like to include in their national motifs represent the tears of the Blessed Virgin, who gave eggs to the soldiers at the foot of the Cross. As she begged them to be less cruel to Our Lord she wept, and the drops fell on the shells, flecking them with brilliant dots of colour.[2] Another pattern, geometrical and divided in forty sections, is called the 'Forty Days of Lent'.[3]

In France eggs might be painted with a daisy, the *paquerette*, which is given to every child before attending Easter Mass.[4] The daisy is a conventionalized symbol of the innocence of the Holy Child, and its popular usage started towards the end of the

[1] Information kindly supplied by Dr Wolfhilde von König of Munich.
[2] Dmytrikw, 96.
[3] Information kindly supplied by Mrs Olena Jenkala, formerly of the Ukraine.
[4] Information kindly supplied by Miss I. M. Kaplan, formerly of France.

fifteenth century in Western art.[1] Lithuanians use rue, the national flower of virtue; when girls marry they wear it as a wreath.[2]

Flower designs in general are highly popular, executed not only pictorially, but from an actual floral imprint on the shell. This method, as we shall see, provided the most common type of English *pace* egg; it was presumably a popular style because it was easy to do, the ingredients being readily to hand for country folk anywhere. In Switzerland the custom is unfortunately disappearing; a middle-aged friend writes that it is almost forgotten today, though his grandmother knew it well.[3] Hungarian egg patterns which mostly repeat embroidery designs[4] are also often based on flowers, and indeed they appear on many items of the national folk-art – chairs, tables and garments, even on houses. Eggs from Ormánság region are decorated with the same floral motifs that women paint around the shutters when the house receives its annual spring-clean and whitewash.[5] The tulip is specially popular in Hungary. It is also put on eggs decorated by the Pennsylvania Dutch. A settler of the Moravian sect, travelling from Nazareth to Sumneytown one day in 1829, wrote to his local newspaper that he had seen '*Die alten kritzelten Tullpanen darauf*'[6] (Old folks scratching tulips on Easter eggs). One might argue that this motif was taken to Hungary and Pennsylvania by settlers from the same German area. But other people use it too, so more probably it is just popular as a flower that blooms in springtime.

The use of floral patterns from other branches of folk-art is not confined to Hungary. In Hessen (Germany) the designs, generally small and fine, derive from embroidery used on shirts, aprons and handkerchiefs, as well as knitting patterns for stockings.[7] The Hutzuls are indebted to embroidery too – even the colours are similar.

Moldavians turn to local pottery for inspiration,[8] and at one time Croatians used motifs from skin-tattooing. Herodotus and

---

[1] Ferguson, G., *Signs and Symbols in Christian Art*, New York, 1961, 30.

[2] Information kindly supplied by Miss Marina Gorodeckis.

[3] Information kindly supplied by Herr Willy Hess of Winterthur. See colour plate XXII.

[4] Viski, 48.

[5] Information kindly supplied by Dr Wolfhilde von König. See colour plate XVI.   [6] Shoemaker, 51.   [7] Hain, 71–2. See colour plate XXI.

[8] Oprescu, George, *Peasant Art in Rumania*, London, 1929, 176.

Strabo knew this ancient Balkan tradition, which has been preserved into modern times by the Bosnian Catholics. The period
lasting from St Joseph's Day (19 March) until shortly before
Easter was specially set aside for this purpose. In Turkish times
the tattoos were used as a protection against conversion to Islam,
which is why crosses were so often used, as well as half-moons,
circles with spreading rays – these conceivably having a Bogomil
origin – and the ancient gammadion cross.[1]

Egg-painters inevitably tend to draw on what is familiar. The
Rumanians have named designs: 'holy water', 'the hand of the
beggar' and 'the grass that the lamb eats', which reflect different
facets of peasant life. They loved the flowers and leaves of their
native countryside, and many songs begin 'Oh! green leaf of the
oak tree' or some such refrain. It is not surprising that the same
plants have also found their way into the egg designs, for
Rumanian dances are often named after flowers, as well as after
animals and objects.

Some of these patterns are again taken from embroidery.
Others, highly symbolic, are intended only for eggs, and it is
often very difficult to say, simply by looking at them, what they
are meant to portray. Taking a part to represent the whole – the
stork's beak, the flail's handle, the oak leaf – they then reproduce
it in so stylized a fashion that any semblance of realism disappears.
The design 'goose's foot', for instance, could equally well be mistaken for a spider, type of plant, or pieces of bread.

The patterns are handed down from mother to daughter, some
so obscure that even the artists do not know their names. The one
universally known exception is the ploughshare, generally the
first design to be used when decorating. This is because, so they
say, all work in the fields begins with ploughing.[2]

In 1963 I visited the local museum of Radauţi near Suceava in
the Bukowina, and found a large collection of Easter eggs, many
with a single motif on a plain background. Each was named:
priest's belt, star, snowdrop, flower in a pot, melon seed, butterfly,
goat's hoof, cat's paw, goat's ear, the wrong road, small drops,
comb, crab apple – this particular egg was completely plain – oak
leaf, cock's comb and mistletoe. I list these patterns in full because

[1] Eterovich, F. H., and Spalatin, Christopher, *Croatia: Land, People and
Culture*, Toronto, 1964, i.239–40.

[2] Slătineanu, 184–5.

they so closely resemble those recorded by a Rumanian folklorist more than sixty years ago, at the beginning of this century.[1]

Some of the designs have a rich, concealed symbolism. In the Bukowina a woman in childbed is given an egg with a toad to help her recovery.[2] It seems a curious choice but Shakespeare writes:

> *Sweet are the uses of adversity,*
> *Which, like the toad, ugly and venomous,*
> *Wears yet a precious jewel in his head.*[3]

Heads of old, big toads contain a stone called *erepaudia*, which in England was thought to cure any venomous bite from snake or insect; they were sometimes set in rings.[4]

Croatians use egg patterns, too, in reviving strength and fertility: a wheatsheaf design is fed to a childless wife. If this does not help, her husband is assumed to be at fault, and he is given a pattern of roosters; old men get oak leaves in any case, because their vigour is waning – both are common symbols of virility. Farmers assist the crops by placing an egg painted with wheat-ears at the beginning of the first furrow when ploughing begins: another goes in the end of the last, and so the opening and closing of the season is marked.[5]

Nature is an endless source for motifs; bracelets, fences and fir branches are also usual Croatian designs.[6] Pine needles are beloved by the Hutzuls, too, for conifers grow profusely on their native mountains, and, being evergreen, symbolize eternal youth and health.[7] The ladder, a common but rather puzzling design, probably, like the rake, represents good husbandry and prosperity.

The rake has been traced back to a very early date in Hungarian designs. It appears on an egg-shaped toy, apparently a kind of rattle, found at Bia, near Budapest, and dating from the Bronze Age.[8] Similar rattles have been discovered in Russian graves. An egg of clay with a rattle beside it turned up in a first- to second-century A.D. grave in the middle course of the River Kuban in

---

[1] Murgoçi, Agnes, 'Rumanian Easter Eggs', *Folk-Lore*, xx (London, September 1909), 301–3.

[2] Information kindly supplied by Dr Wolfhilde von König.

[3] *As You Like It*, ii.i.12–14.

[4] Brewer, E. Cobham, *Dictionary of Phrase and Fable*, London, 1896, 1,232.

[5] Hosking, Clement, *Old Tales in a New Land*, Sydney, 1957, 143.

[6] Eterovich, i.239–40.   [7] Dmytrikw, 110.   [8] Sándor, 178.

north Caucasia; a rattle egg also appeared in a first-century A.D. grave close to Kiev. Nilsson believed these objects were some kind of toy.[1]

Rakes and combs are common on Hungarian, Czech, Slovak, Ukrainian, Hutzul and Rumanian eggs. Cirlot relates the symbol to the fleshless tail of a fish – an emblem of death.[2] In the Easter context it would be the burial of winter, a possible but rather far-fetched interpretation. Other agricultural and pastoral motifs from the Ukraine include a double spiral figure resembling the letter V, with curved ends denoting the horns of the ram. The hen, which lays eggs, represents fertility and fulfilment of wishes. The Hutzuls are a mountain-dwelling people, and for them the deer represents wealth and prosperity. The wolves, which threaten the herds, appear as a protective: a design utilizing their teeth will keep these savage creatures away from farm and fold.[3]

Ukrainian eggs are well known for exquisite geometrical patterns. Often various types of ribbon or belt are portrayed encircling the egg and, since these are continuous, without a beginning or end, they are called the 'Endless Line', and represent eternity. An undulating curve, rather rare on eggs, but common on medieval embroideries and funeral palls, stands for death.[4]

Rumanians, too, have many designs of this kind, some related to the myth of ancient Greece. *Calea Rătăcită*, an unusual wavy pattern, reminiscent of a partially finished jigsaw puzzle, signifies 'the Lost Road'. The name has overtones of the minotaur, and the mysterious labyrinth where the monster lurked. But it also assists wandering souls, deprived of the Last Rites of the Church, to find the way to their rest.[5]

It is difficult to distinguish between myth and nature in these designs. At some stage they meet and merge. The Ukrainian star, in Rumanian the star-flower, like the circle with protruding curved spokes, is often referred to as a sun symbol, with how much basis in fact it is difficult to say. Typical Latvian patterns suggesting a stylized representation of a daisy, and used for pottery,

[1] Nilsson, Martin P., 'Das Ei im Totenkult der Alten', *Archiv für Religionswissenschaft*, ii (Leipzig, 1908), 534–5.

[2] Cirlot, J. E., *A Dictionary of Symbols*, London, 1962, 58. See colour plate XVI.

[3] Information kindly supplied by Mrs Olena Jenkala. See colour plates XI, XVI.   [4] Dmytrikw, 108.   [5] Slătineanu, 184.

carving, textiles, embroidery, weaving and knitting, are also referred to as sun patterns.[1] A Rumanian folklorist claims that
objects of ordinary appearance are often ancient symbols transformed, and that, for instance, the representation of the reel or
winder is really a sun symbol.

In my own collection of eggs a wheel-like pattern of radiating
spokes, said to represent the sun's rays, occurs all along the Car-
pathians, and the sunflower itself – another related symbol – is
popular in Ukrainian design. The ancient sun god Dazhbog was
an important Slav deity. In Galicia, until quite recently, people
used to say to someone they hated, 'May the sun make you
perish!' and in Croatia, 'May the sun avenge me on you!'[2]

But are there any really valid grounds for assuming that these
patterns – the gammadion cross so popular in northern Ruthenia,
the spoked circle, the radiating rays and so forth – were sun
symbols as depicted on Easter eggs? Equally the wheel of spokes
could be a copy of a daisy transfer motif. Since dyes were obtained
naturally in the past, flowers were probably tied to the egg as a
means of obtaining colour. With these yielding imprints by
transfer, the idea of floral patterns might have developed as a
result. The design of radiating spokes is very widespread, and is
found in Lithuania, Poland, the Ukraine, Czechoslovakia,
Dalmatia, Lausitz and elsewhere.

Sometimes the type of tool used has considerable bearing on
the style in which the egg is decorated. With the tip of a metal
funnel you can trace a design of uniform thickness. But a pin,
which is a popular instrument, produces a slanting, comma-like
mark. These are arranged concentrically in the shape of many-
angled stars, which usually draw attention to the ends of the egg
and are sometimes described as sun patterns. They are well known
in many countries of Europe.

Polish eggs are often decorated with the spider, which is a
variant of the ancient gammadion cross or swastika, another sun
symbol, but modern Polish folklorists believe it is purely decorative and that there is no reason to assume a magic or symbolic
significance.[3] The same no doubt applies to the swastikas, which
appear on Latvian and Lithuanian eggs.

[1] Information kindly supplied by Mrs Terēza Budiņa Lazdiņa.
[2] *Larousse Encyclopaedia of Mythology*, London, 1959, 296.
[3] Seweryn, 174. See colour plates XI, XII, XIV, XVI, XVII, XXIII.

In these more sophisticated times when, like so much else, egg-decoration becomes an expression of nationalism, the artists who do this work like to attach an age-old significance to every single pattern. Often, I think, there is a basis of truth in this, but sometimes it is far-fetched. However, it is not only egg-decorators living in exile who become nationalistic. The distinguished folk-lorist Arnold van Gennep put forward a very improbable, and incorrect, theory that Easter egg gifts arose in Alsace in the late fifteenth century and thence spread throughout western Europe.[1]

The prevalence of the gammadion cross on Slav Easter egg designs attracted the attention of Dr Milovan Gavazzi, a Yugoslav scholar, who wrote at some length on the subject in 1929, without, however, drawing any particular conclusions. He had noticed it on other Slav folk-objects, especially embroidery. The essay draws by way of illustration on the large collection of swastika-decorated eggs in the Ethnographic Museum of Zagreb.

He saw a swastika pattern or variants of it in forms which would seem at first glance to be something else – chiefly fragments of swastikas or ones that have lost their hooks. Again, he regarded other figures as swastikas whose members had been brought into contact or linked together. The essay, though interesting and exceedingly detailed in its analysis, proves little one way or the other about this type of design[2] (see colour plates XII, XXIII).

One last Slavic pattern deserves a mention. A distinguished Latvian friend, striving in exile to keep the culture of her country alive, decorated a few eggs for me with the design of the Tree of the Dawn. She could tell me nothing about it, except that it was popular in Latvian embroidery and folk-art.

The tree is a common traditional symbol, often, as here, of no particular species. Early Slavonic mythology refers to a primitive god of joy, Kupala, who was closely associated with fertility. He was worshipped beneath a sacred tree, generally the birch, which was stripped except for the upper branches, leaving a kind of crown around the top. It was garlanded during his festival and, at dawn on the morning of that day, purple loosestrife had to be found and plucked, for it had the power to frighten away demons.[3]

[1] Van Gennep, *Manuel*, 1.iii.1,323.

[2] Gavazzi, Milovan, 'Svastika i Njezin Ornamentalni Razvoj Na Uskrsnim Jajima Sa Balkana', *Zbornik Za Narodni Život i Običaje Južnih Slavena*, xxvii (Zagreb, 1929), i.1–23.　　　　[3] *Larousse*, 305–7.

Conceivably, this Slavic Tree of the Dawn, then, is a blend of the two observances, for the worship of vegetable life was a prominent feature in the cult of this god.

ENGLISH PACE-EGGS

The Wordsworth Museum in Grasmere, Cumberland, contains eleven pace-eggs from Rydal Mount, Wordsworth's home, dyed and decorated by James Dixon, the gardener, for the poet's grandchildren. The dates of these eggs span the period 1868–78, and that from the first year is marked accordingly. The decorations include a swan framed in a border of flowers, two long-tailed birds and other pastoral motifs. On one there is a representation of the Wordsworth family crest.

Sometimes such eggs were kept carefully in corner cupboards and handed down as family heirlooms. They were also strung in garlands on the mantelpiece, as many as twenty at a time.[1] This custom is to be found on the Continent. In Denmark, on Fionie Island, egg garlands were made by blowing out the contents of the eggs, decorating the shells and threading them together in a wreath. Coloured ribbons might be used as interspersions. These garlands were hung at Easter-time on the roofs of houses, churches and schools.[2] Czechs threaded the eggs and placed them in the windows of their homes.[3] In Safien egg garlands of this kind were often suspended in the living-room at New Year, when people came to visit.[4]

In England paste-eggs, as they are called, were a popular part of the Easter festival. Today, unfortunately, English people tend to buy chocolate eggs in the confectioners. But in the northernmost counties, such as Northumberland and Cumberland, the old tradition has kept alive. My husband, who was born near Hexham in Northumberland in 1930, remembers decorating eggs when he was a boy. They were made into miniature parcels, with petals or little flowers pressed carefully against the shell. Next, scraps of

---

[1] Thiselton-Dyer, T. F., *British Popular Customs*, London, 1876, 169. Jewitt, Llewellynn, 'On Ancient Customs and Sports of the County of Derby', *Journal of the British Archaeological Association*, vii (London, 1852), 205.

[2] Uldall, 4.

[3] Hazeltine, Alice, and Smith, Elva, ed., *The Easter Book of Legends and Stories*, New York, 1947, 219.

[4] Wildhaber, *Wir färben*, 18.

material in various different colours from the sewing basket were wrapped around and, finally, something to hold it all in place, such as a piece of linen. This bundle was put into boiling water, where it remained for about half an hour. Meanwhile the colours in the material came out and stained the eggs in pretty tints, leaving the outline of the flowers.

But this was before the Second World War. Today the custom is kept going by the north-country Women's Institutes – or perhaps one should say that it was. Last Easter, for the first time, local members in my husband's village on the South Tyne did not prepare paste-eggs for the children. Looking back through the *Women's Institute Book* for Cambo, Northumberland, an entry reads:

> This year, 1922, prizes were offered for the three prettiest eggs shown at the W.I. meeting in April. Onion peeling is largely used, and they are tied up with whin and other flowers, cretonnes, ribbons, etc. Specimen eggs are kept for years. Mrs Keith has a dozen eggs on which her grandfather, Mr Henry Codling, the late joiner, had drawn with a sharp penknife, swans, a boat-house, a squirrel, owls, and dates from 1882–1886. They were dyed with logwood and onion peeling.[1]

Today a champion egg-decorator in Northumberland is Mrs Herdman of Acomb village on the North Tyne. Each year when the season comes round, her grandchildren are sent out into the fields to gather certain plants and herbs. Results are best if the leaves are allowed to wilt a little before applying them to the egg. Now, of course, it is not so easy to dye by the traditional method. Most modern materials have fast colours which do not stain the shells. Scraps of old cloth must be searched out from cupboards and drawers instead.

I have in my collection beautiful eggs in red and blue and yellow, decorated by Mrs Herdman and her daughter, who has learnt the craft. They are imprinted with leaves of vetch, burnet, wild carrot, lupin, rose, lady's mantle, yellow corydalis and fern. Sometimes the natural green of the leaves appears upon the surface of the egg. The effect is curious and striking, reminiscent of beautiful artistic fossils (see colour plate XXII).

[1] Bosanquet, Rosalie E., ed., *The Cambo Women's Institute Book*, Newcastle, 1929, 17–18.

This plant-appliqué method is also known on the Continent, and has been recorded in Switzerland, Austria, Germany, Portugal, France, Sweden, Latvia, Hungary, Bulgaria, Greece and Yugoslavia (Slovenia and Macedonia). A Lebanese Christian told me that her family boiled Easter eggs with flowers, but thought that, like so many present-day habits, this was borrowed from Europe. Most spring plants are in fact suitable for the purpose, especially those with finely jointed leaves. Sometimes the warmth of the egg itself enables the plant to stick, or it may be bound in place. An old lady from the northern Border country uses golden syrup very effectively.

Mrs Herdman's parents had the milk-delivery business in the village, and used to give a coloured egg to each of their customers on the Easter round. Her father also worked in the local coalmine. A traditional Northumbrian song runs:

> *And to please the pit laddies at Easter*
> *A dishful of gilty paste eggs.*[1]

In those days miners were lit at work with tallow candles. Using hot wax from one of these, Mrs Herdman's father wrote each client's name upon an egg, which was then dipped in dye, and finally polished with butter. Two generations later Mrs Herdman's son-in-law, who is from the same district, remembers a similar custom: at school every member of his class received an egg before going home for the Easter vacation. Each had his name written on it with a candle, and they were coloured with coffee grounds. This inscribing of names on the shell was, again, not peculiar to England. Danes wrote names or initials with melted wax and the Pennsylvania Dutch also used a candle; Germans preferred soap.[2]

'Paste' or 'Pace' is simply a corruption of 'pasche', meaning 'paschal', though the original meaning is now entirely forgotten. When I talked to Mrs Herdman, she used it quite literally to mean paste in the sense of glue, though no such substance is utilized in the process. This is in contrast with the 'painted eggs' which Northumbrians despise, using the term to describe those decorated by any method other than their own.

A year or two ago Mrs Herdman's daughter had her entries

---

[1] 'The Pitman's Courtship', a local Northumbrian song, published in 1818.
[2] Uldall, 2. Information kindly supplied by Herr Karl-Heinz Vick of Rostock.

ruled out of order in the Institute competition, because the judge believed that they were painted. In fact, they were not, and she was paying the penalty for exquisite workmanship. Earlier, before they were made largely for entry in such competitions, pace-eggs played a lively part in Northumbrian Easter celebrations. If a woman refused a man a pace-egg, he seized her boots, and if a man refused a woman, she snatched his cap. In each case a ransom had to be paid.[1]

Today these traditional pace-eggs have mostly been replaced by confectionery, introduced by the Dutch and French at the beginning of the century. Till then it was a slow and expensive process making chocolate eggs. They were shaped by hand, using tin-plate moulds in two separate halves, and trimmed. Modern mechanical processes then speeded up the operation and enabled hundreds to be made in the time it originally took to make one. The early creations were huge shells of smooth, glossy chocolate, adorned with ribbons and flowers of edible coloured sugar.[2]

Next on the market came smaller marzipan eggs, with pink icing piped along the seam. These were occasionally decorated with appropriate paper patterns of different Easter animals: a rabbit or a chicken. There were milk-chocolate eggs as well, the size of ordinary hen's eggs and wrapped in pretty coloured foil paper – mauve, gold, red and green – with creamy yellow filling and marshmallow representing the yolk and the white. They were prepared in baskets and laid in nests of coloured straw. Others contrived from sugar resembled the spotted eggs of birds, presented in nests of chocolate. Today these eggs are made from almost anything from jelly to toffee.

THE SCRATCH TECHNIQUE

In 1959 the Opies were told: 'In Cumberland we take more notice of the pace-eggs than of the chocolate ones.'[3] They found that many English children could still decorate eggs in traditional styles, including scratching with a steel pen, after the manner of engraving. At one time a penknife was used partially to remove

---

[1] Ditchfield, P. H., *Old English Customs*, London, 1896, 80.

[2] Daiken, Leslie, *Children's Toys throughout the Ages*, London, 1953, 179.

[3] Opie, Iona and Peter, *The Lore and Language of Schoolchildren*, Oxford, 1959, 251.

the dye and mark out the shell into several compartments: one with, perhaps, the recipient's name and age, another containing a landscape, and a third a Cupid. The last motif must have been quite common, for it sometimes happened that pace-eggs were used on St Valentine's Day.[1] But these more elaborate creations have long disappeared. A modern child would not attempt to produce such a thing unless he was very painstaking, though I have seen some fine recent specimens done by adults from Cumberland, mostly with animal designs.

By contrast, the earliest egg of this kind preserved by the Pennsylvania Dutch is simply inscribed 'M.B.' and dated 1774.[2] Since modern American history virtually begins with the Declaration of Independence in 1775, this one is of particular interest. Perhaps there were also more elaborate patterns, but the earliest written reference, in Thomas Anburey's *Travels Through the Interior Parts of America*, published a little later in 1789, gives no details of the designs on these early eggs.

Scratch-carving is the most popular technique in certain Slav countries: north Poland, where they are called *skrobanki*, Lithuania, Slovenia, Latvia and the Sorb areas around Hoyerswerda and Cottbus.[3] Czechs adopted it in the late nineteenth century, utilizing mainly designs of plants with an occasional rhyme, and Germans in Bohemia, Silesia and Slovakia (Zips) did much the same.[4] In Bulgaria this method was confined to the monasteries.[5] It is also found among the Bethlehem mother-of-pearl workers, who dye their eggs brown and use religious motifs.[6] The method is simple. All that is necessary is to stain an egg one colour and use a sharp object to carve a pattern. Leaving the contents intact is advisable, since the shell is all too easily pierced and it is brittle if blown.

ETCHING AND APPLIQUÉ

Konrad Noll, a Rhineland priest, noted in 1601 how teachers were giving their schoolchildren coloured eggs in class: 'Often the eggs

[1] Thiselton-Dyer, 163. Hone, i.426.

[2] Shoemaker, 53.

[3] *Ibid.*, 51–62. Seweryn, 173. Information kindly supplied by Miss Marina Gorodeckis. See colour plates XIII, XXIII.

[4] Pranda, 5–6. Also personal observation. See colour plate XVIII.

[5] Vakarelski, 187.

[6] Wilson, C. T., *Peasant Life in the Holy Land*, London, 1906, 46.

were painted and the colour afterwards etched out in acid, producing all kinds of figures on the egg. No expense was spared.'[1]

The method he describes is rather unusual and limited to certain countries – they know it, for example, in Styria, Estonia, Bosnia, Czechoslovakia, Switzerland, Hessen, and in the Sorb Lausitz. The most primitive technique necessitates placing the coloured eggs in an ant-hill. The insects will sprinkle the eggs with their own natural acid so that the shells are brightly speckled. But most people today use nitric acid – the Sorbs prefer sauerkraut juice, which is just as effective and safer for children to handle.[2]

Perhaps it was the slight risk involved that prevented this method from spreading. Appliqué eggs, on the other hand, are most suitable for children, since they do not require immense concentration or skill. Many countries make these with the most unlikely materials. The Portuguese use sea-shells,[3] and Austrians little strips of dough, to achieve raised patterns.[4] Serbs have little circles of coiled metal called *kezap* and *srma* or tufts of brightly coloured wool;[5] and the Poles make paper-cuts called *wylepianki*, but only around Lowicz.[6] Made to resemble a little jug with paper base and handle and spout, they are usually decorated with roosters or flowers and the whole effect is charming.

In western Poland and in Silesia they make eggs with rush-pith and wool appliqué. These reed eggs were once popular in many parts of Germany too. The supplement of wool is peculiar to Poland, but a very elaborate style is found near Brno, with the addition of ribbon, bead and paper ornamentation. In Eisenach a reed-pith-covered egg was once publicly carried on a rod adorned with a cockerel of dough.[7] Moravians use them as toys – putting pebbles inside to make a rattle. Sometimes they hang all the year from the ceiling and an Easter dove with pith decorations is suspended over the cradle.[8]

---

[1] Von König, Kostbare Ostereier, 206.

[2] Schmidt-Kowar, E., *Sorbische Ostereier*, Bautzen, 1965, 10.

[3] Oliviera, Ernesto Veiga de, 'Folares et Œufs de Pâques au Portugal', *Schweizerisches Archiv für Volkskunde*, LIII (Basle, 1957), ii–iii, 156.

[4] Information kindly supplied by Miss I. M. Kaplan.

[5] There are some examples of this style in the Belgrade Ethnographic Museum.   [6] Seweryn, 174. See colour plate VIII.

[7] Weinhold, Gertrud, *Das schöne Osterei in Europa*, Kassel, 1965, 37–8.

[8] Kunz, Ludvik, 'Mährische Ostereier', *Schweizerisches Archiv für Volkskunde*, LIII (Basle, 1957), ii–iii.165. See colour plate XXIII.

At one time these may well have served some magic protective purpose. According to Bächtold-Stäubli the reeds must be picked at full moon, since it is then that they contain pith, whereas when it wanes they will be empty.[1] The Chinese used reeds for purposes of divination: to obtain an augury, one picked a certain number and flung them down. They would then arrange themselves in one of the sixty-four diagrams of ancient Chinese philosophy.[2]

In Ireland reeds are lucky. Picked on St Bride's Eve without a cutting instrument, they are made into crosses, blessed in church, and placed above the entrance to house and byre. In England they have curative powers and are used to get rid of warts and ulcers.[3] Traditionally the significant feature of a reed, and probably what gave rise to these ideas, is its reputation of regaining its green colour in the rain. For this reason it was a symbol of immortality – a very ancient idea, recorded as long ago as the tenth century.[4]

Of course, rush-pith – they call it *binsa graws* in Pennsylvania – is easy to find at Easter-time. Over there it is either used on its own, or combined with strips of material to cover the egg.[5] The best way to get the pith out is by pushing with a matchstick. Its natural colour, pale white and yellow, is generally left unchanged, though in the Odenwald they occasionally stain it with water-colours. In Siegerland they hang this kind of egg upon the May Tree.[6]

Czechs also used material, but not in combination with rush-pith. This idea originated in religious houses and urban areas at the end of the nineteenth century. Specifically in Moravia straw-covered eggs are made. Little tubes of barley straw are soaked in water, cut lengthways to form a flattened surface and then into different shapes, which are coloured and stuck on the shells. Once widespread in much of Slovakia as well, this method can now be found only in the western and southern parts of the country.[7] Again it may have had some magical origin – straw as part of the

---

[1] Bächtold-Stäubli, i.1,333–4.

[2] Giles, Herbert A., *Confucianism and Its Rivals*, London, 1915, 25–6.

[3] Hole, Christina, ed., *Encyclopaedia of Superstitions*, London, 1961, 292.

[4] Grimm, Jacob and Wilhelm, *Deutsches Wörterbuch*, Leipzig, 1860, ii.37.

[5] Shoemaker, 27–30. See colour plate XXIII.

[6] Mössinger, Friedrich, 'Odenwälder Binseneier', *Schweizerisches Archiv für Volkskunde*, LIII (Basle, 1957), ii–iii.74.

[7] Pranda, 5–6. See colour plate XIII.

sustaining corn, source of food and thus of life; straw dollies and crosses have often a special significance. As we saw earlier,[1] a Croatian woman who is barren is offered an egg with a wheat-sheaf design as a cure.

Since the beginning of the twentieth century Moravian and Bulgarian blacksmiths and goldsmiths have embellished Easter eggs by applying various miniature metal ornaments – without breaking the shell.[2] In Hungary they fitted metal hangers or little metal shoes and spurs.[3] Magyars have always been famed for horsemanship, so it is interesting that even eggs are equipped for riding. But they are seldom to be seen. The very extensive collection at Basle lacks examples and a Hungarian friend had not even heard of them. It is a rare technique, known chiefly in the south.

At Bernece horseshoes, crosses, flowers and other metal fittings have been known since the beginning of the century. Holes are bored through the shell and the metal attached with coloured pins. In Verebely (Bars Komitat) these 'lucky eggs' are pierced by a nail to which four horseshoes and two spurs have been attached – commonly they are made by gipsies and itinerant blacksmiths. Similar metal objects in India, Israel and North Africa are fixed to the door of the house or a tree as charms against witchcraft of any kind,[4] and, of course, the significance of horseshoes is well known.

INSCRIPTIONS

Inscribed eggs too are occasionally to be found in certain Slav countries – Moravia, Slovakia, Yugoslavia and Poland – but they are not at all common, and do not exist in the Ukraine, probably because lettering would not combine well with the elaborate geometrical patterns. It is rather in Germany – greater Germany – that this technique is practised to any extent. Mozart is said to have composed one of his first songs as an Easter-egg embellishment,[5] and Dr Wolfhilde von König, who has written extensively

---

[1] See earlier section in this chapter which deals with designs.

[2] Vakarelski, 187–8.

[3] Viski, 48.

[4] Sándor, István, 'Das beschlagene Osterei', *Schweizerisches Archiv für Volkskunde*, LIII (Basle, 1957), ii–iii, 179–80.

[5] 'Vom Osterei und seinen wundersamen Geheimnissen', *Pro*, v (Basle, April 1966); no author; no pagination.

on the subject, collected various other references from the eighteenth century.[1] But there seems to be nothing earlier, so in fact this must be one of the later methods of Easter-egg decoration.

Religious verses, which are common and must pre-date the secular love rhymes, were generally not invented by the decorators themselves, who collected and wrote them down for later use. It was customary for a godparent to present his charge with this kind of inscribed egg, and some of the verses are suitably solemn and admonitory:

> *Keep the dress which Jesus gave you*
> *Lily white.*
> *You got it clean from Him*
> *And clean you must return it.*[2]

> *Christ lies in His grave*
> *For three days*
> *With wounds on hands and feet.*
> *Sinner, you must atone.*[3]

A Styrian egg gloomily points to the transience of this worldly life:

> *The roses in the garden*
> *Flower every year;*
> *Man flowers only once*
> *And then it is all over.*[4]

The tone can be reminiscent of the kind of Victorian sampler which little girls were expected to stitch for their general edification:

> *Hold your soul in high esteem,*
> *For Jesus does.*
> *He has given His precious life*
> *To redeem it.*[5]

Some are more like hymns:

> *As you have arisen from the dead*
> *Let us too arise, Lord Jesus Christ,*

---

[1] See her article, 'Ostereierverse', already referred to.
[2] Hain, 73.
[3] Von König, 'Ostereierverse', 85.
[4] Kretzenbacher, 107.
[5] Von König, 'Ostereierverse', 85.

Then through your Ascension
Like You we shall arise from our graves.[1]

Sophie Lechner of Switzerland, remembering her childhood with her brothers and sisters, recalls how her father used to put a black 'sinner's egg' in their stockings on Easter Monday, inscribed with dire warnings – an unpleasant reminder that the holiday had ended.[2]

Those which girls presented to their sweethearts were often a way of conveying feelings that the donor did not dare to express:

Sweet is what this egg conceals,
But sweeter far a kiss from you.[3]

Another egg from Styria laments:

The sky is high,
The fields are wide,
And being alone
Is no joy.[4]

In north Tyrol boys and girls exchange eggs simultaneously, so that the inscriptions work almost as question and answer.[5] Sometimes they were parting gifts, for in the summer German boys often went to the North Rhine–Westphalia industrial region for seasonal employment. Such an egg from Hessen reads:

Even if distant places part us,
Remain in love
With the one who wrote these words
Upon this Easter egg.[6]

It could be a way of plighting one's troth:

For Easter you will get this egg
For Whitsun my promise,
For Shrovetide my hand,
That I promise you.[7]

---

[1] *Ibid.*

[2] Lechner, Sophie, 'Beim Eiermalen', *Heimatwerk*, xxxii (Zürich, February 1967), i.8.

[3] Wildhaber, *Wir färben*, 30.

[4] Kretzenbacher, 107.

[5] Becker, 9.

[6] Hain, 73.

[7] Kretzenbacher, 107.

Or of snubbing a suitor:

> *If this egg were my heart,*
> *I certainly would not give it to you.*
>
> *See, you have an egg!*
> *I know you would rather have two.*
> *But I would be a fool;*
> *You and I would still not be as one.*[1]

The reference to a pair of eggs is to this method of avowing engagement.[2] Some young men took this kind of rebuff very much to heart and dashed the offending egg to pieces.

---

[1] Von König, 'Ostereierverse', 86–7.
[2] See earlier section in this chapter which deals with tokens of love.

Chapter 12
Artificial Techniques

Ovum est candidum; et omnes tamen colores
admittat: scribi potest, pingi potest, tingi
potest et nunc flavum, nunc rubrum, nunc
caeruleum patrii ritus faciunt.
Erycius Puteanus, *Ovi Encomium* (1617)

A shallow courtier present, impatient of the honours paid to
Columbus, abruptly asked him whether he thought that in
case he had not discovered the Indies, there were not other
men in Spain who would have been capable of the enterprise.
To this Columbus made no immediate reply, but taking an
egg, invited the company to make it stand on end. Everyone
attempted it, but in vain, whereupon he struck it upon the
table so as to break the end and left it standing on the broken
part; illustrating in this simple manner that when he had
once shown the way to the New World, nothing was easier
than to follow it.

W. Irving, *Life of Columbus*

EARLY ART EGGS

The Bavarian priest Andreas Strobl gives a detailed account of
contemporary Easter eggs in his collection of sermons, *Ovum
Paschale Novum Oder Neugefärbte Oster Ayr* of 1694, in which he
writes:

The whole year eggs do not receive so much honour as at Easter;
they are gilded, silvered, painted with spots and figures, they are also
painted and decorated with beautiful colours in relief, they are
scratched; they are made into Easter lambs or into a pelican who
feeds his young with his own blood, or they carry the picture of
Christ or something else; they are boiled, they are dyed green,
red, yellow, gold, etc. They are made up and then given as gifts
by one good friend to another. They are even carried in large
amounts to the church to be blessed, and there are many who now
eat or drink a soft boiled egg, rather than anything else.

Columbus, in the little anecdote at the beginning of this chapter makes the point that nothing is easier than imitation. And the great flood of work produced by peasant art was, in time, taken up, sophisticated and generally embellished. Those with a skilled trade or master craft tried their hand at Easter eggs – the glass-blowers of Bohemia, wood-carvers, workers in enamel and precious metals, the famous Kutahya potters and many others. Some made little knick-knacks and curiosities, fantasies around the idea of an egg: table-ware, beauty requisites, ornamental boxes, and items of genuine usefulness.

A particularly usual example, which turns up all over western Europe, is the pomander. In the nineteenth century these were carved by prisoners and sailors from boxwood in two halves that unscrewed for easy filling with potpourri: some people substituted coriander seeds – a moth-repellent. Different examples, which are not pierced and do not open, are purely ornamental. Containers of other kinds were often of this particular shape. The famous Bavarian Nymphenburg factory made a sponge-box in the form of an egg, and there is a French eighteenth-century box in the Guildhall Museum, covered with calf leather, hand-tooled in gold and lined with silk – perhaps it was intended for an Easter egg. Even watches, invented there around 1500, were known as Nuremberg eggs.

The art eggs *par excellence* are, of course, those created by the famous Carl Fabergé, court jeweller to the Tsar of Russia. Strictly speaking, they belong to this section. But because they are so obviously linked with the basic religious life of the country generally they have been dealt with in ch. 8.

The forerunners of these art eggs are to be found in the remote past. Dr H. R. Ellis Davidson has drawn my attention to the remarkably beautiful Knossos fresco, 'Partridges', housed in the Museum at Heraklion, and dating from 1500 B.C. Beneath the two birds are a number of oval objects, resembling eggs and striped in brilliant shades of red, green, blue, yellow and white. Archaeologists excavating at Wonseradeel in Friesland made extensive finds inside small hills, dated at about 500 B.C. and apparently built to provide dry ground in wintertime, when the sea surged in and flooded the land. The contents included pottery and pottery eggs, and it has been suggested that these might have been intended to encourage the hens in their laying. But there was also a peewit's egg, made of baked earth and painted,[1] and no one could possibly have been interested in encouraging a peewit to lay.

It is conceivable that it was in fact intended as some kind of magic. Even today there is a considerable folklore in the Netherlands surrounding the bird. Annually people search for its first egg, and when this is found the news is printed on the front page of the Press, for it means that spring has come. The local burgomaster of the district where this occurs telephones the Queen, and an audience is arranged at which the successful person presents it to her.

The purpose of the prehistoric peewit's egg is too obscure to be clearly defined in the light of present evidence. But observations made elsewhere in Europe suggest a possible connection between early eggs and rites for the dead. Nilsson, who has written extensively on the subject, collected much valuable material from Etruscan burial-sites. He notes six ostrich eggs from Vulci, scratched or painted with scenes of animals, warriors and chariots.[2] These, of course, are real eggs, but they probably served a purpose similar to artificial examples, which he also describes. A large egg made of clay was, in fact, found in a grave at Corinth. It is decorated with the figure of a flute-player, seated on a chair and surrounded by five mourning women.[3]

Several smaller clay eggs, covered in white and striped with black and red on either side, were excavated at Praeneste (Palestrina), which dates from the seventh century B.C.[4] Decorated eggs from the same period were discovered in the Athens cemetery by German archaeologists, and are housed in the museum, Kerakimos. Two more from a well-documented grave at Worms (Germany), and dated approximately A.D. 320, are ornamented in the same fashion.[5] The sarcophagus, which was Roman Germanic, contained the remains of a child. I wrote to the local museum, but the Director told me that it is not possible to ascertain whether or not this was a Christian burial.

---

[1] Information kindly supplied by Henk Arends from the *Bulletin of the Royal Netherlands Association of Antiquaries*, June 1966.

[2] Nilsson, Martin P., 'Das Ei im Totenkult der Alten', *Archiv für Religionswissenschaft*, ii, (Leipzig, 1908), 532.

[3] *Ibid.*, 533.

[4] *Ibid.*

[5] Wildhaber, Robert, *Wir färben Ostereier*, Berne, 1957, 2.

Others of glazed clay, with what appears to be a feather design in slip, turned up in eleventh-century graves on Gotland.[1] Specimens like them are numerous in the neighbourhood of Kiev. Perhaps this was a Swedish borrowing from the Russians: earlier there was a Viking kingdom at Kiev and a rattle-egg of clay was also excavated there from a first-century Slavic grave.[2]

The usage of an egg in funeral rites has already been discussed in general terms. But do these artificial examples have a special significance of their own? Were they thought to be more durable, perhaps? The highly elaborate specimens referred to above were probably intended to serve a similar purpose to the burial paintings adorning the walls of tombs, which depict the earthly life of the dead and honour their memory. Dominant features are selected – the musician and his flute, a warrior's chariot. Simpler motifs, such as the stripes and dots, are again insufficient to build on – though, of course, we do know what they mean to modern Ukrainians – but the colours are of some interest. Black and white are shades of mourning, and red, the symbol of blood and life, is common in early burials. Palaeolithic grave finds show that the corpse was sometimes smeared with a red substance, and Brandon suggests that we may here have the first example of the endeavour to prevent – or reverse – the consequences of death. Physical disintegration could be avoided by what he describes as 'contagious magic'.[3]

EGGS OF GLASS, PORCELAIN, WOOD, STONE AND PRECIOUS MATERIALS

In modern times eggs of various artificial materials are very popular. One seldom passes a gift-shop without seeing a multi-coloured selection of them, in imitation marble, intended as paper-weights or ornaments. They are pleasant to hold, and indeed the aristocracy of old Russia used them as hand-coolers, made from jade, malachite, and other semi-precious stones from the Urals; malachite, which was worked by prisoners, is found in

[1] Oxenstierna, Eric, *Die Wikinger*, Stuttgart, 1959, pl. 78.
[2] Nilsson, 534–5.
[3] Brandon, S. G. F., *History, Time and Deity*, Manchester, 1965, 14. Becker, Albert, *Brauchtum der deutschen Osterzeit*, Jena, 1937, 44. I am indebted to F. J. Collins for first drawing my attention to this point.

conjunction with uranium, and the convict workers who died in those mines were often killed, probably not by poison gas, but by radiation. Since the Russian revolution the idea has been copied in the Belgian Congo, where malachite is also found, and in Germany.

The Prussian Court likewise borrowed from the Russians the custom of presenting porcelain Easter eggs, as a result of Charlotte's marriage with Tsar Nicholas I. She was the daughter of Friedrich Wilhelm II, who wrote to her in 1820: 'You will receive a lot of porcelain Easter eggs, made after the design of those at Petersburg.'[1]

The Berliner-Porzellan-Manufaktur is the only factory in Germany which ever produced eggs in this style. They were made with a hole on top, since they often also served as scent-bottles. The stopper was generally surmounted by some typically German emblem – a helmet or eagle, shaped in brass. Representative designs, in keeping with this, tend to be secular and often illustrate contemporary Berlin life, its famous buildings and monuments. In pattern they resemble tea or coffee services from the same factory, the design framed in an oval on a white or gilded base with gold ornamentation; the famous Berlin blue is lavishly used.

In Imperial Russia there were many porcelain-makers; large quantities of eggs were produced in Volhynia, now part of the western Ukraine, at the Baranowka Factory, founded in 1801 by Michael Mezer and his brother. From 1895 until the Revolution it was run by the Gripari family at the estate of Prince Gargarin. Their porcelain resembled work from the Russian Imperial Factory.[2] Eggs were adorned with Biblical subjects: scenes of the Resurrection, ikons, portraits of cherubs and saints. Western influence sometimes creeps in: a portrait of St Evgenia dressed as a nun is reminiscent of Pre-Raphaelite painting, and certain floral examples could be mistaken for Limoges.

The Danish Royal Family have a few art eggs in their personal collection at Rosenburg Castle. A hen's egg, covered in silver filigree, carries the monogram of Christian V, who ruled at the

---

[1] König, Wolfhilde von, 'Kostbare Ostereier', *Die Waage*, iii (Stolberg, June 1964), 209. See colour plate I.

[2] Haggar, Reginald G., *The Concise Encyclopaedia of Continental Pottery and Porcelain*, London, 1960, 58. See colour plates II, III, IV.

end of the seventeenth century. Another, in gold and ivory, was a toilet-table article, and belonged to Queen Anna Sophia, who lived at a slightly later date.[1]

Generally, of course, only royalty could afford eggs made of precious materials. But in 1717 Liselotte, Countess of the Rhenish Pfalz, sent the Princess of Wales an Easter present 'to make you laugh'. Her gift, two eggs of tortoiseshell, was filled with little rings.[2] Indeed, in sophisticated times the original purpose of such offerings becomes increasingly overlooked. Instead of commemorating our Redeemer, they foster nationalism or just serve as a joke – and, as in ancient times, are tokens of love.

Further upstream, Alsatian glass-blowers gave eggs to their sweethearts. One from Solbach dated 1765 and coloured in pretty shades of blue, red, yellow and purple, reads:

> *With all my love and all my faith*
> *This Easter egg I give to you.*[3]

German glass-makers in Bohemia used to produce this kind of thing too – sometimes in highly elaborate patterns – and simple examples are still blown in Thuringia. Young Alsatian carpenters made wooden eggs for their girl-friends, embellished with carving or poker-work. In Strasbourg they were presented at Christmas and were known as Nazareth eggs. Later in the year they were changed into Easter gifts by replacing the Christmas tree which topped them with an Easter hare.[4]

Being unbreakable, wooden eggs were widely made for children, especially in Czechoslovakia, where they were never regarded as an art form deserving much skill and effort. Those from the Ukraine are often decorated with poker-work, and show scenes of costumed children playing egg-tapping. Others are inlaid with mother-of-pearl, yet another example of how various different folk-arts were so often employed in making Easter eggs: this particular craft is still a living art in the modern Ukraine, though the standard has deteriorated in Soviet times. In an

---

[1] Uldall, Kai, 'Les Œufs de Pâques au Danemark', *Schweizerisches Archiv für Volkskunde*, I IV (Basle, 1958), 3–4.

[2] Becker, 48.

[3] Pfleger, Alfred, 'Osterei und Ostergebäck im Elsass', *Schweizerisches Archiv für Volkskunde*, LIII. (Basle, 1957), ii–iii 118.

[4] *Ibid.*, 117.

Colour Plate XIX Eggs decorated by the batik, or wax-resist, technique. The upper row were made at a Mennonite village in the Pfalz, using rust and whey dye. The two right-hand eggs in the second row, the whole of row 3, and the right-hand egg in row 4, were made by an East Prussian (German) craftsman; certain of the designs show similarity with those used in Poland. In the second row, the two left-hand eggs are the work of a Lithuanian artist (Marina Gorodeckis); tea was used as a dye. The left-hand egg in row 4 is Austrian, and the remaining six, predominantly black eggs (rows 4 and 5) are from the Ober Krain, or Kranj district in Slovenia. Black colour is generally achieved with oak bark by the Slovenian mountaineers, and the usual batik technique is sometimes varied by substituting oil for wax.

Colour Plate XX Batik (wax-resist) eggs from Upper Lusatia (Ober Lausitz, Germany). The three exceptionally fine eggs in the second row are the work of Martin Drabent of Grossräschen. Both he and his son do this work, and have won many prizes in egg-decorating competitions. Sorb craftsmen, the partly Slav-speaking inhabitants of this area, traditionally use a trimmed goose feather to achieve the effect of triangular stippling.

attractive variant the inlay is filled with coloured paint, reproducing the intricate geometrical patterns beloved by Ukrainian Hutzuls (see colour plate XII).

Few art eggs will have had any magic significance: they were largely intended for the amusement of children and the pleasure of adults. The famous faience eggs of the Kutahya potters are a notable exception. Isnik and Kutahya are two towns in northwest Asia Minor famous for pottery manufacture. Both places appear to be connected with sacerdotal eggs – Isnik with Moslem, Kutahya with Christian rites. A great deal of mosque furnishings were made in Isnik, and probably the eggs of 'Damascus porcelain', with blue and purple markings, which Bassili describes as hanging in Cairo mosques, were really from there.[1]

Dr F. R. Martin believes 'Damascus' ware did not come from that city at all; that the name was given by Armenian merchants who traded in it. By way of support, he points out how it differs in paste and glaze from Syrian ware of the fourteenth and fifteenth centuries. The famous blue work in any case originates some fifty or more years after Damascus fell to Selim I (1517), upon which all craftsmen of any note were deported to Constantinople. The ware known by this name was, in his opinion, more probably made at Isnik; the general style and designs of the work done there support this view.[2]

Isnik is the old Nicaea, where the First Ecumenical Council was held in A.D. 325 and the Nicene Creed was promulgated. Today only a village, in 1333 – before the Turkish conquest – it was once capital of Asia Minor. Tabah Zade, one of the last master-workers who lived there, flourished in the early seventeenth century. When he died his craftsmen settled in Kutahya, whence came certain of their basic materials, and where, in any case, they could earn more money. Extant examples of their work date from the early eighteenth century and onwards – the peak of the local craft.[3]

---

[1] Bassili, William, *Sinai and the Monastery of St Catherine*, Cairo, 1962, 139, note 1, and 140.

[2] Martin, F. R., 'The True Origin of So-called Damascus Ware', *The Burlington Magazine*, xv (London, April–Sept. 1909), 269–70.

[3] *Ibid.*, 270. Boulanger, Robert, *Turkey*, Paris, 1960, 183.

The influx of craftsmen, many of them Armenian, deported to western Asia Minor from Tabriz after the Turkish conquest in 1514, must already have made an impact on local workmanship. But though, even in recent times, the majority of the Kutahya potteries were in Armenian hands – in fact the place was the seat of an Armenian bishop and the doyen of Armenian music, Komitas, was born there – most of their work is Islamic in style. No doubt this catered for the predominantly Turkish market. Rare examples have pictures of saints and Armenian inscriptions; a saucer with the figure of St Sergius is dated 1719.[1]

Eggs, evidently intended for hanging in churches and mosques, originate from the same period. Pierced for the purpose, they are generally decorated in several colours; green and yellow are the most usual – it is less common to find combinations of blue and purple – and the outlines are painted with thin black lines. The mosque eggs show flowers,[2] as a rule; on the Christian eggs the design is of seraphim, perhaps alternating with sepia crosses.[3] In Western art these beings are coloured red, but Armenia would fall outside this tradition. Blue in the Middle East – of different shades and combined with purple – is used to ward off the evil eye. Other Armenian eggs, the *ova de crucibus*, eggs of the Cross, were plain white.[4]

WAXING METHODS

It will seem strange to include a type of decorated shell egg with these examples of the craftsman's art. But the spectacular wax-resist method, which very closely resembles batik, is so complicated that it merits consideration outside the primitive rustic techniques common to peasant work in this field. The high degree of skill involved is implied in a Rumanian phrase, 'tormented eggs' – because of the time and trouble involved – and we will

[1] Ormanian, Malachia, *L'Eglise Arménienne*, Paris, 1910, 182. Boulanger, 293. Hobson, R. L., *A Guide to the Islamic Pottery of the Near East*, London, 1932, 92.

[2] Louvet, Marie-Hélène, 'Pâques – dites le avec des Œufs,' *ABC Décor*, No. 54 (Paris, April 1969), 33.

[3] Rackham, Bernard, *Islamic Pottery and Italian Maiolica*, London, 1959, 52. Other data kindly supplied by R. H. Pinder Wilson, Deputy Keeper of Oriental Antiquities at the British Museum. See colour plate VII.

[4] Leland, C. G., *Gypsy Sorcery and Fortune Telling*, London, 1891, 78.

see something of the sophisticated methods employed to achieve such elaborate results.

These beautiful 'embroidered' eggs – a Greek expression – are common in central and eastern Europe. Melted wax, generally bees-wax, for candle-grease is not satisfactory – is applied in desired patterns to the shell of the egg. The instrument used is a thin stylus or needle; earlier it would have been a thorn. Peasants often made a crude wooden tool with a pig-bristle fixed to the end.

Sorbs heat their wax by putting it in the bowl of a spoon, bent at right angles over a candle, the handle secured in a slice of beet-root or large potato.[1] It is essential to use it quickly and skil-fully, for mistakes cannot be put right. Even if the wax is wiped off, it leaves a greasy place, which prevents colour from taking. The Bulgarians generally mix a little soot with the colourless wax, because it is difficult to see on the surface of the egg shell.

Beginning with the palest colour, the egg is immersed in dye for half an hour, removed and dried. Gentle heating melts the wax, which is carefully wiped off with a warm, soft rag. On no account should it be scraped with a knife or other sharp object, as this would damage the pattern. Different areas are now re-waxed, depending how many colours are used, and the egg placed in another dye. After each dipping, wax is put on the area where preceding colours are to remain. Some designs may contain as many as seven shades. Rumanians washed the eggs in yoghourt first, so they would take both colours and wax more easily.

Another variant on the batik method is to remove the wax, not during decorating, but at the end of the process, so that a nega-tive white ornament is produced. Wax is laid on the egg in the shape desired and it is put to soak in the dye. When it has been lifted out and dried, this wax is removed. If a single-shade egg of this type is intended to carry coloured decorations on a white background, it is dyed first and the required patterns drawn on the surface in wax. If it is then soaked in sauerkraut liquid or vinegar solution – methods favoured in Czechoslovakia – the acid in the water will remove all dye from the exposed areas, leaving a coloured pattern under the wax. Sometimes the finished egg is polished with melted lard or bacon fat, which gives it a nice shine.[2]

[1] Schmidt-Kowar, E., *Sorbische Ostereier*, Bautzen, 1965, 6–7.
[2] Pranda, Adam, *Kraslice v Slovenskej L'udovej Umeleckej Výrobe*, Bratislava, 1958, 4.

Rumanians elaborate this method by applying the design with melted wax and placing the egg in strong wine-vinegar for a period of about ten hours. This slightly corrodes the shell, but leaves the waxed design untouched. The egg is now dipped in the chosen colour, and when the wax is removed the pattern remains in slight relief. Peasants in Vrancea – a mountainous region – do this type of work in several colours. A different relief effect is achieved in Bulgaria, Slovakia, and the Bavarian Alps as well as in Rumania itself. Bees-wax tinted with soot or brick dust is applied to the egg with a pin, and is left permanently in place.[1] A modern innovation is to follow the batik process, but apply coloured instead of neutral wax at certain stages, enabling rich colours, not suitable for overlaying on each other, to be used in unison.

Russians make a different type of egg entirely from wax, a method which was probably originally developed at the candle works of the Orthodox Church, now in Novodyevichi Monastery. They would have made the eggs there and the sisters no doubt decorated them at Easter, as now. The method – minute coloured beads embedded in the surface of the wax – is a tradition of the Russian Church taken to the Holy Land, and from there to this country. It is now being done by Arab Orthodox sisters both in Jerusalem and England. A factory-produced transfer of the Resurrection appears on one side; on the other, embroidery-based patterns of flowers or the Cross, worked out in the little coloured beads. Ribbons attached to one end are to hang them beside the family ikons (see colour plate V).

EGG CURIOSITIES

These solid-wax creations are a far cry from the traditional Easter egg as we all know it. Equally, in England, something over 100 years ago, it became popular to present one's sweetheart with an Easter trifle patterned like a bird's egg. They were made in Sunderland at one of the big pottery works, and were earlier produced in lustre-ware, later as imitation birds' eggs with the natural speckles and coloration. In about 1885 these were slightly modified as vinaigrettes or scent-bottles. Another variant on the same

---

[1] *Ibid.*, 3. Slătineanu, Barbu, 'Les Œufs de Pâques en Roumanie', *Schweizerisches Archiv für Volkskunde*, LIII (Basle, 1957), ii–iii.183.

motif were the salt- and pepper-pots shaped and coloured like birds' eggs. These too were very popular in Victorian times.

Prettily decorated pottery eggs with floral designs were also made at Sunderland during the same period, but these were generally for children. They were marked with the name of the recipient and date of the gift. There are a few in the Sunderland Museum, but one seldom sees them in the antique shops. Some, decorated with horses and foals, were sold as 'fairings' – the old-fashioned word for a love-token – at the big horse fairs in the north. Others, hinged and made of ivory, contained sewing materials.

Many of these knick-knacks served a useful purpose. Battersea enamel eggs, made from 1753 to 1756, and again in the early nineteenth century, were generally prepared as vinaigrettes or snuffboxes; others were nutmeg-graters. These were also made in wood, usually quite plain, with only a few lines of reeding around the joint. They were at most two inches long and weighed less than an ounce. Around 1775 to 1780 brightly-cut engraving was introduced, and some of these examples are reminiscent of Easter eggs (see colour plates V, VI).

At that period in England nutmeg was popular for putting into bad wine and spicing ale, as well as for improving foods in general. Also from the Far East, and perhaps, in its own sphere, as essential to ordinary life is a commodity which strikes us as distinctly luxurious – incense. *Kogo* is the Japanese word for an ornamental incense-box, and sometimes a crane's egg was converted for this purpose. A red-and-gold lacquer egg in my collection, with a Japanese design and a gilt clasp, was probably intended for the same use (see colour plate VIII).

Eggs also appear as water-containers. Among the Bushmen in South-West Africa ostrich egg-shells, sometimes inscribed with geometrical patterns, are employed in this way.[1] In sixteenth- and seventeenth-century Europe they were also popular drinking vessels. The British Museum have a number of fine examples from Germany, Bohemia and England. There is the Aston tankard embossed and chased with silver-gilt mounts, and one from Augsburg, emblazoned with the owner's name, is fitted with chains for picking it up.

[1] Information kindly supplied by William Lockwood of Fresno, California.

At that time in western Europe ostrich eggs were very rare and much sought after by the rich, but there are also legends which imply that the substance in proximity to the liquid was of importance. It is said, for instance, that the Holy Grail was formed by angels from an emerald which fell from Lucifer's forehead as he was hurled into the abyss.[1] And it was an accepted gesture of munificence to drop a gem into the cup from which someone was about to take a draught:

> *The king shall drink to Hamlet's better breath,*
> *And in the cup an union shall he throw,*
> *Richer than that which four successive kings*
> *In Denmark's crown have worn.*[2]

Albertus Magnus notes that 'in its nest the griffin lays the agate for its help and medicine', and in the Middle Ages the 'gryphon's egg' was a valuable curiosity, used as a goblet.[3] Perhaps these attractive ostrich-egg tankards once had some similar significance.

---

[1] Cirlot, J. E., *A Dictionary of Symbols*, London, 1962, 115.

[2] *Hamlet*, v.ii. 282–285.

[3] Brown, Robert, 'Remarks on the Gryphon, Heraldic and Mythological', *Archaeologia*, xlviii, (London, 1885), ii.355–76.

Chapter 13
The Egg Tree

Awake! Raise up before the Beloved's house
A lofty May tree, brightly coloured.
Red cloth strips blow in the wind
From the branches.

Hungarian love-song

THE AMERICAN EGG TREE

Decorated eggs are often very beautiful. The effect is especially attractive when they are attached to threads and used to make an egg tree. In Sweden, at Easter, birch twigs are hung with dyed eggs, feathered birds called *påskaringar*, and small witches on broomsticks – all this in place of the coloured feathers which had decked the fronds in Lent.[1]

Such delightful Easter customs, unfamiliar in England, are especially popular in Germany, and are found in America, among the many European traditions which survive. The Pennsylvania Dutch (Deutsch) area, containing strongholds of the Moravian Church – a sect originating at Herrnhut on the borders of Silesia – is still thoroughly German in character, and German is widely used. Many of these families make egg trees, sometimes in the house and with coloured eggs, or more often in the garden with plain egg-shells impaled on a bush.

Both types seem to date from the late nineteenth century, though the house version is spoken of as less of a novelty than the garden tree, which may go back a little further. The earliest account, from a local paper, *The Reading Eagle*, is dated April 1876:

> R. D. Lingle, druggist, at Tenth and Chesnut, has in his parlour, for the pleasure of his little daughters, a new kind of tree, which was placed there on Easter Eve, and has been called an Easter Egg Tree. It is probably the only one of its kind put up in this city, and is apparently a new idea. Spruce boughs are hung with egg shells

[1] Arnott, Margaret, 'Easter Bread of South Eastern Pennsylvania', *Expedition* (Philadelphia, Spring 1961), III, iii, 26.

beautifully ornamented with paint, gilt and coloured paper. Beside these are paper ornaments representing bouquets . . . baskets, banners, flags, etc., all tastefully arranged. Excepting the eggs, the tree presents very much the appearance of a Christmas tree.[1]

There was another description, the following year, in the *Lebanon Daily Times*:

> At Christmas-time evergreen trees laden with choice and rare gifts, etc., are very common, but a similar tree adorned with mottled and vary-coloured eggs is an unusual ornament for the house, to please the children and excite their fancy. It made a beautiful appearance and was quite as appropriate as the time honoured Christmas tree.[2]

A third report, dated some ten years later, describes a tree set up in an indoor garden, and the great pleasure it gave to the children:

> Ex-Councilman Harry C. Smith celebrated Easter yesterday at his home, No. 505 Aston Street, by having a large cedar tree placed in his parlour, standing in the middle of a miniature garden. The tree was tastefully festooned with Easter eggs, all handsomely decorated, and presented a very pleasant and attractive scene. Rabbits and little ones [*sic*] were pleased as well as the crowds of little folks who thronged his residence yesterday afternoon.[3]

Old people interviewed in the area by Shoemaker had early memories of putting plain egg-shells on an outdoor bush at Easter-time. Their recollections, which are not accurately dated, probably go back to the latter part of the nineteenth century.

The Egg Tree,[4] a prize-winning children's book which appeared in 1950, has undoubtedly helped to spread the custom throughout America. It is a study of the Pennsylvania Dutch community, and the author describes in some detail their traditional egg designs: the 'bright and morning star', the 'deer on the mountain', the 'pomegranate' and the 'horn-blowing rooster'. She encourages her young readers to carry on the tradition for themselves, and to decorate egg trees for their homes, schools and churches.

In 1964 the custom had even reached Alaska. I saw children – including Eskimos – in the town of Anchorage decorating egg

---

[1] *The Reading Eagle*, 24 April 1876.
[2] *Lebanon Daily Times*, 3 April 1877. See Egg Tree in plate 16.
[3] *The Norristown Register*, 11 April 1887.
[4] Milhous, Katharine, *The Egg Tree*, New York, 1950.

trees, and the local Chamber of Commerce organized an exhibition of their work in the National Bank. This is not surprising, for Alaskan settlers are naturally mainly from the 'Lower Forty-eight' – as they call the rest of the continental United States – and carried the tradition north with them, sharing it with the indigenous population.

A GERMAN CUSTOM

The Pennsylvania Dutch are of German origin, and in fact Germany seems to be the country most closely associated with this custom. At Easter-time most German families prepare an egg tree, with blown shells or tiny wooden eggs. A friend living in Rostock (Mecklenburg) writes: 'Many people here, also ourselves, are accustomed to collecting empty eggs, to paint them and to fasten them on birch branches. These branches are then put into a big vase.'[1]

This is usually prepared about a fortnight before Easter, and the vase is carefully chosen; some people prefer those traditional brown glazed pots, inscribed with homely sayings, such as 'God with us'. Another friend in Stralsund (Pomerania) sent a description of the custom:

> In Germany we are familiar with it [the egg tree] only on a smaller scale. We prepare branches with fresh green leaves, birch twigs are a great favourite . . . and stand them in flower vases, hung with small Easter eggs. The custom in this form is known everywhere in Germany. In the art emporia it is possible at Eastertime to purchase beautifully decorated tiny wooden Easter eggs for this purpose.[2]

A publication put out by the Sorb minority of Lausitz,[3] east Germany, describes how the schoolchildren colour and blow eggs, hanging them on sprays of birch leaves in their schools and homes. The Sorbs are an isolated remnant of the Slav tribes, left behind during the great migrations across Europe, and are located mainly in the surroundings of Bautzen and Cottbus. It would be very difficult to say whether, in this case, the egg-tree custom was taken from, or given to, the surrounding Germans. The first

[1] Information kindly supplied by Herr Karl-Heinz Vick of Rostock.
[2] Information kindly supplied by Herr Hans Zühlke of Stralsund.
[3] Schmidt-Kowar, E., *Sorbische Ostereier*, Bautzen, 1965.

seems more likely, since the practice appears all through Germany, whereas in Slav countries – despite the popularity of Easter-egg decoration – it is comparatively unusual.

In 1966 a young Slovenian girl, recalling her childhood, remembered blown, painted eggs hung on a pine tree.[1] But although Slovenia is now part of Yugoslavia, it was formerly linked to Carinthia in Austria-Hungary, and German cultural influence used to predominate.

Egg trees are well known in villages of the Elbsandsteingebirge – what we call the Saxon Switzerland – but this is fairly recent. On Maundy Thursday children around Bastei hang coloured shells or roots on a fruit tree in the garden. Schandau people do not use a growing tree, but place the trunk of a birch in the ground near their house, or tie it to the fence; round the Landsbach they use coloured paper and ribbons for decoration.[2]

In Rathmannsdorf, also near the Landsbach, young boys and girls walked round the easter tree on Easter night and presented it to the Easter Virgin; she gave them cake and coffee in return. Once it was usual to fell young beech trees for the purpose, but, since the First World War, fruit trees have replaced them. If Easter is not too early, and the blossom is out, the effect must be delightful.[3]

In parts of the north Franconian Alps, a tree adorned with ribbons, flowers and coloured eggs is erected above the village well. Everyone gathers to sing and draw Easter water at midnight.[4] An important occasion for Christians, at one time this must have been a notable ritual. It is the moment when the font is blessed, and people say all water becomes holy and miraculous; at one time they used to gather round fountains and springs to drink and benefit from these healing properties.

Today the girls and boys pelt each other with water and get a soaking. At Neumühle there is a custom, kept going as a curiosity, for a virgin to draw the water at midnight in complete silence;

---

[1] Information kindly supplied through the assistance of Miss Jacqueline Simpson.

[2] Information kindly supplied by Dr Siegfried Kube of the Institut für Deutsche Volkskunde, Dresden.

[3] Information kindly supplied by Dr Siegfried Kube.

[4] Kunstmann, Hellmut, *Der Osterbaum an Quellen und Dorfbrunnen*, Kulmbach, 1958, 1–2.

it is shared out and drunk the following morning – Easter Day.[1]

CONFUSION OF FESTIVALS

At New Year in certain villages of Alsace a fountain was decorated with a 'May'. This was a small fir tree, hung with ribbons, eggshells and the figure of a man beating his wife. Local girls danced around it and the tree was preserved for the rest of the year.[2]

Despite the hint here of unhappy married life, the May tree was often a love gift from a young man to his girl friend. Well within memory it was usual in many Czech villages for boys to place a May tree in front of their sweetheart's window. It was done secretly at night, the tree lavishly decorated with ribbons and coloured egg-shells, and local tradition held that it represented the girl's life: she would live as long as the tree.[3] The most popular girl was given an extra tree.

Hungarian boys sang:

> *Awake! Raise up before the Beloved's house*
> *A lofty May tree, brightly coloured*
> *Red cloth strips blow in the wind*
> *From the branches.*[4]

This was *hajnalfa*, tree of the dawn[5] – small, slender, and all its branches removed, except at the very top, where the leaves were tied with ribbons and coloured scarves. A boy would put it in front of his girl-friend's home, and in some villages the tree was so small that it stood on the gate or the roof of the house. The Matyó of Mezokovesd divided the task more evenly: the boys brought the tree and the girls then decorated it with bottles of wine and coloured eggs.[6]

Sometimes in Hungary May Day and Easter observances were confused and the distinction blurs between egg and Easter egg trees. This is not unusual when two festivals occur close together,

---

[1] *Ibid.*, 'Der Osterbaum', *Schönere Heimat*, iv (Munich, 1960), 269.
[2] Miles, C. A., *Christmas in Ritual and Tradition*, London, 1913, 269–70.
[3] Spicer, Dorothy, *The Book of Festivals*, New York, 1937, 88–9.
[4] Viski, Károly, *Volksbrauch der Ungarn*, Budapest, 1932, 63.
[5] Sándor, István, 'Das beschlagene Osterei', *Schweizerisches Archiv für Volkskunde*, LIII (Basle, 1957), ii–iii.180.
[6] Viski, 63–4. Károlyi, Alexander, *Hungarian Pageant*, Budapest, 1939, 80–1.

especially if one is not fixed. The tree, festooned with coloured eggs, might be set up on Easter night, when it was known as the boy's 'coat of arms'.[1]

The egg-tree custom does not seem to have been general all over Hungary and May trees were not so numerous in every village. Sometimes there was only one, in front of the church, as in some places in Germany where it was a permanent feature, decorated for May every year with sausages, cakes and eggs.[2]

At home and in Ireland there are a few scattered references to such trees. An account, recorded 100 years ago of the Grimsby May-pole, says: 'It formed, I assure you, a very gay scene; the pole decorated with garlands of flowers, various coloured ribbons and streamers, green boughs and festoons of painted egg-shells.'[3]

This not unlike an old Swedish custom of selling May-poles in the market, decorated with coloured paper and gilt egg-shells.[4] Another description of an English May Day, this time at King's Lynn in 1894, tells how groups of children carried garlands around the town. These were made with two wooden hoops, fastened together at right angles and supported on the end of a pole. Flowers and green boughs were arranged over the hoops, and a strand of bird's eggs hung from the ensemble.[5]

An Irish reference, again nearly 100 years old, comes from County Antrim:

> In the course of a walk taken on an Easter morning some years ago, I came upon a small settlement of 2 or 3 houses. A large midden occupied a central position, and stuck firmly into this was a bush or large branch bare of leaves, but bearing an empty egg shell on each of its small twigs; there were probably 40–50 egg-shells on the bush. Since then, on another Easter Monday, I observed a bush of egg-shells in a garden in front of a cottage in the adjoining County of Down.[6]

Probably what the writer had seen was a local confusion of May Day and Easter tradition. The Irish like to have a May tree, and

[1] Viski, 52.

[2] Philpot, J. H., *The Sacred Tree*, London, 1897, 155.

[3] Gutch, Mrs, and Peacock, Mabel, ed., *Examples of Printed Folk-Lore Concerning Lincolnshire*, London, 1908, 201.

[4] *Dictionary of Folklore, Mythology and Legend*, New York, 1949, i, 341.

[5] 'May Ladies, King's Lynn', *Folk-Lore*, x (London, December 1899), 443–4.   [6] *Notes and Queries*, 12 April 1879, 5th Series, ii.287.

often cover a convenient bush near the house with egg-shells the evening before. They do this in all the provinces except Munster, and in Ulster it is not only found in the east, where the Easter tree has been noted, but also in Armagh, Tyrone and Donegal.[1]

At Gainsborough there used to be a derivative of the egg tree on Royal Oak Day. Local boys collected all the birds' eggs they could find, and made a flower garland like a crown. Adorned with gilded oak-apples, flowers and swathes of eggs, this hung across the street.[2]

In fact, the egg tree and its variants figure at a number of festivals: Easter, May Day, Whitsun, Summer Solstice, Royal Oak Day and Christmas. Dr Siegfried Kube of Dresden believes the German Easter egg tree is the result of a confusion with the Christmas tree which took place in the nineteenth century. He may well be right, for the egg tree appeared among German settlers in America during the same period, at a time when emigration from Germany was in full flood.

Today Ukrainian friends in England have made a similar adaptation, decorating their Christmas tree with coloured egg-shells, and the Poles have a special technique for embellishing eggs with appliqué paper cuts. The designs are usually flowers or roosters, and a small stand, handle and spout, all made of paper, are attached to make the egg resemble a little jug. The handle is provided so that these eggs can be hung on the Christmas tree (see colour plate VIII).

In west Germany and parts of France, a green branch is selected at harvest and prettily decorated with foodstuffs, including eggs.[3] People in the Rhineland and Eifel Mountains hang shells on a small tree at Whitsun, which they call the Whitsun bush or St John's Crown[4] – for in Germany egg trees were also erected on St John's Day. The tree, called a St John's tree, is garlanded with flowers and lit with numerous candles. Quite often the egg-shells are hung in long chains.[5]

---

[1] *Complete Atlas of the British Isles*, London, 1965, 127.
[2] Gutch, 205–6.
[3] Philpot, 150–1.
[4] Bächtold-Stäubli, Hanns, ed., *Handwörterbuch des deutschen Aberglaubens*, Berlin, 1929–30, ii.612.
[5] Spamer, Adolf, 'Sitte und Brauch', *Handbuch der Deutschen Volkskunde*, ii (Potsdam, 1936), 99.

At this time, which coincides with the Summer Solstice, there is dancing around the tree in the Erzegebirge; in the Upper Harz Mountains they strip the lower bark off certain fir trees and hang them with red and yellow eggs. Then young people dance around them in daytime, the old in the evening. That same night boys in the Eifel parade through the streets with a bundle of branches, begging for egg-shells to hang on it.[1]

The use of a tree or tree-substitute, such as these branches, is often linked with gifts of eggs. Here they are to decorate the tree. In Nassau after the May tree was erected, people gave the local boys eggs to eat,[2] and in Alsace the tree was carried round while a collection of eggs was made.[3] Boys and girls in parts of Poland decorated green branches with coloured egg-shells and toured the houses on May Day, singing and begging for money and eggs.[4]

Around Dresden and Eisenach egg trees were usually erected on the third Sunday before Easter (Laetare), on Maundy Thursday, and on Easter Day itself, according to the traditions of a particular village. German folklorists believe that these trees are a relic of older processional customs, which were forbidden around 1860 and as a result disappeared altogether. In the early nineteenth century a decorated tree was carried through the streets on Laetare Sunday, but in some areas the custom was prohibited and this seems to have led to the placing of trees in front of individual houses by way of substitute. Eggs came to be used on them instead of other ornaments, but in the German places where tree processions were never prohibited, they were not introduced.[5]

Easter egg trees do seem to have influenced the Laetare tree in certain areas; for instance, in Moravia, where it was adorned with coloured egg-shells and flowers, and the village girls escorted it to every house. We know that certainly as early as the seventeenth century egg-shells were used to decorate branches symbolic of summer, carried into German villages at Laetare. Still today, in villages north of Dresden, egg trees are erected on this occasion, and some people say that this will induce the hens to lay more eggs.[6]

[1] Miles, 269. Spamer, 99. *Dictionary of Folklore*, i.341.
[2] Bächtold-Stäubli, ii.612.   [3] *Dictionary of Folklore*, i.341.
[4] Spicer, 261.
[5] Wähler, Martin, *Thüringische Volkskunde*, Jena, 1940, 433.
[6] Information kindly supplied by Dr Siegfried Kube.

In Heidelberg at Laetare school children received *Pretzels* with eggs, if they toured the houses, singing:

Winter heraus
Sommer herein[1]

The *Pretzel*, a huge affair, shaped like an inverted heart, with fronds on top, has coloured streamers suspended from the bottom and a white egg embedded in the centre. As we know them, *Pretzels* are salted outside. But they were always made with salt and flour, because these were foods permitted in Lent. All three – eggs, salt and flour – were richly symbolic. In France there was a tithe called *sal i ous (sel et œufs)*.[2] At one time bread and salt were eaten when swearing an oath; together with a white egg, they formed the three traditional 'White Offerings' of Germany.

Bread has a peculiar significance in corn-growing countries, for it is the staple food. Frazer collected many legends of the corn spirit, absorbed in Christian times into the sacrament of the Eucharist. Our Lord spoke of this Himself: 'I am the bread of life: he that cometh to me shall never hunger',[3] and used it at the Last Supper to symbolize His Sacrifice: 'And He took bread, and gave thanks, and brake it, and gave unto them, saying, This is my Body which is given for you: this do in remembrance of me.'[4]

In the same way He made Himself known to the disciples at Emmaus: 'He took bread, and blessed it, and brake, and gave to them. And their eyes were opened, and they knew Him.'[5] Modern Catholic children are told that if they waste bread, and do not eat it up, they will make Our Lady cry.[6] *Pretzels*, which more or less correspond to our own hot-cross buns, resemble the unleavened bread which Jews eat at Passover: 'And they baked unleavened cakes of the dough which they brought forth out of Egypt, for it was not leavened; because they were thrust out of Egypt, and could not tarry, neither had they prepared for themselves any victual.'[7]

[1] Information kindly supplied by Dr Wolfhilde von König of Munich.
[2] Van Gennep, Arnold, *Manuel de Folklore Français Contemporain*, Paris, 1947, 1.iii.1,252.
[3] John vi.35.
[4] Luke xxii.19.
[5] *Ibid.*, xxiv.30–1.
[6] Hole, Christina, ed., *Encyclopaedia of Superstitions*, London, 1961, 65.
[7] Exod. xii.39.

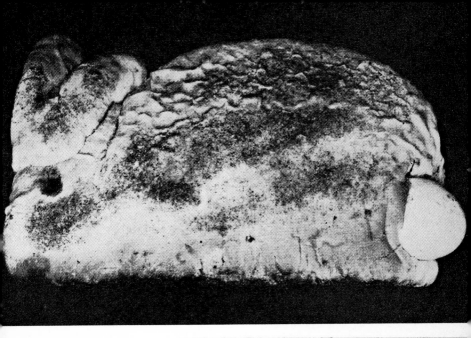

13a (above) Easter cake from the Pennsylvania Dutch community, showing an Easter rabbit (*Oschter Haws*) laying an egg
13b (below)   Easter cake from the Greek island of Hydra showing three red eggs, symbolic of the Trinity. Hydra is populated by Greek Albanians but the custom is common to much of Greece, and the cake is called a *Christopsomon*

14 A Pennsylvania Dutch woman dyeing Easter eggs (late nineteenth century)

15　Countrywomen selling decorated eggs and *Dynovaca* (Easter
switches) in Prague, Easter 1959

16 Mrs Huyett of Lancaster County (Pennsylvania) decorating an
egg-tree with her own Pennsylvania Dutch *binsa graws* (rush-pith)
eggs. The tree is wrapped in cotton, and the eggs are covered with
rush-pith and fabric. An egg in colour plate XXIIIb was prepared
by Mrs Huyett using this method, and she also made two of the
eggs shown in colour plate XVIb

17   Traditional egg-chandelier made by the bachelors of Beuel-
Kuedinghoven, a village near Bonn (1962). It contains 3,000 eggs
and hangs in the main street until the harvest is won

18 King Constantine tapping eggs with Greek sailors at Skara-manga (Easter 1967)

19 Marta Jenkala, when she was 13, wearing her Ukrainian national
costume and holding a handful of Easter eggs decorated by her
mother, Mrs Olena Jenkala. Mrs Jenkala decorated many of the
eggs shown in colour plate XI, and some of them were made by her
daughter. Miss Jenkala also prepared the bottom row of eggs in
colour plate XIV

20a (above)   Pace-Egging at Mirfield, Yorkshire, March 1967
20b (below)   Egg-Rolling at Selby, Yorkshire, April 1961

Palm Sunday, a week before Easter, commemorates Our Lord's ride into Jerusalem, when fronds were cast beneath His feet. Bavarian children, returning from church, bring palms; their families must step over these and give them an egg. Dutch children carry the *palmpaas*, a wooden pole on which traditional decorations, baked from bread, are mounted. These are often shaped like a hen surrounded by its chickens, with an egg embedded in the dough. As a rule the *palmpaas* is elaborately garnished with dyed eggs, apples, coloured paper, plaited bread and great strands of raisins, sweets, chocolate biscuits, dried apples, plums, and sprigs of green. Children walk about carrying this, singing and asking for money and eggs. A friend from Amsterdam writes that they still do it today.[1]

CARRYING OUT DEATH AND BRINGING IN SUMMER

We need not look too far to find the source of the processions from which the egg tree has descended. For in Germany they were closely connected with the ceremony of Carrying out Death from the village. This generally took place on Laetare Sunday, but the date varied. Depending on the locality, it might be Shrove Tuesday, Ash Wednesday, or the third or fifth Sunday of Lent. Frazer tells us the fourth Sunday of Lent was called Dead Sunday for this reason.[2] Perhaps the movable nature of the ritual depended on variable tokens of the approach of spring, like the date of the first swallow.

In old Bohemia children celebrating *Todaustragen* (Carrying out Death) processed with a 'sun tree', decorated with painted eggs. In Czech-speaking areas *Smrt*, an effigy of Death, also called *Mařena* further to the north, was taken from the village. Girls who were in charge of this straw figure dressed in old clothes sang:

> *We carry Death out of the village,*
> *And bring summer back into our homes.*

In the north they burn the figure, but first boys try to seize its hat, which the girls protect. In some areas they throw the dummy in the water on Palm Sunday, and sing:

---

[1] Information kindly supplied by Henk Arends, of Amsterdam.
[2] Frazer, Sir James G., *The Golden Bough*, London, 1911, iv.221.

On the water flows Death
Summer breaks the spell of winter
With Easter bread and red eggs
We celebrate summer.[1]

Often this is done at sunset. The Ethnographic Museum in Prague has one of these Death figures from Ořechovičky in Moravia, wearing a rich, many-stranded necklace made entirely of egg-shells.[2] The figure, which can also be decorated with coloured rags, is destroyed either by fire or by tossing it into the water. The Whitsun Knave – an effigy carried in procession in Alsace, with a garland of egg-shells around its neck – resembles this Death.[3]

On Laetare Sunday in German Moravian villages, such as Jassnitz and Seitendorf, girls and boys dressed Death in a fur-cap and old leather breeches; carrying the dummy into the fields on a pole, they flung it roughly down, and circled round, shouting and screaming and tearing the figure to pieces. After the remains had been burnt, everyone danced and rejoiced in the coming of spring. Then they returned to the village, begging eggs as payment for Carrying away Death.[4]

Green boughs were usually brought back as tokens of spring, and it is interesting that, while a demand for eggs accompanied the return of spring, the figure of Death was dressed in egg-shells. There is probably a contrast between the whole eggs, representing new life, and the empty shells, symbolic of death. This distinction cannot be pressed too far, as the differentiation between the whole egg and the shell is not always so clear. For instance, on May Day in Westphalia cowherds drove the cattle by slapping them with rowan switches. They were given eggs to eat as they did this, and used the shells to adorn the fronds. Here the egg-shell appears to be a protective symbol. But it is worth noting that the Beltane Carline, a figure of terror associated with witchcraft, was traditionally pelted with egg-shells, in order to destroy his powers of evil.[5]

---

[1] Information kindly supplied by Herr Hans Zühlke from *Babička*, by Božena Němcová, Prague, 1885. See plate 12.
[2] See Šourek, Karel, *Folk Art in Pictures*, London, n.d., pl. 27.
[3] Bächtold-Stäubli, ii.612.
[4] Frazer, iv.238–9.
[5] James, E. O., *Seasonal Feasts and Festivals*, London, 1961, 313.

Ceremonial return to the village was called Bringing in Summer. In parts of Bohemia girls cut down a young tree with a bursting, green crown, hung a female figure on it, decked it with green, red and white ribbons, and marched in procession back to the village with this *Lito*, the Summer figure, singing:

> *Death swims in the water,*
> *Spring comes to visit us,*
> *With eggs that are red,*
> *With yellow pancakes.*
> *We carried Death out of the village,*
> *We are carrying Summer into the village.*[1]

Red and yellow are interesting because they correspond to the colours used for decorating egg trees in the Harz Mountains. Probably they signify the warmth of the sun and renewed life after winter.

In Silesian villages, after Death had been thrown in the water, young people cut down a fir tree, peeled the bark from its trunk and decorated it with garlands, paper roses and egg-shells. They called this Summer or May, and boys carried it round the houses, singing and asking for gifts. The tree used was similar to the bough, decked with eggs, found in Saxony.[2]

German girls in Moravia, like the Saxons, performed this task on Laetare Sunday, but sometimes the rituals took place a little later in the year. In parts of Westphalia two girls led a third adorned with flowers around the houses. As usual, they sang and asked for eggs: the flower-crowned girl was the Whitsun Bride. At Waggum in Brunswick, all the village girls accompanied her; arrayed in flowers, they represented spring, inducing fertility in man and beast, just as the Easter tree and its man-made derivative, the May-pole, represent the fructifying spirit of vegetation, which helps the crops to grow.[3] The eggs associated with both must be an additional charm to strengthen the magic fertility of girls and trees.

Laetare Sunday, when these rituals are often enacted, suggests that once again the Church took note of earlier pagan custom and Christianized it. The fourth Sunday in Lent, so called from

---

[1] Frazer, iv.246.
[2] *Ibid.*
[3] *Ibid.*, ii.63, 6.

the first word of the Introit, 'Rejoice [*laetare*] ye with Jerusalem, and be glad with her, all ye that love her',[1] is a day when the Pope used to bless a special rose, sculptured in pure gold, presenting it to the Queen or Princess who had done most for the Church in the previous year;[2] woman – who gives birth to life – and a plant figure in this unusual Christian observance.

The green tree is a common emblem of fertility, symbol of nature's continuous renewal, and in countries throughout the world, an egg is a primitive symbol of increase. We saw earlier how Slovakians hung Easter egg-shells in their fruit trees to increase the yield.[3] Hence no doubt the association of the egg tree with festivals of increase – spring, Summer Solstice, harvest-time – and the custom of erecting a young tree, branch, or garland on the roof of a new house, to fructify those within.[4] The Slovak National Museum contains an interesting variation on the custom: a nineteenth-century wedding candlestick, carved in wood, and supported on a little table, on which stands the figure of a man on horseback. Tied to this is a long branch, representing a decorated tree, and hung with miscellaneous items – apples, nuts and birds, but chiefly coloured eggs.[5]

THE GIFT-BEARING TREE

The origins of the egg tree seem lost in oblivion, but in different countries there are scattered examples of gifts offered to trees. In many parts of the world there has been a belief in tree spirits, and tree worship was common among European races. The old German laws dealt savagely with anyone damaging the bark of a young shoot. The offender's navel was cut off and his entrails wound round the mutilated trunk.[6]

Russians supposed that the souls of their ancestors went into the trees, a belief they shared with natives of north-west Papua, who hung offerings – strips of red and white cloth and baskets of food – on the branches. The Yakuts living in a land where trees

---

[1] Isa. lxvi.10.

[2] Brewer, E. Cobham, *Dictionary of Phrase and Fable*, London, 1896, 723.

[3] Pranda, Adam, 'Die slowakischen Ostereier', *Schweizerisches Archiv für Volkskunde*, LIII (Basle, 1957), ii–iii.170.

[4] Philpot, 156.

[5] Šourek, pl. 34.

[6] Frazer, ii.9.

are rare, put objects of iron and brass, and other precious items, on any outstanding specimen.[1]

The Padaythabin tree of Burma was hung with gifts. Its original grew in the heaven of the *nats* – spirits – and bore on its boughs whatever one desired. These trees were sometimes made of silver, and had silver coins or jewels on their branches. They are often taken in Buddhist processions and presented to monasteries.[2] Egyptian cosmology refers to a jewel-bearing tree, and this is how Arabians imagined the zodiac, with the stars as its fruit.[3] Probably the idea of a golden tree hung with jewels, which is common throughout the East, derives from the conception of a star-bearing world tree.

Sometimes the tree carried, not the source of light, but food, without which we die. The Tree of Life is common to many cultures. There is the Celtic apple tree, the Chinese peach, the date palm of the Semites, and so on. The Jewish *menorah*, or branched candlestick, is probably a stylized version of the same idea.

In the fourth century A.D. there was a famous pear tree at Auxerre, hung with trophies of the chase and venerated as a god; an Arabian tree on which the people of Mecca hung weapons, garlands and ostrich eggs is identified with the acacia of Nakhla, dwelling-place of the goddess Al-ʿOzza. A sacred date palm at Nejřan, also in Arabia, was worshipped annually, and hung with beautiful clothes and jewellery.[4] Charles Darwin, when he was in South America, on the borders of Patagonia, saw the famous Tree of Walleechu. It was winter-time, and the tree had no leaves, but votive offerings were hanging from it. Those Indians who were too poor to bring gifts tied on a thread instead.[5]

The ancient Greeks put offerings and consecrated fillets on the boughs of certain trees. Statius, writing in the second century B.C., describes a notable example covered with weapons, boars' heads, lions' skins, and great horns, given as hunting trophies.[6] The famous story of the Golden Fleece tells how Phryxus, carried by

---

[1] Porteous, Alexander, *Forest Folklore, Mythology and Romance*, London, 1928, 54, 172.

[2] *Ibid.*, 186.

[3] Philpot, 117, 119.   [4] *Ibid.*, 20, 45.

[5] Porteous, 237.

[6] *Theb.*, ix.585.

a wonderful ram across the Hellespont, sacrificed it to Areas, and hung its golden fleece on the boughs of a sacred beech. Here the suspended object was something which had been of service. Conversely, escaped prisoners who sought sanctuary in the cypress grove at Phlius in the Peloponnesus put their chains on the branches.[1]

Even in the nineteenth century Estonian peasants thought certain trees were sacred and laid wreaths on them,[2] and in the era of revolutions in France, Italy and America, a tree of liberty became a popular idea. This was a tree set up by the people, decorated with flags and other items. At the top they placed a cap of liberty. Americans planted them during the War of Independence as symbols of growing freedom; Italians during the battles of 1848. The Jacobins selected their first in 1790 and put on it triangles of equality, circles of unity, and tricolour ribbons.[3] Liberty, especially during that period, was the most revered ideal, and in these offerings hung on the symbolic tree we see a modern version of an old idea, revived today in yet another form through the children's Easter egg tree.

[1] Philpot, 51.
[2] *Ibid.*, 19.
[3] Brewer, 1,244.

Chapter 14
Easter Egg Pastimes and Games

I'll warrant you for an Egg at Easter.

Old English Saying

MAGICAL SIGNIFICANCE

Easter egg games are legion and are enjoyed by people in countries throughout the Christian world, often with little variation. Their original magic purpose, if such there was, has now largely disappeared, although some hints remain. Germans, for example, used to play a curious game, which consisted of pelting eggs placed on a roof-beam with small missiles.[1] The middle one was known as the King's Egg. So placed, it was thought an effective charm, guarding the house against hazards from above, such as lightning. These talismans were often kept permanently, but sometimes they were changed each year, and this was perhaps a way of doing so.

Here the egg was probably once a protective; just as the old Welsh custom of putting an egg-shell filled with water, meat and flour on the neighbour's window-sill could have been a survival from earlier witchcraft rituals. The shell itself was called *crochan grawys*, a Lent cauldron, and the offender, if caught, was punished by having to clean the family's shoes.[2]

Fertility cults, however, could possibly provide a basis for the majority of Easter games. For instance, the German custom of throwing a flower garland to ring an egg, as in hoopla, and the curious, uncomfortable sport of Easter switches. This was popular in Czechoslovakia on Easter Monday, where they called it *Velikonočni Pondĕli* or *Pomlazka*. Boys wove willow or birch branches and made *dynovacka*, small whips, which they decorated

---

[1] Bächtold-Stäubli, Hanns, ed., *Handwörterbuch des deutschen Aberglaubens*, Berlin, 1929–30, ii.625, note 305.

[2] Davies, J. C., *Folklore of West and Mid-Wales*, Aberystwyth, 1911, 72.

with ribbons and flowers. With these the girls were struck on the legs, and were obliged to hand over decorated eggs to stop the beating.[1]

Reasons suggested for this sport vary considerably: to ensure that the girls are energetic and free from fleas, and to keep them healthy all the year. Sometimes boys and girls beat each other indiscriminately with pussy willows, and both then proffered gifts of coloured eggs.

In Upper Silesia boys went early on Easter morning to their girl-friends' rooms and whipped them out of bed, calling to the parents: *'Glück zu, Glück zu, Ustra; ich kumm eier Techterla schmak-kustrn'* (Good day, Happy Easter. I've come to give your daughter her Easter beating). Any girl who suffered such treatment would have good luck. This slightly immodest version of the custom was known in the fifteenth century, but was later forbidden.[2]

People in northern East Prussia would visit their nearest neighbour as early as possible. Anyone still asleep had the bedding dragged off and the soles of his feet switched. As a reward, or perhaps as a penalty, the intruder received a gift of coloured eggs stained with onion peel, a piece of cake, or some apples. Usually a group of young people, rather than an individual, was responsible and any spoils were divided between them.[3]

In eastern Pomerania children chased their parents out of bed with a birch twig which had a loop on the end. They could only win freedom from this noose by handing out gifts of Easter eggs.[4] In Austria the beating was omitted. Catkins, consecrated on Palm Sunday, were kept in the garden until Easter Day, when children got up before dawn to bring them in. First back received the first Easter egg as a reward.[5]

Green branches, common to all these sports, suggest ideas of fertility – transferring the perennial freshness of the trees to human beings. As a rule, boys beat girls, who propagate the human race. The idea of competition between the sexes, common

[1] Spicer, Dorothy, *The Book of Festivals*, New York, 1937, 87–8. Hazeltine, Alice, and Smith, Elva, ed., *The Easter Book of Legends and Stories*, New York, 1947, 210–26. See colour plates VIII, IX; plate 15.
[2] Lehmann, Hedi, *Volksbrauch im Jahreslauf*, Munich, 1964, 37–8.
[3] *Memeler Dampfboot* (Oldenburg, 7 April 1966).
[4] Information kindly supplied by Herr Hans Zühlke.
[5] Layard, John, *The Lady of the Hare*, London, 1944, 171.

to many Easter games, was probably a relic of old spring rituals, in which rough games were used to stimulate plant life and the forces of reproduction.

This element of struggle and challenge appears in other forms. In Bavaria, as early as 1532, there is a reference to *Eierwalgen*, when one peasant knocked a hatful of eggs out of another's hand; other sixteenth-century records suggest that this sport was even the subject of litigation.[1] A French child playing *chiche d'œufs* says to another: 'Tell me I am mean with eggs.' If the challenge is accepted and repeated, the first child throws an egg into his opponent's face.[2]

Young men and women of Savoy wager a dozen eggs that one will take the other by surprise, saying:

> *Coque gagna*
> *Caréma via*

(Eggs have come, Lent is gone). The loser must pay for a meal of omelette and French toast.[3] In the valley of Doron, also in Savoy, they say:

> *Cristé, Cristé*
> *La Caréma iè via*
> *D'e gagne l'uya*

(Christ, Christ; Lent has gone. I have won an egg); and around Gers whoever manages to say the first 'Alleluia' on Easter morning receives an egg.[4]

EGG-BRINGERS

Competitions are hard work. South German children faced an obstacle of a slightly different kind. Eggs hidden on Easter morning were put in an awkward position, concealed in a prickly place where there were nettles, thorns or holly, and children were stung or scratched before they could reach them.[5]

The poet Friedrich Matthison has left us an account of an

[1] Moser, Hans, 'Brauchgeschichtliches zu Osterei und Osterbrot in Bayern', *Schweizerisches Archiv für Volkskunde*, LIII (Basle, 1957), ii–iii.83.

[2] Van Gennep, Arnold, *Manuel de Folklore Français Contemporain*, Paris, 1947, I.iii.1,340.

[3] *Ibid.*, I,341.

[4] *Ibid.*

[5] *Notes and Queries*, 12 May 1906, 10th Series, v.375.

Easter-egg hunt in the garden of a friend. This was in 1783 and the friend was Goethe, who arranged it to give pleasure to his children on Green Thursday.[1]

Children of German settlers in Pennsylvania found a hare as well as eggs in the shrubbery.[2] This traditional Easter animal was a symbol of fertility, for hares multiply exceptionally fast. They mate when very young, and the females can produce several litters in one year. In traditional Christian art the hare represents lust. Paintings of the Blessed Virgin sometimes show one sitting at her feet, to signify that she overcame all temptations of the flesh.[3]

In Poitrou, according to Van Gennep, they hunt the hare on Maundy Thursday,[4] and there used to be ritual hunts in England at Leicester and Coleshill; there is still a Hare-pie Scramble at Hallaton on Easter Monday. But the first extant reference to the Easter hare and its eggs appears to be German, in a book dating from 1572: 'Do not worry if the Hare escapes you; should we miss his eggs, then we shall cook the nest.'[5]

A Heidelberg doctor, Georg Franck, wrote scathingly in 1682 that only simple people and children believed such stories. He felt strongly on the subject, perhaps because several patients had been very ill after eating Easter eggs: a monk had actually died and a small girl barely survived. A third, who tried to stuff a red egg whole into his mouth, had – naturally – choked.[6] One of his contemporaries calls the Easter hare 'an old fable',[7] and 100 years later Swiss children sang about it;[8] young men of Beuern, who traditionally rang the bells at Eastertime, called this 'ringing the hare' – another eighteenth-century custom which has not survived.[9]

In Pfalz, if an Easter egg hatches, people say the baby bird will have a hare's head.[10] Hare-shaped cakes, sometimes with eggs

[1] Becker, Albert, *Brauchtum der deutschen Osterzeit*, Jena, 1937, 55.

[2] Lichten, Frances, *Folk Art of Rural Pennsylvania*, New York, 1946, 231.

[3] Ferguson, George, *Signs and Symbols in Christian Art*, New York, 1961, 20.

[4] Van Gennep, *Manuel*, I.iii.1,324–5.

[5] Quoted by Weiser, Francis X., *The Easter Book*, London, 1955, 189.

[6] See Franck, Georg, *XX Satyrae Medicae*, Heidelberg, 1682.

[7] Cruickshank, Constance, *Lenten Fare and Food for Fridays*, London, 1959, 84.

[8] Bächtold-Stäubli, vi.1,330.

[9] *Ibid.*, 1,331, note 44.   [10] *Ibid.*, 1,328.

baked into them, are a popular seasonal treat in Germany, so it is surprising to find certain areas where the Easter hare is quite unknown: Bächtold-Stäubli mentions west Bohemia, Saxony, Wenden and east Prussia.

However, most German children enjoyed building nests for it with flowers and hay, gathered from the woods – often under the fruit trees, where consecrated shells used to be burnt to increase the yield. Swabian villagers made little gardens with moss and willow roots, especially for these nests,[1] and people in the Odenwald put a miniature house covered with moss in the real garden;[2] children were told that the Easter hare would come and put coloured eggs in it.

Probably through German influence, the custom came to Denmark, especially to the Baltic island, Langeland, where eggs marked with children's names are hidden in the garden. They call these *hareaeg*.[3] In fact the Easter hare comes and lays its eggs in the garden in many European countries. But in Yugoslavia it was the stable. Children of the Harz region found theirs in shoes put outside the bedroom door; in Aargau they arrived through the window and rolled along the floor.[4] Modern greeting cards show the hare carrying a small basket of coloured eggs. But around Karm, the animal itself is often red or green. Mother cuts the egg sack off its back on Saturday evening, and inside is an egg for each member of the family.[5]

This magic animal – in L'Auxois they thought the hare was a sorcerer who could speak on Easter Day[6] – varies the time of its arrival. It could be Palm Sunday, Green Thursday, or any other day of Lent. In parts of Switzerland father must whistle on Easter morning, and the children then find eggs concealed in small baskets around the house.[7] Pennsylvania Dutch children search everywhere – indoors as well as in the garden and the barn; for the *Oschter Haws* may have left eggs anywhere – maybe in someone's hat or on a window-sill. Ever since the first wave of

---

[1] Spicer, 133.

[2] Personal observation, spring, 1967.

[3] Uldall, Kai, 'Les Œufs de Pâques au Danemark', *Schweizerisches Archiv für Volkskunde*, liv (Basle, 1958), 7.

[4] Wildhaber, Robert, 'Der Osterhase und andere Eierbringer', *Schweizerisches Archiv für Volkskunde*, LIII (Basle, 1957), ii–iii.114.

[5] *Ibid.*   [6] Van Gennep, *Manuel*, i.iii.1,325.

[7] Wildhaber, Robert, *Wir färben Ostereier*, Berne, 1957, 30.

settlers at Germantown in 1680, their children have continued to prepare for the coming of the hare. But if someone badly behaved puts out a nest, he will probably find it full of rabbit-dung in the morning.[1]

In some places children prepare specially carefully to receive the Easter hare. In Hettingen they collect green leaves, left over from the autumn, to make him soup.[2] This is in Germany proper. In another part of America, Frederiksburg in Texas, German settlers and their descendants light bonfires on Holy Saturday on the tops of nearby hills. Children are told the Easter hare is burning flowers to make dye for colouring eggs.[3]

Possibly this custom is all that remains of the burning Easter wheel, common in Germany. Near Bad Pyrmont, at Lügde, an old town on the Saxon boundary, such wheels are still prepared from oakwood and decorated with straw and green branches. On the night of Holy Saturday they are taken to the top of a local mountain, set on fire, and sent spinning on their way into the valley.[4]

These remnants of fire worship are of extreme antiquity, but their link with Easter, and especially Easter eggs, is rather tenuous; though it is worth noting that the charred remains of such a wheel, spread on the fields, is said to make them fertile. In Westphalia they call Easter fires *Poskefür*, and if they are to be effective the wood must be stolen. Records date these back to early Christian times – the ninth century.[5]

The hare, with or without a bonfire, is often displaced by other egg-bringers. Westphalians have an Easter fox and birds are a widespread substitute – or, really, a more obvious choice. Swiss children believe it is the cuckoo, and in Styria, though the hare tradition has recently been adopted, they also prepare nests for the red-egg bird, which flies down in Easter week. Other popular birds are the Tyrolese Easter chicken and the rooster of Schleswig-Holstein, which lays red eggs on Easter morning. Thuringia has an Easter stork, Westphalia a crane as well as the Easter fox, and

---

[1] Shoemaker, Alfred L., *Eastertide in Pennsylvania*, Kutztown, 1960, 48–9.

[2] Bächtold-Stäubli, vi.1,329–30.

[3] Hole, Christina, *Easter and Its Customs*, London, 1961, 41.

[4] Boehle, Bernd, *Handy Guide to Western Germany*, Gütersloh, 1958, 300. Also information from Herr Willy Hess.

[5] Lehmann, 34.

Czechs a lark. In Carinthia the red-egg-laying bird is a Heavenly Hen.[1]

Perhaps there is a link between these birds and the dove of the Holy Spirit. Egg-bodied models were made as gifts, for example in Eisenach at midsummer. These were made from the pith of rushes and prettily coloured. Odenwalders made head, tail and wings of folded paper and called them Easter birds. They were hung in people's homes, especially in the corner reserved for saying prayers.[2] In Moravia they were fastened over the baby's cradle, often for the rest of the year.[3]

The Ukrainian Hutzuls make a similar bird from a coloured egg-shell and folded paper, the head being of grey wax which was also used as adhesive for the other portions. It is hung from the living-room ceiling or in front of the ikons as a reminder of the birth of Christ, when a dove, it was said, came down from Heaven and soared above the infant Jesus.[4]

In the German Pfalz and the Hunsrück Mountains, the Easter bird, again suspended from the rafters, was made from a large blown egg, usually a goose egg, with coloured paper wings. Saxon peasants hung a carved wooden dove above the table.[5] As with so many Germanic customs, this reappears among the Pennsylvania Dutch. The bird, made from an Easter egg with paper wings, head and tail, was called an *Oschter Feggel*, and placed near an open window, where it would turn in the breeze.[6]

In some parts of Germany God, Christ, or St Nicholas brings the Easter eggs, but it is unusual. And there is no mention of egg-bringers in Orthodox countries, except in Greek Macedonia, where *Paschalia*, the Easter Spirit, slips red eggs under children's pillows after the midnight Resurrection service, when they are fast asleep.[7]

---

[1] Bächtold-Stäubli, vi.1,329. Wildhaber, *Der Osterhase*, 115. Van Gennep, *Manuel*, I.iii.1,324.

[2] Mössinger, Friedrich, 'Odenwälder Binseneier', *Schweizerisches Archiv für Volkskunde*, LIII (Basle, 1957), ii–iii.77.

[3] Kunz, Ludvik, 'Mährische Ostereier', *Schweizerisches Archiv für Volkskunde*, LIII (Basle, 1957), ii–iii.165.

[4] Hodgson, M. L., 'Some Notes on the Huculs', *Folk-Lore*, xvi (London, March, 1905), 53. Dmytrikw, Olga, *Ukrainian Arts*, New York, 1955, 97.

[5] Bächtold-Stäubli, vi.1,332.

[6] Shoemaker, 31.

[7] Abbott, G. F., *Macedonian Folklore*, Cambridge, 1903, 37–8.

The church bells are silent in Catholic countries from Maundy Thursday until Easter. Children are told that they have gone to Rome to see the Pope and collect eggs for Sunday. They will return, bringing the eggs, and drop them down for all good children – into houses and gardens, on window sills and into clogs. They are to be found everywhere, even in the road.[1]

In some French villages children actually watch for the return of the bells. Their parents take them into the fields or on to a hillock, and they then face towards Rome, watching for the bells to descend. In other districts they are told about the chariot drawn by four white horses, on which the eggs arrive. It moves so fast that no one can see it, except a good child.[2]

In Liège they arrive in a boat on the River Meuse; Belgian children are sometimes told that an old man has flown with the birds to Rome, to collect eggs from the Pope. Townspeople open all their doors and windows so that the eggs can come in, and then the children search for them in vases and saucepans, perhaps even under the mattress. On small Flemish farms, as soon as they hear the bells ring again on Easter Day, they go out and hunt for the eggs hidden in the garden and hedgerows, or among the sprouting rye and evergreens – box trees and yew.[3]

The green setting is reminiscent of a custom from Russia and the Baltic. In Latvia and Estonia barley sown in a bowl, or in a plate on a layer of soil, several weeks before Easter, provides a nice green background for the eggs.[4] Again the germinating green of nature stresses the original significance of the egg – a symbol of life reborn.

SOCIAL IMPORTANCE

Gradually Easter eggs lost their early meaning and dwindled into

---

[1] Bächtold-Stäubli, vi.1,329. Wildhaber, *Der Osterhase*, 115–16. Hole, *Easter*, 47. Meertens, P. J., 'Ostereier und Ostergebäcke in den Niederlanden', *Schweizerisches Archiv für Volkskunde*, LIII (Basle, 1957), ii–iii.125. Pieters, Jules, 'Œufs de Pâques en Belgique', *Schweizerisches Archiv für Volkskunde*, LIII (Basle, 1957), ii–iii.121. Van Gennep, Arnold, *Le Folklore du Dauphiné*, Paris, 1932, i.284–5.

[2] *Ibid., Manuel*, 1.iii.1,214.

[3] Wildhaber, *Der Osterhase*, 116. Pieters, 121.

[4] Information kindly supplied by Miss Salme Pruuden and Mrs Terēza Budiņa-Lazdiņa.

something of purely social significance. In England after the Reformation they were used much less in church ceremonies, more in egg games played during Easter-tide;[1] in many countries they became a popular part of farm and village life.

Millers in Ruchaux, Belgium, calling at clients' houses on Easter Monday with grain which had been ground, were given eggs known as 'The Miller's Easter Faring'. In Flanders farm servants, knocking on the house door at midnight, called out: 'Easter has come. Lent is over.' Whoever heard them first received two or four extra eggs from the other farm-dwellers next morning. People in Broekhom had the reputation of giving three eggs at this time of year, when only two were expected. Hence the saying 'a Broekhom couple', which means three of anything.[2]

Staff did well; in Denmark each servant received from the farmer's wife a certain number of eggs inscribed with his name – peasant girls gave them to their lovers.[3] They did this in Sweden too, and sometimes got cakes in return.[4]

German girls in the Eifel made a similar present to their boy-friends, saying:

> *Two eggs are 'a disgrace',*
> *Three eggs are 'a favour',*
> *Four eggs are 'for show',*
> *Five eggs bring 'a courting',*
> *Six eggs bring 'a marriage'.*[5]

In Spain it is the young men who approach the girls. At Easter-time in Barcelona they bring a basket, decorated with ribbons and mounted on a stick; the eggs are put into it.[6]

Hutzuls made it a communal occasion. Everyone gathered in front of the church on Easter Day with food for the priest to bless, offering one another coloured eggs and begging forgiveness for past wrongs. Later on boys tried to snatch these eggs from the girls. But if a girl made a gift of one to a boy, it showed how much

---

[1] Wright, A. R., *British Calendar Customs: England*, London, 1936, i.90.
[2] Pieters, 124–5.
[3] Uldall, 2.
[4] Eskeröd, Albert, 'Ostereier in Schweden', *Schweizerisches Archiv für Volkskunde*, LIV (Basle, 1958), 2.
[5] Lehmann, 36.
[6] Information kindly supplied by Frau Gertrud Weinhold.

Colour Plate XXI Acid-etch eggs from Slovakia, Austria and Germany. The two eggs top left and top right were made by Germans from the Zips area of northern Slovakia. Both are dyed with onion-peel and have a floral pattern on the reverse. The red egg between them, dated 1962, is from a Croatian village in Burgenland (eastern Austria) and bears an Easter greeting in Croat. Bottom left and bottom right are eggs from Silesia (German), and the remaining seven eggs (1967–8) were made at Mardorf in Hessen. This is among the most active areas in Germany for this particular craft.

Colour Plate XXII English Pace eggs with plant imprints and natural-colour dyes. The onion-peel eggs, top left and top right, were made by Mrs Herdman of Acomb and Mrs Cyril Thompson of Newbrough. Both are prize-winning egg decorators in Northumberland, where their villages are situated. Except the second row left-hand egg, the remainder of rows 1 and 2 are from Newbrough, and are prize-winning eggs. The left-hand egg in row 2 and all of rows 3, 4 and 5 are by Mrs Herdman, in a style with which she has won numerous competitions. The three eggs in the bottom row are by Mrs Beattie Allison of Halton-Lea-Gate, on the border of Cumberland and Northumberland. Her eggs have been exhibited by Carlisle Museum.

she liked him.[1] Hungarian boys and girls also exchanged coloured eggs on Easter Sunday afternoon; if they were old enough, it signified an engagement.[2]

There is a charming early account in the diary of Thomas Hoby, who visited Venice in 1549, and observed the young gallants tossing eggs filled with 'Sweet waters and damask powders' in through the ladies' windows.[3] This was in fact during the winter, not at Easter, but it is interesting that these eggs were a kind of love gift. Gay though it must have been, this meeting of lovers was purely formal: the lady was up at her window, the gentleman down below. In Norway, even 100 years ago, when social customs were often so prudish, the bestowal of an egg gift was much more daring. Lovers walked to church on Easter Sunday; the girl first hid a coloured egg inside her bodice, or among her other clothes, and a favourite boy-friend was allowed to search and take it – or she might present it secretly on the walk. Norwegian children did this as a game.[4]

In Hungary – chiefly Transdanubia and Upper Hungary – two little girls might seal their friendship with a 'bride's plate', which one presents to the other. It contains a bottle of wine and a *Pretzel*, surrounded by decorated eggs. A group of girls, usually about eight, accompany the plate. The girl who is the 'bride' takes a few eggs and puts down several of her own.[5]

Apart from such formal exchanges, the actual business of eating eggs was often a popular sport. Throughout north-west Germany peasants held competitions to see who could eat the most,[6] and *émigrés* in Pennsylvania have many stories of such feats. One man remembered that, after being challenged, his father had eaten fourteen and won. The loser could only manage twelve. A woman who ate the same amount became quite ill: 'I often heerd of people eating 12 eggs and I thought I'd try. I ate eleven but I stuck on the yaller of the twelfth. But, oh! I was so sick. I never

---

[1] Hodgson, 53.

[2] Sándor, István, 'Ostereier in Ungarn', *Schweizerisches Archiv für Volkskunde*, LIII (Basle, 1957), ii–iii.179.

[3] Information kindly supplied by Arthur Hulme.

[4] Weiser-Aall, Lily, 'Osterspeisen und Osterei in Norwegen', *Schweizerisches Archiv für Volkskunde*, LIII (Basle, 1957), ii–iii.133.

[5] Sándor, 179.

[6] Spicer, 134.

want to try it again.'[1] This was in 1893. Farm-labourers in Sweden enjoyed this game as well, and champion 'eaters' gained a name in their own district.[2]

These competitions perhaps derived from earlier ritual feasts. In many parts of France children, shepherds and groups of young men toured the houses, singing, merry-making and collecting eggs, which they made into an omelette. In Dauphiné it was prepared when the sun rises on St John's Day.[3] Sometimes a number of small omelettes were customary, but in many villages a single huge one was cooked, and everyone ate a share. Depending on the district, this might be on May Day, St John's Day or the Feast of St Peter and St Paul.

One hesitates to suggest that such ceremonies carry any solar significance. But Runeberg, describing a ritual in the village of Andrieux,[4] directly links it to the returning sun, which does not shine in this Alpine region for 100 days. At the beginning of the nineteenth century the villagers formally welcomed its return on 10 February. Four shepherds played fifes and trumpets at dawn, and ran through the village to the home of the oldest inhabitant. Then everyone prepared an omelette. At ten in the morning they all assembled in the market-place, formed a circle around the oldest inhabitant, and danced, each holding a plate with his omelette. Next, everyone went to a stone bridge and put their omelettes on the parapet. Dancing continued until the sun appeared, when everyone, including the old man, offered their omelette to it. Then it was time to go home. The crowd dispersed and people returned to their houses to eat the omelettes. Here the solar connection is too close to be accidental, and one must assume that the omelette and therefore the egg was in this case originally a magic offering to the renovated sun at the close of winter.

It seems possible that modern eating competitions which one finds in many countries had their origin in such an idea. More recently such pastimes were, of course, intended to give pleasure to children, and cooking and eating eggs out of doors was meant as a treat.

[1] Shoemaker, 34. [2] Eskeröd, 10.

[3] Chambers, E. K., *The Mediaeval Stage*, Oxford, 1903, i.128.

[4] Runeberg, Arne, 'Witches, Demons and Fertility Magic', *Commentationes Humanorum Litterarum*, XIV (Helsinki, 1947), Nos. 1–4, 202.

Irish children in Ulster prepared roasted eggs over an open fire,[1] and in Denmark children of pre-Confirmation age made quite a ceremony of something similar. This was mainly found on small Baltic islands south of Fionie, and was still to be seen at Strynø in 1957. Each child's parents give him eggs marked with his name, and a supply of bread and butter, and then boys go round the village, begging for straw and an iron cooking-pot. Then, with the girls, they go to the beach and make a stone furnace to hold the cooking-pot, filled with the eggs.

The boys do the cooking, boiling the eggs until they are hard, while the girls dance in a circle and sing. Then some of the boys light small seaweed fires along the beach, making sure that there is more smoke than flame. Bolder children used to jump back and forth across these until their parents stopped them. When the eggs were ready, everyone sat on the sea-wall to eat them. But first each child tossed his egg in the air and caught it again. Afterwards they all went back to the village, and danced round the May-pole. This generally was on either Maundy Thursday, Easter Monday or Easter Day itself.[2]

EGG-TOSSING

In the game described above, each child tossed his egg up in the air before eating it. In Denmark Easter marks the beginning of a time when everyone – especially children – can again amuse themselves out of doors, winter being over. Egg-throwing in England, on the other hand, seems originally to have been an indoor sport. It is recorded that in 1839 the Bishop and Dean of Chester Cathedral threw eggs to the choir-boys inside the church.[3] Later the game was played outside on the village green.

It still survives in parts of France, or did within living memory. Eggs are tossed in the air, and anyone who lets his fall is disgraced and must pay a penalty. Children had to wait until their parents gave the signal to begin. Sometimes they made bets with each other, to see whose egg remained intact.[4] At one time everybody took part, so perhaps originally the game was to ensure that

[1] *Complete Atlas of the British Isles*, London, 1965, 127.

[2] Uldall, 6–7.

[3] Hardwick, Charles, *Traditions, Superstitions and Folklore*, London, 1872, 72. Wright, i.90.

[4] Van Gennep, *Manuel*, 1.iii.1,342.

the hens would lay well, or to protect the community from witches and other evil influences by collective effort.

In a grassy meadow an egg can often be thrown in the air and allowed to fall without breaking; in Switzerland they did this to test the strength of the shell.[1] German children found a way of cupping it in their hands and giving a twist as they made their toss, so that the egg descends on the tip, still spinning, and does not break. This game, conceivably intended to transmit fertility to the grass, was called 'Egg-guggling'.[2]

On the Dutch Frisian island of Schiermonnikoog children go to a special Easter meadow and play at 'Egg Sales'. One player sells his egg for a few pennies to another. The second player throws the egg into the grass, hoping to break it. If it remains whole he must return it to the original owner.[3] Inevitably this sometimes degenerates into a battle. French children at Montbéliard armed themselves with egg ammunition on Easter Day.[4] Nearer home, old people in Carmarthenshire still remember children colouring eggs with herbs and then 'for half of the day they kept throwing the eggs at each other'. This informant had been to Argentina and seen local people throwing eggs and water at each other on the same occasion, even in the streets of Buenos Aires.[5]

The combination of eggs and water implies some sort of spring fertility ritual. In Wales, at Whitchurch, they had what must have been a similar custom, omitting the water. Childless married women went to the churchyard on Easter Monday, taking two dozen tennis balls, twelve covered with white leather, twelve with black. They tossed them over the church, and all the people, gathered specially for that purpose, tried to catch one. This was repeated every year until a child arrived.[6] It seems likely that these tennis balls were a later substitute for eggs.

EGG-ROLLING

Egg-tossing was often linked with egg-rolling. Boys played both games indiscriminately in the meadows of Cumberland and

---

[1] Liebl, Elsbeth, 'Ostereierspiele im Atlas der schweizerischen Volkskunde', *Schweizerisches Archiv für Volkskunde*, LIII (Basle, 1957), ii–iii.64.

[2] Bächtold-Stäubli, ii.622.   [3] Meertens, 127.

[4] Van Gennep, *Manuel*, 1.iii.1,341.   [5] Davies, 72.

[6] Owen, Trefor M., *Welsh Folk Customs*, Cardiff, 1959, 87, note 2.

Westmorland, and Danish children on Amager Island roll their eggs before tossing them in the air with the aid of a sling.[1] Danish folklorists detect no magic or protective measures in this sport. But in origin it could have been a charm to fertilize the earth or to assist in human reproductive powers. At Connel Ferry in Scotland girls and boys vied with one another to see who could roll their egg farthest and most smoothly. Whoever did so would marry first.[2]

Both rolling and slinging occur in different parts of north Friesland, rolling being common to most of the islands. Played on some traditional spot, it is not unlike billiards, and the eggs are eaten after they break open. They have a slinging rhyme on Föhr:

> *Arken wahre san Toop*
> *Man Toop as frei*[3]

('Everyone watch out for his head; my head is loose'.)

There are some attractive religious legends associated with this game. Hutzuls of the western Ukraine say that the Blessed Virgin filled her apron with eggs. But when she appeared before Pontius Pilate to plead for Our Lord, she dropped to her knees and the eggs rolled out over the world's surface, until they were distributed throughout all nations.[4]

More general is the belief, shared by Orthodox and Protestant, that the rolling of an egg symbolizes the rolling away of the stone which closed Christ's tomb, and hence the Resurrection. The Swedes have a semi-miraculous legend, reported in 1624 and thought to relate to the end of the sixteenth century, of a boy who stole a coin from a holy well in order to buy eggs for a rolling. At once, so the legend goes, his hand became paralysed. It was not until his mother had done penance in the same place that the hand was healed and the boy could go and play.[5]

Other early records of the game exist elsewhere. In Paris there is a reference from 1587,[6] and Danish folklorists also trace it to

---

[1] Uldall, 5. Thiselton-Dyer, T. F., *British Popular Customs*, London, 1876, 159.
[2] Banks, M. Macleod, *British Calendar Customs: Scotland*, London, 1937, i.40.
[3] Jensen, Christian, *Die Nordfriesischen Inseln*, Lübeck, 1927, 445.
[4] Dmytrikw, 96.
[5] Eskeröd, 13–14.
[6] Van Gennep, *Manuel*, 1.iii.1,347.

the sixteenth century, if not earlier.[1] In England an account by
Thomas Hyde, dated 1694, refers to boys in the north of England
who begged for eggs the evening before Easter, boiled them hard,
dyed them with herbs and rolled them in the fields:

> *Ovis hoc modo paratis, pueri in Campos exeuntes Ovorum Ludum exercent,*
> *magno cum gaudio, Ovis tinctis variè ludendo; scil. vel in aërem ad instar*
> *Globulorum humi volvendo, plerumque ita ut sint obvia aliorum Ovis, et eis*
> *occurrentia frangant: et alia id genus factitando, quae à Borealibus hominibus*
> *melius inquirantur.*[2]

Egg-rolling has been a popular sport in the British Isles for
many years. Children in Ramsey (Isle of Man) still climb the
Fairy Mound on Ballastowell on the morning of Easter Monday.
It is an old burial site and probably convenient; but it is worth
noting that the same game was played on two prehistoric mounds
at Birkenhead Park.[3]

E. K. Chambers compares egg-rolling with the custom of
sending a burning wheel downhill among the vineyards – a solar
emblem. On the strength of this, he assumes the rolled eggs are
also sun symbols.[4] But the evidence is surely too scanty. In
Scotland, however, the game conceivably represents a last echo of
the Beltane rites, a Celtic fire festival honouring the sun. Bonfires
were lit on a hill-top at daybreak and various dairy products,
including eggs, were brought as offerings. Within living memory
children celebrated Beltane with eggs and bannocks. The eggs
were merely roasted, but the bannocks, marked with a cross, were
rolled downhill three times.[5] It is easy to imagine that egg-rolling
developed from this, especially as Beltane was observed on 1 May,
which is not so far removed from Easter. A correspondent of
Folk-Lore wrote in 1917:

> I used to roll dyed eggs on 'Egg Monday' when I was a boy in Ross
> and Cromarty, and we had an 'Egg Sunday'. We afterwards burned
> whin and searched for shellfish. In Edinburgh here, I find the dyed
> eggs are rolled in Bruntsfield Links. The custom was quite common

[1] Uldall, 5.

[2] Quoted by Opie, Iona and Peter, *The Lore and Language of Schoolchildren*,
Oxford, 1959, 255, note 1.

[3] Gill, W. Walter, *A Third Manx Scrapbook*, London, 1963, 268. Gill, *A
Second Manx Scrapbook*, London, 1932, 140.

[4] Chambers, i.128.

[5] McNeill, F. Marian, *The Silver Bough*, Glasgow, 1961, ii.62.

all over Scotland until recently. It has been stamped out by un-imaginative school-teachers and parsons.[1]

An earlier account from Bervie, Scotland, notes that the custom of rolling 'paiss eggs' was still in existence, but slowly dying out. Young people collected eggs from their friends well in advance and went to the 'paiss braes' near a famous spring on Easter Sunday. The eggs were dyed with such plants as whin, logwood or tea leaves, and ribbons or tapes were tied round before boiling, so that each person would know their own. As a rule, the eggs were boiled at least half an hour, to make them really tough. After the rolling, everyone sat at the foot of the braes and ate their eggs.[2]

Girls and boys on Harris Island put their eggs in a row and rolled them all downhill. It meant good luck for the rest of the year if the eggs remained intact, bad luck if any broke.[3] On Barra, a Catholic island, they also had egg-rolling, and it was known in Shetland, but did not survive the Second World War. In north-east Scotland, where the game was unknown, children saved their Easter shells, and sailed them on the pond like boats.[4]

Yorkshire people referred to 'Paste Egg', or 'Troll Egg Day', which became Easter Monday, but at one time was Easter Day itself. 'Troll' means 'to roll' and probably derives from broad Yorkshire, 't'roll'. This was in the North Riding. An account from Whitby, dated 1901, describes a fair held between the parish church and the Abbey on Easter Monday and Tuesday. Children 'trolled' their coloured eggs, marked with their initials and gilded with dots, in the neighbouring fields.[5]

In the East Riding 'Throwl Egg Day' was celebrated at the beginning, not the end, of Lent on Shrove Tuesday. A newspaper account, also from the beginning of the century, remarks that if young men did not roll eggs successfully on either Shrove Tuesday or Easter Monday they would become ill at harvest-time.[6]

---

[1] Mackenzie, D. A., 'Note', *Folk-Lore*, xxviii (London, December 1917), 450.

[2] Banks, *Scotland*, i.45.   [3] *Ibid.*, 40.

[4] McNeill, ii.49. Banks, *British Calendar Customs: Orkney and Shetland*, London, 1946, 20–21. *Ibid., Scotland*, i.46.

[5] Blakeborough, Richard, *Wit, Character, Folklore and Customs of the North Riding of Yorkshire*, London, 1911, 73. Gutch, Mrs, ed., *Examples of Printed Folk-Lore Concerning the North Riding of Yorkshire*, London, 1901, 245–6.

[6] Gutch, *Examples of Printed Folk-Lore Concerning the East Riding of Yorkshire*, London, 1912, 92. *Ibid., North Riding*, 246.

Egg-rolling is popular elsewhere in the north of England. It was common in and around Hexham, Carlisle, Newcastle, Berwick-on-Tweed and other parts of the Border country, and Westmorland. In Northumberland they often called it 'booling'. The game has survived to the present day but, according to the Opies only in areas north of the Trent. Sometimes only a few children take part, and competitors show much more interest in eating the eggs afterwards. The Opies quote a traveller in 1957 among the remote dales of Cumberland: 'There were signs of accomplished egg-rolling on the grass banks at the side of the road, even in Troutsdale.'[1]

Certain towns have a special site traditionally used for the game: Bunker's Hill in Derby, the castle moat, Penrith, Barney's Hill in Chester, and the 'Valley' in Scarborough. The most publicized event takes place in Avenham Park, Preston, on Easter Monday afternoon. Children roll coloured hard-boiled eggs down the grassy slopes of the park to the Ribble River which flows through it. Originally the idea was to keep one's own egg intact as 'victor', and seize other people's broken ones. But this is impossible now, as so many take part in the game.[2] However, in smaller places the custom still retains its character of a contest. At Lancaster, where once not Monday but Easter Day was the chosen occasion, there is an 'Easter field' called Giant Axe. A certain Jeremiah Wane, much offended that these games took place on a holy day, hired a field and a band to tempt away all the children. Those who came were given books. This was in 1828.[3]

The Opies found this game in west Ulster, Limerick, Kilkenny and Wicklow, where children stained them with whin blossom first.[4] They called it 'egg-trundling' at Holywood. Women and children played, picking up the broken bits afterwards, and eating them. Thiselton-Dyer says only Presbyterians took part,[5] but he must be wrong, as several of the areas mentioned above are almost exclusively Catholic. On the contrary, we know that Dissenters who emigrated to Pennsylvania completely shunned

[1] Opie, 253. Wright, i.90–1. Information kindly supplied by Cyril Thompson of Newbrough, near Hexham. See plate 20 (Selby).

[2] Opie, 254. Hole, *Easter*, 46.

[3] Lofthouse, Jessica, *Portrait of Lancashire*, London, 1967, 203.

[4] Opie, 254.

[5] Thiselton-Dyer, 178.

these sports, and did not even celebrate Easter Day,[1] though our own Presbyterians must sometimes have been more lenient.

The game is popular all over Europe. Children still play it in Austria, sometimes using wooden eggs, sometimes real ones, and smashing them with sticks when they reach their destination.[2] We find it in adjoining areas, in Friuli (north Italy) and in Switzerland, where in French-speaking districts it is still a lively community sport and not something which has degenerated into a children's pastime.[3]

Rules vary slightly from one country to another. Often the egg which went furthest was winner, as on the Dutch Frisian island, Ameland, where children rolled their eggs down a sand-dune.[4] This rule was duplicated in east Slovakia, but if one egg hit another its owner had won.[5] French children played the same way. Young girls took part at the Chauny Lent Carnival. The winner became Queen, and paraded with her companions through the streets. Afterwards the eggs were sliced and eaten with dandelion salad.[6]

In north Bohemia the egg which rolls fastest wins. Round eggs were specially selected as good rollers, which could be aimed more easily.[7] If an egg happened to stop rolling, German children whipped it like a top. Presumably the success of this depended on having the egg facing the right way up. They called the round end 'angel', the point the 'devil'.[8]

Though common in Germany, this is so widespread a custom in Britain that perhaps it was taken to the United States by British settlers. A rolling ceremony has taken place on the White House lawn since 1877, when it was introduced by Dolly Madison, and they say that over 100,000 eggs used to get broken. But today they are mostly plastic, and there is no mess to clear up.[9]

[1] Shoemaker, 4.

[2] Information kindly supplied by Herr Karl-Heinz Vick.

[3] Liebl, 64–5. Perusini, Gaetano, 'Uova e Pani di Pasqua in Friuli', *Schweizerisches Archiv für Volkskunde*, LIII (Basle, 1957), ii–iii.144.

[4] Meertens, 127.

[5] Pranda, Adam, 'Die slowakischen Ostereier', *Schweizerisches Archiv für Volkskunde*, LIII (Basle, 1957), ii–iii.171–2.

[6] Van Gennep, *Manuel*, 1.iii.1,346–7.

[7] *Dictionary of Folklore, Mythology and Legend*, New York, 1949, i.341.

[8] Lehmann, 36. Bächtold-Stäubli, ii.625.

[9] *Daily Telegraph*, 12 April 1966.

In this particular form the game no longer has any significance, beyond a jolly entertainment for the children. But an account set down within this century describes how the *fellahin* of Egypt played it to honour their local saints. The eggs, coloured bright red or yellow, were also used on the Coptic Easter Monday. They were rolled, not down a slope, but across the ground towards a row of eggs some distance away, rather in the style of bowling. Whoever cracked one could claim them all. As is so often the case in oriental societies, women took no part in the sport.[1]

A Victorian traveller in a different part of the East saw Christian boys in Baku (Azerbaijan) – then, as now, in Russian control – playing egg-rolling games in the street with red hard-boiled eggs.[2] In Russia proper, especially if Easter was early, snow might still be on the ground. At any rate it would be very cold, which explains a local variation called *katanyi*. A narrow slide, propped up at one end, is set up indoors and eggs are rolled down it from a little platform at the top. Each player has a different-coloured egg, and the idea is to bump someone else's. If this happens, then the opponent's egg is forfeit, and the game continues until all the eggs are taken.[3]

The same sport appears in Latvia, long under Russian domination, with slight modifications. Two players take part, and if the eggs roll to the right they become the property of the first player; if to the left, of the second. Sometimes Latvian children take two sticks, propping one end on a box, with a narrow gap between them. The eggs are rolled down, and if one hits another and does not break, its owner is the winner.[4] Children in Styria have a similar game. Eggs are rolled along two thin strips of wood, which form a sloping incline. An egg which is either thrown off this by another or jumps is called 'the beggar' and is lost.[5] In Slovenia they use one board only.[6]

---

[1] Blackman, Winifred, *The Fellahin of Upper Egypt*, London, 1927, 253.

[2] Simpson, William, *The Buddhist Praying Wheel*, London, 1896, 285.

[3] Information kindly supplied by Miss Natalia Grushy, formerly of Moscow.

[4] Spicer, 212. Information kindly supplied by Mrs Terēza Budiŋa-Lazdiŋa.

[5] Kretzenbacher, Leopold, 'Vom roten Osterei in der grünen Steiermark', *Schweizerisches Archiv für Volkskunde*, LIII (Basle, 1957), ii–iii.109.

[6] See Vučo, Julijana, *Folk Traditions in Yugoslavia*, Izdavavacki Zavod, n.d.

Danish children sometimes played indoors, and sometimes out, depending on the weather. *Trille påskeaeg* was on Easter day; they took it in turns to roll an egg down a slope. Whoever succeeded in touching another's egg won either it or a small sum of money. But the rules varied: this might have to be repeated three times, or perhaps the shell of the other egg had to be cracked. When the game was finished everyone ate their eggs with bread and butter. A small plank or a sandy slope served the purpose, depending on whether the game was played indoors or out.[1]

Off Denmark, remote in the North Sea, Heligoland children used to be given eggs and oranges, which they took to the peak of the island and played a rolling game throughout Easter afternoon. Further north, in the stormy, wind-swept Faroes, children also played out of doors, despite the weather. From a high point of the Rógvukollur Ridge they rolled their eggs down, stained with an infusion of their native moss, *steinamosi*, which, as its name suggests, grows in profusion among the rocks.[2]

Fishermen's children from the south-east villages of Schonen in Sweden played in the open too. They met on 'egg hill' with pockets full of eggs, and rolled as many as they could as far as possible. Any which happened to break were immediately eaten. Town-people in the same country made a row of eggs, and tried to hit one, by knocking a second against them with the help of a board.[3]

Sorb children in Lausitz dig a pit for their egg-rolling, which they call the 'Waleien'. It is deeper at one end than the other, and the first player puts his egg at the further end. The next has to roll his against it. If he misses, his egg is forfeit, but if he succeeds he can keep both eggs. At first it is difficult to hit the target. So later in the game, when a lot of eggs have accumulated, one player may strike several at once, and perhaps win two or three. In parts of Friuli they dig an egg-shaped ditch for their version of this game.[4]

Sometimes other activities followed. Children in Hornback, north Seeland, play rolling on a wooded hill and then build *påskestuer*, small huts made from pine branches. These little houses contain simple furniture – a table and a stone bench,

---

[1] Uldall, 4–5.

[2] Williamson, Kenneth, *The Atlantic Islands: a Study of the Faroe Life and Scene*, London, 1948, 129–30.   [3] Eskeröd, 12–13.

[4] Perusini, 147. Schmidt-Kowar, E., *Sorbische Ostereier*, Bautzen, 1965, 13.

decorated with moss and shells. Grown-ups are invited in the evening to an Easter meal of eggs, bread and butter. The custom in this form must be fairly recent, since pine trees did not appear in the region until 1800. But it is interesting that shepherd-boys in Jutland build small huts made of turf-sods and branches for the feast of Pentecost.[1] Dr Alan Gailey says that the practice was also known in Ulster. Children dyed eggs yellow by boiling them with whin blossom; they played egg-tossing or egg-rolling, and in some areas built little houses in which they boiled the eggs. They were called 'Easter houses': 'booley huts' in Lecale, County Down.[2]

Though there is unlikely to be any direct link, this is reminiscent of the Jewish Feast of Tabernacles, an autumn harvest festival. It was and still is celebrated by living in rustic booths for seven days. These must be built in such a way that stars are visible through the branches at night. The Psalmist links the idea of a booth with a high place: 'Lord, who shall dwell in thy tabernacle? who shall dwell in thy holy hill?'[3] and St Peter referred to this custom on the mountain of the transfiguration: 'Lord, it is good for us to be here: if Thou wilt, let us make here three tabernacles; one for Thee, and one for Moses, and one for Elias.'[4]

[1] Uldall, 6.
[2] Gailey, Alan, 'Edward L. Sloan's "The Year's Holidays"', *Ulster Folklife*, xiv (Belfast, 1968), 54. Buchanan, Ronald H., 'Calendar Customs' (Part 1), *Ulster Folklife*, viii (Belfast, 1962), 22–3. O'Danachair, Caoimhin, 'Distribution Patterns in Irish Folk Tradition', *Béaloideas*, xxxiii (Dublin, 1965), 102–4, fig. 3.
[3] Ps. xv.1.
[4] Matt. xvii.4.

Chapter 15
More Pastimes and Games

We sing, we sing the Easter song:
God keep you healthy, sane and strong.
Sickness and storms and all other harm
Be far from folks and beast and farm.
Now give us eggs, green, blue and red;
If not, your chicks will all drop dead.

Austrian Pace-Egging Song

EGG-TAPPING

Egg-tapping is a widespread Easter custom – it appears all over Europe with a wonderful variety of names. Norwegians call it *'knekke'*, meaning 'knock', and English players, depending on the area, refer to 'shackling', 'jarping', or 'dumping'. It is *'eiertikken'* in Holland, *'pötjerin'* on Föhr, *'njötjerin'* on Amrum – both parts of north Friesland – *'Kippen'* in Germany, *'tutsanye'* in Yugoslavia, and *'pigge påskeaeg'* in Denmark. An early reference comes from Poland, where a game called *'w waletke'* was played in the fifteenth century.[1] Hyde, writing in 1694, describes how it was enjoyed by Christian children in Mesopotamia during Easter and the following period up till Ascension Day.[2]

The principle of the game is to hold an egg firmly and tap other people's so briskly that they break. Obviously, in order to win, one's own egg must not get damaged. The rules varied slightly from one country to another. Alsatians had very few egg games, but this was popular with the boys, and in Strasbourg egg-picking fortnight spanned the weeks before and after Easter. Players struck the ends, first point to point, then broad end to broad end, crying earthily: *'Arsch uf Arsch!'*[3] This sport disappeared with the First World War.

---

[1] Seweryn, Tadeusz, 'Les Œufs de Pâques Polonais et Hutsules', *Schweizerisches Archiv für Volkskunde*, LIII (Basle, 1957), ii–iii.173.

[2] Hyde, Thomas, *De Ludis Orientalibus*, London, 1694, 237.

[3] Pfleger, Alfred, 'Osterei und Ostergebäck im Elsass', *Schweizerisches Archiv für Volkskunde*, LIII (Basle, 1957), ii–iii.118.

In the Tyrol it is the only traditional egg game of its kind that still exists. This decline is partly due to the fact that coloured eggs have acquired a certain value. Then food difficulties after the defeat of the First World War disinclined many people to lavish eggs on Easter games. But tapping was played immediately before a meal, so the egg, which was then eaten, was not wasted, as it might perhaps have been at a rolling out in the meadow. The rule was to crack the losing egg three times, using both the pointed end and the '*Guf*', or blunt one.[1]

Austrian boys in Styria play the same way and obtain their supply of eggs about ten days before Easter. On the Friday before Palm Sunday, known as 'painful Friday', palm branches are prepared for blessing. Pussy willows are bound round a large branch – as many as can be fitted on, for, after the service is over, the housewife will give as many red eggs for the tapping game as there are strands of pussy willow.[2]

In certain Orthodox countries egg-tapping has a semi-religious significance. In Greece, where it is known to have existed since the thirteenth century, many broach their eggs in this way at the midnight Easter Service, when they are still in church, after the ritual blessing, 'Christ is risen', is pronounced. By breaking the shell of the eggs, which are always red, they say that the blessing can escape.[3]

Greeks eat their eggs point upwards, together with Easter bread. If one survives the tapping game and remains intact throughout the Easter period it will bring good luck for the whole of the following year, for it symbolizes strength. It would be put carefully in front of the family ikon.[4] Everyone loves this little ceremony, and even the King and Queen take part. A photograph of King Constantine cracking eggs with naval ratings appeared in the British Press at Easter, 1967.[5] Family and friends like to do it, especially husband and wife. Each makes a wish, and

[1] Ilg, Karl, 'Sitte und Brauch um Osterei und Osterbrot im Tirol', *Schweizerisches Archiv für Volkskunde*, LIII (Basle, 1957), ii–iii.95.

[2] Kretzenbacher, Leopold, 'Vom roten Osterei in der grünen Steiermark', *Schweizerisches Archiv für Volkskunde*, LIII (Basle, 1957), ii–iii.104.

[3] Arnott, Margaret, 'Die Ostereier in Griechenland', *Schweizerisches Archiv für Volkskunde*, LIII (Basle, 1957), ii–iii, 193. Woolley, R. C., in the *Sunday Times*, 26 December 1954.

[4] Arnott, 193.   [5] See plate 18.

whoever wins will see their wish come true. Two red eggs tapping against each other is a common motif on Greek Easter cards.

In Rumania, another Orthodox country, there was often a family ritual on Easter morning. Everyone went to greet the head of the household, taking a red egg, which they struck against his, exchanging the ritual greeting at the same time. This was called '*ciocnirea ouălor*', and was performed during the three days of Easter, whenever visitors came to the house. On the first day, just the pointed ends were struck, but on the Monday and Tuesday it was either end, and even the sides. The person whose egg remains whole is supposed to outlive the other.[1] Are there echoes here of the ancient pagan life egg, whose preservation was closely linked with the life of its owner?

If two friends or relations were playing, it was accepted practice for the younger to proffer his egg, with the pointed end uppermost, while the elder person struck it with his own. Meanwhile, the ritual greetings were exchanged:

'Christ is risen!'

'He is risen indeed.'[2]

In Albania, where there were considerable numbers of Orthodox Christians, this custom was also observed. But it was not restricted to Christians. A Moslem friend from Tirana remembers playing the game as a child at Easter-time.[3] Albanian Moslems used to celebrate Easter and Christmas with as much pleasure and unself-consciousness as their own feast days, harking back to pre-Turkish times, when the whole country was Christian.

In Switzerland, *Eier tütschen*, which is *Eier düpfen* to the Bernese – it has various dialect names – is very popular. Whoever breaks his own egg must surrender it to the winner. If the egg is very hard, a good many can soon be won. In the western part of the country innkeepers may provide as many as 1,000 coloured eggs to use in this sport.

In Berne Canton, and especially around Emmental, it was a public occasion; until recently, when someone was caught using

---

[1] Slătineanu, Barbu, 'Les Œufs de Pâques en Roumanie', *Schweizerisches Archiv für Volkskunde*, LIII (Basle, 1957), ii–iii.181. Spicer, Dorothy, *The Book of Festivals*, New York, 1937, 276.

[2] Murgoçi, Agnes, 'Rumanian Easter Eggs', *Folk-Lore*, xx (London, September 1909), 296.

[3] Information kindly supplied by Vera Bloshmi, formerly of Tirana.

an egg with a cement core. Since then the Canton government has
banned the game as a public sport, though it continues un-
officially.[1] This sort of behaviour was quite usual. Van Gennep
points out that in late eighteenth-century Provence cheats used
marble or alabaster eggs.[2] Rhinelanders used warm pitch as a
filling, and this they called a '*Judasei*' – the traitor egg.[3]

Egg-tapping was an early sport in England. Hyde mentions
it in his *De Ludis Orientalibus* (1694) in a way that suggests it was
originally a pastime of the north: '*Hic Ludus non retintur in mediis
partibus Angliae.*'[4] Dorset children during the last century played
the game at Shrovetide, but in a modified form. Everyone put
their eggs in a sieve and shook them gently together. As the eggs
cracked, they were removed, until only the winner's remained.[5]
In Martock (Somerset) the winner took all the cracked eggs, and
in Taunton Deane the prize was an Easter cake; at Langport in
1870 broken eggs were given to the schoolmaster. The champion
dressed in a fool's cap made of patchwork, and headed a procession of schoolchildren collecting money.[6] The game is still played
around Sedgemoor.

A Cumberland hotel recently held a popular 'dumping' competition, which was reported in the local Press:

> Customers at the Black-a-Moor Hotel were able to 'dump' to their
> heart's content on Sunday night, and when the pasche eggs creaked
> under the strain there was salt supplied so they could be eaten up.
> Stanley Brag, the landlord, told the *News* that everyone enjoyed this
> annual event. 'I supply all the eggs and they each bear my special
> mark, just in case someone tries to introduce pot or wooden ones.'[7]

Sometimes the proper method was to break the egg on your
neighbour's forehead – as in Spain.[8] If done quickly and correctly,
it does not hurt, though the echo is said to resound in one's skull.
It is tempting, though far-fetched, to assume that this is an oriental custom introduced into Spain by the Moors, for Iranian Jews

[1] Information kindly supplied by Herr Willy Hess of Winthertur.

[2] Van Gennep, Arnold, *Manuel de Folklore Français Contemporain*, Paris,
1947, I.iii, 1,344.

[3] Müller, J., *Rheinisches Wörterbuch*, Berlin, 1928, iii.1,214.

[4] Hyde, 238.

[5] Dacombe, Marianne, ed., *Dorset*, Dorchester, 1935, 98.

[6] Briggs, K. M. and Tongue, R. L., *Somerset Folklore*, London, 1965, 157.

[7] *Cumberland Evening News*, 25 April 1957.

[8] Urlin, Ethel L., *Festivals, Holy Days and Saints' Days*, London, 1915, 85.

break their Passover eggs by banging them on the forehead,[1] and Jewish children in Kurdistan play egg-tapping.[2] But this can hardly be so. A young Slovenian girl in 1966 remembered how, as children, her brothers and sisters had broken eggs on each other's foreheads,[3] and in Sweden, another unconnected area, it is also occasionally done.[4] In fact, most children would probably enjoy this, if they happened to think of it.

American Syrians in Boston test the shells first with their teeth, to find the strongest. They call the sharp end the 'head', the other, the 'heel'. One player says to the other: 'I shall break your head with my head!' But if the egg is really hard, he says: 'I will break your head with my head, and your heel too.' The second player, concealing his own egg in his hand, so that only the tip shows, says: 'Well, break it.' The first player may try to do this, or persuade him to reveal a little more of the surface of the egg. But if the first player thinks he will not win he exchanges eggs with the second, who takes the initiative in the game. Whichever egg remains intact wins, and the game continues with a replacement egg. Final victory goes to his opponent when a player runs out of eggs.[5]

Dutch children played *eiertikken* on Easter Monday with coloured eggs borrowed from their mothers. Three eggs are called a *'paschei'*; they are first stained with coffee, onion or beet-juice, then taken to a meadow and matched against each other. Nowadays this game is often played with nuts, like English 'conkers' or chestnut-tapping.[6]

A German from Cologne, resident in this country, remembered playing *Kippen* as a child before the First World War with coloured eggs left by the Easter hare. Nearby villages were filled with people competing in market squares on Easter Day, and an umpire compèred the matches. In this version victory was difficult:

---

[1] Information kindly supplied by Mrs V. F. Sharp of London.

[2] Information kindly supplied by the Rev. Vassily James of London.

[3] Information obtained through the kind assistance of Miss Jacqueline Simpson.

[4] Eskeröd, Albert, 'Ostereier in Schweden', *Schweizerisches Archiv für Volkskunde*, LIV (Basle, 1958), 12.

[5] Wilson, Howard R., 'Syrian Folklore Collected in Boston', *Journal of American Folklore*, XVI (Boston, 1903), 139.

[6] Meertens, P. J., 'Ostereier und Ostergebäcke in den Niederlanden', *Schweizerisches Archiv für Volkskunde*, LIII (Basle, 1957), ii–iii.126–8.

the winner had to break both ends of his opponent's egg. The German informant's father told him, rather prosaically, that the game was to encourage poultry-farmers to give their livestock better food – presumably more grit, to strengthen the shells.[1]

This, if true, was very commendable. But not everyone approved of such games. The following paragraph appeared in a Pennsylvania newspaper in 1868:

> Egg-picking prevailed to a great extent yesterday. In all parts of the city juveniles could be seen with their favourite eggs in hand, challenging whoever might come along to try their metal. Would it not have been better for these young folks to postpone their games until after Sabbath day. Certainly today [Easter Monday] would have been more appropriate – if such proceedings are to take place at all.[2]

Egg-picking, as they called it, was actually popular with the Pennsylvania Dutch. Sometimes the children broke eggs against their own foreheads. A local newspaper, *The Norristown Montgomery Watchman* (1856), gloomily observes:

> Eggs had to suffer yesterday, but nary one did we see as of old in a youngster's hand, bantering to fights. Alas! that all the sports of bygone days are past. Young America has taken to cigars, tight breeches and big cravats, instead of keeping alive the time honoured custom of fighting coloured wooden eggs against the fruit of the chicken. Truly the human race is degenerating, and the country is in danger.[3]

Apart from Pennsylvania, the game is played by Negroes in the Southern States, perhaps introduced by French settlers.[4] In France itself, and Belgium, it used to be popular. At the village of Denain people played on Palm Sunday, Easter Sunday, Easter Monday and Low Sunday in a road leading to the church. It lasted three or four hours; vendors came and sold eggs specially for this purpose.

Some people strengthened the shells by boiling them or standing them in either powdered lime or alcohol for a week. Guinea-fowl eggs, tougher and more difficult to obtain, were very expensive – about five times the cost of a hen's egg. So many people

---

[1] *Sunday Times*, 26 December 1954, letter from H. J. Reifenberg.

[2] *Allentown Lehigh Valley Daily News*, 13 April 1868.

[3] 25 March 1856.

[4] Puckett, N., *Folk Beliefs of the Southern Negro*, Chapel Hill, 1926, 55.

took part in the sport that a single vendor might sell up to 5,500 eggs, testing them first, and charging more for the hard ones. Successful players resold their surplus eggs to bakeries at half price.[1]

In Nantes (Brittany) workers used red eggs. Elsewhere in France it appears in a less proletarian guise – rather like roulette, with a 'banker' who struck each egg. If his broke, he forfeited one, but otherwise his opponent did. This continued until he had run out of eggs or the contestants – usually a group – had done so. The 'banker' could often win several hundred.[2] This custom, called the '*toquette*' and recorded by Van Gennep, has disappeared.

Whenever the game was played, in the Baltic States, the Ukraine or Slovakia, central or western Europe, the principle was much the same. Only the rules varied very slightly. Latvians, for instance, always tapped pointed end against pointed end and made a wish. If the egg remained whole, the wish was granted.[3] North Frieslanders tapped in the same way, but the owner of the whole egg won the loser's, as in Switzerland.[4]

Most people had their own secret recipe for success. But Germans said the best kind of 'victor' egg – Bulgarians gave it the same name, *boretz*, or champion – is one which has been laid on Good Friday. Drawing strength from the holy day, it will certainly beat all the rest.[5]

COIN-AND-EGG GAME

Some people call this game 'egg-spicking'. It is played on the same principle as tapping, but one player substitutes a coin for an Easter egg. German children held an egg almost concealed in the fist, with only a small portion showing. The other player had to throw a coin, so that it stuck securely into the egg – a coloured one in Austria, which was stabbed with a florin.[6] Hungarian boys

---

[1] Van Gennep, *Folklore de la Flandre et du Hainault*, Paris, 1935, I.213–14.

[2] *Ibid., Manuel*, 1.iii.1,343, 1,345.

[3] Information kindly supplied by Mrs Terĕza Budiņa Lazdiņa, formerly of Riga.

[4] Lehmann, Hedi, *Volksbrauch im Jahreslauf*, Munich, 1964, 36.

[5] Vakarelski, Christo, 'Œufs de Pâques chez les Bulgares', *Schweizerisches Archiv für Volkskunde*, LIII (Basle, 1957), ii–iii.186. Bächtold-Stäubli, Hanns, ed., *Handwörterbuch des deutschen Aberglaubens*, Berlin, 1929–30, ii.626, note 317.

[6] *Ibid.*, 623. Kretzenbacher, 108. Layard, John, *The Lady of the Hare*, London, 1944, 173.

used a kreuzer and, if it stuck, the egg was given to whoever had aimed the coin. If the thrower was unsuccessful, and allowed his coin to fall to the ground, it was forfeit to the owner of the egg.[1]

In western Slovakia they called this 'hacking'. Competitors had to break the shell, and whoever lost forfeited the egg or the coin.[2] The game, which has died out now, was also played in Russia. Italian children in Friuli put the egg on the ground instead of holding it.[3]

Swiss players used the same technique, but *Eierspiggis* has disappeared in their country too.[4] Players in the east Tyrol attempt to throw a coin into an egg laid on the ground. In this, called *'Guffen'*, winners kept both egg and coin.[5] Before the First World War it was a popular sport, though it must have been difficult.

In most egg games the idea was to break the shells and eat the contents, but the point of the egg dance was to do as little damage as possible. It needed a great deal of skill. Indeed, whenever anything is especially difficult to do, Germans say, 'It's like the egg dance.'

There is no particular reason to believe that this custom was connected with a specific time of year, but affinities with certain Easter games are sufficiently pronounced for it to be worth mentioning in this section. Then, too, the fact that it was performed as a means of clinching an unsanctioned engagement suggests a possible connection with spring and the reproductive cycle.

It was in fact performed on an Easter Monday in the late fifteenth century, at the wedding of Margaret of Austria and Philip the Handsome, Duke of Savoy. The year was 1498. One hundred eggs were laid out and two young couples, who had been told

---

[1] Jones, William H., 'Magyar Folk-Lore and Some Parallels', *The Folk-Lore Journal* (London, November 1883), 357.

[2] Pranda, Adam, 'Die slowakischen Ostereier', *Schweizerisches Archiv für Volkskunde*, LIII (Basle, 1957), ii–iii.172.

[3] Perusini, Gaetano, 'Uova e pani di Pasqua in Friuli', *Schweizerisches Archiv für Volkskunde*, LIII (Basle, 1957), ii–iii.144.

[4] Liebl, Elsbeth, 'Ostereierspiele im Atlas der schweizerischen Volkskunde', *Schweizerisches Archiv für Volkskunde*, LIII (Basle, 1957), ii–iii.64.

[5] Ilg, 95.

that they might marry if they could finish without breaking an egg, performed the dance together. But the test had to be repeated three times.[1]

Perhaps there is a link between this ceremony and the eggs which are such an important feature at weddings in many parts of the world. Alternatively, the original intention may have been to set a revealing test. For the egg was at one time a mystically significant object: a peasant woman of Mecklenburg was put to death because she refused to swear while holding an egg in her hand, and bore false witness.[2] Bächtold-Stäubli refers briefly to the children at Eberswald, who used to run around a magic circle traced on the ground, holding an egg; this game might be connected with the same idea.[3]

The egg dance seems to have been an ancient custom, once popular in parts of western Europe, which died out over a century ago. It is referred to in an Elizabethan comedy by William Wagner, called *The Longer Thou Livest, the More Foole Thou Art*:

> *Upon my one foote pretely I can hoppe*
> *And daunce it trimley about an egge.*[4]

Dancing upon one foot was a favourite feat of the Saxon gleemen and Norman minstrels, and hopping matches for prizes occasionally took place in the sixteenth century. John Heywood in his *Proverbs* (1566) says:

> *Where wooers hoppe in and out, long time may bring*
> *Him the hoppeth best at last to have the ring*
> *I hoppyng without for a ring of a rushe.*

During the sixteenth and seventeenth centuries the egg dance was performed in northern Holland. A circle was marked out in chalk, and green leaves, flowers and a pile of eggs placed inside it. Performers worked the eggs out of the circle as they danced, and whoever was the quickest won a basket of them as a prize. The person capable of eating most was then taken through the village on a wagon.[5] Hone, in his *Year Book*, describes an egg

[1] Van Gennep, *Manuel*, 1.iii.1,354-5.

[2] Bächtold-Stäubli, ii.596.   [3] *Ibid.*, 622.

[4] Quoted by Strutt, Joseph, *The Sports and Pastimes of the People of England*, London, 1801, 225.

[5] Meertens, 128. Information kindly supplied by Henk Arends from the *Folkloristisch Woordenboek*.

dance which he saw at the Utrecht Fair in July 1828, performed by a ten-year-old girl who was blindfold: 'Fourteen eggs were arranged on the ground at about two feet distance from each other . . . it must have required considerable skill and practice to avoid, as she certainly did, treading on the eggs.'[1]

When Dr Johnson visited the Continent he saw an egg dance performed in the streets of Paris (1775), but gives no further details.[2] Laborde's *Views of Spain*, published in 1809, describes such a dance among the Valencians: 'In the first they place on the ground a number of eggs, at small intervals from each other; they dance round the eggs in these intervals; it seems as if they must crush them every moment, but notwithstanding the celerity and variety of the steps they display, they never touch one of them.'[3]

Strutt's *The Sports and Pastimes of the People of England*, published in 1801, refers to roughly the same period:

> This performance was common enough about 30 years back, and was well received at Sadlers Wells; where I saw it exhibited, not by simply hopping round a single egg, but in a manner that much increased the difficulty. A number of eggs, I do not precisely recollect how many, but I believe about 12 or 14, were placed at certain distances marked upon the stage; the dancer, taking his stand, was blindfolded, and a horn-pipe being played in the orchestra, he went through all the paces and figures of the dance, passing backwards and forwards between the eggs without touching one of them.[4]

Eighteenth-century memories of the egg dance also come from Denmark. *Aeggedans* was performed at Carnival time before Lent; it took various forms. An early account, dated 1745, describes how an egg was placed on a goblet, which was standing upside down on a small pile of sand. The performer – presumably an acrobat – was required to shift the egg from its pinnacle to the floor in the course of the dance and then, walking on her hands, put it back in its original position.[5]

---

[1] Hone, William, *The Year Book*, London, 1832, 481.

[2] Johnson, Samuel, *Diaries, Prayers, and Annals*, New Haven, 1958, 236. Entry for 16 October 1775, 'At the Boulevard saw nothing, yet was glad to be there. Rope dancing and farce. Egg Dance.'

[3] *Notes and Queries*, 24 November 1900, 9th Series, vi.404.

[4] Strutt, 225–6.

[5] Uldall, Kai, 'Les Œufs de Pâques au Danemark', *Schweizerisches Archiv für Volkskunde*, LIV (Basle, 1958), 8.

A different description from Amager Island is dated 1758. In this version the dancer kicked the goblet, so that the egg fell on to the sand. Then he picked the goblet up in his feet and inverted it over the egg. The dance, which has not survived, was also performed at Carnival time. It is thought that it was imported by the Dutch, for the Danish King had summoned people from Marken, north Holland – then an island – to come and settle in 1521.[1]

If the egg dance was performed at Sadlers Wells, it was also arranged as training for the Royal Corps de Ballet in Copenhagen. First a man, then a woman, and finally a couple had to dance between a fixed number of eggs laid out on the floor without breaking them: this version was from Seeland.[2]

Although there does not seem to be any definite evidence that the egg dance as such was an Easter dance, Carnival occasions and the fifteenth-century performance referred to above establish a link with that time of year. A correspondent of *Notes and Queries* noticed in Lausanne in 1870 a procession which took place on Easter Monday. The local butchers donned fancy dress and carried emblematic banners, together with a glass case containing, rather surprisingly, a baby and a cow. They paraded to the public promenade, where Easter eggs were placed on the ground at certain distances. Various games were played and one consisted of leaping backwards through the eggs without a breakage, whoever was successful winning them.[3]

Perhaps the most detailed description of the egg dance which we possess is the one in Goethe's novel, *Wilhelm Meister*:

Mignon had been waiting for him; she lighted him upstairs. On setting down the light, she begged that he would allow her, that evening, to compliment him with a piece of her art. He would rather have declined this, particularly as he knew not what it was; but he had not the heart to refuse anything this kind creature wished. After a little while she again came in. She carried a little carpet below her arm, which she then spread out upon the floor. Wilhelm said she might proceed. She thereupon brought four candles, and placed one upon each corner of the carpet. A little basket of eggs which she next carried in made her purpose clearer. Carefully measuring her steps, she then walked to and fro on the carpet,

---

[1] *Ibid.*   [2] *Ibid.*
[3] *Notes and Queries*, 23 July 1870, 4th Series, vi.68.

spreading out the eggs in certain figures and positions, which done, she called in a man that was waiting in the house, and could play on the violin. He retired with his instrument into a corner; she tied a band about her eyes, gave a signal, and like a piece of wheel-work set a-going, she began moving the same instant as the music, accompanying her beats and the notes of the tune with the strokes of a pair of castanets.

Lightly, nimbly, quickly, and with hairsbreadth accuracy, she carried on the dance. She skipped so sharply and surely along between the eggs, and trod so closely down beside them, that you would have thought every instant she must trample one of them in pieces, or kick the rest away in her rapid turns. By no means! She touched no one of them, though winding herself through their mazes with all kinds of steps, wide and narrow, nay even with leaps, and at last half kneeling.

Constant as the movement of a clock, she ran her course; and the strange music, at each repetition of the tune, gave a new impulse to the dance, recommencing and again rushing off as at first. . . .

The dance being ended, she rolled the eggs together softly with her foot into a little heap, left none behind, harmed none; then placed herself beside it, taking the bandage from her eyes, and concluding her performance with a little bow.[1]

Here we have a full account of what was evidently a popular contemporary amusement. But it is worth noting that, in the context of the tale, the egg dance represents a concealed love-offering, made by the gipsy-like Mignon to Wilhelm Meister.

A recent German book[2] seems to infer, perhaps unintentionally, a special connection between the egg dance and gipsies. There is, it is true, a certain formal similarity between the dance of Mignon and that performed by far-removed entertainers in Bengal. To both of these the authors, Mode and Wölffling, draw attention. The appeal of the idea is increased by Bengal being the home of an important gipsy group, the Bediyā. Unfortunately the authority cited by the authors[3] provides no real support for such a theory. Although the Indian dance, like Mignon's, is basically a pure display of dexterity, there is no suggestion that it was performed particularly by gipsies, skilled while they are at this type of

[1] Goethe, Johann Wolfgang, *Wilhelm Meister's Apprenticeship and Travels*, tr. Thomas Carlyle, London, 1874, I.2.viii.98–9. First published 1796–7.
[2] Mode, Heinz, and Wölffling, Siegfried, *Zigeuner*, Leipzig, 1968, 39, 119–20.
[3] Schlagintweit, Emil, *Indien in Wort und Bild*, Leipzig, 1880, i.219–21.

activity. But not all Bengali entertainers belong to this group, and the festivities of Durga, for example, recounted alongside the original reproduction of the dance, would certainly have been graced by non-gipsy virtuosos. Schlagintweit, source of the illustration,[1] explains it as follows: On the artist's head is balanced a hoop to which are attached 24 looped cords. As she dances, she takes raw eggs one by one from a basket she is holding, and fixes them into each of the loops. The cords, tautened by the weight of the eggs, are raised and splayed outwards by the motion of her body, to form a wheel. The skill lies in keeping the cords revolving uniformly, with the eggs the same distance apart and thus unbroken. If they survive, they are then detached from the loops and replaced in the basket as she continues to perform.

In England certain destructive children's games resembled the egg dance. At the beginning of summer, boys living in the Chilterns used to play 'egg-hopping'. They searched for birds' eggs and spread them out on a path, far or near apart, according to the rarity of the species. Then the 'hopper', blindfold, tried to break as many eggs as possible in a given number of jumps. Although it was only a game, players absolutely refused to part with these eggs for money.[2]

'Blin' Stam', played in Argyllshire, was not dissimilar. An egg was put on the ground about fifteen yards from a stand, and blindfolded players took it in turn, holding a stick and trying to guess the distances. The object was to strike the ground an agreed number of times, in the hopes of smashing the egg. Maclagan, who collected this game, thought it likely that it was played at Easter.[3]

What could have been the significance of the egg dance? It is always tempting to convert every puzzling survival into a fertility ritual, and one can often make mistakes in doing so. But in this particular case there is conclusive evidence from four centuries ago, linking the egg dance to the theme of fertility. There is in Amsterdam's Rijksmuseum a painting by Pieter Aertsz, dated 1557 and entitled *Eierdans* (Egg Dance).[4] In the foreground a

[1] See plate 11.
[2] *Notes and Queries*, 19 December 1863, 3rd Series, iv.492.
[3] Maclagan, R. C., *The Games and Diversions of Argyllshire*, London, 1901, 44.
[4] I am greatly indebted to Dr H. R. Ellis Davidson, who first drew my attention to the existence of this painting. See plate 6; also plates 7–9.

gay young man sits with his hand hanging suggestively over the shoulder of a young woman. Behind them is a table with various objects lying upon it, including two wooden tablets, one bearing the head of a jester, the other a leaping roebuck. Details like this were not included in a painting of this period unless they possessed a special significance, and the jester was a symbol of folly, the roebuck of lust. Other elements in the painting emphasize these themes. A jug of garlic hangs outside the window and garlic leaves are scattered over the floor, a plant popularly regarded as an aphrodisiac. Hence a jug hung up in this fashion was the sign for a brothel.

Another important feature of the painting is a reel used for winding thread as it is spun. This is probably an allusion to the sixteenth-century Dutch saying: 'to be as silly as a spinner's reel'.[1] It presumably refers to the egg-dancer, who has removed his sword, cap, and wooden shoes, and is performing amid the litter strewn on the floor: broken egg-shells, garlic, leeks, onion flowers, and empty mussel shells. There is a circle chalked out on the flagstones, an upturned bowl, and an egg. The dancer begins by pushing away the bowl, which initially supports the egg, so that it rolls to the floor without breaking. Then it must be worked back into the circle, and the upturned bowl placed over it. All this is done with the feet, in time to the music, without touching the many objects. Anyone who could do this was given a prize.

In the sixteenth-century eggs, mussels, garlic and onion all symbolized debauchery, because of their supposed aphrodisiac properties. Hence even the dance itself was regarded as sinful. Contemporary etchings by artists like Aertsz and Bruegel, which represent the fools' dance, were given such texts as:

> The fools dance has no measure, for each
> Follows his lust wherever it leads.
> Whoever can keep this measure and rule in everything
> Can escape this dance of the fools.[2]

The man in this picture, therefore, is a fool who cannot resist

---

[1] For this and other material relating to the egg dance in the Netherlands, I am indebted to D. N. Snoep, Scientific Officer, Rijksuniversiteit, Utrecht, the Netherlands.

[2] *Ibid.*

temptation, and the egg dance keeps him from a proper sense of moderation. An unknown Flemish writer notes:

> It's all a silly business, as you can see.
> As the old folk sing and make music
> The foolish youngsters prance over the eggs.[1]

A current German colloquialism is '*Warum dieser Eiertanz?*' meaning, 'Why all this silly nonsense?'[2]

Mrs Ruth Noyes, of the English Folk Dance and Song Society, tells me that the performance of the reconstructed egg dance, included in the 1968 Albert Hall Folk Festival, was largely thanks to the efforts of the Egg Marketing Board, who had contacted her in order to discover if such a dance actually existed. The Humberside Egg Dancers,[3] who appeared on this occasion, also perform locally. Blindfolded after noting the position of the eggs, they dance in the manner of a Morris jig, one man performing a figure, followed immediately by a second dancer, who repeats it. Public interest in these performances was considerable.

EGG-GATHERING

This is a very popular sport in all Germanic countries, so much so that it was carried to German communities abroad. Settlers from the south-west part of the country, where such egg-collecting games proliferated, took them to Bessarabia, the Ukraine and the Dobrudzha; there they flourished until the *Volksdeutsch* homecoming in 1940–3. They are also favourites in other Germanic countries – the Tyrol, Switzerland, Denmark – and in France.[4]

Basically, the game falls into two parts, the job of the 'reader' and the job of the 'runner'. The reader has to collect a large number of eggs, generally about 100, which are laid out at intervals along the ground. Often every tenth is coloured or boiled. The eggs must be taken and put in a tub while the runner covers a specified distance, generally to the next village. He might be told to visit a certain inn, drink a glass of wine, and return.

[1] *Ibid.*

[2] For example, in the newspaper *Memeler Dampfboot*, Vol. 118, No. 11; Oldenburg, 5 June 1967, 142.

[3] Information kindly supplied by Mrs Kathleen Mitchell of Hull.

[4] Lanz, Josef, 'Das Eierlesen in [den ostdeutschen Sprachinseln', *Jahrbuch für Volkskunde der Heimatvertriebenen*, vi (Salzburg, 1961), 98.

Sometimes it was a late Carnival amusement, as in Switzerland, and competitors wore fancy dress. They might represent traditional figures – vicar, doctor, sweep – while a clown daubed the crowd with soot, and a newly married couple enacted vulgar jokes.

Miss Violet Alford has very kindly drawn my attention to a most interesting print in the Landesbibliothek, Berne, which may date from the middle of the last century. It shows a few gentry – men in tall hats – and country people in local costume. Two young men hold fir trees stripped nearly to the top, and many eggs hang on the remaining boughs.[1] Another young man, holding an egg in each hand, is running along a track between two lines of eggs which have been laid out on the ground. Behind him, with one knee bent, is a fool, with a cap and frill, holding what could be a gun. A large crowd of spectators looks on.

The number of players taking part varies, and nowadays the 'runner' may use a bicycle. In the Black Forest they ride on horseback.[2] These games usually end with a public egg meal and general merry-making. Swiss scholars think that this is why their innkeepers are preserving the sport today. Athletic clubs, riding, bicycle, gymnastic societies and guilds, butchers and apprentice millers have also at one time or another been in charge of the organization.[3]

Germans settled in the Ukraine in the late eighteenth century, and this game appeared in Crimean communities – Samau, for example. Players, who kissed Russian style before and after the occasion, wore white shirts, dark trousers, women's stockings gartered with red ribbons, and red and blue ribbons across the shoulders. Ribbons worn over the forehead were always green.[4]

German emigration to Bessarabia began in 1814, and the game of egg-gathering spread from there to the Dobrudzha. In both areas there were two girls for every male player: one caught eggs in her apron, the other transferred them to a basket. Sometimes four 'policemen' supervised the game, carrying decorated whips or truncheons. Generally there was a flag – a substitute for the

---

[1] See also Newall, Venetia, 'Some Notes on the Egg Tree', *Folklore*, lxxviii (London, Spring 1967), 39–45. Further, see plate 10.

[2] Spicer, 134.

[3] Information kindly supplied by Herr Willy Hess, Liebl., 65–7.

[4] Lanz, 102.

egg tree in the Swabian motherland, possibly because suitable trees are harder to come by in Bessarabia. Decorated with small bells, ribbons and a cut-out metal cockerel, it was carried at the head of the procession to the place where the game was to be played. Then it was erected, marking the start of the run.

Sometimes scarves or bottles of wine were hung up on the flag, and seized during the traditional dance performed before the game. At the end the winner carried it home. According to the rules, every tenth egg was coloured red. All of them had to be collected, the plain ones thrown into a girl's apron, the red ones over the flag. In Lichtenthal they hurled both kinds over the flag, and caught them in tablecloths on the other side. Whichever group caught the most had won.[1]

Danes call this game *'aeggeløb'*. They often played it at Carnival time with two groups. The eggs, laid out in two rows, three metres apart, are picked up one by one and put in a basket at the end of the line. Sometimes only one team did this, while the other wound a rope round and round a post,or something of that kind.[2] Local methods varied considerably. In Alsace the eggs were set out in front of the Mayor's residence. This and egg-tapping were the only two egg games known there. Once widely popular, it has since largely died out, though it was recorded at Sierentz as late as 1957.[3]

Some commentators see in this game relics of the old spring competitions in which young men and women took part, originally for magical fertility purposes, and later to assist in choosing a bride. Certainly the composition of the teams picked varied. And while young men often battled, guild against guild, craft against craft, and laying wagers, young men and girls sometimes took part together, at one time perhaps playing in competition against each other: in 1845 there was an event at Baden where teams of boys and girls competed on the ice of a frozen lake.[4]

There was a wave of German emigration to Hungary in the early eighteenth century, and at Inselneudorf, near Budapest, two boys would collect eggs from the girls on Easter Monday. They gathered in the churchyard after the service, and brought a

[1] *Ibid.*, 102–5.
[2] Uldall, 8.
[3] Pfleger, 118. Van Gennep, *Manuel*, 1.iii.1,354.
[4] Bächtold-Stäubli, ii.624.

bucket of water. The eggs, laid out along the road, had then to be collected and thrown into it. A band played, and meantime the second competitor fetched a bottle of wine from a neighbouring village. Afterwards both eggs and wine were given to the priest.[1]

Swabian boys in Sathmar collect eggs one day earlier, on Easter Sunday itself. Each farm provides six – ten if there are marriageable girls – and a red boiled one as an extra. In the afternoon they are all laid out in a long row along the village street. Players, who wear special white trousers and a broad red sash, pelt each other and the crowd with eggs. As a rule, sound ones are put in the basket and specially selected bad ones, marked in advance, are thrown into the crowd. The good ones are cooked and eaten at the dance which follows.[2]

The part played by girls is purely nominal, probably because the game was so strenuous. Indeed, in Birsigtal it was forbidden because one player suffered a stroke.[3] In Bessarabia local people circumvented a similar prohibition by going out on to the distant steppe. Apart from the civic authorities, clergy also spoke out against it. In 1779 the ecclesiastical convention at Bitz prohibited the game; and earlier still, in 1640, hostile sermons were preached at Strasbourg.[4] Johann Conrad Dannhauer, a seventeenth-century Lutheran cleric, also fulminated against what he called the 'heathen-papist' egg-running.[5]

However, the Church did not always disapprove, and some commentators have even attempted to point a link with the humorous Apostles' Run. This appears in certain Passion plays, documented since 1100, and is based on the following passage: 'Peter therefore went forth, and that other disciple, and came to the sepulchre. So they ran both together: and the other disciple did outran Peter, and came first to the sepulchre.'

In Belgium the sport had definite religious associations, for it was connected with a big pilgrimage to the church at Loos. Mothers of sick children, people wishing to be relieved of their

---

[1] Lanz, 101.
[2] *Ibid.*, 101–2.
[3] Bächtold-Stäubli, ii.624.
[4] Lanz, 98–9, 103.
[5] Becker, Albert, *Brauchtum der deutschen Osterzeit*, Jena, 1937, 61.
[6] John xx.3–4.

Colour Plate XXIII (a) Various North European scratch-technique eggs. The two left-hand rows (vertically) are from Lower Lusatia (Nieder Lausitz, Germany). The method is employed by Sorb egg-decorating craftsmen in this area. The third row (vertically; upper part) shows two eggs by a Lithuanian master, who also did the lower two eggs in row 4. The last of these shows a bird above its nest of eggs. At the bottom of row 3 is a Silesian (German) egg, and at the top of row 4 an example of Latvian work. Adjacent to this on the right (stylized swastika in row 5) is another Latvian design, while the final row (vertically) shows three Estonian eggs. In row 5, beneath the swastika egg, are two examples from Cumberland, evidently given as Christening presents in a family named Foster. The upper of the two is inscribed *Fanny Mabel Foster, Born at Allonby on the 27th Oct. 1879*; on the reverse is a pair of scales, the words *Fear Not*, and a cross. The lower of these eggs bears the wording *Eleanor Foster, Carlisle 1882*, with a sailing ship on the reverse. The member of the Foster family who made them was a sailor, and this was his ship.

(b) Rush-pith and coloured-fabric covered eggs. Among the Pennsylvania Dutch this type of egg is designated *binsa graws*. The top centre example, the work of Mrs Huyett (see plate 16), is from this area. The vertical row on the left shows Polish work, in which the rush-pith is interspersed with strands of red, green and mauve wool. The vertical row on the right, with the bottom centre egg, is from Eisenach (Thuringia). The remaining egg, the elaborate example in the centre, is from Ochoz near Brno (Moravia).

Colour Plate XXIV (a) Engraved emu eggs from Australia, that on the left showing an emu; it is blank on the reverse. The reverse of the centre egg shows a bucking horse throwing its rider, and that of the egg on the right, a bull and a mounted horse. Preparation of these eggs probably originated as a herdsman's hobby, but they became well thought of as objects for presentation and were sometimes elaborately mounted. An example exists which was originally a prize to Edward Blundell at the Eagle Farm Sabbath School, Queensland (1875).

(b) Chinese painted eggs, recent examples of a long established art. The eggs, which are made in Peking and Shanghai, are generally emptied with a syringe, and the hole is then refilled with plaster to give the impression of an intact egg. Alternatively, they are mounted singly or in pairs in tiny, specially constructed glass-sided cabinets, often made of rosewood.

fears, and lovers becoming formally betrothed joined in. The game itself was played on Easter Monday. Twenty-six eggs were laid out, three or four steps apart, and the 'reader' gathered them in a basket while the 'runner' headed for his destination. Sometimes players were blindfold, and even used wheelbarrows. Those with covered eyes had to go to a certain spot, and break the coloured eggs there with a stick. If a wheelbarrow was involved, three players were blindfold. One sat in it, another held it by a rope, and the third pushed with the aid of a shoulder strap.[1]

Early accounts of the game exist in Holland. '*Eiergaren*', as it was called, was played in the sixteenth and seventeenth centuries. A large tub of water was placed in the middle of the village street on Easter Monday, and twenty-five eggs, provided by the local innkeeper, were laid along the road at twelve-foot intervals. As usual, two players are chosen, but while one gathers the eggs into a basket the other has to eat an apple floating on the surface of the tub. His hands are tied behind his back. The eggs, which are the winner's reward, are consumed at the celebration afterwards.[2]

The sport was popular at the same period in Bavaria. Races at Remlingen, which still exist, were introduced by the Count of Castell in 1650, who made one part of his egg tithes over to the young boys for this purpose. Here there seems to be a direct link between the game and earlier egg tithes. The system of exacting rent survived the days of pure barter and, since the standard number of eggs, which is 100, sometimes occurs in the games too, it has been suggested that the one may derive from the other.[3]

In 1723 a rich Bavarian farmer donated 50 guilders a year for the Easter service and for a race involving four boys and 100 eggs spread out at intervals of a yard.[4] A certain Georgius Stengelius noted similar customs as early as 1634.[5] Tyrolese egg-running had died out before 1885, probably as a result of the reforms of Joseph II. The teams, which were often huge, with as many as eighty players, wore Carnival clothes and masqueraded as witches, wild men and gipsies, Turks and Moors. One hundred and three

[1] Van Gennep, *Folklore de la Flandre*, 212–13.

[2] Meertens, 128. Spicer, 242–3.

[3] Moser, Hans, 'Brauchgeschichtliches zu Osterei und Osterbrot in Bayern', *Schweizerisches Archiv für Volkskunde*, LIII (Basle, 1957), ii–iii.79, 83.

[4] *Ibid.*, 83.

[5] *Ibid.*

eggs were used and they were only permitted to break three. Losers paid for the celebration meal that followed.[1]

Drinking and merry-making are closely associated with this game. In Switzerland the stipulation that the 'runner' must drink a glass of wine at a particular ale-house before returning is common. Moreover, as the loser had to pay for this, it was not unusual to have a quarrel which ended in a fight.[2] In France the winner received a hogshead of cider, which was shared with everybody.

La Motte du Pougard was an old Druidical barrow not far from Dieppe. On Easter Monday 100 eggs were placed in a basket at the foot, and a circle formed. One person took an egg, which he carried to the top of the mound. This continued till all the eggs were brought up. Then they were carried down again, one by one. Meanwhile the runner ran to the village of Bacqueville and back, about one and a quarter miles away.[3] It does not seem too far-fetched to see a link between this unique game and the egg-rolling on similar barrows in the Isle of Man and at Birkenhead. We are in Normandy now, and perhaps some common tradition is to be sought with the Norsemen, who came to Man and the western shores of Britain.

PACE-EGGING

In order to have a good supply of eggs for the Easter games, it was usual in a number of countries to go out begging. In Ireland children collect goose and duck eggs during Holy Week, and there is a traditional saying: 'One egg for a true gentleman, two for a gentleman, three for a churl, four for a tramp.'[4] Germans called them '*Dingeier*', the eggs which are owing, and Lithuanians gave Easter eggs to the *Khristukas*, 'the singers of the little Christ'.[5] English people spoke of pace-egging, and the Easter plays are pace-egg plays.

Groups of young men, the pace-eggers, travelled around North Country villages at Easter, asking for coloured eggs at all the houses. They were amateur actors, dressed in costume or clothes

[1] Ilg, 96.
[2] Information kindly supplied by Herr Willy Hess.
[3] Jones, William, *Credulities, Past and Present*, London, 1880, 456–7.
[4] Weiser, Francis X., *The Easter Book*, London, 1955, 184.
[5] *Lietuvin Enciklopediga*, Boston, 1959, xii.309–11.

decorated with ribbons, their faces blacked or masked. St George was a popular figure, and there was generally a female character, portrayed by a youth, and known as Old Miser Brown Bags. They performed simple plays, and the custom, though it suffered a setback during two world wars, still exists in various places today.[1]

It was very popular in Lancashire, especially in the Blackburn area, where the actors wore animal skins, and a character called Old Toss Pot carried a basket for the Easter eggs. Harland and Wilkinson give an account of the custom in Blackburn around 1843:

> Young men, in groups varying in number from three to twenty, dressed in various fantastic garbs, and wearing masks – some of the groups accompanied by a player or two on the violin – go from house to house singing, dancing and capering. At most places they are liberally treated with wine, punch or ale, dealt out to them by the host or hostess. The young men strive to disguise their walk and voice; and the persons whom they visit use their efforts on the other hand to discover who they are; in which mutual endeavour many and ludicrous mistakes are made. Here you will see Macbeth and a fox-hunter arm-in-arm; Richard III and a black footman in familiar converse; a quack doctor and a bishop smoking their pipes. . . . A few years ago parties of this description were much subject to annoyance from a gang of fellows styled the Carr-laners (so-called because living in Carr-lane, Blackburn) armed with bludgeons, who endeavoured to despoil the pace-eggers. Numerous fights, with the usual concomitants of broken eggs and various contusions, were amongst the results. This lawless gang of ruffians is now broken up, and the serious affrays between different gangs of pace-eggers have become of comparatively rare occurrence. An accident, however, which ended fatally, occurred last year [?1842]. Two parties had come into collision, and during the affray one of the young men had his skull fractured and death ensued.[2]

This sort of thing was not unique. Rival parties, armed with

[1] Wright, A. R., *British Calendar Customs: England*, London, 1936, i.87–8. James, E. O., *Seasonal Feasts and Festivals*, London, 1961, 305. Robinson, M., 'The Calder Valley Folk Festival', *Folk-Lore*, lxvii (London, Dec. 1956), 234–6. For the origin of the word 'pace', see ch. 7. The alternative 'peace' also occurs.

[2] Harland, John and Wilkinson, T. T., *Lancashire Folk-Lore*, London, 1882, 229–30. See also Wright, i.87–8. Myers, Miles W., 'Letter', *Folk-Lore*, xlix (London, Sept. 1938), 298–9. Ogden, J., 'Pace Egging', *The Antiquary*, xli (London, 1905), 162–3.

wooden swords, were apt to clash in the streets. But, despite the rough-and-tumble, Harland and Wilkinson continue: 'It is not unusual to discover one or two of the fair sex in male habiliments, supporting the character admirably.'[1]

Children were less reckless, but very importunate: 'Houses are literally besieged by these juvenile troops from morning till night! "God's sake! a pace egg!" is the continual cry. There is no particular tune, but various versions of pace-egging and other songs are sung.'[2] A version, collected from Cheshire, went as follows:

> *Here comes three or four jovie lads all in a row,*
> *We've come a pace eggin', we hope you'll prove kind;*
> *Prove kind, prove kind, with your eggs and small beer.*
> *We hope you'll remember its pace eggin' time.*
> *For the diddle dol, for the day, for the diddle dol de day.*
>
> *The next that comes in, is Lord Nelson, you see,*
> *With a bunch of blue ribbon tied under his knee;*
> *With a star on his breast, like a diamond do shine.*
> *I hope you'll remember its pace eggin' time.*
> *For the diddle dol, for the day, for the diddle dol de day.*
>
> *The next that comes in is the miner, you see,*
> *With his round hat and candle, he works under ground;*
> *He works under ground, to get neighbour's coal,*
> *At six in the morning, he pops down yon'd hole.*
> *For the diddle dol, for the day, for the diddle dol de day.*[3]

In September 1966 the Headmaster of Calder High School, Mytholmroyd, in Yorkshire, wrote to Arthur Hulme, who supplied me with the above verses: 'Yes, we perform the play [pace-egg play] eight times on Good Friday each year – wet or fine.'[4] Christina Hole quotes a malicious rhyme sung by little girls in Cheshire:

> *Please, Mrs. Whiteleg,*
> *Please to give us an Easter egg.*

[1] Harland and Wilkinson 230. [2] *Ibid.*

[3] Collected from Arthur Hulme of Marple, Cheshire, in 1966, when he was eighty years old. He remembered it being sung by children during the years 1895–1900.

[4] Written by John Muschamp, Headmaster of Calder High School, Mytholmroyd, near Halifax, Yorkshire, on 5 September 1966.

An Egg at Easter

If you won't give us an Easter egg
Your hens will all lay addled eggs
And your cocks all lay stones.[1]

The Pace Egg was a mummer's play, and it was the original intention of the pace-eggers to act it. Cawte, Helm and Peacock, in their *English Ritual Drama*,[2] give details of localities where the play is or has been performed, and further information appears in Helm's *The Chapbook Mummers' Plays*.[3]

Modern though the text and some of the characters may be – the hero, Lord Nelson, after all, dates from only about 150 years ago – the basic theme is probably of great antiquity. A text, forerunner of such a play, was found at Ras-Shamra, inscribed on cuneiform tablets 3,000 to 4,000 years ago. It describes how the god of vegetation emerges victorious from combat with the god of death. This embodies the annual struggle between summer and winter, which includes the ritual of getting rid of death;[4] in a European context we have noted[5] the tradition of carrying out death and bringing in Summer, and the accompanying ceremonies.

Costumes worn by the pace-eggers are very striking, and consist of a tunic adorned with paper rosettes and elaborate headgear. In this overlapping arches are mounted on a flat cardboard base; these are similar to the arches on the Midgley Wassail Bow, which the children carried round the houses at Christmas-time. The whole hat is decorated with coloured tissue, a few bells hang from the arches, and long strands of coloured beads reach down as far as chest level. The swords used are also decorated with coloured paper. Toss Pot, who represents the Devil, wears a long straw tail.

Apart from this one disreputable figure, they are usually quite an attractive sight, and local people in Midgley once referred to anyone lavishly dressed as 'donned like a Pace Egger'. The version noted by Arthur Hulme lacks a reference to Toss Pot, but the Headmaster of Calder High School substitutes one for the verse about Nelson:

> *The next that steps in is old Toss Pot, you see,*
> *He's a gallant old man and he wears a degree,*

[1] Hole, Christina, *Traditions and Customs of Cheshire*, London, 1937, 77.
[2] London, 1967.
[3] Leicester, 1969.
[4] Harwood, H. W. and Marsden, F. H., ed., *The Pace Egg: the Midgley Version*, Halifax, 1935, 3–4.　　　　　　[5] See Ch. 13.

He powders his hair with a dredging tin box,
He wears a pigtail and you see how it cocks.[1]

Here he cuts quite an elegant figure, but Chambers quotes him as saying:

Although I am ragged and not so well dressed,
I can carry a pace egg as well as the best.[2]

Invariably the performances end with a demand for money and eggs:

Come, search up your money,
Be jubilant and free,
And give us your Pace egg
For Easter Monday.

Go down in your cellars,
And see what you'll find.
If your barrels be empty
I hope you'll provide.

I hope you'll provide
Sweet eggs and strong beer,
And we'll come no more to you
Until the next year.

These times they are hard
And money is scant,
One Pace egg of yours
Is all that we want.

And if you will grant us
This little small thing,
We'll all charm our voices,
And merry we'll sing.[3]

In Westmorland the Pace Eggers are called 'Jolly Boys'. Six performers are mentioned, providing their own costumes – this was presumably the general practice in the old days. *The New Hutton Women's Institute Book*, compiled in 1955 by Mrs M. F. Alexander, lists the six characters as the Singer, Lord Nelson,

---

[1] Muschamp, John. See note 4 on page 367.
[2] Chambers, E. K., *The English Folk-Play*, Oxford, 1933, 70.
[3] Harwood and Marsden, 23.

Toss Pot, Molly Brown Bags, Paddy Fra Cock and Jolly Jack Tar, but notes that the play has not been performed there within the last fifty years.[1]

Mary Danielli, writing in *Folk-Lore* in 1951, describes the performance as a hereditary affair, handed down by parents to their children. The group, exclusive and clannish, would not permit anyone else to take part.[2] Children, on the other hand, who performed *The Lancaster Pace Egg Play*, were 'of the poorer classes ... dressed up in scraps of wall-paper, and any tawdry ornaments they could procure'.[3]

Material comes from widely scattered areas of Great Britain. A correspondent of *Notes and Queries* in 1916 observed boys pace-egging on Good Friday at Rochdale, and thought that more Pace Eggers could be seen there than anywhere else in the country.[4] Thiselton-Dyer quotes a pleasant rhyme from Cheshire, nearby:

> *Eggs, bacon, apples, or cheese,*
> *Bread or corn, if you please,*
> *Or any good thing that will make us merry.*[5]

The Opies wrote in 1959 that Easter preparations in the West Riding of Yorkshire and in the North of England culminate with the schoolboy Pace Egg Play.[6] Up in Scotland, on the island of Islay (Argyll), the custom dwindled to a simple demand for eggs. Boys at one time called round the houses on Easter Sunday, begging eggs for their *Dòmhnach Càisg*, the Easter Sunday feast. They were seldom refused, and most people gave more than one, so that they built up a big supply.[7]

Children with wooden clappers must have been very tiresome; they were common in Wales. This was called '*clepian wyau*' in Anglesey, and '*clepio wyau'r pasg*' in Caernarvonshire. They sang:

[1] Information kindly supplied by Miss Margaret Musgrove. See also *Folk-Lore*, xlix (London, 1938), 36–46, for a version of the Pace Eggers play. *English Ritual Drama* (see page 368, above) details places of performance in Westmorland.

[2] Danielli, Mary, 'Jolly Boys or Pace Eggers in Westmorland', *Folk-Lore*, lxii (London, 1951), 463.

[3] Helm, Alex, ed., *Five Mumming Plays for Schools*, London, 1965, 37.

[4] *Notes and Queries*, 1 July 1916, 12th Series, ii.12.

[5] Thiselton-Dyer, T. F., *British Popular Customs*, London, 1876, 169.

[6] Opie, Iona and Peter, *The Lore and Language of Schoolchildren*, Oxford, 1959, 251.

[7] Banks, M. Macleod, *British Calendar Customs: Scotland*, London, 1937, i.41.

Clap, clap gofyn ŵy
i hogia' bach ar y plwy.

('Clap, clap, ask for an egg for little boys on the parish.') But quite often the wooden clappers made such a noise that the rhyme was omitted, and it is not surprising that unfriendly housewives sometimes replied: *''Dydi'r gath ddim wedi dodwy eto'* – 'The cat hasn't laid yet' – and sent them away empty-handed. Children in Y Brython sometimes collected as many as 200 eggs in the course of Holy Week. Then the dishes were removed from the kitchen dresser, and those of the eldest child put on the top shelf, those of the second on the second, and so on.[1]

Moving southwards, one finds the same custom in the Channel Islands. Old people interviewed in Guernsey in the middle of the last century remembered children begging for eggs, and they called it *'demander la mouissole'* – *mouissole* from the old Norman *mouisson*, meaning 'a bird'.[2]

On the continent of Europe – and especially in the Germanic area and surrounding countries – collecting eggs has been popular, though there are seldom indications of costume or any dramatic performance. As in Wales, it seems to have been a noisy affair. But generally the rattles which were used were operated for a special purpose. They announced the times of services in church during the period when, in Catholic lands, church bells do not ring until Easter Day.

These rattle-boys were known as *'klepperaars'* in Belgium; and in Arlon, where they call the rattles *'klekken'*, they tour the streets at 7 a.m., noon and 7 p.m. Each one is wooden – with a handle, surmounted by a horizontal surface, on which a movable hammer strikes, going from left to right. In Germany clapper-boys operated the *Ratschen* and eggs were given as a reward. People were generous, and whole clothes' baskets might be filled with eggs.[3]

Occasionally a secular element crept in. An old farm-worker from Pankow (Berlin) remembered that the group was led by a man with a chain wrapped round his waist. He carried a drum,

---

[1] Opie, 252. Owen, Trefor M., *Welsh Folk Customs*, Cardiff, 1959, 86.

[2] MacCulloch, Edgar, *Guernsey Folklore*, London, 1903, 46.

[3] Pieters, Jules, 'Œufs de Pâques en Belgique', *Schweizerisches Archiv für Volkskunde*, LIII (Basle, 1957), ii–iii.122. Cruickshank, Constance, *Lenten Fare and Food for Fridays*, London, 1959, 80.

and his companion, who was hung with bells, played on the accordion.[1] I myself saw an identical couple eking out a pathetic existence as street entertainers in East Berlin in 1962. Caught behind the Wall when it was constructed in 1961, they were trying to amuse holiday crowds during May Day celebrations.

Clappers were not always used. At Louvain, in Brabant, boys knocked on the shutters and doors on Holy Saturday night, calling out, *"T is Pasen"* (It is Easter). In western Flanders, they sang a verse:

> *Lent is over,*
> *Kyrie Eleison.*
> *At Easter we shall eat eggs*
> *And so Lent will be forgotten,*
> *Kyrie Eleison.*[2]

Children in Picardy, who recited the times of the services, knew a pretty rhyme:

> *Good women, who to God would fare,*
> *Bring us each of eggs a pair,*
> *A good ham too, for a gift this day*
> *Makes sure, good women, that your hens will lay.*
> *And you'll go straight to your heavenly rest*
> *As the hen herself goes straight for the nest.*[3]

A less demanding version runs:

> *Eggs for the little children, pray!*
> *Four for me and eight for my pal –*
> *And you'll go straight to Eternal Day*
> *As a stone to the bottom of the well.*[4]

And another:

> *I've a little cock in my basket;*
> *It'll sing for you if you ask it*
> *With eggs red and white. Alleluia!*[5]

In Savoyard villages young men used to sing the Passion on

---

[1] Information kindly supplied by Herr Karl-Heinz Vick.

[2] Pieters, 122.

[3] Robson, E. I., *A Guide to French Fêtes*, London, 1930, 77. Watts, Alan W., *Easter, Its Story and Meaning*, New York, 1950, 113.

[4] *Ibid.*

[5] *Ibid.*

the evening of Holy Saturday. Any eggs they were given were eaten with green salad the following day. Sometimes they were all pooled for a great feast at a neighbouring café. The words they sang varied, often containing a veiled threat in case the treat was withheld, and occasionally were semi-mystical:

> *Donnez un œuf à ces petits*
> *Qui vous diront trois mots De Profundis*
> *Qui vous mèn'ront en Paradis.*[1]

(Give an egg to these little ones, who tell you three words from the depths, which will lead you to Paradise.)

At times the custom must have been a great public nuisance. In the Thônes Valley (Savoy) young men sang all night with a violin in front of the houses. This was done, not once, but on the first three or four nights of Holy Week:

> *Réveille-toi, peuple endormi*
> *Sors de ton lit, prends tes habits*
> *Apportez des œufs dans nos paniers*
> *S'il y a des filles à marier*
> *Nous vous prions des vous lever*
> *Apportez des œufs dans nos paniers.*[2]

(Wake up, sleeping people, leave your beds, dress, bring eggs for our baskets. If there are marriageable girls, we beg you to get up and bring eggs for our baskets.) Some of these eggs were sold to pay for wine, which was drunk later on; others were kept and used to make an omelette. In France, quite often on such occasions, an enormous omelette was made, symbolizing, according to van Gennep, fertility, many children, and a rich profusion of crops. It might contain as many as 100 eggs.[3]

Conscripts at Romain de Jalionas preferred a different delicacy. Instead of making an omelette, they visited the farms, begging eggs and fat to make *coques* (what we would call 'French toast') – slices of bread soaked in beaten egg and fried.[4] Young men in Alsace asked the girls for eggs. This was thought to be a

---

[1] Information kindly supplied by M. Jacques Picot of Paris.
[2] *Ibid.*
[3] Van Gennep, *Manuel*, 1.iii.1,281. *Ibid.*, *Le Folklore du Dauphiné*, Paris, 1932, 1.242.
[4] *Ibid.*, 69.

compliment, and people laughed at a girl who was ignored. She would have to hatch her own eggs, they said.[1]

Throughout France at one time it was customary for anyone with a certain profession – a shepherd, miller, or sweep – to go out pace-egging. They called on their customers, who could not very well refuse them.[2] In most countries where this was practised pace-eggers formed a specific class or age group. In Sweden, on the other hand, it was usually the poor who begged for eggs at Easter-time, though young people dressed in costume also liked to do so.[3] In Belgium, the Netherlands and Denmark children sang for eggs at the farmyard gate. The Danes called it *'synge for aeg'*.[4]

At Denekemp in the eastern Netherlands a boy – representing Judas – leads the group collecting eggs on Palm Sunday. His helper, Krioter, probably a distortion of Iscariot, assists him in looking after the Easter fire. The eggs they receive are sold to buy wood for this, and any surplus is spent on raisin bread. Later a blaze is kindled on Easter Mountain and the children play there with coloured eggs.[5]

Once the sexton, teacher's wife and priest's servant all received a share. Indeed, it was not unusual for members of the church staff, like the sacristan, to go pace-egging: again it is difficult not to see a connection here with the ancient egg tithes, when such people used to come collecting them. Boys gathering, not for the monasteries, but for themselves, are recorded in Bavaria as early as the seventeenth century: in 1619 the St Veit Monastery gave four crowns to 'Boys who sang for eggs'.[6]

A few days before Easter, boys in southern Holland went out carrying a basket for eggs, and armed with a supply of bread and pancakes. Their song stresses the thought found in the Dutch *eiertikken*, that several eggs are needed to make an Easter egg:

> *Little wife, do your best,*
> *Take the eggs from the nest*
> *Of the white hens.*
> *God can tell them*
> *From the white and the black.*
> *Give some from each little hen.*

[1] *Ibid., Manuel*, 1.iii.1,274.   [2] *Ibid.*, 1,273, 1,292.
[3] Eskeröd, 11.   [4] Uldall, 4.
[5] Meertens, 126–7.   [6] Moser, 80.

One egg is no egg;
The second is half an egg;
The third is an egg;
The fourth is an Easter egg.[1]

The play on numbers is to persuade the housewife to give as many eggs as possible. If none was produced, a much ruder song was sung, and windows and doors bumped with sticks and stones. Afterwards the spoils were divided out. On the island of Sylt (north Friesland) they used a similar rhyme, though these children were a little less demanding:

Hans Ajen ging me Trummer om Biin,
Hans Ajen seid' : Guddei!
Jen Puaskei es nönt,
Tau es wat,
Tri es en hiile Puaskei.[2]

(I have an egg decked on its shell with bunting. I have an egg says, 'Good Morning.' One paste-egg is nothing, two are a bit, three are a whole paste-egg.) Coloured strands used to decorate the eggs were saved from left-over pieces, gathered up by the children when their mothers were weaving material for the colourful Frisian costumes. On Föhr, south of Sylt, at the end of the last century, children were still collecting coloured eggs and cakes on Easter morning, going from house to house, but without singing.[3]

CONCLUSION

Performances of the kind just described, if they survive, may continue to exist as curiosities or tourist attractions. For those who do not object to the commercialization of these old traditions, there is already a rather sophisticated – and certainly very attractive – version of a pace-egging song from Heysham (Lancashire) in a recording by a Yorkshire vocal group.[4] Where the thought behind such folk-practices has long been lost, the superficial externals can at least be given permanence in this way, and, since

[1] Information kindly supplied by Henk Arends from the *Folkloristisch Woordenboek*.
[2] Jensen, Christian, *Die Nordfriesischen Inseln*, Lübeck, 1927, 445.
[3] *Ibid.*
[4] The Watersons on a gramophone record entitled 'Frost and Fire'.

we are now often left with nothing better, we can, up to a point, try to deduce what went before. In collecting together between one cover a proportion of the material available on egg customs and beliefs, I have put forward various suggestions as to the basic ideas contained in them, but I hope that others will elaborate on what I have done.

In conclusion, I want to stress the value of a comparative study of the symbols used by mankind at different times and in different places. Symbols are an important manner of expression, and at their best put forward ideas of considerable profundity. Early, unsophisticated man lacked verbal means of setting out his more esoteric thoughts, which we have developed – nor need his methods be outmoded. The current confidence in our own articulacy, which in fact usually obtains on a very superficial level, leads to the error that humanity on its own is capable of grasping the truths of existence. Hence the tendency towards secularization and the increasing arrogance of mankind. The intervention of symbols helps make it clear that mysteries exist which are hard for us to express and to comprehend. Once that inevitable truth is grasped, man cannot be other than humble.

One could cite many interesting examples of how, in the current phase of humanism run wild, old symbols and customs are actually perverted to serve the new outlook – something which has certainly also occurred in the past, but not in the context of the absolute break we now have with former values. It is perhaps here that the greatest danger in popularizing folklore can lie. We are presented with a misinterpretation of these ancient modes of behaviour as mere expressions of humanism, and in this way it is sought to show, misleadingly, that the new outlook does not lack roots, but is an essential human characteristic.

Where the real idea behind the old-established symbols is out of keeping with current dogma, the meaning is simply twisted beyond recognition; ikons in Russia are described as 'Moving beyond the realm of cold, Christian portraiture, towards humanism'. The treatment of the Cross is also a good case in point. Atheists like to dismiss it as a revolting emblem, an instrument of torture; separating it from Our Saviour, they ignore its role as a daily reminder not only of His Passion, but of our sinfulness.

This being so, it is not surprising to find the communists equipped with a 'humanized' version of the same symbol. For this must surely be the origin of their hammer and sickle, especially since, as originally drawn, it was dominated by a sword,[1] and would have been still closer to the Orthodox cross than in the present version. Lenin apparently thought a warlike weapon might create a poor impression and ordered its removal. Curiously, in the original portrayal of the hammer-and-sickle motif, painted by a well-known Belgian pacifist named Wiertz in 1855,[2] they are held aloft by a girl and a youth, while a sword slips out of his hand.

Lenin, or one of his associates, must have seen the painting in Brussels, and had it adapted into the cross-like emblem we now know. The humanist aspect of the symbol is again underlined in the variant erected by the Russians at the Paris Exhibition in 1936, and now to be seen in Moscow. In this, two gigantic, heroic figures advance, brandishing these weapons of man's determination to subdue the universe.

The Easter token, the egg, has not, as far as I am aware, been debased into an appendage of any of the modern pseudo-philosophies. It is true that, in the Lausitz in east Germany, the local crafts in general, and perhaps Easter egg customs foremost amongst them, are kept going for political reasons to stress the old Slav connections of the region. From Nazi Germany, too, there is a distasteful picture in a Party publication, showing children decorating a May tree with traditional items, and also with anti-Semitic paraphernalia; presumably egg trees suffered in the same way.

From the humanist point of view the, for them insignificant, egg as an emblem of creation and life is probably not appealing, since it does nothing to inflate the dignity of man – quite the opposite. It is worth noting that most of the traditions encouraged in the Soviet Union are those in which the people play an active part. Man's function within his environment must be stressed, since he is – or will become – master of it. An egg, on the contrary, expresses concretely the manner in which it is simple to grasp how things happen, yet why they do so remains unknown – an idea quite unacceptable to modern politico-scientific dogma.

Evolutionism in itself, though no longer subject to doubt,

[1] *Soviet Weekly*, 7 January 1967. Reply to a reader's inquiry.

[2] I am indebted to Andrew Rothstein for kindly drawing my attention to this.

fails to solve this problem, and attempts to propound a dialectical pattern of development do not hold their own. This method of thought is not exclusive to the sophisticated. A paper by Annie Lebeuf, 'Le Système Classificatoire des Fali',[1] shows something of the same in a primitive symbolic form. Since a portion relates to eggs, the context is of interest. The Fali are a tribe of north Cameroon who see the development of the universe in opposition and alternation, primarily a classification of beings and things. In the first place, the male egg of a tortoise, representing terrestrial animals, and the female egg of a toad, representing aquatic animals, revolved in opposite directions in the eastern and western parts of the hemisphere. This rhythm in double time, intended to throw into relief the significant contrasts of the universe, is succeeded by the development of the centre. Te Dino, the first man – owing his origin, one presumes, to the tortoise as earthly creator – is saved from the Flood by the aquatic toad. At this privileged point – seen as a moment of synthesis – the beginnings of life will be concentrated, and from it they will spread out, organizing themselves into hierarchical order.

One can see how such ideas, fascinating as a real expression of the untutored mind, could be bowdlerized to fit in with dialectical materialism. The Communist Chinese have been peculiarly adept at bringing old beliefs into line with the New Order, though Hitler made use of Wagner in the same way. Mao's famous dictum, 'The east wind will prevail over the west wind', and the anthem of the Cultural Revolution, 'The East is Red', no doubt both derive from the ancient Chinese theory that the East is the birthplace of life.[2] It is well known, too, that Chinese 'advisers' in the Congo made a show of providing native Simbas with an enchantment against bullets. Even eggs might have been useful, for among the Cewa tribe, who inhabit an area east of the Livingstone Memorial, an egg wrapped in black cloth is buried at a doorway to repel intruders; this will cause the house to appear doorless and in darkness, like the talisman.[3]

At the 1967 Conference of the International Folk Music

[1] Published in *African Systems of Thought*, ed. Fortes, M. and Dieterlen, G., London, 1965, 329–30.

[2] Giles, Herbert A., *Confucianism and Its Rivals*, London, 1915, 122.

[3] Mitchell, J. Clyde, 'The Meaning of Misfortune for Urban Africans', in *African Systems of Thought*, 195. See note 1, above.

Council, Dr Hoerburger[1] spoke of the distinction to be drawn between folk-practices as wholly belonging to the innermost life of the people, or as something adopted or imposed for some understood or ulterior reason. This he categorized as the first and second existences of the custom. In treating eggs, I have not confined myself to the first existence – my final chapters on games are an obvious exception, where the ulterior motive nowadays is fun. This study also deals with art eggs and the egg as an abstruse philosophical symbol. With eggs it is not difficult to draw the line between the symbol in its first and second existences. But in concluding I have tried to suggest yet another type of experience – possibly it could be called the third existence – where the custom is still accepted at face value by the participants, but receives its direction from a subtle psychological approach on political, or sometimes commercial, grounds.

---

[1] Dr Felix Hoerburger of the Institute for Musical Studies, Regensburg. Dr Hoerburger has elaborated elsewhere a more detailed scheme of ethnomusicological classification.

Appendix 1: Egg-colouring Substances

The following is a list, not intended to be exhaustive, of some egg-colouring substances used in certain countries.

ALSACE
red   carrot.

BOSNIA
In villages near Zepče strands of different-coloured thread are wrapped around the eggs; cooking enables the colour to come out in geometrical patterns. Around Bugojno plum root, ash root, cherry bark, walnut husks, a grass called *broč* and soot are used.

BRITISH ISLES
red   cochineal.
yellow   furze and gorse flowers (including the Isle of Man), whin (Scotland and Ulster).
green   spinach and leaves of the pasque flower, a purple anemone, so called because it blooms at Easter-time.
purple   log wood, beetroot (Scotland).

CZECHOSLOVAKIA
red   crushed, burnt brick-dust soaked in water.
yellow   ears of grain, crocus, apple rind.
green   boiled hay, young grass or young alder bark.
brown   plum skins, red onions.
black   old alder bark, coffee essence, rusty iron boiled in cabbage water.
A few drops of vinegar might be added to make the colours adhere better.

DENMARK

red   carrot.
yellow   narcissus, onion.
brown   coffee grounds.

In north Seeland dye and butter are put on scraps of linen and secured to the egg, producing a multi-coloured effect.

ESTONIA

green   young sweet-corn, rye.

FRANCE

red   carrot, madder wort.
pink   radish peel.
yellow   marigold, mignonette, starwort.
green   artichoke leaves.
mauve   beetroot.
purple   anemone.
brown   coffee grounds.

GERMANY

red   crushed red clay, boiled teak-wood shavings; in the eighteenth century, brazil.
yellow   crab apple bark, young wheat, caraway seeds.
green   grass, spinach juice, rye, winter corn; in the eighteenth century, gentian flowers with alum, dark red poplar flowers.
brown   young oak bark, coffee, bark of plum tree.
black   alder twigs.

These colourings, other than those from the eighteenth century, are in fact used by the Sorbs in Lausitz. No doubt German villages use much the same method, though commercially-produced dyes are available in special Easter packs in most shops. One interesting method still in use at a Mennonite village in the Pfalz is a rusty nail soaked in whey, producing a rich brown colour (see colour plate XIX).

HOLLAND

red   red cabbage.
green   rye, spinach.
brown   coffee grounds.

HUNGARY

yellow   cow's whey mixed with alum, wolf's milk boiled in water, crab apple bark, saffron.

green   hemlock.

black   gall nuts.

Before starting work, Hungarians mixed dyes with vinegar and alum to make them last longer, and sometimes did not even place the egg in the colouring, but applied it by hand.

ITALY

green   sage.

LATVIA

Bits of coloured yarn or cloth are bound around the eggs before boiling.

LITHUANIA

yellow   hay.

green   small, tender birch leaves.

grey   old oak bark.

MACEDONIA (Yugoslav)

red   roots of *Rubia tinctorum*, soaked overnight, boiled and alum added.

yellow   euphorbia petals, boiled with ash; leaves of *Lycium halimfolium*; roots of *Arum maculatum*. Alum keeps the colour fast.

PENNSYLVANIA DUTCH

red   madder root, called *grabb*, provides a pale shade of this colour.

yellow   alder catkins, called *alla hecka schwens* and the local hickory bark.

green   shoots of young sweet-corn.

brown   coffee grounds, walnut shells.

Scraps of coloured calico are also fastened to the shell before boiling in soap lye – *saifa lawk* – to bring the colour out.

POLAND

orange   crocuses.

green   moss.

black   alder bark, fresh plane tree leaves.

PORTUGAL

yellow   gorse.

green   mint, ivy leaves.

mauve   fleur-de-lys.

RUMANIA
red   marjoram, St John's Wort, logwood.
yellow   wild apple leaves.
green   unripe sunflower seeds, leaves of the pasque flower, meadow saffron, nettles.
blue   cornflower mixed with alum.
black   shells of nuts.

SLOVENIA
yellow   saffron.
grey-red   young alder bark, cherry bark.
black   oak bark.

SWEDEN
The philologist Johan Ihre refers to egg colouring in his *Glossarium Sviogothicum* (1769) but provides no details of materials used.

UKRAINE
red   logwood.
yellow   apple tree bark, mistletoe leaves, aspen and dried flowers of the woadwaxen picked before the Feast of St John (7 July, Orthodox style).
green   sprouting rye, wheat.
violet   sunflower seeds, elderberry fruit and bark.
black   old walnuts, oak bark.

Onion peel is almost universally used to obtain shades from yellow through red to dark brown.

The custom of preparing Easter eggs with water or oil colour paints is now too widespread to need description, and local or topical designs often appear. Indian Christians, for example, prepare eggs in this way, using local motifs. Especially beautiful painted examples in my own collection show floral patterns (from Czechoslovakia) and the Paschal Lamb or Christian fish (from the Convent of Eichstätt in Bavaria) (see colour plate X).

Appendix 2: The Goddess Eastre

In a book dealing with so central a feature of the Easter season, mention must be made of Eastre, the pagan goddess of spring. The hare, on grounds that are not clearly established, was said to be sacred to her. In fact, we know virtually nothing of this goddess. Eostre or Ostara, as she is variously called, is a mysterious, shadowy figure. Her cult was probably common to the West Germanic tribes, but no specific reference occurs, except in Anglo-Saxon literature: Bede, in his *De Temporum Ratione*, in the eighth century, mentions her briefly, but only to say that April was then named after her: '*Veteres Anglicani populi vocant Estormonath paschalem mensem, idque a dea quadem cui Teutonici populi in paganismo sacrificia fecerunt tempore mensis Aprilis, quae Eostra est appellata.*'[1]

Dr Robert Wildhaber, the Swiss authority on Easter lore, believes that no connection between this goddess and the spring festival, with its eggs, has been satisfactorily established.[2] According to Hermann Paul,[3] the ancient and rather obscure German spring goddess Austrô is probably Eostre, known through the *Ostermonat*: Old High German, *Ôstarmanoth*; Anglo-Saxon, *Éosturmónath*. *Ôstarmanoth* is found in Eginhart, a contemporary of Charlemagne.[4] Some authorities, discussing the origins of the word 'Easter', believe that Bede invented it.[5] This seems unlikely.

[1] Grimm, Jacob, *Teutonic Mythology*, London 1883, i.289, note 1.

[2] Wildhaber, Robert, *Wir färben Ostereier*, Berne, 1957, 1.

[3] Paul, Hermann, *Grundriss der Germanischen Philologie*, Strasbourg, 1891, i. 1,111.

[4] Grimm, i.290.

[5] Helm, K., *Altgermanische Religionsgeschichte*, Heidelberg, 1914, ii.ii.277ff.

Bede, who regarded paganism as a sin, would not have invented a heathen goddess in order to explain the name of the month of Easter.[1] In any case, there are calendar references to the Easter period in Germany which are virtually contemporary with Bede. Friedrich Kluge infers certain facts from the writings of Wulfila (*c*. 311–83), Bishop of the West Goths, founder of German-Arian Christianity and the most important source of the early Gothic language. Wulfila's writings date from the latter part of his life (*c*. 369 onwards), and he did not use the name of the pagan goddess for Easter. However, Kluge points out that, while Wulfila uses *paska*, and not *austrôns*, at approximately his period, or soon afterwards, the name of the heathen spring celebration of the goddess Austrô could well have given rise to a Germanized naming of the Christian festival among his people. In the Main district during the eighth and ninth centuries the expression '*ôstarstuopha*' came into use in court circles instead of Latin terminology. It denoted a seasonal tribute to the king, and suggests an even earlier popular use of the word in connection with the calendar.[2]

The name Eostre seems to be connected with the Indian *usrâ*, meaning 'dawn', and the Latin Aurora, Roman goddess of the dawn.[3] Austri, in the *Edda*, is a spirit of light, a male being; as Grimm says, a female equivalent might have been called Austra.[4] Paul points out that here there is a connection between *Oster* and the Indo-German root-words for 'dawn', e.g. Old Indian, *usás*; Lithuanian, *ausra*; Middle Indo-German, *ausos*; Greek, *eos*; Latin, *aurora* (from *ausos-a*);[5] on this basis he postulates that she must have been a goddess of the dawn from time immemorial. This being so, the words *Ost*, East, etc., could derive originally from the goddess. In Old High German the adverb *ostar* did in fact express movement towards the rising sun, and similarly the Old Norse *austr*.[6] Kluge's dictionary supports the derivation of *Ost* from the ancient word for 'dawn', which presumably referred to the dawn goddess.[7] Other scholars endorse this view. Feldmann

[1] Stenton, F. M., *Anglo-Saxon England*, Oxford, 1943, 98.

[2] Kluge, Friedrich, *Deutsche Sprachgeschichte*, Leipzig, 1925, 189.

[3] *Ibid*. and Götze, Alfred, *Etymologisches Wörterbuch der deutsche Sprache*, 1st edition, 1881; republished Berlin, 1951, 541.

[4] Grimm, i.291.   [5] Paul, i.1,111.

[6] Grimm, i.291.   [7] Kluge and Götze, 541.

suggests the specific Old High German meaning 'to the east' for *ostara*,[1] and Max Gottschald explains *Ost* (Old High German *Ostan*) as follows: 'Mythological meaning: sunrise, spring (among the Anglo-Saxons a Spring Goddess, *Eostre*).'[2]

Aurora, Latin for Eos, the Greek personification of the dawn, was a purely mythological figure, not a goddess with a cult. Hesiod tells us she was the daughter of the Titan Hyperion and Theia, and mother of the winds Zephyrus, Notus and Boreas, of Hesperus and the stars. Homer represents her as rising each morning from the couch of Tithonus, drawn out of the east in a chariot, bringing light to gods and to mankind. He calls her 'rosy-fingered'. Aurora was also the paramour of the hunter Orion, and represented the constellation that disappears at the flush of dawn; by the hunter Cephalus she was the mother of Phaeton. In art Eos is traditionally represented as a young woman, walking rapidly, with a youth in her arms; sometimes she rises from the sea in a chariot drawn by winged horses; sometimes, as the goddess who disperses the dews of the morning, she has a pitcher in each hand. In Latin works – Virgil, for example – *Aurora* was used to signify the east.[3]

In Hindu mythology the dawn is *Ushas*, daughter of Heaven and sister of the Adityas. The friend of men, she visits every household, no matter how lowly. Smiling and bringing wealth, she is herself unchanging and immortal, but causes men to grow old. Max Müller points out that all this may be purely allegorical language, but he also postulates a possible link between dawn and the Sanskrit word for bright:

> In the *Veda* the gods are called Deva. This word in Sanskrit means bright—brightness or light being one of the most general attributes shared by the various manifestations of the Deity, invoked in the *Veda*, as Sun, or Sky, or Fire, or Dawn, or Storm. We can see, in fact, how in the minds of the poets of the *Veda*, *deva*, from meaning 'bright', came gradually to mean 'divine'.[4]

[1] Feldmann, Joseph, *Ortsnamen*, Halle, 1925, 74.

[2] Gottschald, Max, *Deutsche Namenkunde*, Berlin, 1954, 457.

[3] *Encyclopaedia Britannica*, London, 1963, ii.767–8.

[4] Müller, F. Max, *Chips from a German Workshop*, London, 1867, i.25.

A List of Books Cited and Consulted

I HISTORY, TOPOGRAPHY AND ARCHAEOLOGY

Ainsztein, Reuben, 'The Jewish Background of Karl Marx', *Jewish Observer and Middle East Review*, London, 23 October 1964.

Alexandrov, Victor, *The Tukhachevsky Affair*, London, 1963.

Blackman, Winifred, *The Fellahin of Upper Egypt*, London, 1927.

Boulanger, Robert, *Turkey*, Paris, 1960.

Canziani, Estella, *Through the Apennines and the Lands of the Abruzzi*, Cambridge, 1928.

Cles-Reden, S. V., *The Realm of the Great Goddess*, London, 1961.

Complete Atlas of the British Isles, London, 1965.

Craine, David, *Manannan's Isle*, Douglas, 1955.

Daiken, Leslie, *Children's Toys Throughout the Ages*, London, 1953.

Dalton, O. M., *A Guide to the Early Christian and Byzantine Antiquities*, London, 1903.

Doolittle, Justus, *Social Life of the Chinese*, London, 1866, 2 vols.

Durham, M. E., *Through the Lands of the Serb*, London, 1904.

Eterovich, F. H., and Spalatin, Christopher, *Croatia: Land, People and Culture*, Toronto, 1964, 2 vols.

Frazer, Sir James G., *Pausanias's Description of Greece*, London, 1913, vol. 3.

Goff, A., and Fawcett, H. A., *Macedonia*, London, 1921.

Gordon Childe, V., *Skara Brae*, Edinburgh, 1950.

Gray, J. H., *China*, London, 1878, 2 vols.

Grimm, Jacob and Wilhelm, *Deutsches Wörterbuch*, Leipzig, 1860, vol. 2.

Hakluyt, Richard, *The Principal Navigations, Voyages, Traffiques and Discoveries of the English Nation*, Glasgow, 1903, vol. 2.

Hamelius, P., ed., *Mandeville's Travels*, London, 1919.

Hand, Wayland, *A Dictionary of Words and Idioms Associated with Judas Iscariot*, Berkeley, 1942.

Hartley, Dorothy, *Food in England*, London, 1954.

Heslop, Oliver, *Northumberland Words*, London, 1892, vol. 1.

Hodson, T. C., *The Meitheis*, London, 1908.

Holt, Edgar, *Protest in Arms*, London, 1960.

Jensen, Christian, *Die Nordfriesischen Inseln*, Lübeck, 1927.

Jourville, John de, *Life of St Louis*, tr. R. Hague, London, 1955.

Kavadias, G. B., *Pasteurs-Nomades Méditerranéens: Les Saracatsans de Grèce*, Paris, 1965.

Kohl, J. G., *Russia and the Russians in 1842*, London, 1843, 2 vols.

König, Wolfhilde von, 'Die Ausrufer', *Die Waage*, Stolberg, January 1966, vol. 5.

Korea, Its Land, People and Culture of All Ages, Seoul, 1963.

Krünitz, J. G., *Economic Encyclopaedia*, 1777.

Lane, E. W., *Arabian Society in the Middle Ages*, London, 1883.

Lethbridge, T. C., 'Recent Excavations in Anglo-Saxon Cemeteries in Cambridgeshire and Suffolk', *Cambridge Antiquarian Society*, Cambridge, 1931, Quarto Publications, New Series, No. 3.

Lewis, Reba, *Indonesia, Troubled Paradise*, London, 1962.

Lietuwin Enciklopediga, Boston, 1959, vol. 12.

Lofthouse, Jessica, *Portrait of Lancashire*, London, 1967.

Mackenzie, G. Muir, and Irby, A. P., *Travels in the Slavonic Provinces of Turkey-in-Europe*, London, 1867, 2 vols.

Maser, Werner, *Die Frühgeschichte der NSDAP*, Frankfurt-am-Main, 1965.

Mode, Heinz and Wölffling, Siegfried, *Zigeuner*, Leipzig, 1968.

Muller, J., *Rheinisches Wörterbuch*, Berlin, 1928, vol. 3.

Needham, Joseph, *A History of Embryology*, Cambridge, 1934.

Oxenstierna, Eric, *Die Wikinger*, Stuttgart, 1959.

Rawlinson, George, tr., *The History of Herodotus*, London, 1910, vol. 1.

Romanelli, Guido, 'Bela Kun', *Encyclopaedia Britannica*, London, 14th Ed. 1929, vol. 13.

Roucek, Joseph L., ed., *Slavonic Encyclopaedia*, New York, 1949.

St Clair, S. G. B., *A Residence in Bulgaria*, London, 1869.

Salisbury, Jesse, *A Glossary of Words and Phrases used in S.E. Worcestershire*, London, 1893.

Schlagintweit, Emil, *Indien in Wort und Bild*, Leipzig, 1880, vol. 1.

Scofield, John, 'Freedom Speaks French in Ouagadougou', *National Geographic*, Washington, August 1966.

Sommer, Fedor, *Die Geschichte Schlesiens*, Breslau, 1908.

Stefánsson, Vilhjálmur, 'The Stefánsson–Anderson Arctic Expedition', *Anthropological Papers of the Museum of Natural History*, New York, 1919, vol. 14.

Stenton, F. M., *Anglo-Saxon England*, Oxford, 1943.

Stratilesco, T., *From Carpathian to Pindus*, Boston, 1907.
Talbot Rice, Tamara, *Everyday Life in Byzantium*, London, 1967.
Thomson, W. P. L., *Islands of the North*, Lerwick, n.d.
Williamson, Kenneth, *The Atlantic Islands: a Study of the Faroe Life and Scene*, London, 1948.
Wilson, C. T., *Peasant Life in the Holy Land*, London, 1906.
Wissowa, Georg, *Paulys Real Encyclopädie der classischen Altertums-wissenschaft*, Stuttgart, 1942, vol. 18A.
Wyon, Reginald, *The Balkans from Within*, London, 1904.

II LITERATURE AND THE ARTS

Bainbridge, Henry C., *Peter Carl Fabergé*, London, 1949.
Baxter, J. H., *St Augustine: Select Letters*, London, 1930.
Borrow, George, *An Account of the Gypsies of Spain*, London, 1893.
Bossert, H., *Peasant Art in Europe*, London, 1927.
Brown, Alec, ed., *Essays on National Art in Yugoslavia*, London, 1944.
Cawte, E. C., Helm, Alex and Peacock, N., *English Ritual Drama*, London, 1967.
Chambers, E. K., *The English Folk-Play*, Oxford, 1933.
—— *The Mediaeval Stage*, Oxford, 1903, 2 vols.
Christie, Manson and Woods, *Catalogue of a Collection of Objets d'Art*, London, 1934.
Cicero, *Orations*, London, 1852, vol. 3.
Dearmer, Percy, ed., *The Oxford Book of Carols*, Oxford, 1928.
Descargues, Pierre, 'Chefs d'Œuvre à Partir d'un Œuf', *Connaissance des Arts*, Paris, April 1967, No. 182.
Dickens, Charles, *David Copperfield*, London, 1870, 2 vols.
Dmytrikw, Olga, *Ukrainian Arts*, New York, 1955.
Evans, E. P., *Animal Symbolism in Ecclesiastical Architecture*, London, 1896.
Fasold, Hans, *Bunte Ostereier*, Freiburg, 1966.
Feldmann, Joseph, *Ortsnamen*, Halle, 1925.
Ferguson, George, *Signs and Symbols in Christian Art*, New York, 1961.
Gavazzi, Milovan, 'Svastika i Njezin Ornamentalni Razvoj Na Uskrsnim Jajima Sa Balkana', *Zbornik Za Narodni Život i Običaje Južnih Slavena*, Zagreb, 1929, vol. 27, No. 1.
Gimbutas, Marija, *Ancient Symbolism in Lithuanian Folk Art*, Philadelphia, 1958.
Glover, A. S. B., ed., *Shelley*, London, 1951.
Goethe, Johann Wolfgang, *Wilhelm Meister's Apprenticeship and Travels*, tr. Carlyle, Thomas, London, 1874.
—— *Faust*, tr. Wayne, Philip, London, 1949.

Gorky, Maxim, *Childhood*, tr. Wettlin, Margaret, Moscow, n.d.

Gottschald, Max, *Deutsche Namenkunde*, Berlin, 1954.

Haggar, Reginald G., *The Concise Encyclopaedia of Continental Pottery and Porcelain*, London, 1960.

Hahn, Konrad, *Deutsche Volkskunst*, Berlin, 1928.

Hain, Mathilde, 'Bemalte Ostereier in Hessen', *Schweizerisches Archiv für Volkskunde*, Basle, 1957, vol. 53.

Harwood, H. W., and Marsden, F. H., ed., *The Pace Egg: The Midgley Version*, Halifax, 1935.

Helm, Alex, *Chapbook Mummers' Plays, The*, Leicester, 1969.

—— ed., *Five Mumming Plays for Schools*, London, 1965.

Helm, K., *Altgermanische Religionsgeschichte*, Heidelberg, 1914, vol. 2.

Herringham, Christiana J., 'Notes on Oriental Carpet Patterns', *The Burlington Magazine*, London, October 1908–March 1909, vol. 14.

Hesiod, *Théogonie*, Paris, 1928.

Hobson, R. L., *A Guide to the Islamic Pottery of the Near East*, London, 1932.

Hofer, Tamás, *Hungarian Peasant Art*, Budapest, 1958.

Johnson, Samuel, *Diaries, Prayers and Annals*, New Haven, 1958.

Kluge, Friedrich, *Deutsche Sprachgeschichte*, Leipzig, 1925.

—— and Götze, Alfred, *Etymologisches Wörterbuch der deutsche Sprache*, 1st ed. 1881; republished, Berlin, 1951.

König, Wolfhilde von, 'Kostbare Ostereier', *Die Waage*, Stolberg, June 1964, vol. 3.

Lacey May, G., ed., *English Religious Verse*, London, 1937.

Lane, Edward W., ed. and tr., *Sindbad the Sailor*, London, 1896.

Lawrence, D. H., *Selected Poems*, London, 1950.

Lichten, Francis, *Folk Art of Rural Pennsylvania*, New York, 1946.

Lodge, Oliver, *Peasant Life in Yugoslavia*, London, 1941.

Magnusson, Magnus, and Pálsson, Hermann, tr., *Njal's Saga*, London, 1960.

Magoun, Francis, tr., *The Kalevala*, Cambridge, Mass., 1963.

Martin, F. R., 'The True Origin of So-called Damascus Ware', *The Burlington Magazine*, London, April–Sept. 1909, vol. 15.

Meiss, Millard, 'Addendum Ovologicum', *The Art Bulletin*, New York, 1954.

—— 'Ovum Struthionis, Symbol and Allusion in Piero della Francesca's Montefeltro Altarpiece', *Studies in Art and Literature for Belle da Costa Greene*, Princeton, 1954.

Migeon, Gaston, and Sakisian, Arméneg, *La Ceramique d'Asie-Mineure et de Constantinople*, Paris, 1923.

Milton, John, *Poetical Works*, Oxford, 1922.

Morley, Henry, ed., *Thoms' Early Prose Romances*, London, 1889.

Oprescu, George, *Peasant Art in Roumania*, London, 1929.

Owen, Elias, *Old Stone Crosses of the Vale of Clwyd*, London, 1886.

Paul, Hermann, *Grundriss der Germanischen Philologie*, Strasbourg, 1891, vol. 1.

Pliny, *Natural History*, ed. Bostock, John, London, 1856–7, vols. 5, 6.

Rackham, Bernard, *Islamic Pottery and Italian Maiolica*, London, 1959.

Ridgeway, William, *The Dramas and Dramatic Dances of Non-European Races*, Cambridge, 1915.

Roberts, Michael, ed., *The Faber Book of Modern Verse*, London, 1936.

Rogers, Benjamin B., ed., '*The Birds*' *of Aristophanes*, London, 1906.

Rowland, Benjamin, 'The World's Image in Indian Architecture', *Journal of the Royal Society of Arts*, London, June 1964.

Scott, Sir Walter, *Minstrelsy of the Scottish Border*, Kelso, 1802–3, vols. 2 and 3.

Skeat, Walter W., *A Concise Etymological Dictionary of the English Language*, Oxford, 1882.

Snowman, A. Kenneth, *The Art of Carl Fabergé*, London, 1953.

Šourek, Karel, *Folk Art in Pictures*, London, n.d.

Southey, Robert, *Poetical Works*, London, 1849, vol. 4.

Starr, Laura B., 'Decorated Ostrich Eggs', *Strand Magazine*, London, 1900, vol. 20.

Swift, Jonathan, *Gulliver's Travels*, Oxford, 1954.

Tennyson, Lord Alfred, *Works*, London, 1894.

Turner, J. Horsfall, ed., 'The Peace Egg Play', *Yorkshire Notes and Queries*, July 1887.

Tyack, George S., *The Cross in Ritual, Architecture and Art*, London, 1900.

Van Gennep, Arnold, *Les Arts Populaires et Decoratifs de Savoie*, Paris, 1927.

Watts, William, ed., *St Augustine's 'Confessions'*, London, 1919.

Whittick, Arnold, *Symbols for Designers*, London, 1935.

Wilson, Edward M., 'An Unpublished Version of the Pace Eggers Play', *Folk-Lore*, London, 1938, vol. 49.

Wollin, Nils G., *Äggkoppar, Äggstallase och Äggställ*, Stockholm, 1962.

Yershov, P. P., *Конёк-Горъунок*, St Petersburg, 1834.

III RELIGION

Addis, William, ed., *A Catholic Dictionary*, London, 1959.

Agrawala, Vasudeva S., *Sparks from the Vedic Fire*, Varanasi, 1962.

Arrowsmith, R., ed., *The Rig Veda*, Boston, 1886.

Astley, H. J. D., *Biblical Anthropology*, Oxford, 1929.

Aston, W. G., ed., *Nihongi*, London, 1896.

Attwater, Donald, *A Dictionary of Mary*, London, 1957.

Baring-Gould, S., *Legends of Old Testament Characters from the Talmud and Other Sources*, London, 1871.

Bassili, William, *Sinai and the Monastery of St Catherine*, Cairo, 1962.

Birnbaum, Philip, *High Holyday Prayer Book*, New York, 1951.

Brandon, S. G. F., *History, Time and Deity*, Manchester, 1965.

Brasch, R., *The Star of David*, London, 1955.

Bullock, James, *The Life of the Celtic Church*, Edinburgh, 1963.

Burggraff, Aloysius J., *Handbook for New Catholics*, Glen Rock, N.J., 1960.

Caudwell, Irene, *Ceremonies of Holy Church*, London, 1948.

Cruickshank, Constance, *Lenten Fare and Food for Fridays*, London, 1959.

Daniélou, Jean, *Primitive Christian Symbols*, London, 1964.

Davis, Charles, ed., *The Egyptian Book of the Dead*, New York, 1894.

Dawood, N. J., tr., *The Koran*, London, 1964.

Dragomanov, M. P., *Notes on the Slavic Religio-Ethical Legends*, Bloomington, 1961.

Drower, E. S., *Water into Wine*, London, 1956.

Eliade, Mircea, *Patterns in Comparative Religion*, London, 1958.

Fishman, Isidore, *Introduction to Judaism*, London, 1962.

Gardner, James, *The Faiths of the World*, Edinburgh, 1858, 2 vols.

Gaskell, G. A., *A Dictionary of the Sacred Language of All Scriptures and Myths*, London, 1923.

Gaster, Theodor H., *Festivals of the Jewish Year*, New York, 1952.

—— *Passover, Its History and Traditions*, New York, 1958.

Giles, Herbert A., *Confucianism and Its Rivals*, London, 1915.

Glasenapp, Helmuth von, *Non-Christian Religions*, New York, 1963.

Groot, J. J. M. de, *The Religious System of China*, Leiden, 1910, vol. 6.

Guthrie, W. K. C., *Orpheus and Greek Religion*, London, 1935.

Hamilton, Mary, *Greek Saints and Their Festivals*, London, 1910.

Harrison, J. E., *Prolegomena to the Study of Greek Religion*, Cambridge, 1903.

Hasluck, F. W., *Christianity and Islam under the Sultans*, Oxford, 1929.

—— *Letters on Religion and Folklore*, London, 1926.

Hastings, James, ed., *Encyclopaedia of Religion and Ethics*, Edinburgh, 1908–15, 12 vols.

Haughton, G. C., ed., *Mánava-Dherma-Sástra*, London, 1825.

Hershon, Paul Isaac, *Treasures of the Talmud*, London, 1882.

Hume, R. E., ed., *The Thirteen Principal Upanishads*, London, 1931.

Hymnal, The English, Oxford, 1906.

Idelsohn, Abraham Z., *The Ceremonies of Judaism*, New York, 1930.

Isaac, Paul, *Treasures of the Talmud*, London, 1882.

Jamieson, John, *An Historical Account of the Ancient Culdees of Iona*, Edinburgh, 1811.

Jewish Encyclopaedia, The, New York, 1903, vols. 4 and 5.
Joseph, Morris, *Judaism as Creed and Life*, London, 1920.
Kees, H., *Religionsgeschichtliches Lesebuch (Aegypten)*, Tübingen, 1928.
Kellett, E. E., *A Short History of Religions*, London, 1962.
Kraus, F. X., *Real-Encyklopädie der christlichen Alterthümer*, Freiburg-im-Breisgau, 1880.
Levy, Isaac, *A Guide to Passover*, London, 1958.
Missal, The English, London, 1933.
Newman, Louis, *The Jewish People, Faith and Life*, New York, 1965.
Nikhilananda, Swami, tr., *The Upanishads*, London, 1957.
Obolensky, Dmitri, *The Bogomils*, Cambridge, 1948.
Ormanian, Malachia, *L'Eglise Arménienne*, Paris, 1910.
Parsons, E. C., *Pueblo Indian Religion*, Chicago, 1939, 2 vols.
Petschenig, M., ed., *Corpus Scriptorum Ecclesiasticorum*, Vienna, 1888, vol. 17.
Prayer Book of the United Hebrew Congregations of the British Commonwealth of Nations, The Authorized Daily, London, 1962.
Price, Nancy, *High Days and Holy Days*, London, 1954.
Radhakrishnan, S., ed., *The Principal Upanishads*, London, 1953.
Schauss, Hayyim, *The Lifetime of a Jew*, New York, 1950.
Simpson, William, *The Buddhist Praying Wheel*, London, 1896.
Simpson, William, *Jewish Prayer and Worship*, London, 1965.
Soltes, Mordecai, *The Jewish Holidays*, Philadelphia, 1931.
Urlin, Ethel L., *Festivals, Holy Days and Saints' Days*, London, 1915.
Vipont, Elfrida, *Some Christian Festivals*, London, 1963.
Watts, Alan W., *Easter, Its Story and Meaning*, New York, 1950.
—— *Myth and Ritual in Christianity*, London, 1959.
Weiser, Francis X., *The Easter Book*, London, 1955.
Williamson, Robert W., *Religious and Cosmic Beliefs of Central Polynesia*, Cambridge, 1933.
Wilson, H. H., ed., *Rig Veda Sanhita*, London, 1857.
Wright, Richardson, 'Easter Celebrations of the Gypsy Coppersmiths in New York', *Journal of the Gypsy Lore Society*, Edinburgh, 1947, vol. 26.
Zernov, Nicholas, *Eastern Christendom*, London, 1961.

IV FOLKLORE, MYTHOLOGY AND ANTHROPOLOGY

Aarne, Antti and Thompson, Stith, *The Types of the Folktale*, Helsinki, 1964.
Abbott, G. F., *Macedonian Folklore*, Cambridge, 1903.
Abbott, J., *The Keys of Power: a Study of Indian Ritual and Belief*, London, 1932.

Abercromby, John, 'The Beliefs and Religious Ceremonies of the Mordvins', *The Folk-Lore Journal*, London, April–June 1889, vol. 7.

Albanian Notes, Ilford, November 1965, No. 3.

Alexander, M. F., *The W.I. Book for New Hutton*, New Hutton, 1955.

Alford, Violet, *Pyrenean Festivals*, London, 1937.

Alhady, Alwi Bin Sheikh, *Malay Customs and Traditions*, Singapore, 1962.

Antubam, Kofi, *Ghana's Heritage of Culture*, Leipzig, 1963.

Argenti, Philip, and Rose, H. J., *The Folklore of Chios*, Cambridge, 1949, 2 vols.

Arnott, Margaret, 'Die Ostereier in Griechenland', *Schweizerisches Archiv für Volkskunde*, Basle, 1957, vol. 53.

—— 'Easter Bread of South Eastern Pennsylvania', *Expedition*, Philadelphia, Spring 1961, vol. 3, no. iii.

Arundell of Wardour, Lord, *Tradition, Principally with Reference to Mythology and the Law of Nations*, London, 1872.

Ashton, John, *Curious Creatures in Zoology*, London, 1890.

Aubrey, John, *The Remaines of Gentilisme and Judaisme* (1686–87), London, 1881.

Bächtold-Stäubli, Hanns, ed., *Handwörterbuch des deutschen Aberglaubens*, Berlin, 1927–35, vols. 1–6.

Ball, J. Dyer, *Things Chinese*, London, 1926.

Banks, M. Macleod, *British Calendar Customs: Orkney and Shetland*, London, 1946.

—— *British Calendar Customs: Scotland*, London, 1937–41, 3 vols.

Baring-Gould, Sabine, *Strange Survivals*, London, 1892.

Barondes, R. de Rohan, *China, Lore and Legend and Lyrics*, London, 1960.

Bassett, F. S., *Legends and Superstitions of the Sea*, London, 1885.

Bayley, Harold, *The Lost Language of Symbolism*, London, 1912, 2 vols.

Beatty, Bill, *A Treasury of Australian Folk Tales and Traditions*, London, 1960.

Becker, Albert, *Brauchtum der deutschen Osterzeit*, Jena, 1937.

Beckers, Hartmut, *The Myth of the Origin of the World according to the Mashafi Räsh*, Münster, unpublished MS.

Beckwith, Martha, *Black Roadways: a Study of Jamaican Folk Life*, Chapel Hill, 1929.

—— *Jamaica Anansi Stories*, New York, 1924.

—— *Jamaica Folklore*, New York, 1928.

Bellamy, H. S., *Moons, Myth and Man*, London, 1936.

Benet, Sula, *Song, Dance and Customs of Peasant Poland*, London, 1951.

Bett, Henry, *English Myths and Traditions*, London, 1952.

Billson, Charles J., *County Folk-Lore: Leicestershire and Rutland*, London, 1895.

Blakeborough, Richard, *Wit, Character, Folklore and Customs of the North Riding of Yorkshire*, London, 1911.

Bompas, C. H., *Folklore of the Santal Parganas*, London, 1909.

Bonnerjea, Biren, *A Dictionary of Superstitions and Mythology*, London, 1927.

Bonser, K. J., 'Easter in Greece', *Folklore*, London, Winter 1964, vol. 75.

Bosanquet, Rosalie, ed., *The Cambo Women's Institute Book*, Newcastle, 1929.

Bradley-Birt, F. B., *Bengal Fairy Tales*, London, 1920.

Brady, John, *Clavis Calendaria*, London, 1815, 2 vols.

Brand, John, *Observations on Popular Antiquities*, 1st edition, Newcastle, 1777; London, 1810.

Brandon, S. G. F., *Creation Legends of the Ancient Near East*, London, 1963.

Brasch, R., *How did It Begin?* London, 1965.

Bray, A. E., *Traditions, Legends, Superstitions and Sketches of Devonshire on the Borders of the Tamar and the Tavy*, London, 1838, 2 vols.

Brewer, E. Cobham, *Dictionary of Phrase and Fable*, London, 1896.

Brězan, Jurig, *Hochzeitsreise in die Heimat*, Dresden, 1953.

Briffault, Robert, *The Mothers*, London, 1927, 3 vols.

Briggs, K. M., and Tongue, R. L., *Somerset Folklore*, London, 1965.

Brown, Robert, 'Remarks on the Gryphon, Heraldic and Mythological', *Archaeologia*, London, 1885, vol. 48.

Browne, Sir Thomas, *Pseudodoxia Epidemica*, London, 1686.

Buchanan, Ronald H., 'Calendar Customs' (Part 1), *Ulster Folklife*, Belfast, 1962, vol. 8.

Burdick, L. D., *Foundation Rites*, London, 1901.

Burne, C. S., *The Handbook of Folklore*, London, 1914.

Čerbulenas, K., 'Margučiu Menas Lietuvoje', *Mokslas ir Gyvenimas*, Vilnius, March 1967.

Chabas, F. J., *La Papyrus Magique Harris*, Paris, 1860.

Chambers, R., *The Book of Days*, London, 1869, vol. 1.

Cirlot, J. E., *A Dictionary of Symbols*, London, 1962.

Cooper, Gordon, *Festivals of Europe*, London, 1961.

Cormack, J., *Everyday Customs in China*, Edinburgh, 1935.

Cox, G. W., *The Mythology of the Aryan Nations*, London, 1870.

Cox, Marian Roalfe, *An Introduction to Folklore*, London, 1895.

Cremer, William H., *Easter Eggs: a Sketch of a Good Old Custom*, Ipswich, 1870.

Crooke, William, *Popular Religion and Folklore of Northern India*, London, 1896, 2 vols.

Crossland, John, 'Sacrifices in Tudor Buildings', *Sunday Telegraph*, London, 24 January 1965.

Curtin, Jeremiah, *Fairy Tales of Eastern Europe*, London, 1906.

Dacombe, Marianne R., ed., *Dorset*, Dorchester, 1935.

D'Alviella, Goblet, *The Migration of Symbols*, London, 1894.

Dalyell, John Graham, *The Darker Superstitions of Scotland*, Edinburgh, 1834.

Danielli, Mary, 'Jolly Boys or Pace Eggers in Westmorland', *Folk-Lore*, London, December 1951, vol. 62.

Davies, Edward, *The Mythology and Rites of the British Druids*, London, 1809.

Davies, J. C., *Folklore of West and Mid-Wales*, Aberystwyth, 1911.

Dictionary of Folklore, Mythology and Legend, New York, 1949, 2 vols.

Ditchfield, P. H., *Old English Customs*, London, 1896.

Dixon, J. H., 'The Paschal Egg: an Enquiry into Its Origin', *Northumberland Legendary Tracts*, Newcastle, 1844.

Drake-Carnell, F. J., *Old English Customs and Ceremonies*, London, 1938.

Dundes, Alan, 'Earth-diver: Creation of the Mythopoeic Male', *American Anthropologist*, Wisconsin, 1962, vol. 64.

Durham, M. E., *Some Tribal Origins, Laws and Customs of the Balkans*, London, 1928.

Eliade, Mircea, *The Forge and the Crucible*, London, 1962.

—— *Images and Symbols*, London, 1961.

Ellis Davidson, H. R., *Gods and Myths of Northern Europe*, London, 1964.

Elwin, Verrier, *Myths of the North-East Frontier of India*, Shillong, 1958.

Emerick, Abraham J., *Obeah and Duppyism in Jamaica*, Woodstock, 1915.

Eskeröd, Albert, 'Ostereier in Schweden', *Schweizerisches Archiv für Volkskunde*, Basle, 1958, vol. 54.

Espinosa, Aurelio M., 'New-Mexican Spanish Folk-Lore', *Journal of American Folklore*, Boston, October–December 1910, vol. 23.

Evans, E. Estyn, *Irish Folk Ways*, London, 1957.

Fortier, Alcée, 'Louisianian Nursery Tales', *Journal of American Folklore*, Boston, 1888, vol. 1.

Foster, Jeanne C., *Ulster Folklore*, Belfast, 1951.

Fowler, Alice, 'Note', *Folk-Lore*, London, September 1917, vol. 28.

Frazer, Sir James G., *Folklore in the Old Testament*, London, 1919, 3 vols.

—— *Golden Bough, The*, London, 1907–15, 12 vols.

—— *Totemism and Exogamy*, London, 1910, 4 vols.

Freund, Philip, *Myths of Creation*, London, 1964.

Gailey, Alan, 'Edward L. Sloan's "The Year's Holidays"', *Ulster Folklife*, Belfast, 1968, vol. 14.

Garnett, Lucy M. J., and Stuart Glennie, John S., *The Women of Turkey and their Folk-Lore*, London, 1890–1, 2 vols.

Gaster, M., *Rumanian Bird and Beast Stories*, London, 1915.

Gentleman's Magazine, The, London, 1831, and 1883.

Georgieva, Milica, *Бојадисување и шарање на Велигденски Јајца Во Скопје и Околијата*, Skopje, 1960.

Gill, W. Walter, *A Second Manx Scrapbook*, London, 1932.

—— *A Third Manx Scrapbook*, London, 1963.

Gomme, G. L., ed., *The Gentleman's Magazine Library: Manners and Customs*, London, 1883.

Granet, Marcel, *Festivals and Songs of Ancient China*, London, 1932.

Graves, Robert, *The White Goddess*, London, 1938.

Gregor, W., *Notes on the Folklore of North-East Scotland*, London, 1881.

Grimm, The Brothers, *Fairy Tales*, London, 1909.

—— *German Folk Tales*, Carbondale, Ill., 1960.

Grimm, Jacob, *Teutonic Mythology*, London, 1883–8, 4 vols.

Gubernatis, Angelo de, *Zoological Mythology*, London, 1872, 2 vols.

Gutch, Mrs, ed., *Examples of Printed Folk-Lore Concerning the East Riding of Yorkshire*, London, 1912.

—— *Examples of Printed Folk-Lore Concerning the North Riding of Yorkshire*, London, 1901.

—— and Peacock, Mabel, ed., *Examples of Printed Folk-Lore Concerning Lincolnshire*, London, 1908.

Guthrie, E. J., *Old Scottish Customs*, London, 1885.

Haavio, Martti, 'Väinamöinen, Creator of the World', *F.F. Communications*, Helsinki, 1952–3, vols. 61 and 62.

Hackin, J., *Asiatic Mythology*, London, 1963.

Hansen, T. L., *The Types of the Folktale in Cuba, Puerto Rico, The Dominican Republic and Spanish South America*, Berkeley, 1957.

Hardwick, Charles, *Traditions, Superstitions and Folklore*, London, 1872.

Hardy, James, ed., *The Denham Tracts*, London, 1891–5, 2 vols.

Harland, John, and Wilkinson, T. T., *Lancashire Folk-Lore*, London, 1882.

Hartland, Edwin S., *County Folklore: Gloucestershire*, London, 1892.

—— *Primitive Paternity*, London, 1909, vol. 1.

—— *The Science of Fairy Tales*, London, 1891.

Hazeltine, Alice, and Smith, Elva, ed., *The Easter Book of Legends and Stories*, New York, 1947.

Hazlitt, W. C., *A Dictionary of Faiths and Folklore*, London, 1905, vol. 1.

Hellbom, Anna-Britta, 'The Creation Egg', *Ethnos*, Stockholm, 1963, No. 1.

Henderson, William, *Notes on the Folk Lore of the Northern Counties of England and the Borders*, London, 1866, 2nd Ed., 1879.

History of the Witches of Renfrewshire, A, Paisley, 1877.

Hodgson, M. L., 'Some Notes on the Huculs', *Folk-Lore*, London, March 1905, vol. 16.

Hole, Christina, *Easter and Its Customs*, London, 1961.

—— ed., *Encyclopaedia of Superstitions*, London, 1961.

—— *English Custom and Usage*, London, 1941.

—— *Mirror of Witchcraft, A*, London, 1957.

—— ed., *Oxford and District Folklore Society Annual Record*, Oxford, 1962.

—— *Traditions and Customs of Cheshire*, London, 1937.

Hone, William, *The Every-Day Book*, London, 1837, vol. 1.

—— *The Year Book*, London, 1832.

Hosking, Clement, *Old Tales in a New Land*, Sydney, 1957.

Howitt, William, *A Country Book*, London, 1859.

Hrdlicka, V. and Z., 'Daruma, A Japanese Folk Toy', *New Orient*, Prague, March 1966.

Hsu, Francis L. K., *Under the Ancestors' Shadow*, London, 1949.

Hutchinson, Walter, ed., *Customs of the World*, London, n.d., vol. 1.

Huxley, Francis, *The Invisibles*, London, 1966.

Hyatt, H. M., *Folklore from Adams County, Illinois*, New York, 1935.

Hyde, Thomas, *De Ludis Orientalibus*, London, 1694.

Ilg, Karl, 'Sitte und Brauch um Osterei und Osterbrot in Tirol', *Schweizerisches Archiv für Volkskunde*, Basle, 1957, vol. 53.

Ingersoll, Ernest, *Birds in Legend, Fable and Folklore*, London, 1923.

International Folk-Lore Congress, The, Exhibition of Folklore Objects at Burlington House, London, 1891.

Jacobs, J., ed., *The Fables of Aesop*, London, 1889, vol. 1.

Jacottet, E., *The Treasury of Basuto Lore*, London, 1908.

Jagodic, Maria, 'Über Ostereier und Ostergebäck in Slowenien', *Schweizerisches Archiv für Volkskunde*, Basle, 1957, vol. 53.

James, E. O., *The Ancient Gods*, London, 1960.

—— *Seasonal Feasts and Festivals*, London, 1961.

—— *The Tree of Life*, Leiden, 1966.

Jewitt, Llewellynn, 'On Ancient Customs and Sports of the County of Derby', *Journal of the British Archaeological Association*, London, 1852, vol. 7.

Jobes, Gertrude, *Dictionary of Folklore, Mythology and Symbols*, New York, 1961.

Joisten, Charles, 'Le Folklore de L'Œuf en Dauphiné', *Arts et Traditions Populaires*, Paris, January–March 1961.

—— 'Folklore de L'Œuf' (Note), *Arts et Traditions Populaires*, Paris, January 1965.

Jones, William, *Credulities, Past and Present*, London, 1880.

Jones, William H., ed., *The Folk Tales of the Magyars*, London, 1889.

—— 'Magyar Folk-Lore and Some Parallels', *The Folk-Lore Journal*, London, November 1883.

Jung, Carl G., *Man and His Symbols*, London, 1964.

Jungfer, Victor, *Litauen – Antlitz eines Volkes*, Leipzig, 1938.

Károlyi, Alexander, *Hungarian Pageant*, Budapest, 1939.

Kelly, Walter, *Curiosities of Indo-European Tradition and Folklore*, London, 1863.

Kemp, P., *Healing Ritual: Studies in the Technique and Tradition of the Southern Slavs*, London, 1935.

Kittredge, G. L., *Witchcraft in Old and New England*, Cambridge, Mass., 1928.

König, Wolfhilde von, 'Ostereierverse', *Bayerischen Jahrbuch für Volkskunde*, Munich, 1961.

Kramer, S. N., *Mythologies of the Ancient World*, New York, 1961.

Kretzenbacher, Leopold, 'Vom roten Osterei in der grünen Steiermark', *Schweizerisches Archiv für Volkskunde*, Basle, 1957, vol. 53.

Kunstader, Peter, 'Living with Thailand's Gentle Lua', *National Geographic*, Washington, July 1966.

Kunstmann, Hellmutt, 'Der Osterbaum', *Schönere Heimat*, Munich, 1960, vol. 4.

—— *Der Osterbaum an Quellen und Dorfbrunnen*, Kulmbach, 1958.

Kunz, Ludvik, 'Mährische Ostereier', *Schweizerisches Archiv für Volkskunde*, Basle, 1957, vol. 53.

Lanz, Joseph, 'Das Eierlesen in den ostdeutschen Sprachinseln', *Jahrbuch für Volkskunde der Heimatvertriebenen*, Salzburg, 1961, vol. 6.

Larousse Encyclopaedia of Mythology, London, 1959.

Laur, Ernest, 'Verzierte Ostereier', *Heimatwerk*, Zürich, February 1967, vol. 32, No. 1.

Layard, John, *The Lady of the Hare*, London, 1944.

Leather, E. M., *Folklore of Herefordshire*, London, 1912.

Lebeuf, Annie, 'Le Système Classificatoire des Fali', a paper in *African Systems of Thought*, ed. Fortes, M., and Dieterlen, G., London, 1965.

Lechner, Sophie, 'Beim Eiermalen', *Heimatwerk*, Zürich, February 1967, vol. 32, No. 1.

'Qui n'a pas ses Œufs de Pâques?', *Lectures Pour Tous*, Paris, n.d.

Legey, F., *Folklore of Morocco*, London, 1935.

Lehmann, Hedi, *Volksbrauch im Jahreslauf*, Munich, 1964.

Leland, C. G., *Gypsy Sorcery and Fortune Telling*, London, 1891.

Liebl, Elsbeth, 'Ostereierspiele im Atlas der schweizerischen Volkskunde', *Schweizerisches Archiv für Volkskunde*, Basle, 1957, vol. 53.

Liungman, Waldemar, 'Das Mardukneujahrsfest', *F.F. Communications*, Helsinki, 1937–8, vols. 48, 49.

Long, George, *The Folklore Calendar*, London, 1930.

Louvet, Marie-Hélène, 'Pâques – dites le avec des Œufs', *ABC Décor*, Paris, April 1969, No. 54.

Lukas, Franz, 'Das Ei als kosmogonische Vorstellung', *Zeitschrift des Vereins für Volkskunde*, Berlin, 1894, vol. 4.

Lum, Peter, *Fabulous Beasts*, London, 1952.
MacCulloch, Edgar, *Guernsey Folk Lore*, London, 1903.
Mackenzie, Donald A., *Egyptian Myth and Legend*, London, 1913.
—— *Myths and Traditions of the South Sea Islands*, London, 1930.
—— *Myths from Melanesia and Indonesia*, London, 1931.
—— *Myths of Babylonia and Assyria*, London, 1915.
—— *Myths of Pre-Columban America*, London, 1924.
Mackenzie, D. R., *The Spirit-Ridden Konde*, London, 1925.
Mackinlay, James M., *Folklore of Scottish Lochs and Springs*, Glasgow, 1893.
Maclagan, R. C., *The Evil Eye in the Western Highlands*, London, 1902.
—— *The Games and Diversions of Argyllshire*, London, 1901.
Magnus, Leonard A., *Russian Folk Tales*, London, 1916.
Mansikka, V., *Religion der Ostslaven*, Helsinki, 1922.
McNeill, F. Marian, *The Silver Bough*, Glasgow, 1961, vol. 2.
McPherson, J. M., *Primitive Beliefs in the North-East of Scotland*, London, 1929.
Meertens, P. J., 'Ostereier und Ostergebäcke in den Niederlanden', *Schweizerisches Archiv für Volkskunde*, Basle, 1957, vol. 53.
Megas, George A., *Greek Calendar Customs*, Athens, 1958.
Memeler Dampfboot, Oldenburg, 5 June 1967, vol. 118.
Merrifield, Ralph, 'Good Friday Customs in Sussex', *Sussex Archaeological Collections*, London, 1950, vol. 89.
—— 'Witch Bottles and Magic Jugs', *Folk-Lore*, London, March 1955, vol. 66.
Métraux, Alfred, *Voodoo in Haiti*, London, 1959.
Meyerowitz, Eva L. R., *The Divine Kingship in Ghana and Ancient Egypt*, London, 1960.
Middleton, John, and Winter, E. H., *Witchcraft and Sorcery in East Africa*, London, 1963.
Miles, C. A., *Christmas in Ritual and Tradition*, London, 1913.
Milhous, Katherine, *The Egg Tree*, New York, 1950.
Mitchell, J. Clyde, 'The Meaning in Misfortune for Urban Africans', a paper in *African Systems of Thought*, ed. Fortes, M., and Dieterlen, G., London, 1965.
Moser, Hans, 'Brauchgeschichtliches zu Osterei und Osterbrot in Bayern', *Schweizerisches Archiv für Volkskunde*, Basle, 1957, vol. 53.
Mössinger, Friedrich, 'Eierkronen und Eierketten', *Volk und Scholle*, Darmstadt, 1938, No. 16.
—— 'Odenwälder Binseneier', *Schweizerisches Archiv für Volkskunde*, Basle, 1957, vol. 53.
Müller, F. Max, *Chips from a German Workshop*, London, 1867, vol. I.
—— *Contributions to the Science of Mythology*, London, 1897, 2 vols.

Murgoçi, Agnes, 'Rumanian Easter Eggs', *Folk Lore*, London, September 1909, vol. 20.

Němcová, Božena, *Babička, Obrazy Venkovského Života*, Prague, 1885.

Newall, Venetia, 'Decorated Eggs', *Folk-Lore*, London, 1965, vol. 76.

—— 'Easter', *Man, Myth and Magic*, London, 23 July 1970, No. 27.

—— 'Easter Egg Customs and Games', *Viltis*, Denver, March–April 1967, vol. 24.

—— 'Egg', *Man, Myth and Magic*, London, 30 July 1970, No. 28.

—— 'Easter Eggs', *Folk-Lore*, London, 1968, vol. 79.

—— 'Easter Eggs', *Journal of American Folklore*, Austin, January–March 1967, vol. 80.

—— 'Eggs – Easter Food and Folk Belief', *Lore and Language*, Sheffield, August 1970, No. 3.

—— 'Some Notes on the Egg Tree', *Folk-Lore*, London, Spring 1967, vol. 78.

Newberry, J. S., *The Rainbow Bridge*, London, 1934.

Nickel, Johanna, 'Lausitzer Ostereier', *Schweizerisches Archiv für Volkskunde*, Basle, 1957, vol. 53.

Nilsson, Martin P., 'Das Ei im Totenkult der Alten', *Archiv für Religionswissenschaft*, Leipzig, 1908, vol. 2.

Nisizawa, Tekiho, *Japanese Folk Toys*, Tokyo, 1939.

Notes and Queries: 9 June 1855, vol. 11.

   11 December 1858, 2nd Series, vol. 6.

   19 December 1863, 3rd Series, vol. 4.

   23 July 1870, 4th Series, vol. 6.

   12 April 1879, 5th Series, vol. 2.

   4 December 1880, 6th Series, vol. 2.

   22 January 1881, 6th Series, vol. 3.

   15 October 1881, 6th Series, vol. 4.

   30 September 1882, 6th Series, vol. 6.

   9 December 1882, 6th Series, vol. 6.

   21 April 1883, 6th Series, vol. 7.

   10 September 1887, 7th Series, vol. 4.

   21 January 1888, 7th Series, vol. 5.

   11 February 1888, 7th Series, vol. 5.

   5 May 1894, 8th Series, vol. 5.

   2 June 1894, 8th Series, vol. 5.

   24 November 1900, 9th Series, vol. 6.

   22 April 1905, 10th Series, vol. 3.

   8 July 1905, 10th Series, vol. 4.

   14 April 1906, 10th Series, vol. 5.

   12 May 1906, 10th Series, vol. 5.

   15 September 1906, 10th Series, vol. 6.

15 May 1915, 11th Series, vol. 2.

1 July 1916, 12th Series, vol. 2.

17 December 1921, 12th Series, vol. 9.

9 January 1932, vol. 162.

O'Bryan, Aileen, 'The Dîné: Origin Myths of the Navaho Indians', *Bureau of American Ethnology*, Washington, 1956, Bulletin 163.

O'Danachair, Caoimhin, 'Distribution Patterns in Irish Folk Tradition', *Béaloideas*, Dublin, 1965, vol. 33.

Ogden, James, 'Pace Egging', *The Antiquary*, London 1905, vol. 41.

Oliveira, Ernesto Veiga de, 'Folares et Oeufs de Pâques au Portugal', *Schweizerisches Archiv für Volkskunde*, Basle, 1957, vol. 53.

O'Neill, John, *The Night of the Gods*, London, 1893–7, 2 vols.

Opie, Iona and Peter, *The Lore and Language of Schoolchildren*, Oxford, 1959.

Owen, Elias, *Welsh Folklore*, Oswestry, 1887.

Owen, Trefor M., *Welsh Folk Customs*, Cardiff, 1959.

Parsons, Elsie Clews, *Folklore from the Cape Verde Islands*, Cambridge, Mass., 1923, 2 vols.

Partridge, J. B., 'Note', *Folk-Lore*, London, 1914, vol. 25.

Patai, Raphael, ed., *Studies in Biblical and Jewish Folklore*, Bloomington, 1960.

Payne, Charles F., 'Some Romani Superstitions', *Journal of the Gypsy Lore Society*, Edinburgh, 1957, vol. 36.

Payne Knight, Richard, *The Symbolical Language of Ancient Art and Mythology*, New York, 1876.

Percy Anecdotes, The, London, 1868, vol. 1.

Perusini, Gaetano, 'Uova e Pani di Pasqua in Friuli', *Schweizerisches für Volkskunde*, Basle, 1957, vol. 53.

Peters, John P., *Nippur*, New York, 1897, 2 vols.

Petrovíc, Alexander, 'Contributions to the Study of the Serbian Gypsies', *Journal of the Gypsy Lore Society*, Edinburgh, 1938, vol. 17.

Pettigrew, T. G., *Superstitions connected with the History and Practice of Medicine and Surgery*, London, 1894.

Pfleger, Alfred, 'Osterei und Ostergebäck im Elsass', *Schweizerisches Archiv für Volkskunde*, Basle, 1957, vol. 53.

Philpot, J. H., *The Sacred Tree*, London, 1897.

Pieters, Jules, 'Œufs de Pâques en Belgique', *Schweizerisches Archiv für Volkskunde*, Basle, 1957, vol. 53.

Polson, Alexander, *Our Highland Folklore Heritage*, Inverness, 1926.

—— *Scottish Witchcraft Lore*, London, 1932.

Porteous, Alexander, *Forest Folklore, Mythology and Romance*, London, 1928.

A List of Books Cited and Consulted

Pranda, Adam, *Kraslice v Slovenskej L'udovej Umeleckej Výrobe*, Bratislava, 1958.

—— 'Die slowakischen Ostereier', *Schweizerisches Archiv für Volkskunde*, Basle, 1957, vol. 53.

Puckett, N., *Folk Beliefs of the Southern Negro*, Chapel Hill, 1926.

Quaritch Wales, H. G., *The Mountain of God*, London, 1953.

Ränk, Gustav, 'Ostereier in Estland', *Schweizerisches Archiv für Volkskunde*, Basle, 1957, vol. 53.

Ranke, Kurt, *Folktales of Germany*, London, 1966.

Read, John, 'Alchemy and Alchemists', *The Advancement of Science*, London, June 1952, vol. 9, No. 33.

Rhys, John, *Celtic Folklore*, Oxford, 1901, 2 vols.

Robinson, Mary, 'The Calder Valley Folk Festival', *Folk-Lore*, London, 1956, vol. 67.

Robson, E. I., *A Guide to French Fêtes*, London, 1930.

Roheim, G., 'Hungarian Pageant: Hungarian Calendar Customs', *Journal of the Royal Anthropological Institute*, London, 1926, vol. 56.

Roth, Walter, 'An Enquiry into the Animism and Folklore of the Guiana Indians', *Thirtieth Annual Report of the Bureau of American Ethnology*, Washington, 1915.

Rouse, W. H. D., *Greek Votive Offerings*, Cambridge, 1902.

Routledge, Mrs Scoresby, 'The Mysterious Images of Easter Island', *Wonders of the Past*, ed. Hammerton, J. A., London, 1922, vol. 3.

Rudkin, Ethel, *Lincolnshire Folklore*, Gainsborough, 1936.

Runeberg, Arne, 'Witches, Demons and Fertility Magic', *Commentationes Humanorum Litterarum*, Helsinki, 1947, vol. 14, Nos. 1–4.

Ruud, Jørgen, *Taboo, A Study of Malagasy Customs and Beliefs*, Oslo, 1960.

Sándor, István, 'Das beschlagene Osterei', *Schweizerisches Archiv für Volkskunde*, Basle, 1957, vol. 53.

—— 'Ostereier in Ungarn', *Schweizerisches Archiv für Volkskunde*, Basle, 1957, vol. 53.

Schaudel, L., 'Œufs Talismans dans les Murs des Maisons', *Revue de Folklore Français et de Folklore Colonial*, Paris, March–April 1932, vol. 3, No. 2.

Scheidt-Lämke, Dora, 'Die Kirmesbräuche im Koblenzer Land', *Rhein-Lahn-Freund*, Niederlahnstein, 1956.

—— 'Kirmesbräuche im Regierungsbezirk Montabaur', *Rhein-Lahn-Freund*, Niederlahnstein, 1956.

Schmidt, Friedrich Heinz, *Osterbräuche*, Leipzig, 1936.

Schmidt-Kowar, E., *Sorbische Ostereier*, Bautzen, 1965.

Scot, Reginald, *The Discoverie of Witchcraft*, 1st ed., 1584; London, 1654.

Seweryn, Tadeusz, 'Les Œufs de Pâques Polonais et Hutsules', *Schweizerisches Archiv für Volkskunde*, Basle, 1957, vol. 53.

Shaw, M. F., *Folksongs and Folklore of South Uist*, London, 1955.
Sheppard, H. J., 'Egg Symbolism in Alchemy', *Ambix*, London, 1958.
Shoemaker, Alfred L., *Eastertide in Pennsylvania*, Kutztown, 1960.
Sis, Vladimir, *Chinese Food and Fables*, Prague, 1966.
Slătineanu, Barbu, 'Les Œufs de Pâques en Roumanie', *Schweizerisches Archiv für Volkskunde*, Basle, 1957, vol. 53.
Sokolov, Y. M., *Russian Folklore*, New York, 1950.
Spamer, Adolf, 'Sitte und Brauch', *Handbuch der Deutschen Volkskunde*, Potsdam, 1936, vol. 2.
Spence, Lewis, *An Introduction to Mythology*, London, 1921.
Spicer, Dorothy, *The Book of Festivals*, New York, 1937.
Starr, F., *Catalogue of a Collection of Objects Illustrating the Folklore of Mexico*, London, 1899.
Stone, Benjamin, *Festivals, Ceremonies and Customs*, London, 1906.
Strutt, Joseph, *The Sports and Pastimes of the People of England*, London, 1801.
Sykes, Egerton, *Dictionary of Non-Classical Mythology*, London, 1961.
Taylor, Archer, 'Ainu Riddles', *Western Folklore*, Berkeley, 1947, vol. 6, No. 2.
—— 'Das Ei im europäischen Volksrätsel', *Schweizerisches Archiv für Volkskunde*, Basle, 1957, vol. 53.
Taylor, Thomas, tr., *The Mystical Hymns of Orpheus*, London, 1824.
Theal, George McCall, *Kaffir Folklore*, London, 1886.
Thiselton-Dyer, T. F., *British Popular Customs*, London, 1876.
—— *English Folk-Lore*, London, 1884.
Thomas, Northcote W., ed., *Examples of Printed Folklore Concerning Northumberland*, London, 1904.
Thompson, Stith, *Motif-Index of Folk-Literature*, Bloomington, 1966, 6 vols.
Thonger, Richard, *A Calendar of German Customs*, Munich, 1966.
Thorpe, Benjamin, *Northern Mythology*, London, 1851, 3 vols.
Tin Hau, The Birthday of, Hong Kong, 1960.
Tremearne, A. J. N., *The Ban of the Bori*, London, 1914.
—— 'Bori Beliefs and Ceremonies', *Journal of the Royal Anthropological Institute*, London, 1915, vol. 45.
—— *Hausa Superstitions and Customs*, London, 1913.
Trumbull, H. C., *The Threshold Covenant*, Edinburgh, 1896.
Tsereteli, M., 'The Asianic (Asia Minor) Elements in National Georgian Paganism', *Georgica*, London, October 1935, vol. 1.
Turville-Petre, E. O. G., *Myth and Religion of the North*, London, 1964.
Tylor, Edward B., *Primitive Culture*, London, 1903, 2 vols.
Udal, J. S., *Dorsetshire Folklore*, Hertford, 1922.

A List of Books Cited and Consulted

Uldall, Kai, 'Les Œufs de Pâques au Danemark', *Schweizerisches Archiv für Volkskunde*, Basle, 1958, vol. 54.

Urlin, Ethel L., *A Short History of Marriage*, London, 1913.

Václavík, Antonín, *Výroční Obyčeje a Lidové Umění*, Prague, 1959.

Vakarelski, Christo, 'Œufs de Pâques chez les Bulgares', *Schweizerisches Archiv für Volkskunde*, Basle, 1957, vol. 53.

Van Gennep, Arnold, *Le Cycle de Pâques dans les Coutumes Populaires de la Savoie*, Brussels, 1926.

—— *Manuel de Folklore Français Contemporain*, Paris, 1947, vol. 1.

—— *Folklore de la Flandre et du Hainault*, Paris, 1935, 2 vols.

—— *Le Folklore des Hautes-Alpes*, Paris, 1946.

—— *Le Folklore du Dauphiné*, Paris, 1932, 2 vols.

Vegetius, Renatus Publius, *Artis Veterinariae Sive Mulomedicinae*, Leipzig, 1797.

Vilkuna, Kustaa, 'Osterfeiern und Vogeleiersuchen in Finnland', *Schweizerisches Archiv für Volkskunde*, Basle, 1957, vol. 53.

Viski, Károly, *Volksbrauch der Ungarn*, Budapest, 1932.

Wagner, Günter, *The Bantu of North Kavirondo*, Oxford, 1949, vol. 1.

Wagner, Leopold, *Manners, Customs and Observances*, London, 1894.

Wähler, Martin, *Thüringische Volkskunde*, Jena, 1940.

Wallis Budge, E. A., *The Gods of the Egyptians*, London, 1904, 2 vols.

Waterman, Philip, *The Story of Superstition*, New York, 1929.

Weinhold, Gertrud, *Das schöne Osterei in Europa*, Kassel, 1965.

Weiser-Aall, Lily, 'Osterspeisen und Osterei in Norwegen', *Schweizerisches Archiv für Volkskunde*, Basle, 1957, vol. 53.

Wen, Chung-I, 'Bird Ancestor Legends of N.E. Asia, N.W. America and the Pacific', *Bulletin of the Institute of Ethnology*, Taipei, Autumn 1961, No. 12.

Wenzel, Marian, 'Graveside Feasts and Dances in Yugoslavia', *Folklore*, London, Spring 1962, vol. 73.

Werner, Alice, *Myths and Legends of the Bantu*, London, 1933.

Werner, E. T. C., *A Dictionary of Chinese Mythology*, Shanghai, 1932.

Westermarck, Edward, *Early Beliefs and Their Social Influences*, London, 1932.

—— *History of Human Marriage, The*, London, 1921, 3 vols.

—— *Marriage Ceremonies in Morocco*, London, 1914.

—— *Origin and Development of the Moral Ideas*, London, 1917.

—— *Ritual and Belief in Morocco*, London, 1926, 2 vols.

—— *A Short History of Marriage*, London, 1926.

Whistler, Lawrence, *The English Festivals*, London, 1947.

Whittick, Arnold, *Symbols, Signs and their Meaning*, London, 1960.

Wildhaber, Robert, *Wir färben Ostereier*, Berne, 1957.

—— 'Der Osterhase und andere Eierbringer', *Schweizerisches Archiv für Volkskunde*, Basle, 1957, vol. 53.

—— 'Zum Symbolgehalt und zur Ikonographie des Eies', *Deutsches Jahrbuch für Volkskunde*, Berlin, 1960, vol. 6.

Williams, Joseph, *Voodoos and Obeahs*, New York, 1932.

Willoughby-Meade, G., *Chinese Ghouls and Goblins*, London, 1928.

Wilson, E. M., 'Pace Eggers' Play from North Lancashire', *Folk-Lore*, London, June 1941, vol. 52.

Wilson, Howard, 'Syrian Folklore Collected in Boston', *Journal of American Folklore*, Boston, 1903, vol. 16.

Wilson-Haffenden, J. R., 'Ethnological Notes on the Shuwalbe Group of the Borroro Fulani in the Kurafi District of Keffi Emirate of Northern Nigeria', *Journal of the Royal Anthropological Institute*, London, 1927, vol. 57.

Winstedt, E. O., 'Forms and Ceremonies', *Journal of the Gypsy Lore Society*, Edinburgh, July 1908–April 1909, vol. 2.

Winstedt, Richard O., *Shaman Saiva and Sufi*, London, 1925.

Wlislocki, Heinrich von, *Volksglaube und religiöser Brauch der Magyaren*, Münster, 1893.

Wood, Edward J., *The Wedding Day*, London, 1869.

Wood, G. Bernard, 'North Country Amusements of Long Ago', *Country Life*, London, 2 December 1965.

Wright, A. R., *British Calendar Customs: England*, London, 1936, vol. 1.

Yeats, William B., *Fairy and Folk Tales of The Irish Peasantry*, London, 1888.

Yoffie, Leah R., 'Popular Beliefs and Customs among the Yiddish-speaking Jews of St Louis, Mo.', *Journal of American Folklore*, Boston, 1925, vol. 38.

Yueh-Hwa, Lin, *The Golden Wing*, London, 1947.

Zaitsev, Vyacheslav, 'Visitors from Outer Space', *Sputnik*, Moscow, January 1967.

Zimmer, Heinrich, *Myths and Symbols in Indian Art and Civilization*, Washington, 1946.

Zincgref, J. W., *Teutsche Apophtegmata*, Strasbourg, 1626.

Zingerle, Ignaz, *Sagen aus Tirol*, Innsbruck, 1891.

Zmigrodzki, Michel de, 'The History of the Swastika', *Archives of the International Folklore Association*, Chicago, 1898, vol. 1.

Index

Italicized entries denote tale types and motifs. Folktales not being the primary concern of this work, relevant tale types and motifs have been included in alphabetical order within the overall arrangement of this general index, to avoid an unnecessary proliferation of indices. Reference numbers in brackets immediately after the entry and before the page references to the present volume are to Antti Aarne and Stith Thompson, *The Types of the Folk Tale* (Helsinki, 1964), and Stith Thompson, *Motif Index of Folk-Literature* (6 vols.; Bloomington, 1966); tale type reference numbers are preceded by the letters TT.

Bold-faced numbers denote plate numbers (Roman numerals indicate colour plates and Arabic numerals indicate black-and-white plates). These bold-faced numbers are followed by the number, in brackets, of the page opposite which or nearest to which the illustration appears. The illustrations are indexed by subject. Check-lists of illustrations are also indexed under Colour plates and Black-and-white plates, the relevant page numbers being given after the plate numbers in the same way.

The figure in brackets following page references is the footnote number on the given page, from which the passage concerned may be located exactly.

Cheshire, 95, 334, 337, 365, 367, 368, 370
Chicken as Easter egg bringer, 326
China, 3, 5, 14–15, 21, 22, 32, 34, 36, 40, 41, 44, 55, 85–6, 120, 121, 129, 134, 135, 147, 156, 173, 209, 212–13, 238–9, 258–9, 287, 319, 378; eggs from, **XXIV** (363)
Chinook Indians of North America, 28
Chins of Burma, 27
Christmas, 1, 67, 98, 242, 253, 256–7, 268, 297, 312
Chrovotes, 81
Chuvash, 238
Cicero, 145
Cloud(s) from egg, 9, 36
Clytemnestra, from egg laid by Leda, 25
Cochin China, 41
Cock, 70, 71, 116, 130, 256; as Easter egg bringer, 326; cock's egg, 71–3
Cock, Hieronymus: 'Egg Dance', 8 (186)
Collop Monday, 188
Colour plates, **I** (10), **II** (11), **III** (42), **IV** (43), **V** (74), **VI** (75), **VII** (106), **VIII** (107), **IX** (138), **X** (139), **XI** (170), **XII** (171), **XIII** (202), **XIV** (203), **XV** (234), **XVI** (235), **XVII** (266), **XVIII** (267), **XIX** (298), **XX** (299), **XXI** (330), **XXII** (331), **XXIII** (362), **XXIV** (363)
Columbus, Christopher, 292, 293
Comet connected with misshapen egg, 66
Complexion aided by Easter egg water, 247
Conception from divine impregnation (T518), 25 (5)
Conception from extraordinary intercourse (T517), 41 (2)
Conception from falling rain (T522), 37 (4), 121 (1)
Conception from sunlight (T521), 27 (2)
Conflict of good and evil creators (A50), 29 (2, 6)

Congo, 54, 296, 378
Continents originally from egg, 9
Convent of the Annunciation, eggs made by Arab Sisters at, 303, **V** (74)
Copper egg produces lower class, 39
Cornwall, 95, 111
Corpus Christi, 205
Cosmic Egg (A641), 5 (7), 7 (1, 3), 9 (1, 3), 21, (7), 26 (4), 27 (3), 28 (3), 29 (2, 3, 5), 31 (2, 3, 4), 37 (4), 39 (3)
Cow as Creator (A13.1.1), 12 (5)
Cow lays golden egg, 12
Coyote from egg, 5
Crane as Easter egg bringer, 326
Creation from duck's eggs (A641.2), 9 (1)
Creation of angels and devils (A50.1), 30 (1)
Creation of animals (A1700), 378 (1)
Creation of elephant (A1887), 23 (2)
Creation of mountains (A960), 37 (4)
Creation of the sun (A710), 7 (4, 6), 8 (1, 2), 15 (2)
Creator born from egg (A27), 6 (1, 3, 6), 12 (2, 3), 17 (4), 31 (3), 32 (1, 2), 39 (3)
Crete, 293
Crimea, 359
Croatia, 81, 148, 206, 252, 270, 274, 275–6, 277; egg from, **XXI** (330)
Crow: as creator, 27; rain crow's egg, 67
Cuckoo: as Easter egg bringer, 326; exchange of eggs on hearing first, 61
Culture hero born from egg (A511.1.9), 4 (6)
Cumberland, 281, 284–5, 335–6, 339, 347; eggs from, **XXII** (331), **XXIII** (362)
Cups and dishes from egg shells, 81
Cure or cause of illness, egg or part of egg as, 83, 87, 142–8, 253–5
Cyprus, 89–90
Czechs, Czechoslovakia, 55, 59, 76, 214, 237, 249, 259, 260, 269, 270,

Goths, 71, 103, 385
Gotland, 87, 295
Grasshopper egg produces heroine, 41
Great age of dwarfs (F451.3.11), 78 (3, 4)
Greece, 17–19, 25, 37, 47, 119, 121, 136, 150, 151, 152, 160, 164, 168, 169, 172, 174, 181, 189, 195, 210, 214, 219, 220, 221, 222–5, 226, 228, 229, 230–1, 241, 242, 243, 246, 251, 252, 269, 270, 271, 278, 283, 294, 302, 319–20, 345–6, 385, 386; egg cake, **13** (314); egg-tapping, **18** (315). See also Crete; Macedonia; Rhodes
Greenland, 15
Gregory the Great, Pope, 179
Guiana (Guyana), 128
Guinea, 95
Guinea-fowl eggs, 190, 349

Hafenreffer, Samuel, 16
Hail, eggs as charm against, 248–9
Hainan, 34, 41
Haiti, 21, 59, 61, 68, 85, 92, 93
Half eggs fertilize each other, produce world, 22
Halloween, 62, 64
Hare as Easter egg bringer, 324–6
Hausas of West Africa and Sahara, 23, 55, 108, 127, 140
Hawaii, 31
Heaven(s): as egg, 29, 36; originally from egg, 5, 9, 12, 28, 30, 31, 32. See also sky from egg
Heaven and earth from egg (A641.1), 35 (2)
Heavenly Hen as Easter egg bringer, 327
Helen of Troy: from egg dropped from moon, 25; from egg laid by Leda, 25, 162
Hell originally from egg, 30
Helpful toad (B493.2), 378 (1)
Hen and twelve chickens from magic egg, 24
Henry VIII, King, 204, 264

Herero of South-West Africa, 114
Hesiod, 35, 386
Hills originally from egg, 37
Hip egg, 2
Hitler, Adolf, 378
Holger Danske, 41
Holy Land: see Palestine
Holy Water; eggs sprinkled with, 1
Homer, 386
Honey, cup full of, under ice, egg as (in riddle), 20
Hopkins, Gerard Manley, 158
Horace, 162
Horse born from egg (B19.3), 41 (5), 76 (8)
House which has no doors, egg as (in riddle), 20
Hrussos of North-East Frontier Agency (India), 31
Human(s) from egg(s), 9, 21, 40; laid by crow, 27; laid by dove, 34; laid by hawk, 33; laid by thunderbird (thunder egg), 28; laid on waters by giant bird, 34. See also *Mankind originates from eggs*
Hundred eggs laid by woman produce male babies, 38
Hungary, 70, 76, 94, 108, 122, 123, 124, 129, 131, 135, 142, 159, 181, 183, 186, 192, 197, 214, 259, 265, 270, 271, 275, 277, 283, 288, 306, 310, 332, 350–1, 360–1, 381–2; eggs from, **XVI** (235). See also Banat; Transylvania.
Hunger demon from egg, 40
Hutzuls: see Ukraine
Huys, Frans: 'Egg Dance' (after Pieter Bruegel), 7 (186)

Iceland, 33, 72, 104, 105
Idu Mishmis of North-East Frontier Agency (India), 146–7
Iglulik: see Eskimos, Iglulik
Illinois, 253
Immurement, 45–8; of eggs, 48–52
Indelible blood (D1654.3), 69 (1)
India, 2, 5, 9, 12–14, 15, 23, 30, 31, 34, 37, 38, 48, 50, 57, 62, 96, 111,